T0345028

When Public Sector
Workers Unionize

A National Bureau
of Economic Research
Project Report

When Public Sector Workers Unionize

Edited by Richard B. Freeman and Casey Ichniowski

The University of Chicago Press

Chicago and London

RICHARD B. FREEMAN is professor of economics at Harvard
University and the Director of Labor Studies at the National
Bureau of Economic Research. CASEY ICHNIOWSKI is associate
professor at Columbia University Graduate School of Business
Administration and a Faculty Research Fellow of the National
Bureau of Economic Research.

The University of Chicago Press, Chicago 60637
The University of Chicago Press, Ltd., London

© 1988 by the National Bureau of Economic Research
All rights reserved. Published 1988
Printed in the United States of America
97 96 95 94 93 92 91 90 89 88   5 4 3 2 1

Library of Congress Cataloging-in-Publication Data

When public sector workers unionize / edited by Richard B.
    Freeman and Casey Ichniowski.
        p.   cm. — (A National Bureau of Economic Research
    project report)
        "Papers presented at a conference held in Cambridge,
    Massachusetts, 11–15 August 1986"—Pref.
    Includes bibliographies and index.
    ISBN 0-226-26166-2
        1. Trade-unions—Government employees—United States—
Congresses. 2. Trade-unions—Government employees—Law and
legislation—United States—Congresses. 3. Collective bargaining—
Government employees—United States—Congresses. I. Freeman,
Richard B. (Richard Barry), 1943-   . II. Ichniowski, Casey.
III. Series.
HD8005.2.U5W48 1988
331.88'1135'0000—dc19
                                                        88-9669
                                                        CIP

National Bureau of Economic Research

Officers

Richard N. Rosett, *chairman*
George T. Conklin, Jr., *vice chairman*
Martin Feldstein, *president and chief executive officer*

Geoffrey Carliner, *executive director*
Charles A. Walworth, *treasurer*
Sam Parker, *director of finance and administration*

Directors at Large

John H. Biggs
Andrew Brimmer
Carl F. Christ
George T. Conklin, Jr.
Kathleen B. Cooper
Jean A. Crockett
George C. Eads
Morton Ehrlich

Martin Feldstein
David L. Grove
George Hatsopoulos
Franklin A. Lindsay
Paul W. McCracken
Geoffrey H. Moore
Michael H. Moskow
James J. O'Leary

Robert T. Parry
Peter G. Peterson
Robert V. Roosa
Richard N. Rosett
Bert Seidman
Eli Shapiro
Harold Shapiro
Donald S. Wasserman

Directors by University Appointment

Charles H. Berry, *Princeton*
James Duesenberry, *Harvard*
Ann F. Friedlaender, *Massachusetts Institute of Technology*
Jonathan Hughes, *Northwestern*
Saul Hymans, *Michigan*
J. C. LaForce, *California, Los Angeles*
Marjorie McElroy, *Duke*

Merton J. Peck, *Yale*
James L. Pierce, *California, Berkeley*
Andrew Postlewaite, *Pennsylvania*
Nathan Rosenberg, *Stanford*
James Simler, *Minnesota*
William S. Vickrey, *Columbia*
Burton A. Weisbrod, *Wisconsin*
Arnold Zellner, *Chicago*

Directors by Appointment of Other Organizations

Richard Easterlin, *Economic History Association*
Edgar Fiedler, *National Association of Business Economists*
Robert S. Hamada, *American Finance Association*
Robert C. Holland, *Committee for Economic Development*
James Houck, *American Agricultural Economics Association*
David Kendrick, *American Economic Association*

Eric Kruger, *The Conference Board*
Rudolph A. Oswald, *American Federation of Labor and Congress of Industrial Organizations*
Douglas D. Purvis, *Canadian Economics Association*
Dudley Wallace, *American Statistical Association*
Charles A. Walworth, *American Institute of Certified Public Accountants*

Directors Emeriti

Moses Abramovitz
Emilio G. Collado
Solomon Fabricant

Frank W. Fetter
Thomas D. Flynn
Gottfried Haberler

George B. Roberts
Willard L. Thorp

Relation of the Directors to the Work and Publications of the National Bureau of Economic Research

1. The object of the National Bureau of Economic Research is to ascertain and to present to the public important economic facts and their interpretation in a scientific and impartial manner. The Board of Directors is charged with the responsibility of ensuring that the work of the National Bureau is carried on in strict conformity with this object.

2. The President of the National Bureau shall submit to the Board of Directors, or to its Executive Committee, for their formal adoption all specific proposals for research to be instituted.

3. No research report shall be published by the National Bureau until the President has sent each member of the Board a notice that a manuscript is recommended for publication and that in the President's opinion it is suitable for publication in accordance with the principles of the National Bureau. Such notification will include an abstract or summary of the manuscript's content and a response form for use by those Directors who desire a copy of the manuscript for review. Each manuscript shall contain a summary drawing attention to the nature and treatment of the problem studied, the character of the data and their utilization in the report, and the main conclusions reached.

4. For each manuscript so submitted, a special committee of the Directors (including Directors Emeriti) shall be appointed by majority agreement of the President and Vice Presidents (or by the Executive Committee in case of inability to decide on the part of the President and Vice Presidents), consisting of three Directors selected as nearly as may be one from each general division of the Board. The names of the special manuscript committee shall be stated to each Director when notice of the proposed publication is submitted to him. It shall be the duty of each member of the special manuscript committee to read the manuscript. If each member of the manuscript committee signifies his approval within thirty days of the transmittal of the manuscript, the report may be published. If at the end of that period any member of the manuscript committee withholds his approval, the President shall then notify each member of the Board, requesting approval or disapproval of publication, and thirty days additional shall be granted for this purpose. The manuscript shall then not be published unless at least a majority of the entire Board who shall have voted on the proposal within the time fixed for the receipt of votes shall have approved.

5. No manuscript may be published, though approved by each member of the special manuscript committee, until forty-five days have elapsed from the transmittal of the report in manuscript form. The interval is allowed for the receipt of any memorandum of dissent or reservation, together with a brief statement of his reasons, that any member may wish to express; and such memorandum of dissent or reservation shall be published with the manuscript if he so desires. Publication does not, however, imply that each member of the Board has read the manuscript, or that either members of the Board in general or the special committee have passed on its validity in every detail.

6. Publications of the National Bureau issued for informational purposes concerning the work of the Bureau and its staff, or issued to inform the public of activities of Bureau staff, and volumes issued as a result of various conferences involving the National Bureau shall contain a specific disclaimer noting that such publication has not passed through the normal review procedures required in this resolution. The Executive Committee of the Board is charged with review of all such publications from time to time to ensure that they do not take on the character of formal research reports of the National Bureau, requiring formal Board approval.

7. Unless otherwise determined by the Board or exempted by the terms of paragraph 6, a copy of this resolution shall be printed in each National Bureau publication.

(Resolution adopted October 25, 1926, as revised through September 30, 1974)

Contents

Preface

This volume consists of papers presented at a conference held in Cambridge, Massachusetts, 11–15 August 1986, and is part of the National Bureau of Economic Research Labor Studies Program. Support for the project came from the Alfred P. Sloan Foundation. We are grateful to Jane Konkel for assistance in shepherding the volume through the editorial process.

Any opinions expressed in this volume are those of the respective authors and do not necessarily reflect the views of the National Bureau of Economic Research or the sponsoring organization.

Introduction:
The Public Sector Look
of American Unionism

Richard B. Freeman and Casey Ichniowski

After decades in which collective bargaining with the government was considered virtually "impossible" in America,[1] unionization achieved in the 1970s and 1980s greater strength in the public sector than in the private sector. In 1986 over a third of public sector workers were organized into unions, and over 40 percent were covered by collective agreements compared to a union density in the private sector of 14 percent. Nearly one in three union members was a public employee. The National Education Association, the American Federation of Teachers, the American Federation of State, County, and Municipal Employees, and the Service Employees International Union (with nearly half its membership in the public sector) were among the largest unions in the country. Unions of fire fighters and police were well-established exemplars of the craft-type organizations that once dominated American labor. Public sector unionism had become *the* vibrant component of the American labor movement.

Why did union density and collective bargaining prosper in the public sector while declining elsewhere? What does the new public sector "look" of organized labor mean for the economy? Do labor-management relations in the public sector mirror private sector patterns or do they represent something novel on the labor scene? What can the private sector learn from the success of collective bargaining in the public sector?

This volume examines these questions with: new data on public sector labor laws; previously unanalyzed Census/Survey of Governments data

Richard B. Freeman is professor of economics at Harvard University and the Director of Labor Studies at the National Bureau of Economic Research. Casey Ichniowski is associate professor at Columbia University Graduate School of Business Administration and a Faculty Research Fellow of the National Bureau of Economic Research.

1

on state and local government labor relations practices; specially constructed data sets on teachers, police, federal employees, and arbitrators; labor relations histories in particular states; and extracts from the Current Population Survey and other surveys of individuals. These new data permit analyses of public sector unionism that go beyond estimating the impact of a 0-1 union variable on wages that has been the focus of much past work. The research highlights fundamental differences between public and private sector labor relations in the conditions that foster or undermine unionism; the pay and employment outcomes unions produce; and the procedures by which unions secure benefits for their members.

Studies of the growth of public sector collective bargaining attribute the 1970s and 1980s spurt largely to the enactment of comprehensive labor laws that impose a duty to bargain on managers, often with compulsory arbitration to resolve disputes. The greater effectiveness of these laws than that of the National Labor Relations Act, which governs private sector unionism, is explained by the political incentives that keep public sector managers from opposing unions and committing unfair labor practices to the extent done in the private sector.

The studies of union impacts find that public sector unions have different or more pronounced effects than private sector unions in several areas: reducing layoffs and unemployment and increasing employment of members; raising wages of nonunion workers through "spillover" or "threat" effects; and increasing expenditures in organized departments. In addition, teacher unionism has been found to be associated with higher student test scores. As a result of these impacts, the wage differential between union and nonunion workers, commonly used to measure what unions do, *understates* the impact of unionism on the public sector.

Finally, the research shows that public sector unionism affects outcomes in ways that go beyond standard collective bargaining: through lobbying and political campaigning that influence both the goals and behavior of management and citizens' views about desired public services, and through use of final outcome arbitration to resolve impasses rather than the traditional strike weapon.

The Central Role of Labor Laws in Public Sector Labor Relations

Students of the U.S. Labor movement have long debated the role of labor law in unionization. Some argue that laws are a fundamental determinant of union strength, crediting (blaming) the National Labor Relations Act of 1936 and decisions of the War Labor Board for much of the rise of private sector unionism in the 1940s, and blaming (crediting) union decline in the 1970s and 1980s on the ensuing failure of labor law to control illegal management activities in representation elections.[2] Others, noting union successes in periods of legal adversity and the ability of management and labor to circumvent legal restrictions, feel that laws have little effect on unionism.[3]

The variation in public sector labor laws among states and occupations at a point in time and over time—which ranges from outlawing collective bargaining to providing arbitration mechanisms to resolve contract disputes—provides a "natural experiment" to evaluate the role of legal enactment in the evolution of collective bargaining. Accordingly, NBER researchers developed a data set measuring public sector labor law from 1955, when bargaining with the government seemed impossible, to 1984, when many states had enacted comprehensive public sector labor laws; they obtained data on collective contracts in Ohio and Illinois, industrial states whose public sector unionization prior to enactment of laws are oft-cited counter examples to the claim that laws are important; and they determined the dates when police departments first signed collective contracts in cities throughout the country. Analyses of these data yield five broad conclusions about the role of labor law in the rise of collective bargaining in the public sector.

1. The legal environment is critical in determining whether or not public sector employers bargain collectively with their workers.

The evidence is threefold. First, favorable state public sector labor laws increase the probability that a municipal department is governed by a collective contract, even when other diverse determinants of contract status, including extent of union membership[4] and the city in which a department is located, are held fixed (Freeman and Valletta, this volume, chap. 3, tables 3.2 and 3.3). Second, passage of comprehensive public sector labor laws induced sharp increases in the percentage of departments bargaining within a state. Among police, research indicates that the impact of laws is so substantial that within eight years of enactment of laws mandating arbitration virtually all departments bargain contractually with their workers, while in the absence of laws it would take "forever" (252 years) for workers to achieve such coverage (Ichniowski, this volume, chap. 1, table 1.2, figure 1.2). Third, analysis of Ohio and Illinois shows that the 1983 comprehensive public sector laws enacted in these "exceptions" induced dramatic spurts in contract coverage: in Illinois the probability that school districts signed contracts increased by 32 percentage points within a year of enactment (Saltzman, this volume, chap. 2, table 2.4). Moreover, unionism prior to passage of the laws was abetted by favorable court decisions on the legality of collective bargaining. While not "necessary" for unionization, favorable public sector labor laws seem to be a sufficient condition for rapid growth.

2. *Economic benefits and costs do not readily explain the timing of public sector labor laws.*

The trend in public sector labor law has been, first, to legalize union activity and require managers to "meet and confer" with unions; second, to require managers to bargain with unions; and, third, to mandate arbitration or other final closure mechanisms to guarantee a contract (Valletta and Freeman, this volume, appendix B). To the extent that passage of the laws themselves depends on fundamental economic forces, the factors that determine enactment of laws should be part of the economic analysis of union growth. Can we identify such factors?

While cross-state comparisons show that state characteristics such as per capita income and public expenditures are associated with public sector laws favorable to unionism (Kochan 1973; Faber and Martin 1980; Hunt, White, and Moore 1985), analysis of changes over time fail to turn up systematic factors that cause states to enact laws earlier rather than later (Farber, this volume, chap. 5). Different states moved at different speeds toward comprehensive public sector labor laws, apparently for "idiosyncratic" political reasons involving patronage, personalities, and union rivalry rather than broad economic or social factors. That Ohio and Illinois did not enact comprehensive labor laws until 1983 is consistent with this pattern. Viewed negatively, the inability to explain the timing of state labor laws suggests limits to economic analysis of legal developments and the need for detailed legislative histories to understand changes. Viewed positively, the finding suggests that treating the timing of the laws as exogenous does not create significant biases in analyzing the impact of laws on bargaining and thus strengthens the conclusion that laws can be treated as an independent cause of the growth of collective bargaining.

3. *Public sector laws favorable to collective bargaining raise wages in nonunion as well as union departments but have substantial adverse employment consequences only for nonunion departments.*

By spurring collective bargaining, public sector labor laws are indirectly responsible for union-induced changes in wages and employment. In addition, the laws affect economic outcomes by enhancing the bargaining power of unions and altering management decisions in nonunion departments as well.

Indicative of the impact of laws on union bargaining strength, unionized workers in municipal departments in states with laws favorable to collective bargaining receive about 6 percent higher pay than those in states with unfavorable laws and appear to experience a comparable increase in pay following passage of favorable laws.[5] Indicative of the apparent impact of the laws on nonunion departments, the pay of nonunion municipal workers is about 3 percent higher in states with comprehensive public sector labor laws than in other states, seemingly as a result of the "threat" that those workers will also unionize. The employment consequences of strong collective bargaining laws, by contrast, differ between union and nonunion departments: unionized departments experience only marginally lower employment in favorable legal environments despite higher wages whereas nonunion departments suffer considerable job loss, suggesting that unions use some of the power they attain from favorable legislation to maintain employment (Freeman and Valletta, this volume, chap. 3, tables 3.5 and 3.7).

4. Among states that obligate employers to bargain, wages are no higher with compulsory arbitration than with other dispute resolution mechanisms, whereas wages are noticeably higher with strike-permitted laws.

One of the hallmarks of public sector labor relations is the use of dispute resolution mechanisms, including compulsory interest arbitration of various forms, in place of strikes and lockouts. While at one time public sector unions opposed such alternatives to the strike, more recently management has alleged that arbitration favors unions. Dramatizing this complaint in 1977, one Massachusetts mayor stripped to his shorts before television cameras to show that arbitration was "stripping" the city of its money (*New Bedford Standard-Times*, 25 January 1977). Extant research, however, finds that arbitrated settlements are, if anything, lower than negotiated settlements (Ashenfelter and Bloom 1984). This leaves only one possible way for arbitration to raise wages: by creating an environment in which cities agree to high negotiated settlements for fear that arbitrators will impose even higher wages. If this were true, cities in states with compulsory arbitration would pay more for comparable labor (all else the same) than cities in states that simply require employers to bargain with unions; pay would rise especially rapidly when state laws changed from duty-to-bargain to compulsory arbitration. The evidence, however, shows that pay in states with compulsory arbitration laws does not differ noticeably from that in other duty-to-bargain states, whereas pay is on the order of 2–9 percent higher in states that permit strikes (Freeman and Valletta, this volume, chap. 3, table 3.8). That arbitration has little impact on wages in states that encourage bargaining is important in light of evidence that arbitration laws reduce strike rates (Ichniowski 1982), for it suggests that compulsory arbitration resolves impasses without strikes— the aim of these laws—without increasing wages and salaries.

5. *Arbitrators do not favor one side or the other nor respond greatly to the facts of a case when labor and management make "reasonable" proposals; rather, they tend to "split the difference."*

The question of the extent to which arbitrators split the difference between offers as opposed to making independent judgments based on the facts is a long-standing one. One way to evaluate arbitrator behavior is to devise "laboratory-type experiments" in which the researcher asks arbitrators to settle pseudocases that isolate the effect of given conditions on outcomes. In an NBER experiment, the researcher asked arbitrators to resolve cases patterned after actual contract disputes and varied the settlements proposed by labor and management. In a set of identical cases, arbitrators tended to split the difference between offers, giving higher (lower) awards when management or labor offers were high (low) even under identical factual situations (Bloom, this volume, chap. 4). At first blush this might suggest that the best strategy for unions and management is to make extreme proposals regardless of the facts. This would be an incorrect inference, however, as arbitrators do indeed place primary weight on facts when offers and facts are unrelated (Bazerman and Farber 1985). Arbitrators split the difference when they feel the proposals of the two sides reflect the facts. As in actual cases both sides generally base offers on the facts, the result is that arbitrators often split the differences in actual practice.

The Effects of Public Sector Collective Bargaining on Wages

Following the private sector union literature, much research on public sector unionism has examined the impact of unions on wages. Reviewing this extensive body of research, Lewis (this volume, chap. 6) concludes that:

6. *Union/nonunion earnings differences tend to be smaller in the public sector than in the private sector but vary considerably among workers and are far from negligible.*

On average the earnings of union workers exceed those of nonunion workers by 8–13 percent in the public sector, which is about 5 percentage points lower than union/nonunion earnings differences in the private sector. However, some groups of unionized public sector workers obtain as large (local government workers) or larger (public school teachers) earnings advantages over nonunion workers as does the average unionized private sector worker. Looking at demographic groups, union/nonunion earnings differences are higher for women than for men in the public sector but are about the same for black as for white workers. Among occupations outside of teaching, union earnings advantages are smaller for blue-collar workers in the public sector than in the private sector, at least among males, and are modest for police, fire fighters, and most hospital workers.

The new NBER research adds to and modifies the findings of earlier work, leading to three further findings:

7. *Nonunion workers appear to benefit from the presence of unionism in the public sector, receiving higher pay in states with laws favorable to collective bargaining and in cities where other workers are unionized.*

The first bit of evidence of wage spillovers in the public sector is the finding, noted under point 3 above, that the earnings of nonunion workers in states with laws that favor collective bargaining are higher than the earnings of nonunion workers in other states, all else held fixed. The second piece of evidence is that nonunion workers earnings increased especially rapidly in states that enacted comprehensive collective bargaining laws compared to nonunion worker earnings in other states (Freeman and Valletta, this volume, chap. 3, tables 3.5 and 3.7). The third piece of evidence is that workers in unorganized departments of a city receive higher pay when workers in other departments are organized (Zax and Ichniowski, this volume, chap. 12, tables 12.3 and 12.6). Wage "spillover" from organized police to fire fighters, where pay parity is an explicit issue in collective bargaining, is especially pronounced. The interpretation of these relations as resulting from the threat of union organization is supported by other research showing that, among police at least, low-wage departments have the highest chances of being organized (Ichniowski, Freeman, and Lauer 1987).

8. *Public sector wages rise with size of department, partly because larger cities have a greater ability to pay, as reflected in property values and family incomes, while wage differences between union and nonunion public sector workers depend modestly on the city's ability to pay.*

In the private sector, pay increases with the size of firm or establishment, particularly in the nonunion sector, implying that unions raise wages less at large workplaces. Do wages rise with size and union premiums fall with size in the public sector as well? What is the effect of controlling for measures of the size of department or city and the ability to pay on the union wage premium?

Increases in pay with size in the public sector are about as large as the increases in pay with size in the private sector, but they reveal a different pattern by union status, with union effects on wages independent or increasing with size. Data on individuals from the Current Population Survey (CPS) indicate that a 10 percent increase in the size of a government unit is associated with a 0.2 percent increase in wages[6] and a rise in the union wage premium of about 0.4 percent, other factors held fixed. The rise in the union premium at larger workplaces may reflect greater union political power where employment is greater or possibly the ability of strong unions to raise employment as well as wages (see point 10 below). Data from the Survey of Governments (SOG) on municipal departments show a more pronounced relation between size and pay, with a 10 percent increase in size associated with a 0.4 percent increase in pay, but no change in the union premium with size (Brown and Medoff, this volume, chap. 7, table 7.3). As far as can be told, moreover, only about a fifth of the increase in pay with city size results from factors such as property values that measure a city's "ability to pay." Similarly, while some of the public sector union/nonunion wage differential can be attributed to disproportionate unionization of larger departments and of workers in cities with greater ability to pay, the vast bulk of the effect must be attributed to unionism per se rather than to these correlates.

9. *Despite the fact that federal employee unions do not negotiate pay, many federal workers earn more than they would in the private sector, producing queues for federal jobs.*

The question of whether federal employees are paid more or less than otherwise comparable workers in the labor market has generated considerable controversy. Comparisons of wages based on the CPS, which contains information for individual characteristics, show federal employees to be relatively highly paid (Smith 1977), with the greatest differences being among minorities and women (Asher and Popkin 1984). Comparisons of wages in narrowly defined occupations gives, however, the opposite pattern, with significant pay disadvantage to federal workers in the late 1970s and 1980s (Freeman 1988). Which picture of federal pay is right?

Evidence from workers who move between federal and private employment supports the view that federal pay is relatively high for average workers, as those who move from private to federal employment obtain larger wage gains than those who move from one private employer to another. In addition, Civil Service Commission data show sizeable queues for federal employment (Krueger, this volume, chap. 8). As federal worker unions do not negotiate pay, these wage advantages cannot be attributed to collective bargaining. One possible reason for high pay, consistent with the increase in pay by size in the public sector, is that the federal government is by far the nation's largest employer. Another possibility is that the federal government's national pay scale—chosen for reasons of administrative ease, internal labor market mobility, and politics—requires that average pay be high enough to attract labor in high-wage local markets.

The Effects of Public Sector Unionism on Employment, Labor Turnover, Output, and Budgets

Because union wage effects are smaller in the public than in the private sector, it is common to conclude that public sector unions are weaker than their private sector counterparts. NBER research rejects this notion because of the pronounced effects of public sector unionism on other labor market outcomes—employment, layoffs, output, and budgets.

10. Public sector unionism raises employment of organized workers.

It is generally held that private sector union wage gains come at the expense of employment, as enterprises economize on more expensive labor.[7] The pattern in the public sector seems to be quite different. Consistent with earlier work (Zax 1985), comparisons of employment across cities show that with diverse factors held fixed, departments that bargain collectively hire more workers than otherwise similar departments that do not bargain collectively (Freeman and Valletta, this volume, chap. 3, tables 3.5 and 3.6; Zax and Ichniowski, this volume, chap. 12, tables 12.1–12.3). Coupled with the positive impact of collective bargaining on wages, this implies that payrolls are higher in union departments and also produces higher total expenditures in those departments (Zax and Ichniowski, this volume, chap. 12, tables 12.4 and 12.5). Only among teachers have NBER researchers failed to find a positive bargaining effect on employment (Kleiner and Petree, this volume, chap. 11, table 11.6), though here other recent research has detected such effects (Eberts and Stone 1986).

There are two possible reasons why employment of unionized labor might be higher in the public sector despite higher wages. One is that public sector unions shift the demand for members' services through political activity—lobbying and campaigning for additional public expenditures that increase both wages and employment. An alternative explanation is that unions use their bargaining strength to force employers off demand curves in accord with union preferences for jobs (producing so-called efficient contracts), for instance, by demanding contract clauses that specify a minimum number of police per cruiser, or fire fighters per shift or piece of equipment, or pupils per classroom.

Without denying union use of collective bargaining to alter employment, the fact that city councils and legislatures need not appropriate the money to finance negotiated settlements forces unions to complement contract provisions with political and lobbying activities that affect the level of demand. In the public sector unions cannot rely exclusively on collective bargaining behind closed doors to obtain desired agreements, efficient or not.

11. Public sector unionism reduces layoffs and unemployment but has only marginal effects on quits.

The impact of unionism on turnover are strikingly different in the public sector than in the private sector (Allen, this volume, chap. 10). Unions in the public sector reduce substantially temporary and indefinite layoffs, whereas they increase those layoffs in the private sector (Medoff 1979). The magnitudes of the public sector effects are, moreover, quite large: in the mid-to-late 1970s the likelihood that public sector employees would be on temporary or indefinite layoff was 40 pecent less for unionized than nonunion employees, whereas in the private sector unionists were three times more likely to be on temporary or indefinite layoff than nonunion workers (Allen, this volume, chap. 10, table 10.3). On the other hand, quit rates, which unionism lowers markedly in the private sector (Freeman 1980), are barely affected by union status in the public sector (Allen, this volume, chap. 10, tables 10.5 and 10.6). The net of these two effects—reductions in layoffs and modest impacts on quits—is that unionism in the public sector appears to increase job stability and reduce the probability of unemployment for members. This is consistent with the finding that public sector unionism raises employment (see point 10) and is a major element in our conclusion that public sector unions have more substantial economic effects than shown in simple comparisons of union and nonunion wages.

12. Teacher unionism is associated with increased student test scores, but the reasons for this association are not well determined.

Extant research on the impact of unionism on productivity in the public sector presents a mixed picture: some studies show positive union effects, others find negative effects, while others report no effects, leading to the generalization that on net unionism is neutral to productivity in the public sector (Freeman 1986; Methe and Perry 1980). Using special tabulations of student test scores and other indicators to measure outputs in education, NBER researchers found educational productivity to be somewhat higher, other factors held fixed, in more highly unionized states. Longitudinal data that contrast scores in the same state over time show a comparable result, though whether the effects come from the presence of a labor organization per se or from collective bargaining is unclear (Kleiner and Petree, this volume, chap. 11, table 11.8). Working separately with data for individual students rather than states, Eberts and Stone (1986) report comparable results for students with average achievement levels, but more complex ones for more/less able students. Unfortunately neither study is able to identify the particular factors—better management due to union pressures? lower turnover? greater teacher effort?—by which unionism is associated with greater educational productivity.[8]

13. State aid to local school districts does not increase wages or employment in a unionized setting but, rather, reduces taxes.

When a state awards a school district unexpected grants-in-aid, how much of the funds show up in higher teacher pay or employment or other educational expenditures as opposed to reductions in local taxes? Surprisingly, in highly unionized states such as New York (Ehrenberg and Chaykowski, this volume, chap. 9) and Michigan (Murnane, Singer, and Willett 1986), districts have used such money largely to reduce property taxes. Why? One possibility is that school districts were unwilling to make major salary or employment commitments based on state financing that they view as uncertain. Another possibility is that the failure to raise wages or employment is a "period effect" due to the 1970s and early 1980s "tax revolt" at the state and local levels. Finally, it is possible that in these states unions used their lobbying resources to increase educational spending from normal funding sources to such an extent that taxpayers were unwilling to finance additional resources for schooling. Whichever interpretation is correct, the fact that state relief does not augment school spending highlights the limitations on the ability of unions to raise spending through collective bargaining and thus helps explain union pressure for state laws that earmark increased state aid for higher minimum salaries, as in New Jersey, or for general teachers' salaries, as in New York, and the importance of activity outside normal collective bargaining.

14. Public sector collective bargaining raises expenditures on unionized functions but appears to have little impact on total municipal expenditures.

Further evidence on the limited ability of public sector unions to affect outcomes through bargaining is given by the surprising fact that while cities that bargain with unions in four municipal functions (police, fire, sanitation, and street and highway workers) spend more on these activities than other cities, they do not have higher *total* city budgets than cities that do not bargain with unions (Zax and Ichniowski, this volume, chap. 12, table 12.4). The implication is that the bulk of union-induced increases in expenditures on organized activities is funded by reallocating city moneys from nonorganized to organized activities rather than by increasing total spending and taxes. If this finding is correct,[9] public sector unions would seem to have greater ability to alter line items in a given city budget than to increase taxes and budgets, perhaps because taxpayers pay more attention to total tax bills than to expenditures on specific services. By contrast, private sector unions are more likely to impact bottom-line profits than the allocation of moneys within a firm.

Interpreting Public Sector Labor Relations

Despite comprehensive labor laws that mimic the National Labor Relations Act and a tradition of drawing on the experience of the private sector, public sector unions and management have evolved a new and different labor relations system. Why? What explains the features of public sector labor relations found in this volume and in other research?

Our analysis stresses the distinct incentives and constraints that operate in political as opposed to economic markets, in particular the fact that public sector management and labor, unlike private employers and unions, must appeal to voters to support their actions. For unions, this creates an opportunity to affect the agenda of the employers who face them across the bargaining table. At the same time it makes them frame demands and set policies on the allocation of resources to public services broadly defined as well as on benefits to members, and thus go beyond the bargaining table to convince those who ultimately foot the bill of the virtue of their case. Since political influence depends in part on how large a group one can muster, moreover, public sector unions tend to place great weight on employment outcomes (see Courant, Gramlich, and Rubinfeld 1979). On the employer side, the fact that management is beholden to an electorate that includes public sector workers and politically active unions induces management to take a less adversarial approach to collective bargaining than do private sector managers beholden to shareholders. Further reducing the adversarial relation is the fact that unions can be an important ally in convincing the electorate, or the legislature, or other governmental bodies of the need to increase budgets. Finally, the belief that government employees should not have the right to strike has spurred public sector development of arbitration to resolve impasses, which itself alters the nature of the management-labor conflict.

Another important factor that differentiates the public sector from the private sector in the United States (though not in most countries) is the setting of public sector labor law on a decentralized state basis. Decentralization of the law allows areas of the country favorably inclined to unionism to encourage collective bargaining and areas with unfavorable attitudes to restrict it. It also has led to numerous "experiments" with different modes of regulating union and management conduct and conflicts, encouraging institutional innovation and diversity. In contrast to the private sector, where workers and employers have been limited to the traditional model of exclusive representation, bargaining-to-contract, and strikes to settle impasses, the public sector has offered a range of unions and union-type organizations from worker associations with whom employers need not bargain to full-fledged collective bargaining organizations with diverse alternative modes of impasse resolution.

Given the greater success of collective bargaining in the public sector than in the private sector in the 1970s and 1980s, the time would seem to have come for researchers and practitioners to begin to ask what the private sector might learn from the public sector experience rather than the converse.

Notes

1. In 1962 George Meany was quoted as declaring that it is "impossible to bargain collectively with the government." See Kramer, (1962, 41).
2. See, for example, Freeman (1988).
3. John Dunlop, in particular, has argued that union growth occurs in spurts not necessarily related to legal developments (pers. comm. 1987). For the public sector, Burton (1979) has advanced the argument that policy changes are no more important than several other factors.
4. In the public sector there is considerable membership in unions without actual bargaining to a contract, as shown in Freeman, Ichniowski, and Zax (this volume, appendix A).
5. In these calculations a law favorable to collective bargaining is defined as a duty-to-bargain law without arbitration or the right to strike, while an unfavorable environment is defined as a state without any public sector labor law. In the Freeman and Valletta legal index (this volume, chap. 3), these laws have values of about 1.0 and -1.0, respectively, indicating that they are one standard deviation above and below the mean in terms of favorableness to collective bargaining. Hence, we have multiplied the coefficients in their tables by 2 to obtain the figures in the text.
6. Brown and Medoff (this volume, chap. 7) suggest that the "company" employment variable is perhaps a better measure of size of government in the CPS file than the site employment variable, so we concentrate on their company results here.

7. The evidence for a negative employment effect is, however, weak (Pencavel and Hartsog 1984), and models of efficient contracts suggest that it may in fact be negligible if unions are able to redistribute economic rents efficiently.

8. The failure of these studies to identify the mechanism underlying the improved performance of schools in a union environment mirrors the general failure of economists to determine causes of productivity advance and the more specific problem in determining why productivity tends to be higher in unionized settings in the private sector.

9. Valletta (1987) uses a different methodology and obtains comparable results with the SOG data, indicating that this finding is not dependent on a particular model specification. It should, however, be corroborated with other data (tax rates and the like).

References

Ashenfelter, Orley, and David Bloom. 1984. Models of arbitrator behavior, theory and evidence. *American Economic Review* 74:111–24.

Asher, M., and Joel Popkin. 1984. The effects of gender and race differentials on public-private wage comparisons: A study of postal workers. *Industrial and Labor Relations Review* 38 (October):16–25.

Bazerman, Max, and Hank Farber. 1985. Arbitrator decision-making: When are final offers important? *Industrial and Labor Relations Review* 40:76–89.

Burton, John. 1979. The extent of collective bargaining in the public sector. In *Public sector bargaining*, ed. Benjamin Aaron, Joseph Grodin, and James L. Stern, 1–43. Washington, D.C.: Bureau of National Affairs.

Courant, Paul, Ed Gramlich, and Dan Rubinfeld. 1979. Public employee bargaining power and the level of government spending. *American Economic Review* 69(5):806–17.

Eberts, Randall, and Joe Stone. 1986. On the contract curve: A test of alternative models of collective bargaining. *Journal of Labor Economics* 4(1):66–81.

Faber, Charles, and Donald Martin. 1980. Two factors affecting enactment of collective bargaining legislation in public education. *Journal of Collective Negotiations* 9(4):329–42.

Freeman, R. 1980. The exit-voice tradeoff in the labor market: Unionism, job tenure, quits and separations. *Quarterly Journal of Economics* 94(4).

———. 1986. Unionism comes to the public sector. *Journal of Economic Literature* 24(1).

———. 1988. Contraction and expansion: The divergence of private sector and public sector unionism in the U.S. *Journal of Economic Perspectives* 2(2):63–68.

Hunt, Janet, Rudolph White, and T. A. Moore. 1985. State employee bargaining legislation. *Journal of Labor Research* 6(1):63–76.

Ichniowski, Casey. 1982. Arbitration and police bargaining: Prescriptions for the blue flu. *Industrial Relations* 21(2):149–66.

Ichniowski, Casey, Richard Freeman, and Harrison Lauer. 1987. Collective bargaining laws, threat effects, and the determination of police compensation. Typescript.

Kochan, Thomas. 1973. Correlates of state public employee bargaining laws. *Industrial Relations* 12(3):322–37.

Kramer, Leo. 1962. *Labor's paradox—The American Federation of State, County, and Municipal Employees, AFL-CIO.* New York:Wiley.

Medoff, James. 1979. Layoffs and alternatives under trade unions in U.S. manufacturing. *American Economic Review* 69(3):380–95.

Methe, David, and James Perry. 1980. The impacts of collective bargaining on local government services: A review of research. *Public Administration Review* 40(4):359–71.

Murnane, Richard, Judy Singer, and John Willett. 1986. How did teacher salary schedules change in the 1970s? Harvard Graduate School of Education. Typescript.

Pencavel, John, and Cathy Hartsog. 1984. A reconsideration of the effects of unionism on relative wages and employment in the U.S., 1920–1980. *Journal of Labor Economics* 2(2):193–232.

Smith, Sharon. 1977. *Equal pay in the public sector: Fact or fancy?* Princeton, N.J.: Princeton University Press.

Valletta, Robert. 1987. Labor policy and resource allocation in the government sector: Three essays on public school unionism. Ph.D. diss., Harvard University.

Zax, Jeffrey. 1985. Municipal employment, municipal unions, and demand for municipal services. NBER Working Paper no. 1728. Cambridge, Mass.: National Bureau of Economic Research.

I   The Role of Public Sector Labor Law

1 Public Sector Union Growth and Bargaining Laws: A Proportional Hazards Approach with Time-Varying Treatments

Casey Ichniowski

1.1 Introduction

Entering the 1960s, few public sector employees were organized. By 1984, approximately 36 percent of all government employees in the United States were members of unions (Freeman 1986, 41). For certain occupational groups, particularly the protective services, collective bargaining establishes salaries and working conditions for the vast majority of departments in the United States (Freeman 1986, 46). This explosion in public sector unionism has occurred while private sector unionization has declined dramatically. It also coincides with the passage of state laws that provide various degrees of protection of public employees' rights to organize and to bargain collectively. The role that these laws play in the growth of public sector unionism is the central focus of this study.

1.2 Previous Research and Current Methodology

Largely because the coverage of the National Labor Relations Act (NLRA) extends across most areas of private sector employment, econometric investigations of the relationship between policy variables and union growth using private sector data are necessarily very limited. The most convincing studies are perhaps case studies of groups that were at various times covered by the NLRA; for example, supervisors

Casey Ichniowski is associate professor at Columbia University Graduate School of Business Administration and a Faculty Research Fellow of the National Bureau of Economic Research.

The author wishes to thank John Abowd, Richard Berk, Henry Farber and Ann Witte for their comments, and Paul Huo for expert assistance with the research.

in the Foremen's Association of America in the late 1930s and early 1940s (see Ross 1965, 260–62), or agricultural workers in the United Farm Workers in California in the late 1960s (see Kushner 1975). In contrast, the public sector provides a better laboratory for examining the linkages between public policies and union growth because of the extreme variation in public sector collective bargaining laws across states and occupational groups. Despite this, there have been few investigations of the relationship between bargaining laws and union growth in the public sector, and those studies tend to focus on unionization among teachers.[1]

The studies also rely on aggregate state-level data and therefore suffer from three limitations. The state-level percent-organized or percent-covered measures used as dependent variables are affected not only by the formation of new units, but also by subsequent employment effects of collective bargaining. If, as has been recently suggested, public sector unions increase employment as well as compensation levels through their influence on the budget-setting process (Freeman 1986, 52), then percent-organized statistics may increase from relative increases in manning after departments unionize as well as from the formation of new bargaining units. The limited evidence on this point in fact supports the proposition concerning positive employment effects of public unions (Zax 1985). A second difficulty associated with using state-level percent-organized variables as the dependent variable is that these state-level percent-organized variables give equal weight to a given percentage increase in unionization in different states, even though the same percent increase represents very different numbers of bargaining units and covered employees from state to state. For example, a given percentage increase in New Hampshire's percent organized may correspond to the formation of only a very small number of bargaining units covering relatively few employees, while in California the same percentage increase may mean a very large number of new units were formed. Third, state-level analyses cannot provide any information on the kinds of municipalities that are more or less likely to enter bargaining relationships with unions in their departments.

In contrast to this earlier work, in this study I focus on collective bargaining at the municipal level, which is normally the level at which bargaining units are formed for most public sector occupations. I use the data to follow the unionization history of approximately 1,000 municipal police departments with differing characteristics under various state laws. Unlike with most state-level studies, which use cross-sectional data and can only document whether unionization tends to be higher in states that have laws,[2] here I take a longitudinal perspective and ask whether or not the legislation is necessary to permit growth of collective bargaining.

1.2.1   Model Specification: Proportional Hazards Framework

With municipal-level data, more appropriate specifications than have been previously employed can be developed. Specifically, I model the process of bargaining unit formation as a duration study that asks "what determines the length of time that will pass before a department unionizes?" and I use the Cox proportional hazard (PH) model to analyze the data. Let Y_1 measure the number of years municipality i remains nonunion; $f(Y)$ is the probability density function of this duration variable; $F(Y)$ is the cumulative probability function; and $H(Y) = f(Y)/(1 - F(Y))$, the hazard function that describes the rate of transition from nonunion to union status. The PH model assumes multiplicative effects of the independent variables according to:

$$(1) \qquad H(Y) = H(Y)\exp(XB)$$

where X is a vector of municipal and state-level characteristics that affect the decision to unionize. The PH model assumes no specific form for the underlying hazard rate function $H(Y)$. The X variables cause parallel shifts in $H(Y)$.[3]

1.3   Data and Variable Definitions

1.3.1   Dependent Variables: Post-Law Duration and Nonunion Duration

The likelihood function that describes transitions into unionization for each city and town is generated from a duration variable, Y_i. To calculate Y_i, I use responses to two questions to a 1979 survey conducted by Freeman, Ichniowski and Lauer (1985): (1) Does your city have a written labor contract covering wages, hours and conditions of employment for police personnel?; and (2) What year was the first written labor contract signed?. I assume that cities with contracts have been party to a contract since the year given in the response to the second question. This information covers approximately 1,000 municipalities with populations above 10,000 that report municipal police employment in the *Municipal Yearbook* in 1978 (International City Management Association 1978). Police associations that do not bargain for written agreements are considered nonunion. From these survey questions, I construct two different measures of the duration of nonunion status.

The first variable, post-law nonunion duration (PLDUR), is defined as the number of years a city remains nonunion in different legal environments. If laws affect union status, PLDUR will be smaller in the presence than in the absence of a law, and smaller the stronger the law. Because many states do not have laws and because the duration variable is censored for cities that do not unionize, there are some complications in measuring PLDUR. For cities in states *with* laws, there are two components to the PLDUR measure—the value of PLDUR after a law is passed, and the value for PLDUR before the law is passed. For the period *after* passage of the law, PLDUR is either: (1) "year unionized–year of law" for cities that unionize; or (2) "1979–year of law" for cities that do not unionize. For the period *prior* to the passage of the laws, PLDUR is either: (1) "year of law–1958" for cities that do not unionize in the pre-law environment, where 1958 is the year that the first state bargaining law for police was enacted; or (2) "year unionized–1958" for cities that unionize before the law was enacted. For cities in states *without* laws, PLDUR is: "year unionized–1958" for cities that unionize, or, for cities that never unionize, "1979–1958." By defining the duration variable this way, I can contrast unionization in three different environments: in states with a law before and after passage of the law, and in states that never passed a law. Table 1.1 summarizes how PLDUR is defined.

There are two elements of arbitrariness in this definition. First, I chose 1958 as a starting year for calculating nonunion durations, even though I could have chosen earlier years. Second, for cities that do not unionize by 1979, I censor PLDUR at 1979. These two decisions should result in an understatement of the number of years a city is nonunion in an environment without a law and thus bias the estimated effects of the laws downward. That is, had I chosen a year earlier than 1958 as a starting point, the values of PLDUR for cities in environments without laws would be even larger. Moreover, with no particular spurt in police unionization in states without laws since 1979, the number of years that cities remain nonunion in these environments has increased

Table 1.1   Constructing Estimates of Post-law Nonunion Duration (PLDUR)

Law and Unionization Situation	Definition of PLDUR
In states that pass laws:	
After law is passed for cities that unionize after law	year unionized – year of law
After law is passed for cities that never unionize	1979 – year of law (censored)
Before law is passed for cities that do not unionize in the pre-law environment	year of law – 1958 (censored)
Before law is passed for cities that unionize before the law	year unionized – 1958
In states that never passed a law:	
Cities that unionize	year unionized – 1958
Cities that never unionize	1979 – 1958 (censored)

since 1979. One reason why this definition could cause an overstatement of the effects of the laws on unionization is that PLDUR is measured from a starting year of 1958 for cities in states that never enacted a law, while in states that did pass a law, the component of PLDUR for the period after the law is passed is measured from a starting year that is later than 1958. This would result in an upward bias on the estimated effects of the laws, if, as seems likely, the climate for public sector unionization improved over time. However, adding a control variable that measures the year that a law is enacted (YRLAW) will adjust for this bias. By defining PLDUR as beginning in 1958 and including the LAWYR control variable, the analysis should understate the effects of laws on unionization rates.

While analysis of the PLDUR duration variable is designed to give understated point estimates of the effect of the law variables on unionization rates, there is an important limitation on this analysis. The LAWYR control variable is undefined for all no-law observations, and is set to zero for these observations. When the definition of one covariate control variable (LAWYR) directly depends on another covariate (the dummy law variables), the significance of the law dummy variables cannot be determined. Because methods for testing the significance of the parameters on the law variables have not been developed, I estimate several other specifications. First, I analyze a sample with all no-law observations deleted. This addresses a more limited question: within the set of cities that have a law, how do different laws affect unionization rates from the date the law enacted? Since all no-law observations are deleted from the sample (including the set of censored pre-law observations corresponding to the no-law experience of cities that are eventually covered by a law), LAWYR is defined for all observations in the restricted sample. One can therefore test whether the effect of one kind of law on unionization is significantly different from that of a different law.

To extend formal significance testing in a limited fashion to the analyses of the entire sample of municipal observations, I also estimate models of duration of nonunion status using a second duration variable: nonunion duration (NUDUR), which equals the number of years a city remains nonunion after 1955. Again, if a municipality remains nonunion through 1979, the last year of the period being analyzed, the NUDUR variable is censored.

There are several limitations on interpreting parameters on bargaining law variables when NUDUR is the dependent variable. This analysis compares municipalities that were never covered by a bargaining law *and* those that unionized prior to the enactment of a law, with municipalities that did not unionize prior to the law's enactment in states with laws. It tests whether municipalities in the latter group unionized more or less rapidly after the 1955 baseline year, even though the relevant statutes were generally enacted well after 1955. Estimated parameters on the law variables will therefore underestimate the effect of bargaining laws on police unionization. Still, one can test the significance of these underestimates because the definition of NUDUR is the same for cities with and without laws, and because there is no other covariate whose definition directly depends on the law dummy variables. Note, however, that when LAWYR is added to the NUDUR models, it is not possible to perform formal significance testing of the law parameters. Also, including LAWYR in NUDUR models serves a conceptually different purpose than it does in PLDUR models. That is, for observations with laws, NUDUR includes the pre-law years in the dependent duration variable. Thus, where LAWYR is greater, cities have been exposed to the law for less time, implying that the probability of unionization will be lower if laws increase unionization. In NUDUR models, the parameters on LAWYR should therefore be negative, whereas if the climate for police unionization improved during the period under consideration, its coefficient in the PLDUR models should be positive.

In summary, the PLDUR models yield point estimates of the effects of different laws, but to formally test the significance of estimated effects of laws the models must be reestimated with samples restricted to municipalities in states that passed laws. By contrast, the NUDUR models are estimated for the entire sample of municipal observations.

1.3.2   Bargaining Laws: The Timing and Substance of Time-Varying Treatments

In this paper I consider two aspects of state collective bargaining laws as potential determinants of union status: the extent to which the law encourages collective bargaining, and the extent to which the law contains impasse procedures that ensure closure of the bargaining process. My control group consists of states with no collective bargaining laws.[4]

In the case of bargaining laws I distinguish between bargaining permitted (BP) laws that permit but do not obligate employers to bargain with employees, and duty-to-bargain (DTB) laws that require employers to bargain with employees. Bargaining permitted laws often state that employees have some weak form of rights "to meet and confer with" or "to present proposals to" their employers. Duty-to-bargain laws place affirmative obligation on employers to bargain with representatives and thus are more likely to induce unionization.

A DTB provision does not, however, ensure closure to the bargaining process. In the private sector, the strike threat forces negotiators to evaluate impasses and ultimately moves the parties to some resolution of differences in their positions. But, except in very rare circumstances, police strikes are illegal in the United States. One can imagine an employer in a DTB environment bargaining but not conceding to any union demands since the strike threat may be significantly dampened for these public employees. By 1978, fourteen states had enacted some form of compulsory interest arbitration statutes for police negotiations. These environments form another law category (ARB). Under such statutes, police labor organizations need not rely on the final consent of the public employer to determine the terms and conditions of their employment, but rather a neutral third party has power to arbitrate contract terms. If employees believe that interest arbitration produces higher wage settlements, employees would be more likely to organize in these environments. The limited empirical evidence that exists on the impact of arbitration on salaries provides some evidence for such an effect (Olson 1980; Feuille and Delaney 1986). In any case, as long as employees perceive the potential for such an impact of arbitration, it would encourage unionization.

1.3.3   Other Covariates

While there is no comprehensive theory of union growth that clearly identifies other variables that might also influence unionization propensities, previous empirical studies on union growth and representation elections can be used to identify characteristics of police departments and municipalities that might also affect unionization. First, since bargaining laws and policies are defined along state boundaries, it is important to incorporate other state characteristics as controls. State-level controls include four geographic region dummy variables (northeast, north central, south and west), the percentage of state's nonagricultural work force who are public employees, and the percentage of a state's private sector nonagricultural work force that is unionized. The region controls and the percent-union variable will indicate how favorable the climate is toward unionization. If patterns of public sector unionization parallel those in the private sector, one would expect greater public sector unionization for northeastern and north central cities and lower unionization for southern cities. Similarly, the percent-union variable should also have a positive effect on unionization. By contrast, the effect of the proportion of a state's workforce that is in public employment is ambiguous. More public employees constitute a greater voting block likely to pressure states for favorable laws. But, the taxpaying public may find it more important to be represented by public managers who will oppose unionism (and keep labor costs down) where there are relatively more public employees.

Several municipal-level control variables are available for a large proportion of the municipalities in the sample: population, number of departmental employees, per capita income, per capita municipal revenue, central city dummy variable, and three government-type dummy variables (council-manager, mayor-council, and commission).[5] The first two variables acknowledge the importance of unit size in the unionization process. In the private sector, the most common finding is that unit size is negatively related to union support in certification elections (Rose 1972; Chaison 1973; Cooke 1983). The sign of the correlation in this public sector sample may be different for several reasons. First, the private sector samples are generally certification elections from the 1970s or early 1980s. They do not include the earliest unionization campaigns of the 1930s and 1940s, many of which may have had relatively large units. In contrast, this study is designed to consider the process of unionization among all municipalities with populations over 10,000 from the time when virtually no municipal police department was organized. Also, since bureaucratization is likely to increase with city size, employees may need to unionize to obtain a voice in larger municipalities. Since population is available for a slightly larger sample of municipalities than is the department size variable, and since these two variables are highly correlated, I report results for models incorporating only the population control.

Ability-to-pay variables (revenue and income) might indicate an increase in the public employer's ability to satisfy more of the diverse interest groups, including the police department, vying for a share of the municipal budget. In this way, managers in wealthier cities and towns might be better able to avoid unionization. Conversely, the incentive to unionize may be greater where municipal revenues are larger. Thus, these controls play a role similar to firm profitability in private sector unionization studies. The impact of profitability on unionization rates in bargaining-unit-level studies has received little attention in the existing private sector studies.[6]

Central cities may be associated with relatively high area wages, a greater degree of private sector unionization, and perhaps more hazardous duties for the police. If these forces make police more likely to consider unionization, this variable will cause an upward shift in the union hazard function. Finally, different governmental structures might affect the responsiveness of an employer to employee desires, so that certain governmental structures might be more highly correlated with the probability of municipal unionism.

While a number of these controls vary over the period considered, it is necessary to assume that the rankings of municipalities along the dimensions of the controls are reasonably stable over the period (Lawless 1980, 383–94). For example, one must assume that relatively populous cities at the start of the period still rank high in population by the end of the period examined. It is also necessary to assume that unionization of a municipality's police department does not affect that city's relative ranking along the dimensions of the control variables (e.g., if a relatively wealthy suburban town organizes in the early 1960s, it is still relatively wealthy by the end of the period). While these assumptions may be more problematic for some controls (particularly the revenue variables) than for others (such as central city status or government type), these state and municipal characteristics may be correlated with the locus and rate of police unionization and with state bargaining laws. Therefore, they are potentially important controls that help guard against overestimating the impact of bargaining laws on union transition probabilities.

1.4   Empirical Results

Table 1.2 summarizes the basic data that underlie the analysis and reports the percentages of municipalities that unionized before and after enactment of various laws. For each of the law categories, columns 1 and 2 record the number of states that enacted each type of law as its first bargaining law and the number of municipalities in those states with data on their police departments' collective bargaining contract status. Column 3 shows that states that enacted a BP, DTB and an ARB law as their first bargaining law had 65.0 percent, 87.8 percent and 96.2 percent of their police departments organized by 1978. In column 4, one observes that very little of this unionization occurred prior to the enactment of these laws. Only 12.7 percent of the 622 municipalities that unionized did so prior to the enactment of the law. (Any such municipalities are categorized as no-law municipalities in the PH analysis, since they did not remain nonunion past the time of the enactment of the law.) Columns 5 and 6 show that a considerable proportion of the police unionization in states with laws occurred within the first few years of the enactment of a law. This is particularly true for states that had a DTB or an ARB law as their first statute. In those states 52.7 percent and 58.4 percent of all unionization occurred within the first six years of the law, where the year in which the law was enacted is counted as one of these six years (column 6). Of those municipalities that remained nonunion until after a law was passed (column 2 − column 4), 9.7 percent were unionized in BP states, 53.0 percent were unionized in DTB states, and 69.3 percent were unionized in ARB states over the first six years of the initial bargaining law. In sharp contrast, throughout the entire period under consideration, only 9.7 percent of the 237 municipalities in states that never enacted a law had unionized.

This simple analysis, while highlighting sharp differences between police unionization rates in the presence and absence of laws, may be misleading for several reasons. States with laws may have municipalities

Table 1.2   Timing of Unionization Relative to Passage of Bargaining Laws

(1) Type of First Bargaining Law (# of states)	(2) Number of Municipalities	(3) Number Organized by 1978 (as % of col. 2)	(4) Number Organized Pre-Law (as % of col. 3)	(5) Number Organized in First Three Years of Law (as % of col. 3)	(6) Number Organized in First Six Years of Law (as % of col. 3)
For states with a law (34)					
BP (10)	374	243 (65.0%)	15 (6.2%)	12 (4.9%)	35 (14.4%)
DTB (16)	229	201 (87.8%)	29 (14.4%)	50 (24.9%)	106 (52.7%)
ARB (8)	185	178 (96.2%)	35 (19.7%)	74 (41.6%)	104 (58.4%)
Subtotal	788	622 (78.9%)	79 (12.7%)	136 (21.9%)	245 (39.4%)
For states that never enacted a law (14)	237	23 (9.7%)	23 (100.0%)	—	—

that are more prone to unionization. Post-law unionization occurs later in the period under consideration, so that the effects of an improving climate for police unionization must be sorted out before attributing the patterns in table 1.2 to an effect of the laws.

To formalize the analysis, I estimate the principal PLDUR PH model. Of the 1,025 municipalities that have police contract data, 793 have a full set of data on all covariates. Since more than one observation per municipality is included in the sample for any municipality that remains nonunion past the time of the enactment of a law, the total number of observations in the sample for the analysis, N = 1,359, is greater than 793.

Column 1 of table 1.3 presents the complete set of parameters from the PLDUR PH model. Since the magnitudes of the β parameters are affected by the units of measurement for the independent variables, the relative magnitudes of the various β's do not gauge the relative importance of the covariates. Column 2 of Table 1.3 presents the means and standard deviations of the covariates for the N = 793 sample. (The N = 793 sample is used to calculate sample characteristics instead of the N = 1,359 sample since the latter includes more than one observation for certain municipalities and, therefore, would not give an accurate picture of the average municipality.) Column 3 calculates for the dummy variables in the model the quantity $\exp[\beta]$. This calculation yields the ratio of the union hazard rate for a municipality with the given characteristic and one without it (all other covariates the same). Column 4 presents the relative increase in the union hazard rate that would result from a one standard deviation increase in a given covariate. This is given by $\exp[\beta(\bar{x} + \sigma_x)]/\exp[\beta\bar{x}]$. These calculations indicate that the *nature of the bargaining law is the most important factor in influencing unionization rates.*

Specifically, lines 1a, 1b, and 1c of column 3 show that the relative unionization propensity of a municipality is raised dramatically by any of the bargaining laws. Compared to no-law environments, relative unionization propensities are: 15.0 times greater in ARB environments, 13.3 times greater in DTB environments, and 4.2 times greater in BP environments. The magnitude of the effects of laws calculated in this way shows an even more dramatic effect of laws than the simple analysis of table 1.2. Moreover, the calculations in column 4 which compare the magnitude of the effects of the bargaining laws to the effects of other covariates, underscore the conclusion drawn by Saltzman (1985, 345) in his state-level analysis of teacher unionism—that bargaining laws are the single most important determinant of public sector unionization.

Among other covariates, there are significant effects associated with the degree of private sector unionization in the state, the region

Table 1.3   The Impact of Bargaining Laws, State Characteristics, and Municipal Characteristics on Police Unionization

Covariates	(1) β-parameters and (standard errors)	(2) Means and (standard deviations) of Covariates	(3)[a] Relative Increase in Unionization Probability from 0 to 1 increase (dummy variables)	(4)[b] Relative Increase in Unionization Probability from a one standard deviation increase (all variables)
1. Bargaining laws				
a. ARB	2.711[s] (.287)	0.172 (.377)	15.044	2.779
b. DTB	2.590[s] (.262)	0.175 (.380)	13.330	2.676
c. BP	1.442[s] (.218)	0.332 (.471)	4.229	1.972
2. LAWYR	0.092*** (.019)	6.166 (5.639)	—	1.688
3. Region				
a. northeast	0.286 (.217)	0.170 (.376)	1.331	1.111
b. central	0.472*** (.147)	0.328 (.470)	0.624	0.801
c. south	0.459* (.251)	0.281 (.450)	0.632	0.813

4. Percent union	3.692***	—	1.404
	(.913)		
5. Percent public	2.525	—	1.059
	(3.203)		
6. Central city	0.513***	—	1.241
	(.124)		
7. Population	0.050 E-6	—	1.009
	(.210 E-6)		
8. Per capita income	0.043 E-4	—	1.005
	(.370 E-4)		
9. Per capita city revenue	0.357 E-3	—	1.071
	(.222 E-3)		
10. Government-type			
a. mayor-council	−0.068	0.934	0.969
	(.200)		
b. council-manager	0.181	1.198	1.091
	(.196)		

Notes: ssignificance tests not performed on parameters for law dummy variables

acalculated by exp[β]

bcalculated by exp[β($\bar{x} + \sigma_x$)]/exp[β$\bar{x}$]

***two-tailed *p*-value < .01ˣ

**two-tailed *p*-value < .05

*two-tailed *p*-value < .10

variables,[7] and central city status. The insignificant impact of the population variable does not necessarily contradict the observation that the largest cities in the United States are more likely to have unionized police departments. Central city status and population are highly correlated so that with a central city variable in the equation, population has no effect on the propensity to unionize. While the city income and revenue variables both have positive parameters, neither is judged to be significant.

1.4.1 Additional PH Models

While the magnitude of the effects of the bargaining laws is larger than that of all other covariates, formal significance testing of individual parameters on the law variables are not possible for the model in table 1.3. Therefore, several additional PH models are estimated. Parameters on the law variables for these supporting PH models are presented in table 1.4.

As a reference point, column 1 of table 1.4 presents the estimates of the impact of the laws from the model in table 1.2. Column 2 gives estimates of the impact of the laws when NUDUR ("year of unionization–1955" for uncensored observations and "1979–1955" for censored observations) is the dependent variable. In this analysis an observation is classified according to the first legal environment it experiences while it is still nonunion. These estimates show that municipalities with laws unionized earlier in the 1955–78 period than municipalities in the no-law category. Since laws are usually enacted well into the 1955–78 period, the parameters on the law variables are, as expected, noticeably smaller than those obtained in column 1. While these parameters underestimate the effect of bargaining laws, one can test the significance of each parameter relative to the omitted no-law comparison group. Even using these underestimates of the effects of the laws, the estimated parameters on the DTB and ARB variables are significantly different from zero, though the estimated parameter on the BP variable is not.

To illustrate the fact that the column 2 model underestimates the effects of laws because pre-law years are included in the dependent duration variable, I added LAWYR, the number of pre-law years, to the equation. The results in column 3 show that the estimated parameters on the law variables increase dramatically. Again, since LAWYR is undefined for no-law observations, no significance testing of these law parameters is performed.

To judge the significance of the effects of ARB and DTB laws relative to BP laws, the sample in columns 4 and 5 is analyzed. Here, all no-law observations are deleted from the sample, and the observations in the BP category are the comparison group. Whether or not LAWYR

Table 1.4   The Effect of Bargaining Laws on Police Unionization: Estimates
from Proportional Hazards Models

	(1)	(2)	(3)	(4)	(5)
Dependent Variables	PLDUR	NUDUR	NUDUR	PLDUR	PLDUR
Observations	1359	793	793	506	506
1. Bargaining laws					
a. ARB	2.711^s	0.336*	1.856^s	1.915***	1.819***
	(.287)	(.191)	(.399)	(.162)	(.211)
b. DTB	2.590^s	0.445**	1.999^s	1.693***	1.602***
	(.262)	(.211)	(.419)	(.226)	(.259)
c. BP	1.442^s	0.078	1.069^s	—	—
	(.218)	(.171)	(.283)		
2. Years before enactment of law (LAWYR)	0.092***	—	−0.093***	—	−.018
	(.109)		(.021)		(.025)
3. Other controls	a	a	a	a	a
−2* log-likelihood	6410.55	5523.6	5504.2	3885.4	3885.0

Notes: Asymptotically normal standard errors in parentheses. (a): Other controls are: three region dummies; percent of private sector workforce in the state that is unionized; percent of state workforce in public employment; two government-type dummies; central city dummy; population; per capita income; and per capita city revenue.
^{s}Significance tests inappropriate on law dummy parameters in columns marked with s.
***two-tailed p-value < .01
**two-tailed p-value < .05
*two-tailed p-value < .10

is included, significance testing can be performed on the law variables, since LAWYR is defined for all observations in this sample. The analysis does in fact suggest that the DTB and ARB laws increase unionization rates more than do BP laws. Interestingly, once one restricts the sample to observations with some kind of law, the effect of LAWYR is no longer judged to be significantly different from zero. That is, within the range of years that laws were enacted in the United States, post-law durations are not significantly shorter if the post-law duration begins in a later year.

Across all models, it is also interesting to note that the effects of DTB and ARB laws on police unionization are not significantly different from one another. Specifically, in comparing the log-likelihood statistics from any of the models in table 1.4 to a corresponding model in which DTB and ARB categories are collapsed into one variable, there is no significant difference in the performance of the two models.

1.4.2   Survival Plots

A useful way to summarize the data and to underscore the importance of the bargaining laws is to present plots of the survival functions
for various representative cities. Figure 1.1 plots the probability that
a municipality with average characteristics will be nonunion under the
differing legal environments. These probabilities are estimated using
the model in table 1.3 with PLDUR as the dependent variable, with
any LAWYR effect excluded from estimates. The plots for the BP, DTB
and ARB municipalities begin in 1965, 1968 and 1968, respectively.
These years represent the average of the years in which these forms
of bargaining law were enacted. The results are clear. No-law environments are characterized by very little unionization. In 1979, the probability that the average municipality would still be nonunion if it had
not been exposed to a law is approximately .83. Law environments
produce unionization. An average municipality exposed to a BP law
(for fourteen years), a DTB law (for eleven years), or an ARB law (for
eleven years), has .59, .29 and .25 probability of remaining nonunion
by 1979.

In figure 1.2, I plot the probability that a municipality having the
average characteristics of a no-law, BP, DTB, and ARB municipality
will be nonunion at different points in time. Here the municipalities
differ in characteristics across law categories as well as in the law itself.
That the plots are quite similar to those in figure 1.1 underscores the
fact that the legal environment, more than any characteristic, dictates
the union hazard probabilities. The differences between the probability
of remaining nonunion for a no-law municipality and those of municipalities in other legal environments is slightly larger than the differ-

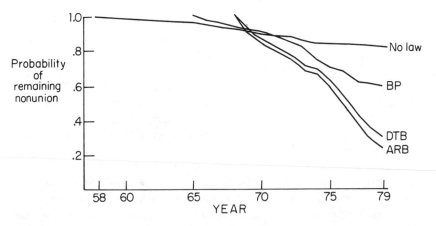

Fig. 1.1   Probability of remaining nonunion for the average municipality under the four different legal environments

ences in figure 1.1. This reflects the fact that no-law cities have lower values of PCTUNION (percent union) and are less likely to be in the northeast region (both of these characteristics are positively associated with the union hazard function). From figure 1.2, one estimates the probability that an average no-law, BP, DTB and ARB municipality will still be nonunion in 1979 as .87, .36, .02 and .01, respectively. These plots depict graphically the central finding of this study: changes in unionization rates among municipal police in the United States occurred after the enactment of bargaining laws.

1.4.3   The Pre-Law Organizers

While the analysis documents the critical role that bargaining laws play in creating an environment that will allow collective bargaining to exist, there are cases where formal collective bargaining contracts are negotiated even though no law exists. To gain further insight into the unionization-bargaining law relationship, I contacted representatives from municipalities that have contracts but are in states that have yet to enact a bargaining law. Of the 793 municipalities included in the PH analysis, 198 are in states that have not enacted a law. Of these 198 municipalities, only 10 have negotiated contracts. However, in several of these cases, the cities enacted a municipal ordinance permitting collective bargaining, emphasizing the importance of protective legislation to allow bargaining. In other cases, municipalities tended to have a strong union influence in private sector employment that made collective bargaining a widely accepted practice in the area. For example, Weirton and Huntington, West Virginia, are communities with strong influences from the steel workers and mine workers, respectively.

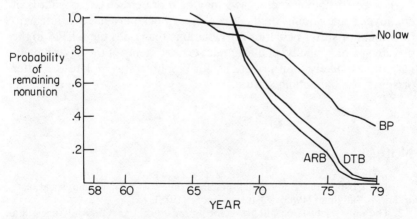

Fig. 1.2   Probability of remaining nonunion for each legal environment's average municipality

Pascagoula, Mississippi (the only municipality with a contract in a state in which police collective bargaining is explicitly illegal by state statute) has a number of craft unions representing workers in its dominant industry, shipbuilding. Management in Pascagoula, because of the state law outlawing police bargaining, has the option of using the courts to void the contract, but has not followed this route because of the strong pro-union sentiment of the citizens in their town. These examples suggest channels through which a variable like PCTUNION influences police unionization rates; however, the examples also suggest that the state-level PCTUNION variable does not adequately capture occasional strongholds of private sector unionization at the municipal level in states with otherwise low levels of private sector unionism.

1.5 Conclusion

Using a PH framework for estimating the rate of unionization among municipal police departments, this study documents the critical role played by the nature of the statutory bargaining environments. The police bargaining laws are clearly not a result of already existing bargaining. The speed with which unionization occurs in the first few years after enactment of laws, particularly laws with some sort of duty-to-bargain provision, does however suggest some form of pent-up demand for unionization. Given the experience in the private sector, where unionism continues to decline in spite of the protections of the NLRA, bargaining statutes are a necessary but insufficient condition for union growth. Other factors specific to the public sector might help to account for the rapid rate of public sector unionization after bargaining laws were enacted. Public sector laws may be more effective safeguards of employees' bargaining rights, since these laws may have stricter enforcement or stiffer penalties for violations than does the NLRA in the private sector.[8] Finally, public employers, as agents of the government, may be less likely than private sector employers to violate the letter or spirit of a bargaining statute.

Notes

1. The most recent study which employs the most rigorous empirical tests to date is Saltzman (1985). Also see Moore (1978).
2. The only analysis on public sector unionism that examines changes in a percent-organized variable is contained in Saltzman (1985, 345). However, the analysis does not correlate this change variable to all categories of bargaining laws.

3. For the original exposition of the proportional hazards framework, see Cox (1972). More recently, see developments in Kalbfleisch and Prentice (1980).

4. A small number of municipal observations in states that eventually enacted a law prohibiting police bargaining are kept in the no-law comparison group.

5. Municipal control variables are available from International City Managers Association, "Master Code" Data Tape (I.C.M.A. 1978). Government type, municipal revenue, per capita income population and department size also appear in the published volume *Municipal Yearbook, 1978* (International City Management Association 1978).

6. In one review of what have generally been industry-level studies, Bain (1981, 3) concludes that profit levels seem to have a positive correlation with union growth and labels this a "prosperity effect".

7. The significance of the set of region controls is judged by comparing the chi-square statistics for the model in table 1.2 with and without the three region variables.

8. For a critical review of the increase in unfair management labor practices and a discussion of the weakness in penalties under the NLRA, see Weiler (1983).

References

Bain, George S. 1981. Certification, first agreements, and decertifications: An analytical framework. Canada Department of Labor.

Chaison, Gary. 1973. Unit size and union success in representation elections. *Monthly Labor Review* 96:51–52.

Cooke, William. 1983. Determinants of the outcomes of union certification elections. *Industrial and Labor Relations Review* 36(3):402–14.

Cox, D. R. 1972. Regression models and life tables. *Journal of the Royal Statistical Society,* Series B, 34:187–220.

Crowley, John and Marie Hu. 1977. Covariance analysis of heart transplant survival data. *Journal of the American Statistical Association* 72(356):27–36.

Feuille, Peter and John T. Delaney. 1986. Collective bargaining, interest arbitration, and police salaries. *Industrial and Labor Relations Review* 39(2):228–40.

Freeman, Richard B. 1986. Unionism comes to the public sector. *Journal of Economic Literature* 24(1):41–86.

Freeman, Richard B., Casey Ichniowski, and Harrison Lauer. 1985. Collective bargaining and threat effects of unionism in the determination of police compensation. National Bureau of Economic Research Working Paper No. 1578.

International City Managers Association. 1978. *Municipal yearbook, 1978* (Washington, D.C.: ICMA).

Kalbfleisch, John D. and Ross Prentice. 1980. *The statistical analysis of failure time data* (New York: Wiley and Sons, Inc.).

Kushner, Sam. 1975. *Long road to Delano* (New York: International Publishers).

Lawless, J. F. 1980. *Statistical models and methods for failure time data* (New York: John Wiley and Sons).

Moore, William. An analysis of teacher union growth. *Industrial Relations* 17(2):204–15.

Olson, Craig. 1980. The impact of arbitration on the wages of fire fighters. *Industrial Relations* 19(13):325–39.

Rose, Joseph. 1972. What factors influence union representation elections? *Monthly Labor Review* 95:49–51.

Ross, Phillip. 1965. *The government as a source of union power* (Providence, RI: Brown University Press).

Saltzman, Gregory. 1985. Bargaining laws as a cause and a consequence of teacher unionism. *Industrial and Labor Relations Review* 38(3):335–51.

Weiler, Paul. 1983. Promises to keep: Securing workers' rights to self-organization under the NLRA. *Harvard Law Review* 96(8):1769–1827.

Zax, Jeffrey. 1985. Municipal employment, municipal unions and demand for municipal services. National Bureau of Economic Research Working Paper No. 1728.

Comment   John M. Abowd

In the private sector the two most important pieces of enabling legislation permitting the formation of collective bargaining units are: (1) the Clayton Act exclusion of coalitions of employees from antitrust regulation and (2) the National Labor Relations Act (NLRA) regulation of the formation of bargaining units and imposition of a duty to bargain on employers. It seems inconceivable that any economist would argue that private sector unionism would have developed its current form or coverage without this protection.[1] The question of which protection is quantitatively more important in explaining the subsequent increase in private sector bargaining units is completely confounded by the uniqueness of the legislative actions. There is simply insufficient statistical variation in the legal environment to permit reliable estimation of the effects of these laws.

Economists presume that private sector bargaining unit formation is a direct result of legal protection not afforded to other forms of collective activity. This presumption is based on a simple before and after comparison of bargaining unit formation around the times of major changes in the legal environment. In the public sector there is also a

John M. Abowd is associate professor of labor economics in the New York State School of Industrial and Labor Relations and the Samuel Curtis Johnson Graduate School of Management at Cornell University, and a research associate of the National Bureau of Economic Research.

1. This is not to argue that collective action by workers occurs only because of the NLRA. Collective action is the regulated activity. Its incidence and form is governed by the costs and benefits of the activity itself. However, the position of recognized bargaining units as a substantial economic force is a direct result of lowering the costs (protection of organizing activity) and raising the benefits (duty to bargain) that occurred because of the form of the regulation.

presumption that the widespread increase in organizing and negotiating activity was due to the legal protection recently granted those activities. Fortunately, in the public sector this presumption can be systematically investigated because the regulation has, for the most part, occurred at the state and local levels of government. The necessary statistical variation in the legal environment is present because the various states acted at different times and with different types of legal protection. The paper by Ichniowski uses this variation in the legal environment to provide striking evidence that it is precisely the form of the legal protection of police bargaining units that has promoted the formation of these units and the subsequent negotiation of collective agreements.

Since many readers may not be familiar with the statistical techniques Ichniowski uses, let me summarize his simplest, but most convincing, results. The unit of analysis is a municipal police force. The definition of unionization is that a bargaining unit exists from the date of signing the first written collective agreement. Ichniowski is studying the time it takes for a bargaining unit to form in the presence of different legal environments: (1) no protection, (2) collective bargaining permitted, (3) duty to bargain, and (4) compulsory interest arbitration. The statistical method is based on the probability of becoming a unionized police force in the next year, given that the police force is not unionized at the start of the year.[2]

From table 1.2 we can deduce that in the absence of any law there is about a 0.4 percent chance of a police union forming in any given year. This is the base against which all comparisons are made. At this rate of unionization, a police force would expect to remain nonunion for 250 years. We can think of this as forever. Turning now to table 1.3, the effect of passing a bargaining permitted law is to increase the conditional probability of union formation from 0.4 percent to 1.6 percent per year. At this rate a police force would expect to remain nonunion for sixty years. The effect of a duty-to-bargain law is to increase this probability from 0.4 percent to 5 percent per year. At this rate a police force would expect to remain nonunion for nineteen years. Finally, the effect of passing a compulsory interest arbitration law is to increase the conditional probability of unionization from 0.4 percent to 6 percent per year. At this rate a police force would expect to remain nonunion for seventeen years. Since the probability of decertification of police unions is essentially zero, if new bargaining units form at a

2. I have taken certain liberties with the statistical terminology in order to promote clarity. Technically, Ichniowski studies the hazard rate, which measures this conditional probability in the next instant given that the union does not currently exist. The "hazard" here is formation of a union. This terminology has its origins in engineering and the life sciences, where the "hazard" is failure of a critical part or death, and leads to somewhat unfortunate connotations in this study.

rate of 6 percent per year, the extent of public sector unionization would reach 27 percent in just five years.

The statistical analysis attempts to control for the independent effects of location, private sector unionization, and other potential correlates of propensity to unionize. In order to gain some feel for the magnitude of the estimated legal environment effects, suppose that there were no public sector enabling legislation. Then, if the extent of private sector unionization increased from 25 percent (the sample average) to 34 percent (one standard deviation above the sample average), the conditional probability of forming a new police union would increase from 0.4 percent to 0.6 percent per year. The length of time a police force would expect to remain nonunion would fall from 250 to 178 years. The effect of increasing private sector unionization is the largest estimated effect on the police unionization rate apart from the public sector bargaining law effects.

Ichniowski's estimated effects of changes in the legal environment are so large that one is compelled to ask: Are these estimates credible? I think the answer to this question is "yes." Most municipalities use standardized personnel policies for police officers already. The formation of a bargaining unit, therefore, has limited benefits unless the police expect to win substantial improvements in the terms of compensation or operating procedures of the force. Without legal protection, police officers may face nontrivial penalties for collective action—termination or denial of promotion, for example. With legal protection, unionized officers are unlikely to lose the benefits of standardized personnel policies, so they no longer risk substantial costs when attempting collective action that might produce other improvements in compensation or working conditions. Therefore, it is believable that police officers would attempt collective action in this low penalty environment. Of course, this does not mean that they will be successful in achieving gains from unionization. The measurement of the gains to the police officers awaits further study.

2 Public Sector Bargaining Laws Really Matter: Evidence from Ohio and Illinois

Gregory M. Saltzman

2.1 Introduction

A generation ago, America had two starkly different legal policies governing collective bargaining and union activity—one for employees of the government and another for employees of private corporations. The erosion of this difference, as more and more states have enacted public sector bargaining laws patterned after the National Labor Relations Act (NLRA), is one of the most important developments in American labor law since 1947. These important legal changes, however, came as a surprise to most industrial relations scholars, and they have not been fully explained even retrospectively.[1]

Two states, in particular, confounded general models of legal policy-making in public sector labor relations: Ohio and Illinois. They were exceptions for two reasons. First, although both were industrialized, highly unionized states located in the North, neither had a statute granting public employees the right to bargain. (The other states lacking such statutes, e.g., Mississippi, North Carolina, and Utah, were generally more conservative states located in the South or the Rocky Mountains.) Kochan (1973, 336–37) noted that the lack of bargaining laws in Ohio and Illinois was anomalous even in the early 1970s, when many states lacked such laws. The Ohio-Illinois anomaly became more striking during the middle of that decade, as the number of other states

Gregory M. Saltzman is assistant professor of economics and management at Albion College and adjunct assistant research scientist at the Institute of Labor and Industrial Relations, University of Michigan.

The author is greatly indebted to William Dickens and Casey Ichniowski for extensive comments on an earlier version of this chapter. He also thanks Malcolm Cohen, Linda Lampkin, and James McCarley for helpful comments. Finally, he thanks the busy practitioners (listed in the references) who agreed to be interviewed for this study.

lacking bargaining laws declined. Second, although neither Ohio nor Illinois had a public sector bargaining statute, they both had many public sector collective bargaining contracts. Burton (1979, 15) cited this fact when he argued that bargaining laws were not the major impetus behind the spread of public sector bargaining.

The exceptional status of Ohio and Illinois ended in 1983, when both states enacted comprehensive bargaining statutes covering most state and local public employees. This chapter examines the reasons why those statutes were finally enacted then and also why previous attempts to secure legislation failed. The analysis of those reasons is based on open-ended interviews with over three dozen union and management lobbyists, legislators, legislative aides, labor lawyers, and other informed practitioners, as well as an examination of legislative documents. Then, the chapter uses quantitative data to measure the impact of these statutes on public sector labor relations in both states. The major conclusions are:

- Bargaining statutes were delayed in Illinois chiefly by the desire of the Chicago Democrats to maintain patronage arrangements and in Ohio chiefly by the insistence of unions that they get a strongly pro-union statute or none at all.
- The enactment of the bargaining statutes in those two states in 1983 was the result of idiosyncratic political events and not of a general trend toward public sector unionism.
- The enactment of these bargaining statutes brought a substantial increase in the extent of bargaining coverage in Ohio and Illinois, even though public sector bargaining had been widespread in both states for years. Some public employers, however, resisted the unionization of their employees even after the 1983 bargaining statutes were passed, which is something that generally did not happen after the public sector statutes enacted earlier in other states.
- The Illinois statute strengthened the bargaining power of teacher unions which had already bargained before the statute. (No baseline data were available on bargaining outcomes prior to 1983 for other employee groups in Illinois or for public employees in Ohio.)

The data underlying these conclusions are presented in the following sections, beginning with the history of public sector bargaining laws in Ohio and Illinois.

2.2 History of Public Sector Bargaining Law in Ohio

Before 1983, Ohio's public sector labor relations were largely unregulated by law. There were, however, some statutes and court decisions that regulated particular aspects of public sector labor relations, as well as a host of bills that failed to be enacted. The first major developments came in 1947, when the same national tide that brought the Taft-Hartley Act brought two efforts to curb public sector unions in Ohio. In January 1947, the Ohio Supreme Court ruled in *Hagerman v. Dayton*[2] that local governments could not permit voluntary deduction of union dues from their employees' paychecks. The court went on to declare that municipal contracts with unions were an improper delegation of governmental authority. A few months later, the Ohio legislature enacted the Ferguson Act,[3] which banned public employee strikes and provided for dismissal of strikers. Furthermore, any striker who was rehired would get no pay increase for one year and would be on probation for two years.

Supporters of public sector unions tried to overcome these two 1947 setbacks, although their efforts accomplished little until 1959. In 1947, shortly after the *Hagerman* ruling, two bills were introduced that would have authorized public sector bargaining,[4] but both bills died in committee. Then, following the Democratic victory in the 1948 legislative elections, the House passed bills to repeal the Ferguson Act[5] and to protect the right of public employees to join unions.[6] The Ferguson Act repeal bill, however, was voted down in the Senate,[7] and the bill protecting the right to join unions never came up for a Senate vote. Several other bills were introduced in the next decade; the most successful of them died in a Senate committee after passing the House.

In 1958, the national tide toward the Democrats was strengthened in Ohio by a right-to-work referendum, which mobilized the labor vote. As a result, the Democrats won simultaneous control of both houses of the legislature and the governorship for the first time since their victory in the 1948 elections, and Ohio's second public sector labor statute was enacted. In 1959, a state senator (who happened also to be a staff representative for the United Steelworkers of America) introduced a bill that would have protected the right of public employees to join a union, authorized informal negotiations, and overturned the *Hagerman* ruling that outlawed union dues checkoff. Amendments narrowed the bill so that it simply authorized dues checkoff. The bill was then passed and signed into law.[8]

In the 1960s, the major legal development was the frequent nonenforcement of anti-union provisions of the law. First to fall by the wayside was the portion of the *Hagerman* ruling that declared public sector bargaining an improper delegation of governmental authority. Cincinnati, which had bargained informally with the American Federation of State, County, and Municipal Employees (AFSCME) ever since the 1940s (Heisel interview), formalized the relationship beginning in 1960. By 1968, all of the other major cities in Ohio (Akron, Cleveland, Columbus, Dayton, Toledo, and Youngstown) had also signed contracts with AFSCME.[9] Teachers and fire fighters began bargaining too.

Meanwhile, employers were becoming reluctant to invoke the Ferguson Act's severe strike penalties. For example, in January 1967 an AFSCME local representing sanitation and snow removal workers in Toledo went on strike. During the strike, the city government "insisted it would enforce Ohio's Ferguson Act . . . [but it later decided] to adopt a 'forgive and forget' attitude."[10] Similarly, in March 1969, when water and sewer workers in the city of Warren, Ohio, struck, the city actually invoked the Ferguson Act and "said it cannot negotiate because the strikers have been fired."[11] After ten days, though, the city settled the strike by signing a new contract, letting the strikers have their jobs back, and indicating that the city would not challenge the strikers' appeal to have the Ferguson Act penalties overturned.[12] Furthermore, there were many cases (beginning in the second half of the 1960s) of strikes by teachers, sanitation workers, and even police and fire fighters where the employer did not even seriously threaten to invoke the Ferguson Act. The Ferguson Act penalties *were* invoked and enforced in a few rare cases, the first of which was a 1967 strike by workers in a county welfare department home,[13] but they generally came to be seen as too harsh to use.

At about the same time, teachers began to press vigorously for bargaining legislation, with the result that a "professional negotiations" bill covering only school employees was almost passed by the 1967–68 legislature. In the beginning of 1967, the Ohio Education Association (OEA) set as its top legislative priority a teacher negotiation bill that provided exclusive recognition to the teacher organization with the largest membership in the district.[14] The Ohio Federation of Teachers (OFT) opposed this bill, preferring recognition by secret ballot election.[15] (The American Federation of Teachers had won the 1965 representation election in Philadelphia[16] and was soon to win the 1967 representation election in Baltimore,[17] despite having a smaller membership in those school systems). Even without OFT support, however, the bill passed the Senate, and its prospects in the House were improved in December 1967 when the OEA raised its dues from $18 per year to $29 (partly to have more money for lobbying).[18] The House passed the bill, after amending it. On the last day of the 1968 legislative session, however, the Senate rejected the House amendments, while the House adhered to them, with the result that the bill died.[19] The chief lobbyist for the OEA claimed that this last minute death in the legislature was the work of Republican Governor James Rhodes, who did not want to have to honor his promise to sign the bill if it reached his desk (Hall interview). (Rhodes was to oppose public sector bargaining legislation more openly a decade later.)

In 1969, the OEA legislative committee recommended that the OEA seek a teacher bargaining law patterned after the NLRA, including the provision for secret ballot representation elections. The OEA's lobbyist recalled that the OEA executive board, still committed to "professional negotiations" rather than "collective bargaining," opposed the recommendation, and a big fight on the OEA convention floor ensued. The convention ultimately accepted the recommendation to seek an NLRA-type statute.

Meanwhile, the Ohio council of AFSCME had also called for public sector bargaining legislation and for the repeal of the Ferguson Act.[20] A bill backed by AFSCME was introduced in the Ohio House of Representatives but made little progress.[21] In 1971, the OEA decided to join forces with AFSCME to seek a bill covering all public employees, rather than one just covering teachers (Hall interview), which strengthened the coalition seeking legislation. The joint OEA-AFSCME bills, however, were killed during the early 1970s by the Republican chairman of the Senate Commerce and Labor Committee (D. Day interview).

The year 1975 brought a major court ruling and an important legislative initiative. The court ruling was the Ohio Supreme Court's decision in *Dayton Classroom Teachers Association v. Dayton Board of Education*[22] that school boards had authority to bargain with their employees and that any contract reached, including a promise to submit grievances to binding arbitration, would be enforceable in court. This ruling established a favorable legal situation for those teacher unions that were strong enough to win recognition. The ruling also reflected the de facto acceptance of public sector bargaining in Ohio during the 1960s and early 1970s, despite the 1947 court ruling in the *Hagerman* case.

Meanwhile, as a result of the 1974 elections, the Republicans lost control of the Ohio Senate, so there was a new chairman of the Senate Commerce and Labor Committee. Ohio's public employee unions united behind S.B. 70, a public sector bargaining bill introduced in 1975 that covered all public employees in Ohio. S.B. 70, a very pro-union bill, passed both houses of the legislature but was vetoed by Governor Rhodes. The House of Representatives failed to override the veto, and the bill died.

In the 1976 elections, the Democrats increased their majority in the Ohio House of Representatives, and Ohio's public employee unions thought that they had gained a "veto-proof" legislature. In 1977, a new bill, S.B. 222, was introduced. S.B. 222 provided a broad scope of bargaining, permitted the agency shop, and legalized most public employee strikes. (Interestingly, both unions and employer organizations preferred the right to strike over binding interest arbitration). Strikes endangering the public health or safety could be enjoined for up to sixty days, and police and fire fighter strikes were banned outright; but employees enjoined from striking could strike when the sixty-day period expired, and police and fire fighters were given interest arbitration. The bill did make two major concessions to management: police and fire fighter interest arbitration awards could be overturned by a three-fifths vote of the city council, and supervisors were excluded from the coverage of the bargaining law unless the individual public employer agreed to include them. Despite the concessions, though, the bill was more favorable to public employee unions than a large majority of public sector bargaining laws in other states.

The 1977 bill had strong backing. The Ohio AFL-CIO and most public employee unions actively supported it, as did one major management organization: the Ohio Municipal League. The leaders of the league had concluded that some sort of legislation was inevitable; they then decided to support the bargaining bill in order to be able to influence its terms. (For example, they had sought the ability to overturn interest arbitration awards for police and fire fighters, as well as the exclusion of supervisors from coverage.) The other management organizations—the school boards association and the county boards association—opposed the bill, as did the Teamsters (which was not ready to win public sector representation elections) (Coleman interview) and the Fraternal Order of Police (which was dismayed by the concessions won by the Municipal League); but opponents were outnumbered in the legislature by supporters. The bill passed both houses of the legislature and was then vetoed by Governor Rhodes. This time, though, supporters of the bill thought that they had the votes to override the veto. To their surprise and dismay, they did not.

Veto overrides took sixty votes in the House of Representatives, and the Democrats had sixty-two. The few Republicans who had voted for the bill initially, however, were unwilling to override a veto by a Republican governor, and three rural Democrats broke party ranks. Thus, only fifty-nine voted to override, and the bill died.

The vote to override the 1977 veto happened to follow shortly after a particularly bitter strike by fire fighters in Dayton. Not only did buildings burn to the ground during the strike, but there were also allegations that striking fire fighters had committed arson. Legislators reacted negatively to the strike; it may have cost the public employee unions the sixtieth and vital vote to override the veto.

One of the three Democrats voting against the override, Bill Hinig, was a committee chairman; both union and management lobbyists I interviewed claimed that the Democratic Assembly Speaker (who appoints committee chairmen) could have swung Hinig's vote (Brandt, Coleman, D. Day, and Smith interviews). A former legislative staff member, by contrast, argued that if Hinig had voted to override, then a different Democratic legislator would have broken ranks. In any case, some labor leaders reacted bitterly to Hinig's defection, and they tried to defeat Hinig in the 1978 primary in order to keep all the Democrats in line in the future. The Speaker, however, raised $70,000 for Hinig and dispatched an aide to manage Hinig's campaign. The challenge to Hinig failed, demonstrating the political weakness of labor. The net result, according to two management lobbyists and two former legislative staff members I interviewed, was that the OEA and the Ohio AFL-CIO lost influence in the legislature. The loss was compounded by the 1978 elections, in which Governor Rhodes was reelected and the Republicans gained enough seats in the Senate to block a veto override.

In the 1982 elections, the Democrats won simultaneous control of the governorship and both houses of the legislature for the first time since 1958. The consequence, in 1983 as in 1959, was that a pro-union public sector labor relations bill was enacted into law. The 1983 bill, S.B. 133, contained several provisions that are common in comprehensive public sector labor relations statutes (e.g., representation elections, a duty to bargain with majority representatives, a prohibition of unfair labor practices, and an administrative agency). In addition, S.B. 133 contained some provisions which made it more pro-union than the 1975 bill, the 1977 bill, and most public sector statutes in other states. Among these are:

(1) fact-finding in cases of bargaining impasses, with the fact finder's report becoming binding unless rejected within seven days by either a three-fifths vote of the total membership of the labor organization or a three-fifths vote of the employer's legislative body;

(2) if the fact finder's report is rejected, a broad right to strike for most public employees, and binding interest arbitration (called "conciliation" to help secure passage of the bill) for groups such as police and fire fighters who are prohibited from striking;

(3) a ban on lockouts;

(4) a broad scope of bargaining (comparable to the NLRA, with the addition that "the continuation, modification, or deletion of an existing provision of a collective bargaining agreement" is also a mandatory subject of bargaining);[23]

(5) mandatory dues checkoff and authorization of the agency shop; and

(6) a mandatory grievance procedure, and a declaration that an employer's repeated failure to process grievances in a timely manner is an unfair labor practice.

In view of these pro-union provisions (particularly binding interest arbitration for public safety employees), the Ohio Municipal League opposed S.B. 133; but this time, labor had the votes even without the Municipal League's support. The bill became law.[24]

2.3 History of Public Sector Bargaining Law in Illinois

In Illinois, as in Ohio, the campaign for public sector bargaining legislation was a long one. In 1945, both houses of the Illinois legislature passed S.B. 427, which authorized public employers to enter into collective bargaining agreements with their employees, provided that these agreements prohibited strikes and lockouts during the term of the contract. The governor, however, vetoed the bill.[25] It would take thirty-eight years before the legislature passed another bill that authorized bargaining for a broad spectrum of public employees.

Despite this setback, unions were able to secure the enactment of several relatively early, but narrow, public sector labor relations statutes, as noted in the Wagner Commission report (1967, D21–22):

1. a 1945 statute authorizing the Chicago Transit Authority to continue the collective bargaining procedures employed when the transit system was privately owned;

2. a 1951 statute authorizing the University Civil Service System to negotiate with organizations representing nonacademic employees on wages and other conditions of employment;

3. a 1951 statute authorizing municipalities to submit wage negotiation impasses with fire fighters to fact-finding;

4. a section in the 1955 State Personnel Code authorizing the State Director of Personnel to negotiate with regard to the pay, hours of work, or other working conditions of employees subject to the State Personnel Code;

5. a 1961 statute authorizing voluntary checkoff of union dues for state employees; and

6. a 1963 statute permitting local governmental agencies to authorize the voluntary checkoff of union dues.

None of these statutes, however, established recognition election procedures, required public employers to bargain, or prohibited public employers from interfering with the unionization of their employees.

The next major legal development came from the courts. When the American Federation of Teachers (AFT) local in Chicago won exclusive recognition from the school board, the National Education Association (NEA) affiliate filed suit. In 1966, a circuit court judge ruled (in *Chicago Division of the Illinois Education Association v. Board of Education of the City of Chicago*) that, even without express statutory authorization, the Chicago school board could grant exclusive bargaining rights to a bargaining agent selected by the teachers. The ruling was affirmed on appeal.[26]

In July 1966, Governor Otto Kerner appointed the Wagner Commission, which was to recommend appropriate policies for public sector labor relations. At the time he appointed the commission, Kerner said that he would try to get a bill enacted provided that the bill did not grant the right to strike. As Milton Derber, vice-chairman of the commission, later pointed out (1968, 552–53), AFSCME was willing to accept a strike ban to get a bargaining statute, but the AFT—which had won gains in Chicago by striking—was not. Moreover, the building trades, afraid that a bargaining statute might threaten their craft jurisdiction, adopted a strong stance against a strike ban as a means of blocking a bill. Despite AFSCME's assertion that labor could not realistically expect Illinois to legalize public employee strikes when no other state had done so (Clark 1969, 171–72), the state AFL-CIO, too, came out against any bill that banned strikes.

The Wagner Commission's report (1967) recommended the enactment of a statute that would declare public sector strikes illegal and explicitly authorize courts to issue antistrike injunctions. They also recommended giving all public employees the right to bargain and establishing an administrative agency to determine units, conduct representation elections, and enforce a prohibition of unfair labor practices; but their proposed statute was doomed to falter on the strike issue. A bill based on the commission's recommendation, S.B. 452, was easily passed by the Senate. Democrats in the House, supported by a minority of the Republicans, amended the bill to delete the strike prohibition. The bill then passed the House. When a conference committee restored the strike prohibition, the House voted down the bill, and the bill died. As Clark (1979, 172) noted: "Despite the explicit backing of Governor Kerner [a Democrat], only two Democrats in the House voted for the bill."

In 1973, another Democratic governor was thwarted in his efforts to get a bargaining bill through the legislature. Daniel Walker, elected governor after making a campaign promise to give public employees the right to bargain, responded to the legislature's defeat of bargaining legislation by unilaterally issuing Executive Order No. 6, which granted bargaining rights to state employees under the jurisdiction of the governor.[27] Although the order did not apply to employees of state universities and employees under the jurisdiction of state officers other than the governor, it still gave bargaining rights to approximately 60,000 Illinois state employees. AFSCME organized most of these employees, thereby gaining additional political clout that would be helpful in future lobbying.

Bargaining bills in the 1970s repeatedly followed a pattern of success in the House, defeat in the Senate. This occurred even after the Democrats took control of the Senate in 1975, chiefly because the Chicago

Democrats resisted legislation. Changes, however, were soon to come in the bargaining policy of Chicago itself.

In 1979, Jane Byrne was elected mayor of Chicago, after making a campaign promise to negotiate collective bargaining agreements with the fire fighters and police. A few months after her election, she appointed a planning board to recommend a collective bargaining policy for city employees.[28] In January 1980, Byrne sent the planning board's proposed bargaining ordinance to the city council. During the same week, the fire fighters union—concerned that Byrne might renege on her campaign promise—threatened to strike if Byrne did not agree to sign a collective bargaining contract.[29] The building trades, however, disliked the planning board's proposal of having only a few large bargaining units (D'Alba interview). In early February 1980, the Chicago Federation of Labor came out against the proposed ordinance.[30] With that, the bargaining ordinance was doomed—it never even came to a vote.

The Chicago fire fighters, however, were not deterred. In February and March, they conducted a twenty-three-day strike, the longest fire fighter strike in U.S. history. The strike, called over the issue of who would be included in the bargaining unit, resulted in an interim agreement on noneconomic issues, with economic issues to be submitted to interest arbitration if the parties could not reach agreement.[31] This interim agreement was the first formal contract that the Chicago fire fighters had ever had, and it was followed a year later by a contract covering the Chicago police.[32]

Meanwhile, the legislature was inching toward a statute providing collective bargaining rights to teachers. In 1973, the legislature enacted a bill (H.B. 1303) requiring school boards to provide dues checkoff to teacher organizations.[33] In 1981, the legislature (despite a Republican majority in the House) went considerably farther, enacting H.B. 701.[34] This latter bill: (1) established a procedure for unit determination and representation elections to select exclusive bargaining representatives, (2) authorized negotiation of binding grievance arbitration, and (3) authorized negotiation of agency shop agreements. Since the Illinois Education Association (IEA)—the chief backer of the bill—stressed its separateness from the rest of the Illinois labor movement, unit determination and the conduct of representation elections were assigned to the regional superintendents of education rather than to a state labor relations agency. H.B. 701, however, stopped short of establishing a duty to bargain, and it did not prohibit unfair labor practices. In some cases, school boards refused to bargain after an H.B. 701 election, such refusal being perfectly legal.

By 1983, the time for comprehensive bargaining legislation had arrived. The legislature voted to approve *two* bargaining bills that established a duty to bargain and granted a broad right to strike (except where the public health and safety would be endangered). The first bill,[35] H.B. 1530, covered employees of public schools, colleges, and universities and was backed enthusiastically by the IEA. The IEA's rival, the Illinois Federation of Teachers (IFT), was less enthusiastic but also backed the bill, perhaps because a bill covering only teachers seemed to have better prospects of passage than the more comprehensive legislation that the IFT preferred. The second bill,[36] S.B. 536, was an AFL-CIO bill covering almost all public employees, including educational employees. As originally passed, the two bills differed in their administrative provisions: H.B. 1530 was to be administered by the regional superintendents of education, while S.B. 536 was to be administered by two special labor relations boards—one for Chicago and Cook County employees and the other for employees of other local governments and of the state. (Chicago Mayor Harold Washington had insisted on the separate board for Chicago and Cook County since he did not want gubernatorial appointees to set labor policy for his city.) H.B. 1530 also lacked some of the management rights provisions which had been added to S.B. 536 in order to get it through the legislature.

When the bills reached the governor, Republican Jim Thompson, he invoked an Illinois procedure known as the "amendatory veto." In this procedure, the governor designates changes in a bill that will make the bill acceptable, and if the legislature enacts those changes, the bill becomes law. Despite a lobbying campaign by management groups, such as the Municipal League, the governor left both bills substantially intact. His amendatory veto did, however, change the educational bill (H.B. 1530) to make it more like the comprehensive bill (S.B. 536): H.B. 1530 was to be administered by a special labor relations board, rather than by the regional superintendents of education, and H.B. 1530 was to include management rights provisions similar to those in S.B. 536.

These changes eliminated the public policy rationale for having a separate educational bill, since Governor Thompson could have achieved similar results by vetoing the educational bill and leaving teachers covered by the comprehensive bill. (His amendatory veto of the comprehensive bill had deleted educational employees from coverage). Furthermore, Thompson's action had the disadvantage of simultaneously creating three separate administrative agencies (one for educational employees, one for noneducational employees of Chicago and Cook County, and one for all other public employees), which might eventually issue inconsistent rulings. Nevertheless, a political rationale for Governor Thompson's action remained: the IEA was eager to have a separate bill, for which it could claim credit, and Thompson owed his narrow victory in the 1982 election to IEA support. He repaid the debt on 23 September 1983, when he signed H.B. 1530 at an IEA meeting before hundreds of cheering IEA members.

Police and fire fighters also ended up with a separate bill, although that was not their original intention. The International Association of Fire Fighters (IAFF) had endorsed the comprehensive bill sponsored by the AFL-CIO (S.B. 536), which banned strikes by public safety employees and substituted binding interest arbitration. The Senate passed the AFL-CIO bill essentially intact, but the House added amendments that the IAFF found unacceptable. Although the House leaders were Democrats friendly to the labor movement, they objected to binding interest arbitration; they therefore amended the bill to allow overrides of arbitration awards by a simple majority of the city council. Furthermore, in order to get Mayor Washington's support for the bill, they added a management rights clause that would have taken away manning rules then present in Chicago's contracts with the fire fighters and police. Finally, the House amended the bill to exclude supervisors, using a broad definition of supervisors that would eliminate many IAFF members from the bargaining unit. Because of these amendments, the IAFF requested that public safety employees be excluded from coverage in the AFL-CIO bill. The House promptly accommodated that request, and the Senate concurred.

In 1985, the IAFF and the (politically less powerful) police unions came back with a new bill, H.B. 1529. This bill, while less desirable from the IAFF point of view than the original 1983 AFL-CIO bill, nevertheless addressed some of the IAFF's concerns about the 1983 House amendments. First, H.B. 1529 required a three-fifths majority of the city council (and not a simple majority) to override an interest arbitration award. Second, it permitted fire fighters (but generally not police) to bargain over manning. Finally, it redefined "supervisor" so that police and fire fighter captains would often remain in the unit—an important change because captains can make up one-third of the fire department work force in a small city.

The IAFF accepted the three-fifths override provision in the 1985 bill for two reasons. First, it might have been impossible to get a bill enacted with fully binding interest arbitration: the House Democratic leaders opposed binding interest arbitration, and Governor Thompson had threatened to veto any bill that required it. Second, the IAFF had simultaneously sponsored a second bill in the 1985 legislature (H.B. 1539) which overturned "little Hatch Acts" that restricted political activities by public safety employees. According to the Illinois state president of the IAFF, H.B. 1539 made the arbitration override provision more palatable by making it easier for fire fighters to campaign against any city council member who voted to override an arbitration award (Walters interview). Although Governor Thompson vetoed H.B.

1539, he did not, according to the Illinois AFL-CIO's chief lobbyist, fight hard to have his veto sustained (Walsh interview). The result was that the legislature overrode his veto on 30 October 1985.[37] With H.B. 1539 enacted, the legislature approved H.B. 1529 the same day.[38]

2.4 Failure and Fulfillment: The Underlying Reasons

What accounts for the long delays in enacting bargaining statutes in Ohio and Illinois? What happened in 1983 that finally brought legislation? The answers for the two states differ slightly, but there are some common elements.

2.4.1 Opposition by Politicians with Political Machines

The first element is political patronage. Some politicians opposed bargaining legislation because the development of collective bargaining would undermine their political machines. Union contracts requiring just cause for discharge would make it harder for officials of one political party to fire workers who had been hired by the opposing party. Similarly, seniority bidding rules would make it harder for officials to use the threat of transfers, job assignments to dirty duty, and assignments to work on holidays to pressure current employees to contribute labor or money to the party in power. Finally, union contracts could also prohibit the assignment of specific patronage duties that had previously been routinely expected. For example, the contract negotiated by the Teamsters with the City of Chicago (*after* the 1983 bargaining law was passed) specified that covered employees need not come out for city parades without pay (Carmell interview).

Ohio has both early and contemporary examples of patronage. A dramatic incident in 1947 demonstrated both the existence of patronage and the potential threat to patronage posed by public employee unionization. According to a monthly publication of the Ohio AFL-CIO:

> One of the events which triggered passage of the Ferguson Act was the firing of 1,000 unclassified highway department workers—all Democrats—in the Chillicothe area. [Republican] Governor Herbert fired them when he took office in January 1947, having defeated Frank J. Lausche. The highway workers . . . thought joining the union [AFSCME] would save their jobs. When union membership didn't protect them from being fired, the highway workers went on strike despite the fact they were no longer state employees. That prompted Ferguson to rewrite New York's Condon-Wadlin Act and introduce it.[39]

According to several of those I interviewed, Ohio still had widespread political patronage even in the 1980s, at least at the county government level. The lobbyist for Ohio AFSCME said, "When a new county engineer is elected from a different party, he appoints new bulldozer operators" (Morgan interview). A management lobbyist added, "In many Ohio counties, the civil service system is, in practice, limited to the welfare department, which is funded and regulated by the federal government" (Coleman interview). In the view of both of these lobbyists, the desire to defend patronage induced many county officials in Ohio to oppose bargaining legislation.

Patronage was an even more important barrier to bargaining legislation in Illinois because it weakened support for bargaining in what would normally be a state's greatest stronghold of pro-bargaining sentiment: the big-city Democrats. Most of the practitioners I interviewed in Illinois attributed the long delay in enacting a bargaining law there to the opposition of the Chicago/Cook County Democratic machine. As an assistant to Governor Thompson put it, "In the old days, only downstate Democrats supported collective bargaining, and they were too small a group to pass anything by themselves. The Republicans and the Chicago Democrats opposed the bills, so the bills never went anywhere" (Bedgood interview).

The monolithic opposition of the Chicago Democrats to any bargaining legislation began to erode in the late 1970s. In part, this stemmed from two federal court rulings restricting patronage. The first case, *Elrod v. Burns*,[40] arose when a newly elected Democratic sheriff in Cook County fired patronage employees appointed by his Republican predecessor. The U.S. Supreme Court ruling in this case, issued in 1976, said that patronage employees in non-policy-making jobs could not be fired solely because a new political party took office. Three years later, a federal district judge issued a ruling in the second case *Shakman v. Democratic Organization of Cook County*,[41] which prohibited basing hiring or promotion on political work for the party in power. (The *Shakman* ruling did not, however, effectively prevent more subtle measures such as better job assignments for active precinct workers.)

Perhaps more important than these court rulings was the December 1976 death of Mayor Richard Daley, who had opposed bargaining legislation and had been able to marshall a solid bloc of Chicago Democratic legislators to support his position. Jane Byrne, campaigning for mayor as an "outsider" in 1979, said she would support collective bargaining if elected. One union leader noted that she changed her mind after she won because she then saw the Democratic machine as a political asset that she could control and not as a barrier to her election as mayor. But a mayor was soon to come who was more resolute in his support for bargaining and his opposition to patronage.

That mayor was Harold Washington, who defeated Byrne in a racially divisive primary election in February 1983. Washington's black supporters saw the Chicago patronage system as a way of perpetuating the white power structure; if bargaining would help dismantle patronage, so much the better. Moreover, AFSCME had been one of the few organized groups to campaign for Washington in the primary, and AFSCME wanted bargaining rights for city workers. Finally, Harold Washington had a philosophical commitment to public sector bargaining; as a state senator in 1979, he was one of two sponsors of a fairly pro-union bargaining bill.[42] With Washington's electoral victory, a substantial block of Chicago Democrats came out in support of bargaining legislation. Despite the continued opposition of Cook County Commissioner George Dunne and some other machine Democrats, the support of the mayor of Chicago gained enough legislative support for a bargaining bill that such a bill soon passed.

2.4.2   Lack of Incentives for Strong Unions

The second reason for the long delay in enacting bargaining legislation in Ohio and Illinois was that many union leaders felt that they could live with the pre-statute legal situation. Unions that were strong enough to win bargaining rights did well without a statute and hence concluded that it was better to have no bargaining statute at all than to have a bad one. In both states, the politically powerful state education associations had already won collective bargaining contracts for most of their members in the absence of a statute mandating recognition and bargaining. Moreover, courts in both states had ruled that these contracts were legally permissible and, in Ohio at least, enforceable in court. A statute would have allowed the state education associations to win recognition in small, rural districts (since the AFT was unlikely to provide strong competition in such districts), and it would have helped them win agency shop agreements. OEA leaders, however, told me in 1980 that they did not think that these gains would be worth accepting restrictions on the then broad scope of bargaining or the establishment of effective penalties against strikes (Barkley and Burgess interviews). This stance had been taken earlier by the Illinois Federation of Teachers, when it helped kill the 1967 bargaining bill in Illinois because it banned strikes and authorized antistrike injunctions.

In both states, AFSCME had more to gain than the teachers' unions from the enactment of a statute, mainly because many large units in their jurisdiction remained unorganized. (In Illinois the biggest unorganized groups were in municipal and county government, whereas in Ohio they were in state and county government.) AFSCME and Service Employees' International Union (SEIU) officials in Illinois estimated at the time the 1983 statute was enacted that an additional 80,000 or 90,000 public employees would soon be bargaining.[43] Similarly, one AFSCME official in Ohio estimated in 1980 that AFSCME's membership in Ohio would rise from its then current 35,000 to 125,000 or 150,000 within five years after a statute was enacted (Morgan interview). Nevertheless, in Ohio at least, AFSCME's already established locals representing municipal employees in big cities opposed any legislation that would weaken their existing contracts. In both AFSCME and the teachers' unions, established locals, being strong, wanted a bargaining statute only if it was as favorable to unions as the NLRA. Thus, in 1977, when Governor Rhodes privately told the Speaker of the Ohio House that he would sign a bargaining bill if certain weakening amendments were added, the governor was told that the weakening amendments were not acceptable.

There were, of course, unions that had trouble winning recognition without a statute. One example was the Ohio Association of Public School Employees (OAPSE), which represents nonteaching employees outside the major cities. One OEA official said that OAPSE would be glad to take almost any collective bargaining law. But precisely because OAPSE was a weak union, it was unable to get the legislation it wanted.

In 1983, however, strong unions in both Ohio and Illinois pressed for legislation. Their motivations were somewhat different in each state.

2.4.3   Illinois: Unfavorable Court Decisions Spurring Cooperation among Unions

In Illinois, unions were jolted into action by threats to their established bargaining relationships. The building trades, for example, had long had "handshake agreements" with Chicago's Mayor Daley. Daley's successors, however, did not honor these agreements as faithfully as Daley had, so the building trades began to see the need for real contracts (Gibson interview). An even greater jolt came in December 1981 when the Illinois State Supreme Court issued two decisions affecting virtually all public employee unions. In the first case, *Peters v. Cook County Health and Hospitals Governing Commission,*[44] the court ruled that public employers were free to withdraw recognition from a union at any time. As one union attorney put it, "Repudiation of a bargaining relationship was old news in theory, but this was the first time that management in a heavily Democratic county actually exercised their power to end collective bargaining. It was a surprise that a friend of unions would do this to them" (Carmell interview). In the second case, *Chicago Board of Education v. Chicago Teachers Union,*[45] the court ruled that a contract provision restricting layoffs was unenforceable because layoffs were a management right granted to school boards by the Illinois School Code. The court suggested that some other contract provisions might also be unenforceable on similar grounds.

According to another union attorney, these decisions threatened even established public sector unions, thereby creating a greater sense of urgency about the need for a bargaining statute (D'Alba interview).

Previous bills in Illinois had failed, in part, because of divisions among the unions, some of which disagreed about the terms of the bills and some of which wanted no bill at all. A few months after these two state supreme court rulings, however, the president of the Illinois AFL-CIO began meeting with the leaders of various unions and their attorneys in an effort to reach agreement on a common bill. By October 1982, they were meeting weekly, and they came up with a draft of a bill by December (Gibson interview). All the unions present agreed to refrain from lobbying for rival bills until after the legislature had made a decision on the common bill.

AFSCME, which had the most to gain from a bill, made the key concession in the interunion negotiations: there would be a historical unit provision to recognize the informal bargaining relationships established by the building trades. This protected the building trades from having their members included in larger bargaining units that AFSCME would probably win. In exchange, the building trades (which had previously opposed public sector bargaining bills) sent not only their lobbyists, but also their local union presidents to tell the Illinois Assembly Speaker and the Illinois Senate President that they supported the AFL-CIO bargaining bill (Carmell interview).

The IEA was not part of the group that had agreed upon this common bill, perhaps because the IEA's intense rivalry with the IFT had strained the IEA's relations with the state AFL-CIO. Early in 1983, however, the Illinois Assembly Speaker informed the IEA and the IFT that a bargaining bill was likely to be enacted that session and that the IEA and the IFT would have to work together if they wanted to have any input (Blackshere interview). The IEA insisted on drafting a separate bill for educational employees (even though the AFL-CIO bill covering all public employees gave employees virtually the same rights), but the educational bill nevertheless had terms acceptable to the IFT. This IEA-IFT agreement marked a major departure from the past, when one teacher union invariably opposed a teacher bargaining bill supported by the other. IEA-IFT cooperation collapsed by the summer—when "traditional organized labor groups" urged Governor Thompson to veto the separate bill for education and let teacher bargaining be regulated by the AFL-CIO's bargaining bill[46]—but by then both bills had at least made it through the legislature.

2.4.4 Ohio: Unified Democratic Party Control of State Government

In Ohio, cooperation among unions had not been as great a problem, perhaps because the OEA's dominance in Ohio was more secure than the IEA's dominance in Illinois and because Ohio had fewer unions that feared the loss of members whom they had represented informally. The key development in Ohio was not an external threat that spurred union cooperation, but rather an unusually favorable political situation that allowed the unions to get what they wanted. The previous problem for unions in Ohio had been that the Democratic party had rarely controlled the state government, and the Republicans generally opposed bargaining legislation. The Democrats won the governorship and majorities in both houses of the state legislature in the 1958 Democratic landslide, but public employee unions had too few members then to get anything more than the dues checkoff statute. Subsequently, more public employees became interested in bargaining, but the political situation became unfavorable. From 1961 to 1982, the Republicans at all times controlled either the governorship or at least one house of the state legislature. Bargaining bills were either killed in Republican-controlled committees or vetoed by Republican Governor Rhodes (who served as governor from 1963 to 1971 and again from 1975 to 1983).

The Democrats made substantial gains in the legislature after the 1971 reapportionment, which was controlled by Democratic officials. (Warren Smith, the chief lobbyist for the Ohio AFL-CIO, estimated that the Democrats gained six to seven seats in the Senate (out of thirty-three) and fifteen seats in the House (out of ninety-nine) as a result of the reapportionment.) The Democrats won a majority in the Ohio House of Representatives in 1973 and a majority in the Ohio Senate in 1975. Unfortunately for the public employee unions, Governor Rhodes was back in office in 1975, and he vetoed their bargaining bills. The Democrats, however, controlled the reapportionment commission again in 1981, and they received a further boost from the economic depression in Ohio in 1982. When the 1982 elections brought simultaneous Democratic control of the governorship and both houses of the legislature, Ohio's public employee unions were finally able to get the strongly pro-union bargaining statute upon which they insisted—even though not a single Republican voted for the bill.

In Illinois, lack of Democratic party control had not been the key barrier to bargaining legislation prior to 1983: Republican Governor Thompson was willing to sign bargaining legislation, and the Democrats controlled both houses of the Illinois legislature from 1975 to 1980. Nevertheless, no bargaining bill acceptable to the unions would have emerged from a legislature like the one in office during 1981–82, when several bills obnoxious to labor (a right-to-work bill, a bill to cut unemployment insurance and workers' compensation benefits, and a bill to require one-year advance notice of strikes) were reported out of committee in the Republican-controlled House. The restoration of Democratic control of the House in the 1982 elections (partly due to unusually active campaign efforts by Illinois unions) made bargaining legislation possible again—once the unions presented a united front and the mayor of Chicago no longer opposed a bill.

2.5. Impact of the 1983 Statutes on the Extent of Bargaining Coverage and Nonwage Bargaining Outcomes

Once the Ohio and Illinois bargaining statutes were enacted, what was their impact on public sector labor relations? Although the statutes may have affected many variables, the analysis here will focus on only two of them: the extent of bargaining coverage and the nonwage outcomes of bargaining.

Quantitative measurement of the impact of the Ohio law is difficult because detailed data for the years before the law was enacted are not available. Thus, there is no baseline against which to measure any changes. A legislative study commission did, however, conduct a survey of local public employers and local public employee organizations in Ohio during the fall of 1984, half a year after the Ohio law took effect. Responses were obtained from about half of the employers and about a fourth of the unions. Although the low response rates mean that these data cannot be used to make inferences about the *proportion* of all public employers or unions that would have given a particular answer, the data nevertheless provide a (probably fairly low) lower bound estimate on the *absolute number* of employers or unions that would have given a particular answer. Results for selected questions are shown in table 2.1.

As table 2.1 indicates, the enactment of the 1983 Ohio bargaining law (S.B. 133) did not overcome all resistance to unions among public employers. Although 54 employers said that they recognized a union after S.B. 133 was passed but before it took effect, 80 said that they adopted solicitation rules (presumably intended to thwart union organizing). Interestingly, 43 of the 80 employers adopting solicitation rules were county governments, jurisdictions where Ohio's public sector unions had been especially weak before the law. When asked what proportion of their employees had to belong to the union before they would grant a fair-share (agency shop) clause, 434 employers (over half the sample) responded that they were ideologically opposed to a fair-share clause. Contracts were common at the time of the survey (514 employers had them), but these contracts were in many cases fairly weak. For example, 153 of the employers responding to the survey said that their contracts did not have grievance arbitration. Although the unions that did not have grievance arbitration (because they had either a weak contract or no contract at all) generally intended to bargain for it, employers not having grievance arbitration generally had no such intention.

Table 2.1   **Employer and Union Reactions to the 1983 Ohio Bargaining Law[a]**

	Employers	Unions
1. As a result of the passage of Senate Bill 133, but prior to 1 April 1984, what changes in the workplace did you institute? (Please check all appropriate responses.)		
a) none	442	NA
b) work rule changes	62	NA
c) job description changes	114	NA
d) supervisor identification	125	NA
e) recognition of union	54	NA
f) adoption of solicitation rules	80	NA
g) offer to renegotiate existing contract	39	NA
h) management training in labor relations	180	NA
i) other	33	NA
2. Do you have a union membership percentage threshold as a determining factor before granting a fair-share [agency shop] clause?		
a) 50 – 59 percent	63	NA
b) over 70 percent	40	NA
c) ideologically opposed to a fair-share clause	434	NA
d) no response	245	NA
3. Do you have a collective bargaining agreement in your unit or units?		
a) yes	514	193
b) no	253	71
c) no response	15	5
4. Does your agreement contain a grievance procedure culminating in final and binding arbitration?		
a) yes	306	146
b) no	153	49
c) no response	323	74
5. Do you intend to bargain for a grievance procedure culminating in final and binding arbitration?		
a) yes	43	95
b) no	214	10
c) no response	525	164

[a]Tabulated from data collected during the fall of 1984 by the Public Employment Advisory and Counseling Effort (PEACE) Commission, a study commission created by the Ohio legislature to review the implementation of S.B. 133. The PEACE Commission sent questionnaires to approximately 1,675 local public employers in Ohio and 1,200 local employee organizations; 782 employers and 269 employee organizations responded. The data in the table indicate the absolute number of employers or unions giving each response.

I supplemented the data obtained from this survey with information obtained from interviews with practitioners. The most interesting finding from these interviews is that some public employers in Ohio have aggressively resisted the unionization of their employees, even after the legislature enacted a bargaining law. This represents a radical break with the previous pattern established by public employers in states that enacted bargaining laws during the 1960s and 1970s. In that era, public employers (unlike their private sector counterparts) did not oppose the unionization of their employees once the legislature declared that it was the policy of the state to protect the right of employees to organize and bargain. Instead, management anti-unionism in the public sector was manifested in disputes about the scope of bargaining. These latter disputes are not absent from Ohio: for example, the City of Cincinnati and the Fraternal Order of Police had a fierce dispute about whether residency requirements were bargainable.[47] What is new is employer campaigning against union representation.

According to one attorney I interviewed, labor relations consulting firms began, shortly before S.B. 133 was enacted, to market their services by conducting seminars explaining why employers would find it advantageous to remain nonunion. Furthermore, the Association of County Commissioners and the Ohio Municipal League, dismayed that the bill was enacted, also allegedly promoted the idea of staying nonunion. A number of local public employers responded by hiring consulting firms to help them defeat unions in representation elections. Most notable was the case of the welfare department in Hamilton County (the county in which Cincinnati is located). This department, several people told me, paid a consulting firm over a quarter of a million dollars to help fight a union-organizing drive during 1983 and 1984, plus substantial additional sums for the legal battles that have followed.

The history of this organizing drive is described in the report of the State Employment Relations Board (SERB) hearing officer on an unfair labor practice charge that the union eventually filed.[48] According to the report, the Hamilton County Welfare Department did not bargain with AFSCME prior to S.B. 133, but it did provide dues checkoff. A substantial number of the employees had signed the dues deduction authorizations, providing a strong base for the organizing drive that AFSCME began in the late spring of 1983 (once it was clear that S.B. 133 would be enacted). The director of the welfare department responded by holding meetings with the managers and first-line supervisors to enlist their support for a campaign to oppose unionization. In the fall of 1983, the welfare department hired a labor relations consulting firm to provide assistance in resisting unionization.

Shortly after hiring the consulting firm, the SERB hearing officer's report continued, the department prohibited the distribution of union literature or authorization cards on the department's premises, even by department employees, and required prior approval before department employees could post notices on the departmental bulletin boards. This policy was relaxed in March 1984 (just before S.B. 133 took effect) to permit solicitation by employees during nonworking time; but solicitation was banned during working time and nonemployees were prohibited from entering the building. The department continued, however, to give unlimited access to the outside consultants, who campaigned among the employees during the employees' working time.

Meanwhile, supervisors used the regular weekly meetings with their subordinates, at which attendance was required, to pass out the employer's representation campaign literature and to discuss election issues. During the two days immediately before the representation election, the department held a series of meetings for all employees at which one of the outside consultants expressed the employer's views on union representation. The notice of the meeting, signed by the director of the welfare department, stated, "If you cannot make the assigned meeting, please arrange to attend one of the other sessions," which created an impression among some employees that attendance was required.[49]

On 11 July 1984, the representation election was held. AFSCME lost by the narrowest of margins: 355 votes for no representation vs. 354 for AFSCME. AFSCME filed an unfair labor practice charge and sought a new election. On 6 February 1986, the SERB hearing officer agreed with the union position on the grounds that the employer's solicitation-distribution rules were unduly restrictive and that the meetings during which supervisors and the outside consultant campaigned against the union involved illegal "captive audience" speeches. The three SERB board members unanimously adopted the hearing officer's recommendation on 12 May 1986, directing that a new election take place; but the Hamilton County Welfare Department challenged the SERB ruling in court.

On 7 July 1986, the Hamilton County Welfare Department's appeal of the SERB ruling was dismissed in county court. Two days later, the AFSCME local chapter president (an employee of the welfare department) requested that a union announcement, printed on 8-½" by 11" paper, be posted on welfare department bulletin boards. (See p. 63.) The welfare department personnel director, however, sent the local chapter president a memo the following day denying the request to post the notice.[50] Thus, the battle over union representation in the Hamilton County Welfare Department continues. Some experienced practitioners familiar with both this case and private sector labor relations told me that Hamilton County's resistance to unionization was as intense as that of most employers in the private sector. The irony

VOTE   VOTE   VOTE

CSEA-AFSCME WELCO CHAPTER

WISHES TO ANNOUNCE THAT A NEW ELECTION
ORDERED BY S.E.R.B. MAY 12, 1986, IS ABOUT TO
HAPPEN!! DATE OF ELECTION WILL BE PUB-
LISHED SHORTLY!!

VOTE   VOTE   VOTE

of the Hamilton County battle is that most of the welfare department's labor costs are reimbursed by the state and federal governments, so that unionization poses less of a threat to the welfare department management than it does to most employers.

Despite this and other cases of management resistance, unions have made considerable gains in winning representation rights in Ohio. The biggest change has come in state government. Before S.B. 133, there had been some "members only" contracts in state government. Indeed, Ohio State University had such contracts with two separate unions for a single classification of employees. These "members only" contracts were, however, generally much more limited in scope than a conventional contract negotiated by an exclusive bargaining agent, if only to avoid inconsistency in the personnel policies applying to members and nonmembers. Exclusive representation contracts, meanwhile, were almost nonexistent in state government in Ohio (the exceptions were one in a home for old sailors and soldiers, and one in a home for the blind).

In the aftermath of S.B. 133, however, AFSCME and other unions very quickly won exclusive bargaining rights for all state employees covered by the new law. The SERB divided the covered state employees into fourteen statewide bargaining units on 25 March 1985. Within five weeks, unions gathered enough employee signatures to petition for representation elections in thirteen of the fourteen units, including two where unions might have been expected to be weak (clerical workers and administrative professionals). The fourteenth unit, state engineers and scientists, was another one that might not be expected to be a union stronghold, but a representation petition for that unit was filed within four months of the SERB unit determination ruling.[51] Unions prevailed over the "no representation" option in all fourteen elections, with the bulk of the state employees going to AFSCME. The speed of these union victories and the inclusion among them of the units for clerical workers, administrative professionals, and engineers and scientists contrasts with the experience of other states, where unionization of the blue-collar employees and the negotiation of one or more blue-collar contracts typically preceded any organizing among clerical workers or professionals. Clearly, there was a pent-up demand for union representation among state employees in Ohio. It took a bargaining statute for that demand to be satisfied.

In Illinois, quantitative assessment of the impact of the 1983 bargaining legislation is more easily done than it is in Ohio, primarily because the Illinois State Board of Education has been collecting data on labor agreements in the public schools since the early 1970s. The state board obtains copies of all signed agreements between school boards and teacher unions and records the presence or absence of various contract provisions. The board summarizes these data in annual pamphlets and also produces data tapes with detailed information for each school district. Copies of these tapes were obtained for this study.

Table 2.2 presents descriptive statistics on the prevalence of signed written agreements between Illinois public school boards and teacher organizations. Several trends stand out:

(1) Agreements were much more common in large school districts (those with large enrollments and, hence, a large number of teachers) than in small school districts. For example, in 1979–80, signed written agreements were in effect in only 15 percent of the districts with enrollments under 500 (which typically had thirty or fewer teachers) but in over 90 percent of the districts with enrollments over 3,000 (which typically had 150 or more teachers.

(2) The percentage of smaller districts with agreements rose only slightly during the four years from 1979–80 to 1983–84.

(3) The percentage of smaller districts with agreements jumped dramatically in 1984–85, the first school year after the 1983 Illinois bargaining law took effect. For example, the fraction of districts having contracts in the under 500 enrollment stratum grew from 15 percent in 1979–80 to only 19 percent in 1983–84, but it then jumped to 56 percent in 1984–85.

Clearly, these data suggest that employer size and legislation both influence whether teachers in a given district are covered by an agreement.

More rigorous evidence of the importance of these factors is presented in tables 2.3 and 2.4, which show logistic regressions aimed at explaining the presence of a substantive contract in Illinois school districts. (Some of the agreements included in table 2.2 were "procedural agreements" in which the school board merely recognized the teacher organization and agreed to negotiate with it, rather than formal

Table 2.2   **Percent of Illinois School Districts with Negotiated Agreements, 1979–80 to 1986–87[a]**

| | District Enrollment | | | | | |
Year	Under 500	500–999	1,000–2,999	3,000–5,999	6,000–11,999	12,000 and Above
1979–80	15%	35%	69%	93%	91%	100%
1980–81	15%	40%	71%	95%	90%	92%[b]
1981–82	19%	42%	74%	95%	90%	100%
1982–83	18%	46%	76%	94%	89%	92%[b]
1983–84	19%	48%	78%	96%	87%	100%
1984–85	56%	83%	93%	97%	100%	100%
1985–86	61%	87%	96%	97%	100%	100%

[a]Data taken from Department of Planning, Research, and Evaluation, Illinois State Board of Education, *Illinois Teacher Salary Study* [title varies], annual editions for 1979–80 to 1985–86.

[b]The changes in the percentage with contracts in the largest enrollment stratum represent the Peoria School District. In 1979–80 and again in 1981–82, the Peoria School District was reported as having a signed written agreement with a coordinating council consisting of representatives of the NEA, the AFT, and independent teachers. In 1980–81, the Peoria School District was reported as developing its salary schedules by meetings between board representatives and representatives of a teacher organization recognized through board policy. In 1982–83, the Peoria salary schedule was reported developed on the basis of meetings between the school board and the superintendent. From 1983–84 onward, the Peoria board was reported as having a signed written agreement with the AFT.

collective bargaining contracts.) The regressions are based on Illinois State Board of Education data for individual school districts, to which I have added county data on the vote for Reagan in the 1984 presidential election. In both tables, the dependent variable was coded as 1 if the school district had a substantive contract, 0 otherwise.

Table 2.3 presents a cross-section estimate of the probability of the presence of a collective bargaining contract in each school district in the fall of 1982 (before the teacher bargaining law was passed). The results were generally as expected. Thus, districts with a small number of teachers (particularly those with 20 or fewer) were less likely to have contracts, while districts with more than 500 teachers were more likely to have contracts. (This confirms the results in table 2.2 even when there are controls for other variables that are highly correlated with district size, such as whether it is an elementary district, a secondary district, or a unit district.) Rural districts were less likely to have contracts, as were districts located outside Cook County. The only surprise was that the probability of a contract was higher in districts located in counties which voted heavily for Reagan in 1984—a result that probably arose because of the high zero-order correlation between the variables *COOKCOUNTY* and *REAGANVOTE* (-0.56). In any case, the coefficient for *REAGANVOTE* was statistically insignificant.

Table 2.4 presents an estimate of the probability of a change from nonunion status to union status. Specifically, the regression in table 2.4 estimates the probability that districts without collective bargaining contracts in the prior year would have collective bargaining contracts in the current year. Data are included for three years: the fall of 1982 (before the bargaining law was passed), the fall of 1983 (after it was passed but before it took effect), and the fall of 1984 (after it had taken effect). The regression includes dummy variables for year, which are proxies for the impact of the law on districts that previously did not have contracts.

The results in table 2.4 differ somewhat from those in table 2.3. In table 2.4, unlike table 2.3, the size of the district and its rural or urban status has a statistically insignificant effect on the probability that the district would sign its first contract. This may suggest that the enactment of bargaining legislation in 1983 reduced the degree to which small unit sizes and location in rural areas posed a barrier to unionization. Meanwhile, the coefficient for *COOKCOUNTY*, which is positive and significant in table 2.3, is negative and significant in table 2.4. Perhaps the districts in Cook County that had not signed contracts prior to 1982 were hard-core nonunion districts for some reasons not controlled for in my model (e.g., enlightened personnel practices that keep a district's employees content). The negative coefficient for *COOKCOUNTY* in

Table 2.3 **Determinants of Contract Coverage in Illinois Public Schools Prior to the 1983 Bargaining Law**[a]

Explanatory Variables	Dependent Variable: Probability of a collective bargaining contract in this school district in the fall of 1982		Impact at Mean of Dependent Variable[b]
	Coefficient	(Standard Error)	
Characteristics of the District			
Dummy variables for the number of teachers in the district:[c]			
20 or fewer (*DIST20*)	−1.358***	(0.173)	−0.330
21 to 50 (*DIST50*)	−0.896***	(0.131)	−0.218
51 to 100 (*DIST100*)	−0.343**	(0.132)	−0.083
500 or more (*DIST500*)	0.499	(0.568)	0.121
Dummy variables for the student population served by the district:[d]			
elementary (*ELEMDIST*)	0.026	(0.114)	0.006
secondary (*SECONDIST*)	0.163	(0.135)	0.040
Dummy variables for the urban or rural status of the district:[e]			
central city (*CENTRALCITY*)	0.416	(0.441)	0.101
suburb (*SUBURB*)	0.434***	(0.120)	0.106
independent city (*SMALLCITY*)	0.357**	(0.123)	0.087
Characteristics of the County			
Dummy variable for districts in Cook County (*COOKCOUNTY*)	0.488**	(0.167)	0.119
Fraction of the county vote for President in 1984 for Reagan (*REAGANVOTE*)	0.615	(1.094)	0.150
Intercept	−0.588	(0.873)	−0.143
−2*LLR		1004	

[a]Logistic regressions based on data obtained from the Illnois State Board of Education on contract provisions in Illinois public school districts. There is one observation for the fall of 1982 for each school district. There are 1,013 observations, 424 of which represent districts with collective bargaining contracts. The dependent variable is coded 1 for districts with substantive contracts, 0 otherwise.

[b]This is the partial derivative of the logit equation with respect to the explanatory variable, evaluated at the mean of the dependent variable. It equals $b*p*(1-p)$, where b is the coefficient of the explanatory variable and p is the proportion of 1's for the dependent variable (42 percent).

[c]The omitted category represents districts with 101 to 499 teachers.

[d]The omitted category represents unit districts which have both elementary and secondary schools.

[e]The omitted category represents rural school districts.

**Significant at the 1 percent level (two-tailed test).

***Significant at the 0.1 percent level (two-tailed test).

Table 2.4   **The Impact of the 1983 Bargaining Law on the Spread of Bargaining in Illinois Public Schools**[a]

Explanatory Variables	Coefficient	(Standard Error)	Impact at Mean of Dependent Variable[b]
	Dependent Variable: Probability that a district that did not have a collective bargaining contract the previous fall will have one this fall (fall 1982, 1983, 1984)		
Bargaining Law			
Dummy variables for the year:			
1984–85 (*LAWEFFECTYR*)	2.353***	(0.203)	0.321
1983–84 (*LAWPASSYR*)	0.449	(0.232)	0.061
Characteristics of the District			
Dummy variables for the number of teachers in the district:[c]			
20 or fewer (*DIST20*)	−0.434	(0.241)	−0.059
21 to 50 (*DIST50*)	0.107	(0.220)	0.015
51 to 100 (*DIST100*)	0.175	(0.236)	0.024
500 or more (*DIST500*)	1.285	(1.204)	0.175
Dummy variables for the student population served by the district:[d]			
elementary (*ELEMDIST*)	−0.286*	(0.120)	−0.039
secondary (*SECONDIST*)	0.212	(0.156)	0.029
Dummy variables for the urban or rural status of the district:[e]			
central city (*CENTRALCITY*)	0.679	(0.986)	0.092
suburb (*SUBURB*)	0.226	(0.141)	0.031
independent city (*SMALLCITY*)	0.293	(0.165)	0.040
Characteristics of the County			
Dummy variables for districts in Cook County (*COOKCOUNTY*)	−0.720**	(0.270)	−0.098
Fraction of the county vote for President in 1984 for Reagan (*REAGANVOTE*)	1.351	(1.179)	0.184
Intercept	−0.706	(1.090)	−0.096
−2*LLR		884	

[a]Logistic regressions based on data obtained from the Illinois State Board of Education on contract provisions in Illinois public school districts. The data consist of observations for each of three years (1982–83, 1983–84, and 1984–85), with one observation for each school district that did not have a collective bargaining contract in the prior year. Thus, all the observations represent school districts that either did not have contracts in the given year or negotiated their first contract in that year. There are a total of 1,727 observations, 281 of which were for first contracts. The dependent variable is coded 1 for districts with substantive contracts, 0 otherwise.

[b]This is the partial derivative of the logit equation with respect to the explanatory variable, evaluated at the mean of the dependent variable. See note b to table 2.3.

[c]The omitted category represents districts with 101 to 499 teachers.

[d]The omitted category represents unit districts which have both elementary and secondary schools.

[e]The omitted category represents rural school districts.

*Significant at the 5 percent level (two-tailed test).

**Significant at the 1 percent level (two-tailed test).

***Significant at the 0.1 percent level (two-tailed test).

table 2.4 could thus reflect the impact of these omitted variables, which are the true reasons for the absence of bargaining.

The major finding from the regression in table 2.4 is that, even controlling for characteristics of the county and characteristics of the school district that might influence whether the district would have a teacher bargaining contract, the 1983 bargaining law brought a notable increase in the subsequent probability of contract coverage. The knowledge that the law would soon be in effect may have brought a small increase in bargaining coverage, as indicated by the positive coefficient (significant at the 5.3 percent level) for the variable *LAWPASSYR* (a dummy variable for school years 1983–84). Much more dramatically, the increase came once the bargaining law took effect, as indicated by the positive and statistically highly significant coefficient for the variable *LAWEFFECTYR* (a dummy variable for school year 1984–85). Moreover, the magnitude of the coefficient for *LAWEFFECTYR* was large—larger than that for any of the other explanatory variables. If the other variables were at their average values, then the probability that a school district would have a contract was 40 percentage points higher in 1984–85 than in 1982–83.[52] By contrast, the nonlegal variable with the greatest impact was *DIST500* (a dummy variable for districts with 500 or more teachers), and its effect on the probability of a contract was less than 20 percentage points. Similarly, the "impact" column in table 2.4 (which reports the partial derivative of the logit function with respect to the explanatory variable) indicates that the law taking effect increased the probability of a contract by 32 percentage points, whereas *DIST500* had an impact of only 17.5 percentage points.

In short, one can be confident that the association between legislation and subsequent increases in contract coverage is real, and it is large enough to be socially important. These results (based on district level data for one state) confirm those reported in Saltzman's (1985) study, which used aggregate statewide data for all fifty states. Obviously, this confirmation with a different data set strengthens the finding.

Does this association between bargaining legislation and subsequent increases in contract coverage demonstrate a causal relationship? In the 1960s and early 1970s, one could argue that bargaining laws were consequences of the same social forces that led to unionization and not an independent cause. By 1983, however, the social forces generating the tidal wave of public employee unionism had receded. As the legislative histories given earlier in this chapter make clear, the Illinois and Ohio bargaining laws were enacted in 1983 not because of a surge in public employee militancy, but because of exogenous political events, such as the breakdown of the Chicago Democratic machine. Moreover, as table 2.2 indicates, in the four years before the Illinois law, there was only a minor increase in the number of Illinois school districts with contracts. It is therefore reasonable to conclude that the substantial increase in bargaining coverage after the 1983 laws was a consequence of the laws per se. Certainly that was the view of the union lobbyists I interviewed, who gave as one rationale for their pursuit of legislation that it would help them win representation rights for additional employees. Thus, as a cause of the growth of bargaining coverage, public sector bargaining laws really matter.

Besides contributing to the spread of bargaining, bargaining legislation could also affect bargaining outcomes. There are two reasons why one would expect that the 1983 teacher law in Illinois should lead to outcomes more favorable to unions. First, the teacher law required that all contracts have binding grievance arbitration. (This was one of the few respects in which the amended version of H.B. 1530 differed from the comprehensive law, S.B. 536, which merely authorized grievance arbitration.) Second, it explicitly legalized teacher strikes, which should have helped unions win favorable contract terms on all issues, even in cases where the union merely threatens to strike.

A different sample of the same data set used to analyze the spread of bargaining was used to analyze the impact of legislation on contract terms. The contract terms sample was based on one observation per contract. Thus, districts with no collective bargaining contracts during the period from 1982–83 to 1984–85 were not included in the sample. On the other hand, districts with two or more contracts during this period were represented by multiple observations. The contract data set used is unusual in having information on contract expiration dates, which made it possible to distinguish records for renegotiated contracts from those for continuations of multiyear contracts.

Table 2.5 uses this sample of the data set to estimate how much of an effect the law actually had on contract terms. The table presents logistic regressions indicating the probability that various contract terms will be present in those cases where there are contracts. These contract terms, each corresponding to a separate regression equation, are: (a) grievance arbitration, (b) fair share, (c) class size limits, and (d) seniority for reductions in force (RIFs).

The results in table 2.5 indicate that the 1983 bargaining law did, indeed, lead to contracts more favorable to unions. The law had its greatest impact on the probability that contracts would include grievance arbitration, which might be expected since the law specifically required the inclusion of this contract provision. In quantitative terms, the probability that contracts included grievance arbitration was 41 percentage points higher in 1984–85 than in 1982–83 (assuming that the other variables are at their average values). The law also increased the probability of fair-share clauses and the use of seniority as the basis for determining who gets laid off during a RIF, although it had no significant impact on the probability of class size limits.

Table 2.5   The Impact of the 1983 Bargaining Law on Contract Language in Illinois Public School Bargaining[a]

| | Probability That the Contract Will Contain: | | | |
| | Grievance Arbitration | | Fair Share | |
Explanatory Variables	Coefficient	(Standard Error)	Coefficient	(Standard Error)
Bargaining Law				
Dummy variables for the year:				
1984–85 (*LAWEFFECTYR*)	2.223***	(0.149)	1.569***	(0.197)
1983–84 (*LAWPASSYR*)	0.115	(0.089)	1.001***	(0.212)
Characteristics of the Bargaining Relationship				
Dummy variable for representation by the AFT (*AFT*)	−0.173	(0.116)	0.060	(0.136)
Dummy variable for first contracts (*FIRSTK*)	0.261	(0.155)	−0.144	(0.135)
Characteristics of the District				
Dummy variables for the number of teachers in the district:[b]				
20 or fewer (*DIST20*)	−0.908***	(0.192)	−0.269	(0.249)
21 to 50 (*DIST50*)	−0.584***	(0.120)	−0.108	(0.158)
51 to 100 (*DIST100*)	−0.368***	(0.102)	0.108	(0.136)
500 or more (*DIST500*)	0.179	(0.290)	0.855**	(0.307)
Dummy variables for the student population served by the district:[c]				
elementary (*ELEMDIST*)	0.038	(0.117)	−0.155	(0.156)
secondary (*SECONDIST*)	−0.067	(0.130)	0.052	(0.162)
Dummy variables for the urban or rural status of the district:[d]				
central city (*CENTRALCITY*)	0.992**	(0.337)	0.193	(0.400)
suburb (*SUBURB*)	0.419**	(0.141)	0.507**	(0.171)
independent city (*SMALLCITY*)	0.429**	(0.137)	0.105	(0.174)

(continued)

Table 2.5 (continued)

| | Probability That the Contract Will Contain: | | | |
| | Grievance Arbitration | | Fair Share | |
Explanatory Variables	Coefficient	(Standard Error)	Coefficient	(Standard Error)
Characteristics of the County				
Dummy variable for districts in Cook County (*COOKCOUNTY*)	0.590***	(0.146)	0.336	(0.194)
Fraction of the county vote for President in 1984 for Reagan (*REAGANVOTE*)	−2.009	(1.163)	−2.070	(1.533)
Intercept	−1.012	(0.761)	2.190*	(0.971)
−2*LLR	1045		698	

| | Class Size Limits | | Seniority for RIFs | |
	Coefficient	(Standard Error)	Coefficient	(Standard Error)
Bargaining Law				
Dummy variables for the year:				
1984–85 (*LAWEFFECTYR*)	0.048	(0.081)	0.284***	(0.077)
1983–84 (*LAWPASSYR*)	−0.009	(0.089)	0.103	(0.084)
Characteristics of the Bargaining Relationship				
Dummy variable for representation by the AFT (*AFT*)	0.078	(0.098)	0.127	(0.091)
Dummy variable for first contracts (*FIRSTK*)	−0.447***	(0.118)	−0.106	(0.087)
Characteristics of the District				
Dummy variables for the number of teachers in the district:[b]				
20 or fewer (*DIST20*)	−1.517***	(0.205)	−0.826***	(0.135)
21 to 50 (*DIST50*)	−0.881***	(0.104)	−0.741***	(0.096)

51 to 100 (DIST100)	−0.537***	(0.086)	−0.453***	(0.089)
500 or more (DIST500)	0.344	(0.261)	0.518	(0.387)
Dummy variables for the student population served by the district:[c]				
elementary (ELEMDIST)	0.125	(0.101)	0.018	(0.088)
secondary (SECONDIST)	0.086	(0.111)	0.214*	(0.100)
Dummy variables for the urban or rural status of the district:[d]				
central city (CENTRALCITY)	0.307	(0.289)	0.869	(0.530)
suburb (SUBURB)	−0.142	(0.117)	−0.071	(0.098)
independent city (SMALLCITY)	−0.089	(0.109)	0.269**	(0.096)
Characteristics of the County				
Dummy variable for districts in Cook County (COOKCOUNTY)	−0.028	(0.127)	0.066	(0.117)
Fraction of the county vote for President in 1984 for Reagan (REAGANVOTE)	3.218**	(1.009)	0.585	(0.861)
Intercept	0.358	(0.667)	−1.410	(0.785)
−2*LLR	1377		1653	

[a] Logistic regressions based on data obtained from the Illinois State Board of Education on contract provisions in Illinois public school districts. There is one observation for each contract reported during 1982–83, 1983–84, or 1984–85 (a total of 1,329). Districts with three contracts during this period thus have three observations, while districts with no contracts are excluded from the regressions. The dependent variable is coded as 1 for contracts where the contract provision is present, 0 otherwise. The number of contracts containing each provision is as follows: grievance arbitration, 828 (out of 1,329); fair share (a public sector term for the agency shop), 129; class size limits, 412; seniority for RIFs, 743.

[b] The omitted category represents districts with 101 to 499 teachers.

[c] The omitted category represents unit districts which have both elementary and secondary schools.

[d] The omitted category represents rural school districts.

*Significant at the 5 percent level (two-tailed test).

**Significant at the 1 percent level (two-tailed test).

***Significant at the 0.1 percent level (two-tailed test).

The one case where a significant effect appeared during the 1983–84 year was fair share (as indicated by the positive and significant coefficient for *LAWPASSYR*), but this effect is subject to two possible interpretations. It might be that knowledge that the 1983 bill would soon go into effect led to the spread of fair-share clauses at the beginning of the 1983–84 school year. (Most school district contracts are signed and ratified shortly after the teachers return from summer vacation. The 1983 law, originally passed by the legislature in June 1983 and signed by the governor in September, went into effect on 1 January 1984.) Alternatively, the spread of fair-share clauses during 1983–84 could reflect the delayed impact of H.B. 701, the bill passed in 1981 that specifically authorized school districts to agree to fair-share clauses. In either case, legislation appears to be an important determinant of bargaining outcomes.

Of the other explanatory variables in table 2.5, perhaps the most interesting is *AFT,* a dummy variable indicating that the teachers in that school district were represented by the AFT rather than the NEA or an independent organization. (The independent organizations were rare, so that the comparison is primarily between the AFT and the NEA.) Although the coefficients for *AFT* were positive in three out of four cases, they were all statistically insignificant. This suggests that, controlling for other determinants of bargaining outcomes, teachers' choice between the AFT and the NEA had little effect on the contract language they won (at least concerning grievance arbitration, fair share, class size limits, and seniority for RIFs). The existence of rival unionism may have substantially affected bargaining outcomes (by spurring *both* the AFT and the NEA to be more aggressive), but these regressions tend to undermine claims that one teacher union is systematically more successful than the other.

2.6 Conclusions

The findings in this study suggest that major political changes—the overthrow of the Chicago Democratic machine in Illinois, the 1983 Democratic triumph in Ohio—may be the prerequisite for the enactment of new public sector bargaining laws in the 1980s. If such political changes occur, then some states in the South or Rocky Mountains might give their employees the right to bargain, or the federal government might enact a bargaining statute for state and local public employees similar to the ones proposed in the mid-1970s. Such legislation would likely bring substantial growth in the extent of bargaining coverage, even though resistance by public employers to unionization may become more common; and (depending on the terms of the legislation) it might also lead to contracts more favorable to unions. As noted at the beginning of this chapter, however, Ohio and Illinois had been "exceptional" cases prior to the enactment of their laws in 1983. Labor's prospects today of winning similar pro-union bargaining legislation in the remaining states that lack it are probably not nearly so bright.

Notes

1. See, however, the quantitative studies by Kochan (1973) and Saltzman (1985), and the case study of bargaining legislation in Wisconsin by Saltzman (1986).
2. 147 Ohio St. 313, 71 N.E. 2d 246 (1974).
3. *Ohio Revised Code* §§ 4117.01–.05.
4. H.B. 92 (1947 *Ohio House Journal* 120, 1303) and S.B. 114 (1947 *Ohio Senate Journal* 116). S.B. 114, incidentally, was introduced by Howard Metzenbaum, who subsequently became a United States Senator.
5. H.B. 5, passage by the House reported in 1947 *Ohio House Journal* 206–7.
6. H.B. 36, passage by the House reported in 1947 *Ohio House Journal* 207–9.
7. 1947 *Ohio Senate Journal* 1086–87.
8. S.B. 209, enacted as § 1321.321, later renumbered as § 9.41 of the Ohio Revised Code (128 *Laws of Ohio* 260 [1959].
9. Ohio Legislative Service Commission, "Public Employee Labor Relations," Staff Research Report no. 96, Columbus, Ohio, February 1968, 28.
10. *Government Employee Relations Report* (hereafter cited as *GERR*), no. 176, 23 January 1967, B-8.
11. *GERR,* no. 286, 3 March 1969, B-8.
12. *GERR,* no. 287, 10 March 1969, B-7.
13. *GERR,* no. 221, 4 December 1967, B-7.
14. *GERR,* no. 175, 16 January 1967, B-7. The bill was numbered S.B. 30.
15. *GERR,* no. 179, 13 February 1967, B-5.
16. *GERR,* no. 74, 8 February 1965, B-2.
17. *GERR,* no. 196, 12 June 1967, B-6; *GERR,* no. 197, 19 June 1967, B-8.
18. *GERR,* no. 222, 11 December 1967, B-8.
19. 1968 *Ohio House Journal* 2219.
20. *GERR,* no. 215, 23 October 1967, B-7.
21. *GERR,* no. 329, 29 December 1969, B-8.
22. 41 Ohio St. 2d 127, 323 N.E. 2d 714 (1975).
23. *Ohio Revised Code* § 4117.08(A).
24. 1983 *Ohio Laws* 140; *Ohio Revised Code* § 4117.
25. *Legislative Synopsis and Digest* (Springfield, Ill.: State of Illinois, 30 June 1945), 176.
26. 127 Ill. App. 3d 328, 468 N.E. 2d 1268 (1966).
27. *GERR,* no. 522, 24 September 1973, B-5 to B-7.
28. *GERR,* no. 820, 23 July 1979, 16.
29. *GERR,* no. 846, 28 January 1980, 20.
30. *GERR,* no. 848, 11 February 1980, 20–21.
31. *GERR,* no. 853, 17 March 1980, 27–28.

32. *GERR*, no. 920, 13 July 1981, 23–24.
33. 1973 *Laws of Illinois, 78th General Assembly* 1:632–33.
34. 1981 *Laws of Illinois, 81st General Assembly* 1:789–93.
35. Enacted as chapter 48, paragraphs 1701–21, *Ill. Stats. Anno.*
36. Enacted as chapter 48, paragraphs 1601–27, *Ill. Stats. Anno.*
37. 1985 *Laws of Illinois, 84th General Assembly* 3:6517.
38. 1985 *Laws of Illinois, 84th General Assembly* 3:7335.
39. *Focus* 11, no. 6 (May 1977):4.
40. 427 U.S. 347 (1976).
41. 481 F. Supp. 315 (1979).
42. S.B. 1387, introduced 11 April 1979. A copy of the bill is available in the Illinois State Library in Springfield.
43. *GERR* 21, no. 1032, 3 October 1983, 1955.
44. 430 N.E. 2d 1128 (1981).
45. 430 N.E. 2d 1111 (1981).
46. *GERR* 21, no. 1032, 3 October 1983, 1954.
47. Paul Furiga, "Cincinnati Using Bargaining Law in Police Strike," *Cincinnati Enquirer*, 6 January 1985, A-1 and A-16.
48. "Hearing Officer's Recommended Determination," *Ohio Civil Service Employees Association (OCSEA) Local 11 v. Hamilton County Welfare Department*, Ohio State Employment Relations Board, Case no. 84-RC-04-0080, 6 February 1986.
49. Ibid., 9.
50. "Motion to Expedite," *OCSEA Local 11 v. Hamilton County Department of Human Services*, Ohio State Employment Relations Board, filed 21 July 1986.
51. *GERR* 24, no. 1145, 6 January 1986, 11–12.
52. Since the logit model is nonlinear, the impact on the dependent variable of a change in one independent variable depends on the values of the other independent variables.

References

PUBLICATIONS

Burton, John. 1979. The extent of collective bargaining in the public sector. In *Public sector bargaining*, ed. Benjamin Aaron, Joseph Grodin, and James L. Stern, 1–43. Washington, D.C.: Bureau of National Affairs.
Clark, R. Theodore. 1969. Public employee labor legislation: A study of the unsuccessful attempt to enact a public employment bargaining statute in Illinois. *Labor Law Journal* 20:164–73.
Derber, Milton. 1968. Labor-management policy for public employees in Illinois: The experience of the Governor's Commission. *Industrial and Labor Relations Review* 21:541–58.
Kochan, Thomas. 1973. Correlates of state public employee bargaining laws. *Industrial Relations* 12(3):322–37.
Saltzman, Gregory. 1985. Bargaining laws as a cause and consequence of the growth of teacher unionism. *Industrial and Labor Relations Review* 38:335–51.
———. 1986. A progressive experiment: The evolution of Wisconsin's collective bargaining legislation for local government employees. *Journal of Collective Negotiations in the Public Sector* 15:1–24.

Wagner, Martin, et al. 1967. Report and recommendations of the Governor's Advisory Commission on Labor-Management Policy for Public Employees. Reprinted in *Government Employee Relations Report,* no. 184, 20 March 1967, D-1 to D-27.

INTERVIEWS WITH AUTHOR

Note: Some interviews listed below were on a "not for attribution" basis and, hence, are not cited in the text.

Arcilesi, Len (president, Cincinnati Teacher's Association, 1966–69; president, Ohio Education Association, 1972–74). Cincinnati, Ohio, 26 June 1980.
Barkley, Bob (supervisor of UniServ staff, Ohio Education Association). Columbus, Ohio, 24 June 1980.
Bedgood, Terry (labor advisor to Illinois Governor Thompson). Chicago, 9 December 1985.
Blackshere, Margaret (lobbyist, Illinois Federation of Teachers). Chicago, 9 December 1985.
Booth, Paul (AFSCME international union area director for Illinois). Chicago, 10 December 1985.
Brandt, John (associate director for labor relations, Ohio School Boards Association). Columbus, Ohio, 25 June 1980.
Burgess, Jack (executive director, Columbus Education Association). Columbus, Ohio, 19 June 1980.
Carmell, Sherman (union attorney). Chicago, 10 December 1985.
Clark, R. Theodore (attorney for Illinois Municipal League). Telephone interview, 3 December 1985.
Coleman, John (executive director, Ohio Municipal League). Columbus, Ohio, 24 June 1980.
D'Alba, Joel (union attorney). Chicago, 10 December 1985.
Davis, Jacky (general counsel, Ohio State Employment Relations Board). Columbus, Ohio, 27 November 1984.
Day, Donald (assistant executive director, AFSCME Council 8, Ohio). Columbus, Ohio, 23 June 1980.
Day, Jack (chairman, Ohio State Employment Relations Board). Columbus, Ohio, 12 August 1986.
De Guise, Earl (international vice president for Illinois and Ohio, International Association of Fire Fighters). Edwardsville, Illinois, 12 December 1985.
Evans, Del (organizer and field representative, Ohio Civil Service Employees' Association, AFSCME). Cincinnati, Ohio, 8 August 1986.
Fix, Helen (commissioner, Ohio State Employment Relations Board, and former assistant minority leader in the Ohio House of Representatives). Cincinnati, Ohio, 11 August 1986.
Frankenfield, Richard (lobbyist, Illinois Education Association). Springfield, Illinois, 12 December 1985.
Gibson, Bob (president, Illinois AFL-CIO). Chicago, 9 December 1985.
Greiman, Alan (assistant majority leader, Illinois House of Representatives). Chicago, 9 December 1985.
Hall, Connie (director of organizing and bargaining, Ohio Education Association). Columbus, Ohio, 12 August 1986.
Hall, John (assistant executive secretary and lobbyist, Ohio Education Association). Columbus, Ohio, 23 June 1980.
Heisel, Don (personnel director for the City of Cincinnati, 1955–68, and assistant personnel director, 1940–55). Cincinnati, Ohio, 26 June 1980.

Jaffy, Stewart (general counsel, Ohio AFL-CIO). Columbus, Ohio, 12 August 1986.

Kiley, Richard (president, Cincinnati Teachers' Union, 1967–69). Cincinnati, Ohio, 20 June 1980.

Looman, John (director, Public Employment Advisory and Counseling Effort Commission). Columbus, Ohio, 26 November 1984.

McPike, Jim (majority leader, Illinois House of Representatives). Alton, Illinois, 12 December 1985.

Marrone, John (associate professor, Labor Education and Research Service, Ohio State University). Cincinnati, Ohio, 21 November 1984.

Moody, Tom (president, Cincinnati Federation of Teachers). Cincinnati, Ohio, 25 June 1980.

Morgan, Tom (legislative director, AFSCME Council 8, Ohio). Telephone interview, 3 July 1980.

O'Reilly, James (labor lawyer). Cincinnati, Ohio, 21 November 1984.

Phalen, Tom (union attorney). Cincinnati, Ohio, 21 November 1984.

Preckwinkle, Steve (lobbyist, AFSCME Council 31, Illinois). Springfield, Illinois, 11 December 1985.

Roe, Charlotte (staff member, Ohio AFL-CIO). Columbus, Ohio, 19 June 1980.

Russell, Harriet (president, Cincinnati Teachers' Association, 1971–75). Cincinnati, Ohio, 26 June 1980.

Schwartz, Lee (lobbyist in the state legislature for City of Chicago, 1971–75 and 1983–84). Chicago, 9 December 1985.

Sheehan, Bill (vice-chairman, Ohio State Employment Relations Board; former secretary-treasurer, Cincinnati AFL-CIO). Cincinnati, Ohio, 21 November 1984.

Smith, Warren (executive secretary-treasurer, Ohio AFL-CIO). Columbus, Ohio, 19 June 1980.

Stallworth, Lamont (member, Illinois Local Labor Relations Board). New York City, 29 December 1985.

Stephens, Roger (president, Cincinnati Federation of Teachers, 1969–79). Cincinnati, Ohio, 20 June 1980.

Toto, John (international representative, AFSCME). Columbus, Ohio 12 August 1986.

Wagner, Martin (chairman, Illinois Educational Labor Relations Board). Chicago, 10 December 1985.

Walsh, Rich (lobbyist, Illinois AFL-CIO). Springfield, Illinois, 11 December 1985.

Walters, Glen (Illinois president, International Association of Fire Fighters). Edwardsville, Illinois, 12 December 1985.

Comment   William T. Dickens

I liked this paper when it was presented at the conference and had very few comments then. Since the author has dealt with nearly all of my complaints, I like the paper even more now and have less to say. My remaining disagreements are very minor.

William T. Dickens is associate professor of economics at the University of California, Berkeley, and a research associate of the Institute of Industrial Relations at Berkeley and of the National Bureau of Economic Research.

First, I still think the paper undersells the results a bit. The paper shows conclusively that bargaining laws can affect the level of union density, at least in the public sector in Ohio and Illinois. A debate has been raging for many years over the question of whether laws matter or just reflect the sentiments of the populations of the countries or states in which they are enacted. We know that the Wagner Act was followed by a great surge in union density, and it has been observed that Canada and the United States—two fairly similar countries with very different labor laws—have very different union densities. Canada, where it is easier to organize, has the higher density. In both cases very respected scholars have argued that it is not the laws which make the difference but public opinion. This question is of immediate importance since there is also a debate over whether changing the labor law in this country could reverse the fortune of the union movement.

As the paper shows, it is hard to argue that the changes in the laws in these two states reflect big shifts in the popularity of unions among the people in the state. The climate in the states is unchanged. In both cases the timing of the laws seems to be due to some chance occurrence in state politics unrelated to the question of public sector bargaining. Nonetheless the changes in the laws seem to be followed by big changes in union density. The only other paper that gets this close to being able to assess causation is Ellwood and Fine's (1983) study[1] of the effects of right-to-work laws. They too find that laws matter. Of course this does not mean that all provisions of state and federal labor laws are of similar importance, but it does add weight to the arguments of those who claim that changing the law could reverse the decline in union density.

My major remaining critical comment pertains to the results presented in table 2.4. The coefficients and standard errors are estimated under the assumption that the errors for each district in each year are independent. This is clearly false, since unobserved factors which make it likely that a district would change in one year also make it likely to change in the next. The most likely effect of the failure of this assumption is to bias the standard errors downward. Thus the results should be interpreted with some caution. Nonetheless, I do not believe that the bias could be big enough for the major finding, the large and significant coefficient on the dummy variable for the year the law took effect, to not hold up. The means in table 2.1 are enough to convince me. If the author wanted to do more he could have estimated the logit model in table 2.3 for each year and compared the intercepts. This would have avoided the error components problem that results from grouping the data as he has.

---

1. David Ellwood and Glenn Fine, "Impact of right-to-work laws on union organizing," National Bureau of Economic Research Working Paper no. 1116, May 1983.

3   The Effects of Public Sector Labor Laws on Labor Market Institutions and Outcomes

Richard B. Freeman and Robert G. Valletta

In this paper we seek to determine the impact of labor laws on the collective bargaining status, wages, and employment of local government workers in the United States. We use the new data on state public sector labor laws described in detail in appendix B in this volume and information from the Survey of Governments (SOG) and the Current Population Survey (CPS) to examine how differences and changes in public sector labor laws across states and among departments in cities affect collective bargaining, wages, and employment.

The major finding is that state public sector laws are a prime determinant of the likelihood that municipal workers are covered by collective bargaining and have a moderate impact on the wages and employment of public sector workers. Comprehensive public sector labor laws raise the probability that workers are covered by collective bargaining contracts and, conditional on contracts, raise wages at the expense of employment. In addition, we find that employment and wages in otherwise identical departments are higher in those with collective bargaining contracts, supporting the notion that public sector unions raise demand for labor as well as increase wages along given demand curves (Zax 1985; Freeman 1986b).

Richard B. Freeman is professor of economics at Harvard University and the Director of Labor Studies at the National Bureau of Economic Research. Robert G. Valletta is a visiting assistant professor of economics at the University of California, Irvine.

The authors wish to thank John Bound, Charles Brown, Harvey Rosen, Jeffrey Zax, and particularly Casey Ichniowski for their advice. We are solely responsible for any remaining errors.

3.1 The Legal Environment for Public Sector Labor Relations

The legal environment for public sector labor relations changed greatly in the United States between the 1950s and 1980s. In the 1950s most states had no explicit legislation covering public sector workers, and the few laws that did exist outlawed strikes or bargaining. During the 1960s a large number of states enacted labor laws that legalized collective bargaining for different groups of public employees. In the 1970s many states amended these laws to impose a duty to bargain on governments, and often followed this with compulsory interest arbitration or, in some cases, right-to-strike provisions designed to resolve impasses in bargaining (see appendix B and Farber, this volume, chap. 5). Other states, by contrast, did not pass such legislation or in some instances enacted anti-union legislation.

For the purpose of analyzing the effects of these different legal settings on public sector labor markets, we develop an index of the favorableness of the state laws toward collective bargaining. Our index is based on provisions regulating bargaining rights and dispute resolution. In the area of bargaining rights, we categorize laws into five groups: bargaining prohibited; no provision for bargaining; bargaining permitted; "meet and confer" or "present proposals"; and duty to bargain. The bargaining prohibited category gives public employers recourse to the courts if workers form unions and try to negotiate over terms and conditions of employment. It is thus the least favorable legal environment for collective bargaining. The no provision for bargaining category is, however, close behind, as courts have often ruled that it also means that workers have no right to bargain collectively. The other legal categories treat collective bargaining more favorably: bargaining permitted allows bargaining but does not require employers to negotiate with workers; "meet and confer" or "present proposals" ensures that employers listen to unions though it still allows them to make unilateral decisions; finally, duty-to-bargain provisions are the most favorable to collective bargaining because they require employers to meet employee representatives at the bargaining table.

In the area of dispute resolution we distinguish between: nonbinding mediation and fact-finding mechanisms that call for a neutral third party to seek to resolve disputes without empowering them to fashion a settlement; compulsory interest arbitration, which gives the neutral party the right to determine the terms of agreement, guaranteeing closure of the process;[1] and laws that permit strikes, which are the traditional private sector mode for resolving bargaining impasses.[2]

The bargaining rights and dispute resolution laws form a hierarchy from least to most favorable to collective bargaining. We combine them into a single index for analysis. First, we divide state laws into the nine categories shown in the first column of table 3.1, from bargaining prohibited at one extreme to strike permitted and compulsory arbitration at the other extreme.[3] As can be seen in columns 2 and 3, there is a wide distribution of municipalities across the nine categories in the years for which we have observations. For reasons of parsimony we further summarize the laws with a single monotonic index of their favorableness to collective bargaining. Specifically, we associate with each legal environment in a city department a value from 9 (= most favorable to collective bargaining) to 1 (= least favorable); compute the mean and standard deviation of these numeric values across cities; and form a standardized Z score as our index measure. The advantage of standardizing categories in this way is that it allows us to simplify presentation of empirical results. The virtue of the Z score is that it gives more extreme values to categories that differ greatly from the mean in their rating and that are relatively rare. None of our results hinge, of course, on this particular way of summarizing the legal codes.

Column 4 of table 3.1 records the Z-score values that we associate with each law category given the distribution of municipal departments in column 2. To illustrate how to interpret the scores consider the movement from no provision ($Z = -1.19$) to duty to bargain with required mediation or fact-finding ($Z = 0.58$) or to arbitration ($Z = 1.29$),—both common changes in state law between the 1960s and

Table 3.1   Distsribution of Survey of Governments (SOG) and Current Population Survey (CPS) Observations Across Legal Categories, by Collective Bargaining Coverage

	% of Observation in Category		Z-Score Value
Legal Category	SOG	CPS	
(1)	(2)	(3)	(4)
1. Duty to bargain and required arbitration	.14	.062	1.29
2. Duty to bargain and strikes permitted	.052	.12	.94
3. Duty to bargain and required fact-finding or mediation	.29	.28	.58
4. Duty to bargain	.040	.072	.23
5. Conferral rights and required fact-finding or mediation	.033	.022	−.12
6. Right to meet and confer or present proposals	.030	.020	−.48
7. Bargaining permitted	.15	.14	−.83
8. No provision for bargaining	.18	.14	−1.19
9. Bargaining prohibited	0.88	.14	−1.54
Number of observations	18,541	17,195	—

1970s. The first change is a 1.77 standard deviation improvement in the legal environment for collective bargaining; the second corresponds to a 2.48 standard deviation improvement. Given the frequency of these changes in the laws we will use a two standard deviation change in the legal index to evaluate the quantitative impact of legal changes on labor market outcomes.

3.1.1 Modelling Effects of the Legal Environment

There are two ways in which laws regarding collective bargaining can affect economic outcomes. First, they can affect outcomes by encouraging collective bargaining (Saltzman 1985; this volume, chap. 2; Ichniowski, this volume, chap. 1) and thus bear *indirect* responsibility for the bargaining-induced increases in wages (Lewis, this volume, chap. 6; Freeman 1986b) and employment (Zax 1985; Freeman 1986b). Second, given collective contracts, the laws can also affect outcomes *directly* by altering the results of bargaining and the decisions of non-union managements. This can occur by changing union power at bargaining tables and by creating greater or lesser threat effects on nonunion employers to match union wage gains.

To analyze the effects of public sector laws on outcomes we develop a model of union behavior in which the legal environment alters the resources the union expends to raise wages at the bargaining table. The model consists of:

i) A labor demand curve that the public sector union can shift through lobbying for greater public spending or other non-bargaining-table activity:

$$(1) \qquad E = -\eta W + X + bRS,$$

where E = ln employment; W = ln wages; η = elasticity of labor demand; X = level of demand for labor; RS = resources devoted by union to lobbying or political activity to raise the demand for public services produced by union members. We assume for simplicity that this activity has a constant proportional effect on demand;

ii) A union objective function that depends on wages and employment:

$$(2) \qquad U = U(W,E);$$

iii) A function relating wages obtained through collective bargaining to the resources devoted to bargaining (RB):

$$(3) \qquad W = W(RB, L, S),$$

where L = the legal environment for collective bargaining, S = labor supply factors, and $RB + RS = R$, the total amount of resources available to the union.

To maximize utility the union divides its resources between bargaining and lobbying/political activity subject to (1) and (3) and the resource constraint. This yields the equilibrium condition that the union divide it resources to equate the marginal rate of substitution in utility to the relevant marginal opportunity costs:

(4) $$Uw/Ue = \eta + b/W',$$

where Uw and Ue are the partial derivatives of the utility function with respect to wages and employment.

How does a more favorable labor law affect wage and employment outcomes in this model? If, as seems plausible, a legal environment favorable to collective bargaining increases the relative effectiveness of resources spent on bargaining as opposed to those spent on raising demand through the political process, W' will be greater at any given level of RB. Therefore, $\eta + b/W'$ will be smaller, inducing the union to shift resources to bargaining and thus to increase wages at the expense of employment. The law acts as if it reduced the elasticity of demand for labor. Since the actual elasticity remains unchanged, this has the consequence of lowering employment.

3.1.2   Reduced Form Estimating Equations

Rather than seeking to estimate a full-scale union maximizing model, we use the model in (1)–(4) as the framework for interpreting reduced-form employment and wage equations. The simplest reduced-form equations that we estimate have the log-linear form:

(5) $$W = aX + cL + dS$$

(6) $$E = a'X + c'L + d'S$$

In some calculations we also include a dummy variable for collective bargaining coverage.[4] With this variable in the regressions, the coefficients on the legal index reflect the direct effects of the laws on outcomes as opposed to the "full" effects in (5) and (6).

3.2   Empirical Analysis

This section presents estimates of what the legal environment does to contract coverage, wages, and employment using data from the SOG for 1977–80 and data from the annual 1984 CPS for six local sector departments: police; fire fighters; sanitation other than sewerage; streets and highways; finance and general control; and teachers.

The SOG contains data on employment, wages, government finances, and diverse aspects of labor relations for municipal departments in the United States. To determine whether a city department in the SOG has a collective bargaining contract, we made use of two pieces of information: the total number of contracts in the municipality and the number of bargaining units. When the number of contracts equals or exceeds the number of bargaining units we specify that each department with a bargaining unit had a collective agreement.[5] When the SOG indicates that a city had no contracts, no bargaining units, and no collective bargaining policy, we infer that no departments have a collective agreement. These two rules enable us to specify the collective bargaining status of departments in 86 percent of the SOG sample. Departments in cities in which the data did not fit these rules have an ambiguous bargaining status, so we deleted them from the sample. By our procedure 21 percent of the sample of department-year observations were covered by collective bargaining. Finally, to take account of the diverse factors beyond state laws that affect municipal labor markets we supplemented the SOG data with detailed information on the economic and demographic characteristics of the populations of 1,153 U.S. cities from Summary Tape Files 1 and 3 of the 1980 Census of Population.[6]

The CPS May files contain information on the demographic and economic position of individual workers and whether they are union members or covered by collective bargaining contracts. In 1984 the file contained this information for the outgoing rotation group from each of the twelve monthly surveys of the year, which we used as our sample. A problem with the CPS is that it does not allow for the possibility that some public sector workers are union members but not covered by contracts, forcing us—like other researchers—to assume that all union members are covered. Because the CPS data are for individuals, moreover, they give greater weight to larger cities and departments than does the SOG. Since larger cities are more likely to be covered by collective contracts, the mean of the coverage variable in the CPS is considerably higher than the mean for the same occupational group in the SOG (see table 3.2).

3.2.1   The Relation of Laws to Coverage

The first issue to investigate is whether public sector laws favorable to collective bargaining are associated with greater contract coverage. If they are not, we would not expect them to have any impact on wages or employment.

To determine the effect of laws on contract status, we estimated linear probability equations linking a 0-1 contract coverage variable to our legal index and diverse controls for various public employee groupings in the CPS and SOG.[7] In the CPS calculations our dependent variable takes on the value one if the worker is a union member or

Table 3.2   **Regression Coefficients and Standard Errors (in parentheses) for the Effect of Laws on Collective Bargaining Coverage (CPS and SOG data)**

| | Panel A: CPS Cross-Section (1984)[a] | | | |
	State Employees	Teachers	Police and Fire	Other Local
Legal index	.13	.10	.10	.11
	(.008)	(.010)	(.020)	(.008)
Mean of 0-1				
coverage variable	.39	.74	.75	.38
R^2	.23	.20	.25	.20
Number of observations	5,340	3,591	741	7,523

| | Panel B: SOG Cross-Section (pooled sample, 1977–80)[b] | | | | |
	Police	Fire	Sanitation	Streets and Highways	Finance and Control
Legal index	.21	.19	.014	.073	.062
	(.008)	(.009)	(.005)	(.007)	(.006)
Mean of 0-1					
coverage variable	.40	.39	.052	.13	.073
R^2	.38	.32	.069	.17	.12
Number of observations	3,904	3,505	3,247	3,906	3,957

[a]Other control variables are: dummy variables for educational attainment, age, region, female, black, city size; fire fighters in the police and fire regression; and alternative wages in the individual's SMSA.

[b]Other control variables are: population (and interactions with three city-size dummies), per capita income, median household income, median property values, percent of population with income below 75% of poverty level, percent black, percent high school graduates, percent with 1 to 3 years college, percent college graduates, percent attended graduate school, region dummies, and year dummies.

covered by a collective contract. In the SOG calculations it takes the value one if the city department has a collective contract according to the procedure described earlier.

Panels A and B of table 3.2 summarize the results of these calculations for the two data sets. While there are differences in the magnitudes of the estimated coefficients on the legal index, both panels tell the same story: they show a significant positive relation between the favorableness of the public sector labor law to collective bargaining and contract coverage. In the CPS calculations the estimated coefficients on the legal index range from .10 to .13, implying that a two standard deviation improvement in the laws (roughly from no laws to duty to bargain or arbitration) would increase the probability of having a collective contract by 20 to 26 percentage points. In the SOG calculations the estimated coefficients vary more widely, from .19 and .21 for police and fire fighters to .07 and .06 for streets and highways, and finance and control, to a bare .01 in sanitation. With the sole exception of sanitation, the estimated effects are quantitatively large relative to the mean coverage. Finally, if the SOG data are pooled into a single sample and dummy variables added for departments, the average effect of the legal index is .12 (column 1 of table 3.3), which is on the same order as the effects found in the CPS data.

The strong relation between laws and the presence of collective contracts that underlies these regressions is shown in figure 3.1, which reports the percentage of city departments or workers in city departments covered by contracts in different legal settings. The coverage proportions range from two-thirds of city departments in the most favorable category to virtually zero in the least favorable, and from three-fourths of workers in city departments in the most favorable category to 19 percent in the least favorable category. Because, as we noted earlier, the CPS data code all workers who are members of unions or associations as having contracts, the 19 percent is undoubtedly a substantial overestimate of the true proportion in that category. The data bias works to minimize the relation between the laws and coverage, making the observed patterns even more striking.

3.2.2   Probing the Law–Collective Bargaining Relation

Should the positive relation between the favorableness of public sector labor law and collective bargaining shown in table 3.2 and figure 3.1 be interpreted as causal, or might it be due to the effect of some omitted variables? One possible explanation of the results is that favorable laws encourage unionization, which leads to collective bargaining, but beyond stimulating workers to organize, the laws then have no further impact. If this were the case, we would expect the estimated coefficient on the laws to disappear if we controlled for union membership in the regressions. Accordingly, we added another labor relations variable from the SOG to our regressions: the percentage of full-time workers who are members of a union or employee association. As can be seen by comparing columns 1 and 2 of table 3.3, addition of this variable reduces the estimated impact of the legal index on coverage from .12 to .07. Still, .07 represents a substantial and statistically significant effect of a change in the legal index on coverage, which implies that even where union and association membership is high, a strong bargaining law serves to legitimize the collective bargaining process. Put differently, worker support for unionism is not enough to guarantee collective bargaining.

A second noncausal interpretation is that the positive relation between public sector labor laws and collective bargaining results from spurious correlation due to the omission of a city- or state-specific variable (call it pro-union sentiment) that is correlated with both the laws and bargaining. To test this explanation we controlled for city

Percent in Category

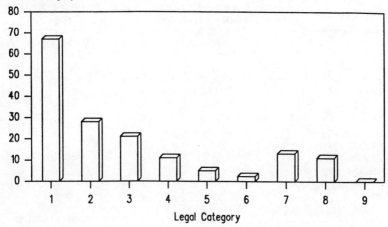

Percent in Category

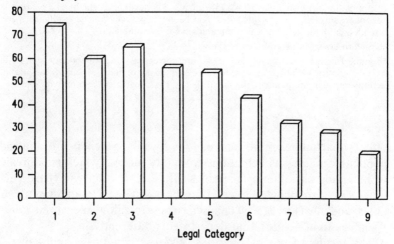

Fig. 3.1   Percent in category of government departments that are covered by collective bargaining (SOG data) (*top*); percent in category of workers that are covered by collective bargaining (CPS data) (*bottom*).

Legal categories are represented by numbers as follows:
1 = Duty to bargain and Required arbitration
2 = Duty to bargain and Strikes permitted
3 = Duty to bargain and Required fact-finding or mediation
4 = Duty to bargain
5 = Conferral rights and Required fact-finding or mediation
6 = Right to Meet and confer or Present proposals
7 = Bargaining permitted
8 = No provision for bargaining
9 = Bargaining prohibited

Table 3.3   Regression Coefficients and Standard Errors[a] for the Effect of Laws on Collective Bargaining Coverage, Controlling for Percent Organized in the Department (SOG data)

	Pooled, 1977–80		Within City Analysis[b]	
	(1)	(2)	(3)	(4)
Legal index	.12	.071	.11	.097
	(.004)	(.004)	(.010)	(.010)
Percent union members	—	.42	—	.20
in department		(.008)		(.009)
Department dummies	yes	yes	yes	yes
City dummies	no	no	yes	yes
Mean of 0-1				
coverage variable	.23	.23	—	—
R^2	.29	.41	.37	.40
Number of observations	13,744	13,744	11,612	11,612

Note: Other control variables are: population (and interactions with three city-size dummies), per capita income, median household income, median property values, percent of population with income below 75% of poverty level, percent black, percent high school graduates, percent with 1 to 3 years college, percent college graduates, percent attended graduate school, region dummies, and year dummies.

[a]Standard errors in parentheses.

[b]Standard errors in columns (3) and (4) are corrected to adjust for inclusion of city-specific control variables. In addition, the models in columns (3) and (4) include interactions between the demographic controls and the department dummy variables.

effects that influence all occupations by taking dependent and independent variables as deviations from city means, which is equivalent to including city dummy variables in the regressions. In these calculations we also included interactions between department dummy variables and measured city characteristics to allow measured control variables to affect different departments differently.

The results of our calculations, given in columns 3 and 4 of table 3.3, show that controlling for city effects has little impact on the estimated coefficient on the legal index, and thus the relation between laws and bargaining cannot be attributed to an omitted city factor. With no control for the percent organized, the coefficient on the legal index in the within-city analysis is comparable to that in the pooled regression, whereas after controlling for the percent organized, it is actually larger. Employee groups governed by more favorable collective bargaining laws are more likely to win contracts than employee groups governed by less favorable laws *in the same city*. We conclude that the relation between the legal environment and contract coverage is more likely to reflect causal factors than to be a spurious correlation due to omitted variable bias.

3.2.3   The Relation of Laws to Wages and Employment

What about the impact of the laws on market outcomes? Do wages and employment differ in departments operating under different collective bargaining laws? To answer these questions we estimated reduced-form equations relating wages to the legal environment in the CPS (table 3.4) and relating wages and employment to the legal environment in the SOG (table 3.5). In both cases we estimated three regressions for each occupation group. The first regression includes the legal index and control variables, but excludes a measure of whether workers are covered by collective bargaining. The coefficient on the legal index thus reflects the direct and indirect effects of the laws as described earlier.

The second regression in each set includes collective bargaining coverage as an additional independent variable. Since coverage is fixed, the coefficient on the legal index variable measures the direct effect of the laws on outcomes. While, as we have seen in figure 3.1, the legal environment and contract coverage are closely connected, there is sufficient variation in the data to allow us to disentangle the effects of the two variables.

The third regression in each set adds a coverage–legal index interaction term to allow for the possibility that the indirect effect of laws is different for workers who gain a contract and those who do not. Each regression also includes the full set of controls described in the table notes. The CPS regressions are limited to wage equations because data on individuals do not permit analysis of the effect of laws on departmental employment.

Turning to the estimates, the first regressions for each group in table 3.4 show that the legal environment has a statistically significant but moderate impact on ln hourly earnings for all groups. The regression coefficients on the legal index are on the order of .03, which translate into roughly 6 percent earnings differentials between states with no laws and those with favorable laws, given the approximately two standard deviation difference between the categories. The second regressions in the table show that much of this is due to the intervening coverage variable: the coefficients on the legal index variable are roughly halved in each case, while collective bargaining is estimated to raise wages by .12 to .15. This is consistent with Lewis's generalization that collective bargaining has sizeable impacts on wages at the local level (Lewis, this volume, chap. 6). Still, the legal index remains significant in all cases, with coefficients that suggest direct effects on earnings of 3 to 4 percent. Finally, the coefficients for the interaction terms in the third regressions in the table range from insignificantly negative to significantly positive, and thus give no indication of a differential effect of labor laws on organized and non-organized workers.

Table 3.4   Regression Coefficients and Standard Errors[a] for the Effect of the
                   Legal Environment and Collective Bargaining Coverage on
                   Ln(Hourly Wage) (CPS, 1984)

Group	Legal Index	Coverage	Coverage-Legal Interaction	R^2	N
State employees	.033	—	—	.36	5340
	(.008)				
	.014	.15	—	.37	5340
	(.008)	(.013)			
	.003	.15	.033	.37	5340
	(.009)	(.013)	(.033)		
Teachers	.029	—	—	.24	3591
	(.009)				
	.017	.12	—	.25	3591
	(.009)	(.015)			
	−.009	.14	.036	.25	3591
	(.015)	(.016)	(.016)		
Police and fire fighters	.033	—	—	.30	741
	(.016)				
	.018	.14	—	.33	741
	(.016)	(.030)			
	.038	.14	−.033	.33	741
	(.024)	(.030)	(.028)		
Other local employees	.037	—	—	.35	7523
	(.007)				
	.020	.15	—	.37	7523
	(.007)	(.010)			
	.015	.15	.015	.37	7523
	(.008)	(.011)	(.011)		

Note: Other control variables are: dummy variables for educational attainment, age,
region, female, black, city size; fire fighters in the police and fire regressions; and alternative wages in the individual's SMSA.
[a]Standard errors in parentheses.

Panel A of table 3.5 reports the results of estimating the effect of
the legal index on wages for city departments in the SOG data, pooled
across departments and years. The estimated impact of the index is
.04, which is of comparable magnitude to the estimate in the CPS data.
The estimated impact of collective bargaining coverage is, however,
noticeably smaller—.06 versus a range from .12 to .15—and its addition
to the equation has a more modest impact in reducing the coefficient
on the legal index. As in the CPS calculations, the interaction term is
negligible, suggesting that state labor laws have a similar impact on the
wages of workers with and without collective contracts.

Panel B of table 3.5 turns from the effect of laws and collective
bargaining on wages to their effect on employment. In these calculations the dependent variable is the log of full-time departmental em-

Table 3.5   **Regression Coefficients and Standard Errors[a] for the Effects of the Legal Environment and Collective Bargaining Coverage on Wages and Employment (SOG pooled cross-section date, 1977–80 (n = 18,382))**

Panel A: Ln (Monthly Salary per Full-Time Employee in Department)			
Legal index	.039	.032	.032
	(.002)	(.002)	(.002)
Coverage	—	.058	.057
		(.004)	(.004)
Legal-coverage interaction	—	—	.002
			(.004)
R^2	.64	.65	.65

Panel B: Ln (Number of Full-Time Employees in Department)			
Legal index	−.056	−.082	−.099
	(.006)	(.006)	(.007)
Coverage	—	.24	.21
		(.014)	(.015)
Legal-coverage interaction	—	—	.076
			(.014)
R^2	.70	.71	.71

Note: Other control variables are: population (and interactions with three city-size dummies), per capita income, median household income, median property values, percent of population with income below 75% of poverty level, percent black, percent high school graduates, percent with 1 to 3 years college, percent college graduates, percent attended graduate school, region dummies, year dummies, and department dummies.
[a]Standard errors in parentheses.

ployment,[8] while the independent variables are the same as in the pay regressions. Here we obtain a surprising result: the estimated coefficient on the legal index is substantial and negative, implying that employment is smaller when laws are more favorable to collective bargaining, whereas the effect of collective bargaining on employment is significantly positive, consistent with Zax (1985).

Why do strong labor laws, which affect wages in the same direction as collective bargaining contracts, have the opposite effect on employment? The positive coefficient on the interaction of collective bargaining coverage and legal enactment in the interaction regression offers one possible answer, for it indicates that the negative relation between the laws and employment occurs largely among city departments that do not sign contracts. If a favorable legal environment induces nonunion cities to raise wages to avoid unionization but does not create pressures for additional government services, one would expect the higher wages to reduce employment. Similarly, if favorable laws raise union power more at the bargaining table than in the political or lobbying arena, as in our model of union behavior, they will induce greater wage increases at the expense of employment under collective bargaining. Put differently, under these interpretations the legal index will measure movements along a demand curve to a greater extent than shifts in labor demand due to union (or nonunion worker) political activity, and thus have negative or nonpositive effects on employment. Since the wage effects of the legal environment are estimated to be about the same in cities with and without contracts, however, this explanation requires the following: either the elasticity of labor demand must be greater in noncovered city departments (as in the private sector, Freeman and Medoff 1981; Allen 1983), or more favorable legal environments must enhance the ability of unions to shift out the demand curve, reducing the negative impact of higher wages on employment.

The second possible interpretation of the employment results is that they are spurious, due to an incomplete specification of the determinants of public sector employment. Perhaps employment is lower in noncovered city departments because these cities have an especially low demand for public services, keeping employment low and limiting the power of unions to obtain contracts.

3.2.4   Probing the Relation of Laws to Wages and Employment

To probe the estimated impact of laws on pay and to examine the possible causes of the inverse relation between the laws and employment, we performed two additional calculations designed to eliminate the potential impact of omitted city variables on the regressions. First, we added city dummy variables to the SOG wage and employment regressions,[9] so that the estimated coefficients on the legal index and collective bargaining reflect the within-city effect of differences in the laws and outcomes among departments. Second, we made use of the 1972 SOG data file to perform a longitudinal analysis of the same city departments over time as state public sector labor laws changed.

Table 3.6 presents the results of our within-city calculations. The dependent variable in panel A is the difference between the log of pay in a department and the average pay in a city for all five departments in the sample. The dependent variable in panel B is the difference in the log of employment in a department and the average employment in the city for all departments. In each panel the independent variables also relate to differences between the variable for a department and the city average. In addition, we allow for likely differences in the effects of city characteristics on departments by including interaction terms between department dummy variables and those characteristics. Controlling for city effects in the wage equation greatly reduces the coefficients on the legal index and on collective bargaining; in the

Table 3.6   Regression Coefficients and Standard Errors[a] for the Effect of the
Legal Environment and Collective Bargaining Coverage on Wages
and Employment Controlling for City-Specific Effects (SOG
pooled cross-section data for 1977–80 (n = 13,960))

Panel A: Ln (Monthly Salary per Full-Time Employee in Department)			
Legal index	.009	.008	.008
	(.004)	(.004)	(.004)
Coverage	—	.008	.008
		(.004)	(.004)
Legal-coverage interaction	—	—	−.003
			(.012)

Panel B: Ln (Number of Full-Time Employees in Department)			
Legal index	.030	.004	.002
	(.020)	(.020)	(.020)
Coverage	—	.24	.24
		(.019)	(.019)
Legal-coverage interaction	—	—	.019
			(.047)

Note: Other control variables are: population (and interactions with three city-size dummies), per capita income, median household income, median property values, percent of population with income below 75% of poverty level, percent black, percent high school graduates, percent with 1 to 3 years college, percent college graduates, percent attended graduate school, region dummies, year dummies, department dummies, and interactions between the city characteristic variables and four department dummies.

[a]Standard errors in parentheses, corrected for inclusion of controls for city-specific effects.

employment equation it reverses the sign on the coefficient on the legal index but has little impact on the estimated effect of collective bargaining compared to our earlier cross-section results. While these changes may be taken as evidence of a significant omitted city-factor bias in the cross-section regressions, they also can be interpreted as reflecting spillover effects across departments within cities that greatly reduce the estimated impact of the laws and of collective bargaining in within-city comparisons. This interpretation is consistent with the Zax and Ichniowski findings of substantial within-city spillovers of wages (this volume, chap. 12).

Table 3.7 presents the results of our longitudinal analysis from 1972 to 1980. Because the SOG did not collect good data on collective bargaining coverage for 1972 our analysis is limited to changes in the legal index over the period. In this eight-year interval approximately 40 percent of our sample changed legal categories, with most of the changes taking the form of movements from simple duty-to-bargain provisions to arbitration, and from meet-and-confer provisions to duty-to-bargain statutes. The regressions we use for our analysis are derived from the following two-equation system:

(7) $$Y_1 = a + bL_1 + cX + \lambda D + u_1$$

(8) $$Y_0 = a' + bL_0 + c'X + D + u_0$$

Here, Y is the dependent variable, wages or employment; D is an omitted city-department variable that is expected to bias cross-section regressions; u_1 and u_0 are independent disturbances; L and X are defined as in eq. (1) and (3). The subscript 1 relates to 1980 and the subscript 0 relates to 1972. This specification imposes similar coefficients on the legal index in the two periods but allows coefficients on the omitted city-department factor and on the control variables (which are available only for one time period and thus have no time subscript) to differ over time. Solving for D in (8) and substituting in (7) yields our estimating equation:

(9) $$\Delta Y = a - \lambda a' + bL_1 - \lambda bL_0 + (c - \lambda c')X + (\lambda - 1) Y_0 + (u_1 - \lambda u_0)$$

in which the omitted city-department factor has been eliminated.

Table 3.7 contains estimates of equation (9) for pay and employment.[10] Panel A gives the coefficients when the dependent variable is the change in pay. The regression shows that the 1980 legal index variable has a positive impact on wages of .024, which is somewhat smaller than the .039 obtained in the comparable table 3.5 regression but still non-negligible and statistically significant. If the specification is correct, the coefficient on the 1972 legal index should be opposite in sign to that on the 1980 legal index, and roughly equal in magnitude to the coefficient on the 1980 index multiplied by one plus the coefficient on the lagged wage term, as is roughly the case. Dividing the departments between those that were and were not covered by collective contracts in 1980 shows similar results.

Panel B of the table gives the coefficients when the change in employment is the dependent variable. Here, we find moderate negative effects for the 1980 legal index in all the regressions, with the separate regressions for city departments by contract status showing greater negative effects to laws without contracts, consistent with the cross-section results given in table 3.5. Note, however, that the 1972 legal index has the same, rather than the opposite, signed impact on employment, suggesting that a more complex model with lagged employment responses is needed to capture the variation in the data. If one assumes that the negative coefficient on the lagged legal index reflects

Table 3.7 **Regression Coefficients and Standard Errors[a] for the Effects of the Legal Environment and Collective Bargaining Coverage on Wages and Employment (Longitudinal model controlling for department-specific effects; SOG data for changes between 1972 and 1980)**

Panel A: ΔLn(Monthly Salary per Full-Time Employee in Department)

	Full Sample (N = 5281)	Covered[b] Departments (N = 1044)	Not Covered Departments (N = 3474)
Legal index 1980	.024	.028	.021
	(.004)	(.008)	(.005)
Legal index 1972	−.002	.002	−.013
	(.005)	(.008)	(.007)
Ln(1972 wages)	−.66	−.62	−.69
	(.012)	(.026)	(.015)

Panel B: ΔLn(Number of Full-Time Employees in Department)

	Full Sample (N = 5281)	Covered Departments (N = 1044)	Not Covered Departments (N = 3474)
Legal index 1980	−.037	−.029	−.037
	(.010)	(.016)	(.014)
Legal index 1972	−.010	−.016	−.029
	(.013)	(.017)	(.019)
Ln(1972 employment)	−.31	−.40	−.31
	(.010)	(.022)	(.012)

Note: Other control variables are: population (and interactions with three city-size dummies), per capta income, median household income, median property values, percent of population with income below 75% of poverty level, percent black, percent high school graduates, percent with 1 to 3 years college, percent college graduates, percent attended graduate school, region dummies, and department dummies.

[a]Standard errors in parentheses.

[b]Refers to departments covered by contract in 1980; coverage data for 1972 are unavailable.

time delays, one would add the coefficients on the two legal index variables to get a full impact of the legal environment.

3.2.5 Arbitration versus Permitting Strikes

The analysis thus far has focused on the relation between the index of the legal environment for collective bargaining and economic outcomes. In states that have enacted duty-to-bargain legislation, the policy-relevant question relates to the more specific issue of the impact of alternative dispute resolution laws on outcomes; specifically, on whether compulsory arbitration or strike-permitted laws raise pay. What does our data tell us about the effects of these provisions on wages and employment in duty-to-bargain states?

To answer this question we estimated wage and employment equations analogous to those given earlier on a sample of departments with duty-to-bargain or stronger bargaining laws in 1980, with dummy variables for arbitration or strike-permitted legislation replacing our legal index. The results of these calculations are summarized in table 3.8 in terms of the coefficients on the key legal category dummy variables. Columns 1 and 2 record the results when the dependent variable is ln wages, while columns 3 and 4 record the results when it is ln employment. The principal finding in the table is the marked difference between the estimated impact of arbitration and strike-permitted laws. In the cross-section analysis, departments covered by compulsory arbitration laws appear to have somewhat lower wages than other depart-

Table 3.8   **Regression Coefficients and Standard Errors (in parentheses) for the Effect of Arbitration and Strike-Permitted Laws on Wages and Employment (SOG cross-section [pooled, 1977–80] and longitudinal data [1980–1972], Duty-to-bargain sample[1])**

| | Dependent Variable | | | |
| | ln Wages | | ln Employment | |
	Cross Section (1)	Longitudinal (2)	Cross Section (3)	Longitudinal (4)
Arbitration 1980	−.023	.005	−.034	−.027
	(.005)	(.010)	(.019)	(.027)
Strikes permitted 1980	.014	.032	−.21	.080
	(.007)	(.015)	(.027)	(.041)
Arbitration 1972	—	−.014	—	−.044
	—	(.012)	—	(.032)
Strikes permitted 1972	—	−.061	—	−.21
	—	(.024)	—	(.062)
ln Wages 1972	—	−.69	—	—
	—	(.017)	—	—
ln Employment 1972	—	—	—	−.26
	—	—	—	(.013)
Sample size	11,396	2,922	11,396	2,922

Note: Other variables controlled for in each regression are: population (and interactions with three city-size dummies), per capita income, median household income, median property values, percent of population with income below 75% of poverty level, percent black, percent high school graduates, percent with 1 to 3 years college, percent college graduates, percent attended graduate school, region dummies, and department dummies. Also, the cross-section regressions include year dummies.

[1]The sample only includes departments in legal categories 1–4 (see table 3.1) in 1980.

[2]Refers only to departments covered by a collective bargaining contract in 1980. Coverage data is unavailable for 1972.

ments. In the longitudinal analysis, departments covered by compulsory arbitration in 1980 have essentially the same pay as other departments, while those that were also covered by arbitration in 1972 are estimated to have slightly lower pay than other departments. At the least these calculations reject the notion that arbitration laws create pressures for higher pay in covered jurisdictions—a result consistent with other findings that compare collectively bargained and arbitrated settlements (Ashenfelter and Bloom 1984; studies cited in Freeman 1986b). By contrast, both the cross-section and longitudinal analyses suggest that pay is modestly higher under strike-permitted laws: in column 1 the coefficient on strike-permitted laws for 1980 is .014; in column 2 strike permitted in 1980 has a positive effect on ln pay, whereas strike permitted in 1972 has a negative effect, as expected given the difference equation. As for employment, the evidence is more mixed: the cross-section and longitudinal calculations show modest negative effects for arbitration laws on employment, but show drastically different effects of strike-permitted laws—negative in the cross-section analysis and positive in the longitudinal analysis—that suggest the need for more detailed investigation. Setting aside the employment results as ambiguous, the conclusion to be drawn from table 3.8 is that *arbitration laws have effectively no impact on pay, while strike-permitted laws raise pay.*

3.2.6   CPS versus SOG Results on Contracts

While it was not the purpose of this study to estimate the impact of union contracts on wages, the surprising difference in the estimated contract effect between the CPS data set in table 3.4—coefficients on coverage of .15—compared to those in the SOG data set—coefficients on coverage of .05—deserves further attention. What might explain the difference? Does collective bargaining in the local public sector raise pay as much as is suggested by the CPS or as little as suggested by the SOG?

We have explored several possible reasons for the divergent estimates of the collective bargaining effect between the two data sets. One possibility is that the CPS data give greater weight to large cities than the SOG data and that coverage effects vary by size of city. To assess this we re-estimated the table 3.5 wage equation weighting the department observations by city size. The estimated coverage coefficients decreased rather than increased, which indicates that union effects are larger for smaller cities, contrary to our hypothesis.[11] A second possibility is that the estimated coefficients differ because the data sets cover different occupations. To see if this is the case, we estimated our cross-section wage equation in the SOG for the two occupations found in both data sets, police and fire, and other local employees,[12] and obtained estimates of coverage effects of .06 and .05, respectively, well below the CPS-based estimates in table 3.4. A third possibility is that the results differ because the SOG sample covers the years 1977–80, whereas the CPS sample covers 1984. To test this possibility we estimated the impact of coverage on wages using the May 1980 CPS. Because this file has fewer observations than the 1984 annual file, we estimated coverage effects for occupations with relatively large numbers of persons: teachers, state employees, and other local employees. The 1980 regression coefficients on coverage exceed the 1984 coefficients for the same groups, rejecting this explanation.[13] In sum, we are unable to account for the difference in estimated coverage effects between the two data sets. Whatever the explanation, however, the message is clear: given the estimated divergence in estimates one should look at both in assessing the impact of collective bargaining on wages and be careful not to mix them in evaluating changes in union wage effects over time.[14]

3.3 Conclusion

This study has found that state labor laws have significant effects on collective bargaining and wage and employment outcomes in the public sector. While there are ambiguities in interpreting some of the empirical relations in the data, the evidence tends to support the following four claims:

1. State laws are a major determinant of whether workers obtain collective bargaining contracts, even after controlling for their union status and for unmeasured city-specific factors.
2. Laws favorable to collective bargaining produce higher wages by encouraging bargaining relations and by creating an environment in which covered and noncovered workers make wage gains. More favorable laws are, however, associated with lower employment, primarily in departments lacking collective bargaining contracts, which we attribute to the departments paying higher wages to avoid unionization.
3. Collective bargaining for local government workers is associated with higher wages and greater employment. The latter is consistent with models of public sector unionism that stress the lobbying and political activities of unions designed to increase demand for public services produced by members.
4. Within cities wage and employment differences between departments covered by more and less favorable public sector laws are relatively modest, consistent with the notion that there are sizeable spillovers of wage and employment decisions across department lines in a city.

Our analysis also raised questions about the magnitude of estimated effects of collective bargaining on wages, which is markedly smaller in the department-based SOG data set than in the individual-based CPS data set for reasons that we were unable to determine.

Notes

1. We do not distinguish between various forms of interest arbitration such as conventional, issue-by-issue last-best-offer, or package last-best-offer.

2. Some laws that outlaw strikes contain specific penalties while others allow courts to decide penalties. As it is difficult to determine which penalties are in practice more severe, we have not attempted to subdivide these laws further.

3. It is unclear whether strike permitted or compulsory arbitration should be viewed as the most favorable category for collective bargaining. In table 3.1 we classified compulsory arbitration as most favorable, but none of our results depend on this choice.

4. Equations (5) and (6) do not allow for supply or demand factors having different effects in cities with and without collective bargaining contracts. As these factors presumably operate differently in the two environments, one might expect them to have different coefficients, and in some of the empirical work we estimate separate equations for covered and uncovered cities to allow for this.

5. For finance and control departments (for which there was no bargaining unit data) we used the data for clerical employee bargaining units.

6. We thank Jeffrey Zax for providing us with this data extract.

7. Given the large samples that we are using it would have been expensive to do logit or probit equations, with little potential gain. As the dependent variables have means well within the 0-1 interval in all samples, we are unlikely to run into serious functional form problems using the linear model.

8. Use of full-time equivalent employment yielded essentially identical results to those reported below.

9. In fact, given the number of cities, we calculated city-specific means for all variables and performed regressions with the difference between a variable in a city and its mean, as in the within-city regressions in our table 3.3.

10. Least squares estimates of equation (9) may still yield inconsistent parameter estimates as the residual u_0 is negatively correlated with Y_0. The coefficient on Y_0 will be biased downward, biasing the coefficient on L_0 as well. While there is no simple correction for this bias unless one is willing to develop a much more complex model, calculations given in Freeman and Valletta (1987) show it to be of negligible magnitude under plausible assumptions.

11. Separate wage equations for departments in cities of different sizes showed the same pattern. In cities with populations over 500,000 the coverage effect is 0.00; in cities with populations between 250,000 and 500,000 it is 0.019; in cities with populations between 50,000 and 250,000 it is 0.015; and in cities with populations less than 50,000, it is 0.071.

12. The other local category differs between the data sets, as there are only three such groups in the SOG: sanitation, streets and highways, and finance and control, while the CPS contains a wider range of departments.

13. The estimated coefficients (standard errors) for 1980 are: 0.21 (0.09) for state employees; 0.19 (0.04) for teachers; and 0.22 (0.07) for other local employees. The latter results are not strictly comparable to the 1984 regressions because prior to 1983 the other local group is confined to public administration employees.

14. Freeman (1986a) reports similar inconsistencies between estimates of changes in union wage effects between CPS- and establishment-based surveys, while Freeman (1985) reports inconsistencies between estimates of public/private sector pay differentials between CPS- and establishment-based surveys of federal employees. Hence, there is growing evidence of inconsistencies between wage differentials based on the CPS and those based on other data sets.

References

Allen, S. 1983. Unionization and productivity in office building and school construction. North Carolina State University. Mimeo.

Ashenfelter, O., and D. E. Bloom. 1984. Models of arbitrator behavior: Theory and evidence. *American Economic Review* 73(1): 111–24.

Ashenfelter, O., and R. G. Ehrenberg. 1975. The demand for labor in the public sector. In *Labor in the public and nonprofit sectors*, ed. D. S. Hamermesh. New Jersey: Princeton University Press.

Courant, P. N., E. M. Gramlich, and D. L. Rubinfeld. 1979. Public employee market power and the level of government spending. *American Economic Review* 69(5): 806–17.

Ehrenberg, R. G. 1973. The demand for state and local government employees. *American Economic Review* 63(3): 366–79.

Ehrenberg, R. G., and J. L. Schwarz. 1983. Public sector labor markets. NBER Working Paper no. 1179. Cambridge, MA: National Bureau of Economic Research. (Forthcoming in *Handbook of labor economics*, eds. Orley Ashenfelter and Richard Layard.)

Farber, H. S. 1981. Splitting-the-difference in interest arbitration. *Industrial and Labor Relations Review* 35(1): 70–77.

Farber, H. S., and H. C. Katz. 1979. Interest arbitration, outcomes, and the incentive to bargain. *Industrial and Labor Relations Review* 33(1): 55–63.

Freeman, R. B. 1981. The effect of trade unionism on fringe benefits. *Industrial and Labor Relations Review* 34(4): 489–509.

Freeman, R. B. 1985. How do public sector wages and employment respond to economic conditions? NBER Working Paper no. 1653. Cambridge, MA: National Bureau of Economic Research.

Freeman, R. B. 1986a. In search of union wage concessions in standard data sets. *Industrial Relations* 25(2): 131–45.

Freeman, R. B. 1986b. Unionism comes to the public sector. *Journal of Economic Literature* 24(March): 41–86.

Freeman, R. B., Casey Ichniowski, and Harrison Lauer. 1985. Collective bargaining laws and threat effects of unionism in the determination of police compensation. NBER Working Paper no. 1578. Cambridge, MA: National Bureau of Economic Research.

Freeman, R. B., and J. L. Medoff. 1981. The impact of the percentage organized on union and nonunion wages. *Review of Economics and Statistics* 63(November): 561–72.

Freeman, R. B., and James L. Medoff. 1984. *What do unions do?* New York: Basic Books.
Freeman, R. B., and Robert Valletta. 1987. The effect of public sector labor laws on collective bargaining, wages, and employment. NBER Working Paper no. 2284. Cambridge, MA: National Bureau of Economic Research.
Hamermesh, D. S. 1975. *Labor in the public and nonprofit sectors.* New Jersey: Princeton University Press.
Ichniowski, C. 1988. Public sector recognition strikes: Illegal and ill-fated. *Journal of Labor Research* 9(1): 183–97.
Lewin, D., P. Feuille, and T. A. Kochan. 1981. *Public sector labor relations: Analysis and readings* 2d ed. Sun Lakes, Arizona: Thomas Horton and Daughters.
Miller, B. 1984. Economics vs. politics: The growth of public sector collective bargaining laws in the American states, 1966–1979. University of South Florida. Mimeo.
Najita, J. 1978. *Guide to statutory provisions in public sector collective bargaining.* Industrial Relations Center, University of Hawaii.
Saltzman, G. 1985. Bargaining laws as a cause and consequence of the growth of teacher unionism. *Industrial and Labor Relations Review* 38(3): 335–51.
U.S. Department of Labor, Labor Management Services Administration. 1981. *Summary of public sector labor relations.*
U.S. Bureau of the Census. 1972, 1976–80. *Annual survey of governments.* Washington, D.C.
———. 1982. *1980 Census of population and housing.* Summary tape files 1 and 3. Washington, D.C.
Wellington, H. H., and R. K. Winter. 1971. *The unions and the cities.* Washington, D.C.: The Brookings Institution.
Zax, J. S. 1985. Municipal employment, municipal unions, and demand for municipal services. NBER Working Paper no. 1728. Cambridge, MA: National Bureau of Economic Research.

Comment   Harvey S. Rosen

The paper by Freeman and Valletta is an econometric investigation of the ways in which different legal environments affect the outcomes of public sector labor markets, where outcomes include: 1) obtaining a contract, 2) levels of unemployment, and 3) wages.

Whatever the model eventually chosen, in order to estimate the effect of the "legal environment" one must be able to measure it. Freeman and Valletta (F&V) devote section 3.1 of the paper to this issue. In this paper, the legal environment encompasses the requirements for bargaining, the provisions for dispute resolution, and strike provisions. Within each category, F&V can order provisions according to how much they constrain the scope of public sector union activity. They then rank all the possibilities along a single dimension. This hierarchy

Harvey S. Rosen is professor of economics at Princeton University, and research associate of the National Bureau of Economic Research.

is described in their table 3.1. To turn this table into a number for each jurisdiction, F&V perform a Z-score transformation of the nine categories.

An alternative strategy would have been to use a system of dichotomous variables to represent the nine categories. There are over a thousand observations, so degrees of freedom would not be a problem. Tests on whether legal environment "matters" would then just be tests for the joint significance of the system of dummies. One advantage of such a procedure is that it would yield quantitative estimates of the impacts of the various arrangements. The other advantage is that it is more familiar to most economists than Z-tests.

F&V use two main sources of data for their analysis, the Current Population Survey and the Survey of Governments. The former is well known to labor economists, but a few words about the latter may be useful. The Survey of Governments is a rich source of data providing almost everything one would want to know about the components of jurisdictions' budget constraints. The main problem that I have had using it arises because various legal jurisdictions can overlap geographically. Consider, for example, a town which pays taxes to a "special district" whose responsibility is to provide education. The town's payments to the special district may be categorized as "intergovernmental grants," and the town's education expenditures recorded as a zero! Unfortunately, the data set provides no obvious way of determining whether such a situation is likely to be important for a given community. It does suggest, however, that some care should be taken in "cleaning" the data, and it would be nice to hear what steps were taken by F&V. (Perhaps such considerations help explain the difficulties that F&V have in reconciling the results from the two sets of data.)

F&V motivate their estimating equation by setting up a model in which the maximand is the union's objective function, which depends on the wage rate and employment. This is maximized subject to the community's demand curve for labor. The twist relative to more conventional models of wage-employment determination in unionized industries is that the union can commit resources to shift out the demand curve for its services. On the other hand, it can also devote resources to raising its wages via collective bargaining; hence, another constraint in the problem is that total union resources must sum to some prespecified amount.

The equations actually estimated are the reduced form of this model. Thus, they estimate:

$$W = a_W X + b_W C + c_W L + d_W S + e_W CxL ,$$

$$E = a_E X + b_E C + C_E L + d_E S + e_E CxL,$$

where E = employment, X = demand variables, S = labor supply variables, L = F&V's measure of the legal environment, and C = a dichotomous variable indicating whether or not there is coverage by collective bargaining. The interaction variables are present to allow for the possibility of "threat effects."

I can think of another way in which the union might affect the economic environment. It might lobby the state and/or federal governments for grants. This suggests that it might be interesting to estimate a grants equation in addition to those for W and E. It also suggests that treating grants as exogenous demand shifters may create econometric difficulties.

It is important to note that the wage variable W does not take into account the accrued value of pensions. In the current context, this point may be of importance for two reasons. First, local managers and politicians may find that the easiest way to deal with the demands of unions is to promise them more money in the future—when someone else will be in charge. Although the evidence is mixed with respect to whether pension underfunding is correctly perceived by current citizens (who might have to pay the price via capitalization), my guess is that this is an important consideration. This also suggests that some measure of the likelihood that current taxpayers will also be future taxpayers might have a role in the model. (Perhaps this could be measured by the proportion of the population that moves away from the community.) Second, if pension practices were more or less uniform across communities, then this issue wouldn't matter very much as a practical matter. However, Frant and Leonard (1984)[1] provide some estimates that there are large cross-community differences. Indeed, different occupations within a community can be treated very differently.

F&V's choices for the X and S variables seem altogether sensible. The only important omission is the community's tax price for local goods and services. In the median voter framework, this is determined in part by the property tax rate, the ratio of the median voter's house value to community property values, and the median voter's marginal federal income tax rate. Presumably, the lower the tax price, the greater the demand for local goods and services, and hence the greater the demand for public sector employees. Some people have argued that local officials' resistance to the elimination of deductibility is due to the fact that it would reduce public employment. Inclusion of such a variable would help shed light on this important issue. Whether the tax price is correlated with the C and L variables, and thus would affect their coefficients, I do not know.

1. Howard Frant and Herman Leonard, "State and local government pension plans: Labor economics or political economy." Memo, John F. Kennedy School of Government, Harvard University, 1984.

F&V estimate the equations using a variety of techniques, with alternative groups of right-hand-side variables. They make a rather strong case that their substantive results are robust. Among these results are that collective bargaining coverage raises wages *and* employment, which is consistent with the notion that public sector unions are able to shift out the demand for labor. However, while a more favorable legal environment leads to higher wages, it does not have much impact on employment in communities that are covered by collective bargaining. F&V explain this by arguing that the main effect of the favorable legal environment is to strengthen the union's position at the bargaining table, which increases its wage rate and moves it back along the demand curve.

F&V's essay joins the growing list of papers suggesting that political and legal institutions do matter in the analysis of a community's economic decisions. The paper will contribute to the debate on suitable ways to quantify such institutions and measure their impact.

4 Arbitrator Behavior in Public Sector Wage Disputes

David E. Bloom

4.1 Introduction

Arbitration is a rapidly growing method for resolving disputes. It is used widely in the United States and other countries to resolve private disputes arising under commercial contracts and collective bargaining agreements, to resolve civil disputes congesting court systems, and to set wages and other terms of new contracts in repeat bargaining situations. Despite the wide range of settings in which it is applied and the numerous forms that it can take, the central feature of virtually all arbitration mechanisms is that they involve a third party: an arbitrator or a panel of arbitrators hearing and deciding how a dispute is to be resolved. Arbitration awards are generally binding either by law or by ex ante agreement of the disputants.

One of the most important characteristics of arbitration mechanisms is that they may be designed in different ways. Indeed, one of the key dimensions along which arbitration mechanisms differ involves the extent to which they constrain an arbitrator's behavior. For example, under conventional arbitration, an arbitrator is simply asked to render a decision that represents his or her best judgment of a fair settlement. The settlement may, but does not have to be, a compromise between the parties' final offers. In contrast, under final-offer arbitration, each party is required to submit to the arbitrator a single final offer and the

David E. Bloom is Professor of Economics at Columbia University, and a research associate of the National Bureau of Economic Research.

The author is grateful to Orley Ashenfelter, Max Bazerman, Leslie Boden, Christopher Cavanagh, Henry Farber, Robert Gibbons, Charles Holt, Morris Horowitz, John Kagel, and Casey Ichniowski for helpful comments, and to Jonathan Backman, Andrew Newman, and Vijaya Ramachandran for helpful research assistance. This research was partly supported by National Science Foundation Grant SES-8309148.

arbitrator is constrained to render a decision that consists of one or the other of those final offers, without compromise. Final-offer arbitration is intended to induce concessionary behavior on the part of risk-averse bargainers, each of whom perceives a trade-off between the probability of "winning" the arbitration and the size of the payoff they receive if they win (Stevens 1966).

Conventional arbitration mechanisms have been objected to on a variety of grounds, the most serious of which is that they "chill" the negotiation process that precedes arbitration. This argument is rooted in the belief that conventional arbitration awards systematically tend to be compromises between the parties' final positions, thereby providing an incentive for the parties to avoid pre-arbitration concessions. This assertion is difficult to evaluate. On the one hand, it might be the case that arbitrators often make decisions by reaching a mechanical compromise between the parties' final offers without paying much attention to the merits of the case (although perhaps with a bit of random noise). This might be an optimal strategy for arbitrators who want to project an image of fairness so they will be hired again by the parties. In addition, since it is almost certainly easier and less time-consuming than weighing the facts in a dispute, mechanical compromise (of which splitting the difference is a special case) is also one way in which arbitrators can engage in shirking. Finally, mechanical compromise might be an optimal decision-making rule for arbitrators if the final offers themselves convey useful information about the nature of efficient settlements. Indeed, if final offers do contain useful information that arbitrators are particularly skilled at extracting, mechanical compromise behavior is not a legitimate complaint against conventional arbitration. Nonetheless, it seems unlikely in practice that an arbitrator could determine whether a pair of final offers contained useful information without at least some reference to exogenous data on the facts of a case. In this situation, arbitration decisions will not be simple mechanical compromises of the parties' final offers, but rather they will be functions of both the offers and the facts.

On the other hand, it is also possible that the parties' final bargaining positions are determined by their expectations about an arbitration award. In other words, if bargainers A and B expect an arbitrator to render a settlement that is relatively favorable to bargainer A, their negotiations will almost certainly take place over settlements that tend to be favorable to A, provided that arbitration is compulsory if they fail to resolve their dispute voluntarily. Thus, arbitration decisions may appear to be mechanical compromises of the parties' final positions, but only because the parties aligned themselves around the arbitrator's preferred settlement point (Farber 1981; Ashenfelter 1985).

The purpose of this study is to analyze arbitrator decision making under conventional arbitration. The main goal is to try to draw inferences about the extent to which conventional arbitration decisions are mechanical compromises of the parties' final offers. This will be done mainly by estimating several simple models of arbitrator behavior that have proven useful in recent empirical studies. These models will be fit to a new set of data on arbitrators' decisions in a series of hypothetical arbitration cases.

The following section will set out the empirical models of arbitrator behavior that have formed the basis for empirical work in this area. Section 4.3 will discuss the conclusions that can be drawn from previous attempts to implement these models. Section 4.4 will describe the experimental design used to generate a new data set on the behavior of conventional arbitrators. Section 4.5 will present and discuss the results of fitting alternative empirical models to these new data. Section 4.6 will discuss and summarize the main conclusions of this study.

4.2   Empirical Models of Arbitrator Behavior

The purpose of this section is to outline several general models of arbitrator behavior under final-offer and conventional arbitration.[1] The fundamental premise of these models is that, under both systems of arbitration, arbitrators form a notion of a preferred wage settlement in one of two ways: just from the facts of the case (X) or from both the facts of the case *and* the employer's and union's final positions (w^e and w^u). Thus, in the first regime, the arbitrator's settlement (i.e., the percent wage increase, w^a) is given by

$$(1) \qquad w^a = X\beta + \epsilon,$$

where β is a vector of weights and ϵ is a random error that captures the effect of unobserved variations in economic environments and differences in arbitrators' assessments of those circumstances. Like previous studies, this study will assume ϵ to be normally distributed with zero mean and standard deviation σ. In the second regime, the arbitrator's preferred settlement ($\tilde{w}^a$) is

$$(2) \qquad \begin{aligned} \tilde{w}^a &= \gamma w^a + (1 - \gamma)[(w^e + w^u)/2] \\ &= \gamma X\beta + (1 - \gamma)[(w^e + w^u)/2] + \gamma\epsilon, \end{aligned}$$

where $0 \leq \gamma < 1$.

Under final-order arbitration, it is assumed that the arbitrator picks the employer's offer when

$$(3) \qquad \alpha(w^a - w^e) \leq (w^u - w^a),$$

if the first regime holds; or

(4) $\alpha(\bar{w}^a - w^e) \leq (w^u - \bar{w}^a),$

if the second regime holds, where $w^u > w^e$, and where $\alpha \neq 1$ implies asymmetric treatment of employer and union deviations from the preferred settlement.

Substituting for w^a and $\bar{w}^a$ in (3) and (4) and rearranging terms leads to expressions (P_1 and P_2) for the probability that the employer's final offer is selected under each regime:

(5) $P_1 = N\{[\alpha/(1 + \alpha)\sigma]w^e$
                      $+ [1/(1 + \alpha)\sigma]w^u - X\beta/\sigma\};$

(6) $P_2 = N[(\delta_1/\gamma\sigma)w^e + (\delta_2/\gamma\sigma)w^u - X\beta/\sigma],$

where $\delta_1 = [\alpha/(1 + \alpha) - (1 - \gamma)/2]$, $\delta_2 = [1/(1 + \alpha) - (1 - \gamma)/2]$, and $N(\cdot)$ is the cumulative distribution function for a standard normal variate.

For regime 1, observe that: 1) $[1 - P_1]$ is an expression for the probability the union's final offer is selected, 2) the probability expressions (P_1 and $[1 - P_1]$) are simple probit functions whose parameters can be easily estimated by the method of maximum likelihood from appropriate data drawn from a series of final-offer arbitration cases, and 3) both α and σ are identified from the coefficients of w^e and w^u, implying that β is also identified. For regime 2, observe that: 1) the probability expressions P_2 and $[1 - P_2]$ are also probit functions although γ and α are not separately identified, 2) the sum of the coefficients of w^e and w^u is an estimate of σ, implying that β is identified, and 3) even though α is not identified, the hypothesis $\alpha = 1$ can be tested from the difference between the coefficients of w^e and w^u (i.e., the difference is zero under H_0: $\alpha = 1$). Finally, observe that the reduced-form probit models suggested by regimes 1 and 2 are identical, even though the interpretation of the coefficients does depend on the regime.

Under conventional arbitration, the theoretical model is conceptually simpler because the arbitrator's preferred settlement is, by definition, either w^a or $\bar{w}^a$, depending on the regime that the arbitrator uses to make decisions. However, the corresponding empirical models are not always equally straightforward. In particular, if arbitrator decisions just depend on the facts of the case, then equation (1) can be estimated directly by ordinary least squares. On the other hand, if arbitrator decisions depend on both the facts and the final offers, it would seem natural to estimate equation (2) directly, also using ordinary least squares. However, that regression ignores the potential simultaneity of the average final offers and the arbitrator's expected decision. In addition, it is not usually possible to fit that regression since w^e and w^u are generally not explicit in actual conventional arbitration decisions. Thus, the term $(1 - \gamma)[(w^e + w^u)/2]$ will become part of the error structure under regime 2. Unfortunately, since w^e and w^u are probably correlated with X, their omission from an ordinary least-squares regression will bias the estimates of β if regime 2 holds.

Two other properties of these alternative models of arbitrator behavior are also worth noting. First, if the decisions of conventional arbitrators are generated by model (1), it would be unnecessary for the parties to formulate and express final positions. Insofar as final offers are an important institutional feature of the arbitration process, model (1) may be too simple a representation of arbitrator behavior. Second, if arbitrator decisions are rendered according to model (2), optimal final offers will always be both divergent and extreme and all bargaining cases will end up in arbitration. However, as a practical matter, the fraction of bargaining cases that ends up in arbitration tends to be less than one-third. In addition, although final offers under conventional arbitration are sometimes extreme, they are typically not more than a few percentage points apart (see Bloom and Cavanagh 1987, table 1). Thus, equation (2) may also be too simple a representation of arbitrator behavior. We will examine this possibility empirically by estimating a more complex model in which the weight that arbitrators place on the final offers (i.e., $1 - \gamma$), depends on the distance between them. These estimates will help us to determine whether arbitrators treat final offers that are further apart as less informative.

4.3 Previous Literature

4.3.1 Review

The main implications of the models discussed and presented in section 4.2 are: 1) that simple regressions of conventional arbitration decisions on the facts of the case and the parties' final offers may lead to incorrect inferences about the true weight that arbitrators place on the parties' final offers (i.e., because of simultaneity bias associated with the effect that expected arbitration decisions may have on the final offers); and 2) regressions that include the facts of the case but omit the parties' final offers (because they are unavailable) may lead to biased estimates of the weights the arbitrators attach to the facts. These problems seriously hinder our ability to test important hypotheses about the nature of arbitrator behavior using data derived from actual conventional arbitration systems.

To date, two alternative approaches have been adopted to circumvent the inherent problems involved in analyzing the behavior of conventional arbitrators. The first approach, due to Ashenfelter and Bloom

(1984), takes advantage of a novel feature of the arbitration system operating in New Jersey. Under that system, unresolved pay disputes between (unions of) municipal police officers and their public employers must be settled by arbitration. However, the form of arbitration is only conventional if both parties agree to it. In the absence of such an agreement, the dispute is settled by final-offer arbitration. Thus, the New Jersey system is a unique laboratory where one can analyze and compare the two forms of arbitration, both of which occur in substantial numbers and involve the same set of arbitrators.

Briefly, Ashenfelter and Bloom (1984) take advantage of the observational equivalence of the regime 1 and regime 2 reduced-form probit models fit to data on the final-offer arbitration cases. In particular, they fit the reduced-form probit model to the final-offer arbitration cases and the regime 1 regression model to the conventional arbitration cases. Under the hypothesis that regime 1 is correct for the conventional cases, the parameters β and σ are common to the two models. Using standard likelihood ratio tests to investigate the commonality of parameters therefore leads to conclusions about whether conventional arbitrators form their preferences according to regime 1 or regime 2 (even though γ is not estimated directly). Thus, estimates of the Ashenfelter-Bloom model provide some evidence of whether arbitrators actually do give weight to the parties' final offers under conventional arbitration.

The second main approach to analyzing the behavior of conventional arbitrators involves an ingenious attempt to overcome the potential simultaneity of arbitration decisions and final offers by exogenously fixing those offers. This approach, due to Bazerman and Farber (1985) and Farber and Bazerman (1986), was implemented by asking professional arbitrators to render arbitration decisions in twenty-five bargaining scenarios, each with a different fictional set of facts and final offers. By their very construction, data generated in this manner do not suffer from the simultaneity or observability problems described above. Thus, a simple regression of the conventional arbitration decisions on the facts and final offers should, in principle, provide unbiased estimates of the parameters of the general model of arbitrator behavior in equation (2).

4.3.2 Critique

As approaches to testing the relevance of the parties' final offers to conventional arbitration decisions, both the efforts of Ashenfelter and Bloom (1984) and of Bazerman and Farber (1985) have their weaknesses.

First, as noted in section 4.3.1, the Ashenfelter-Bloom test is based on the commonality of parameters in the equations describing arbitrator behavior under conventional and final-offer arbitration. This test will fail if regime 2 is the true model for the preferred settlements of conventional arbitrators, but estimation of the regime 1 model biases the estimates of β and σ in such a way that they support the constraints. Although this possibility seems unlikely, it probably is true that at least β is biased in a direction that favors acceptance of the constraints (if regime 2 actually holds) since X is presumably positively correlated with w^u and w^e. Another weakness of this test is that it fails to account explicitly for simultaneity bias involving the final offers under conventional arbitration that could also lead to acceptance of the constraints.

The second set of potentially confounding problems with the Ashenfelter-Bloom model involves the specification of the X vector (i.e., the list of factors that arbitrators consider in rendering an award). For example, arbitrators often report that they are influenced by subjective factors such as the quality of advocacy or the intensity of a particular bargainer's feelings. Alternatively, there may also be important objective factors that arbitrators consider that are not captured in the specifications estimated by Ashenfelter and Bloom. Since either set of factors may vary in some systematic manner across bargaining cases, their omission from the Ashenfelter-Bloom model would bias the estimates they compute and therefore reduce the power of their test for mechanical compromise behavior. The presence of some perverse correlation between the mode of arbitration chosen by the parties (i.e., final offer or conventional) and the random component of arbitrator behavior would have a similar effect.

Overall, the Ashenfelter-Bloom model does not provide a particularly strong test of the mechanical compromise hypothesis. Nor does it provide unambiguous results with regard to this issue. For example, the hypothesis is not rejected in the simple specifications reported, but it is rejected in the richer specifications. However, the great strength of this model is that it tests the mechanical compromise hypothesis using data derived from an operating arbitration system.

Like the Ashenfelter-Bloom study, the Bazerman-Farber approach to testing for mechanical compromise behavior under conventional arbitration also has several problems. First, the twenty-five hypothetical arbitration scenarios sent to actual arbitrators were constructed so that the final offers were orthogonal to the "facts" of the cases. This feature of the scenarios has no analog in actual arbitration where final offers are endowed with information content via their link to the facts of a case. This is unfortunate since it is the information content of the final offers that makes it potentially sensible for the arbitrators to give them weight (see Gibbons 1987 for an interesting model of this communication process). The failure to provide arbitrators with any decision-making criteria is also unfortunate.

Second, according to Bazerman and Farber, the conventional arbitration decision was equal to one or the other of the parties' final offers in 386 out of their 1,522 cases (25.4 percent). This result stands in strong contrast to actual arbitration systems in which arbitration awards infrequently lie on the bounds of the parties' final positions. This boundary problem undoubtedly resulted from arbitrator confusion as to what to do in cases in which the facts suggested a settlement that lay far away from the offers (which happened because of the "pathological" relationship between the facts and the final offers). Although Bazerman and Farber ignore this information in their empirical analysis (as explained below), it represents strong evidence that arbitrators are influenced by the parties' final offers.

Third, Bazerman and Farber report 196 cases (12.9 percent) in which arbitrators' decisions were either greater than the union's final offer or less than the employer's final offer. These cases might be interpreted as evidence that arbitrators are not influenced by the parties' final offers. However, almost all of these cases reflect scenarios in which the "facts" and "final offers" are grossly inconsistent (e.g., the final offers probably looked like typos to the arbitrators). Insofar as arbitration awards rarely lie outside the bounds of the parties' final positions in real-world arbitration, their inordinate prevalence in the Bazerman-Farber data raises serious questions about the external validity of their experiment.

Fourth, Bazerman and Farber try to handle their "extreme" data points by estimating a model that treats as censored all observations that lie on or outside the bounds of the final offers. In other words, all of the Bazerman-Farber results about mechanical compromise behavior are based only on a nonrandom subset of their cases in which arbitrators were either not strongly influenced by the parties' final offers or did not have good reason to ignore the offers entirely.

Overall, the fact that the arbitrator decisions were identical to one or the other of the parties' final offers in roughly one-fourth of the cases is prima facie evidence that arbitrators do pay considerable attention to the parties' final offers, even when they contain literally no information. This finding could be explained in (one or more of) the following three ways. First, arbitrators may not be particularly skilled at identifying cases in which final offers have no information content. Second, arbitrators may engage in mechanical compromise behavior in order to appear fair, but they failed to realize that they had no such incentives in the Bazerman-Farber simulations. Third, the self-selected arbitrators who participated in Bazerman and Farber's study were simply lazy and failed to reveal information about their likely behavior in actual arbitration cases. Nonetheless, because the final offers are exogenously fixed, one conclusion of the Bazerman-Farber study is clear:

the evidence of mechanical compromise behavior is not generated by bargainers positioning themselves around the expected arbitration award.

4.4 Experimental Design

Although Bazerman and Farber's (1985) study has flaws in both its design and its analysis, the basic idea of conducting an "experiment" to learn about arbitrator behavior is quite clever and fundamentally sound. Thus, it seems reasonable to repeat the experiment that they conducted in a way that overcomes as many of the problems they faced as possible. This task was begun in early 1984 by sending a new set of hypothetical arbitration cases to roughly the same population of arbitrators (i.e., members of the National Academy of Arbitrators).

Four cases were prepared for this experiment. These cases were all based on the records of actual bargaining disputes that were arbitrated under the New Jersey Arbitration Law during the years 1980–83. Police officer wages were either the sole or overriding issue in dispute in all of these cases. All of the arbitrators in the sample were provided with the following: 1) general background information on the public employer and the public employee union; 2) information on the bargaining history that led to the arbitration; 3) the final positions of each party and a description of the arguments advanced in support of those positions (or against the other side's position); and 4) statistical exhibits supporting the positions of one or both parties. Arbitrators were asked to examine the information describing the bargaining dispute, to consider that information in light of New Jersey's Arbitration Law, and to render a conventional arbitration award ordering the implementation of whatever salary (or salary increase) they thought to be most reasonable. Arbitrators were also provided with a two-page description of the New Jersey Arbitration Law that included a list of the substantive items they were supposed to weigh in their deliberations (e.g., comparability, ability to pay, cost of living, financial health of the municipality, etc.). Data on police officer salaries in six New Jersey communities and four non-New Jersey communities from 1979 to 1983 were provided as background information for the arbitrators. Finally, arbitrators were provided with a decision form asking them to record their decision and to outline the basis for it. This form also requested information about the professional background and experience of each arbitrator and asked for an evaluation of the arbitration exercise.

In the process of preparing the four abridged arbitration cases, a curious feature of the link between facts and final offers was discovered. In particular, it was observed in the actual arbitration cases that the arguments used to advance a particular position were never so narrowly specified so as to imply a unique final position. In other words, it seemed clear that the arguments could be used to support a range of final positions in the vicinity of the final position actually advanced. This feature of adversariness in interest arbitration was exploited in the experimental design by sending different arbitrators cases that were identical in all respects except for the final positions of the parties (see table 4.1). Since knowing which of the four cases an arbitrator was being asked to decide completely summarizes the facts of the case, any variations in the conventional arbitration decisions that are positively correlated with variations in the final offers may be interpreted as evidence of mechanical compromise behavior.

Unlike the Bazerman-Farber study in which all members of the National Academy of Arbitrators were asked to arbitrate twenty-five hypothetical cases each, the present design asked each arbitrator to consider just two cases (one conventional arbitration case and one final-offer arbitration case, although the final-offer cases are not analyzed here). In addition, arbitration cases were only sent to arbitrators who were not members of New Jersey's panel of interest arbitrators (some of whom might have had considerably more information about the New Jersey municipalities, such as the actual final offers). Of the 527 arbitration exercises mailed out, responses were received to 186. Of these, 131 responses did not include arbitration decisions, either because they indicated that: 1) the arbitrator was deceased, 2) the arbitrator did not have time to participate in the study, 3) the arbitrator would not participate in the study without pay, 4) the arbitrator did not feel competent to resolve wage disputes because of lack of experience with them, or 5) for a variety of reasons, the arbitrator did not think the study could reveal useful information about arbitrator behavior. Overall, the 55 arbitrators who did respond tended to be statistically similar to those who participated in the Bazerman and Farber study: they are generally above the average of all National Academy members in terms of both overall arbitration experience and interest arbitration experience (i.e., the respondents have an average of twenty-two years of arbitration experience and roughly 6 percent of their cases involve disputes of interest). Since interest arbitration presently accounts for only 5 percent of all arbitration cases (only 2 percent before the early 1970s), it is not surprising that many arbitrators chose not to respond to the exercise for lack of expertise.

It is difficult to gauge the potential biases introduced into the study by the self-selection of arbitrators. However, the importance of the results presented herein does not depend critically on the sample of included arbitrators being representative of the population of all labor arbitrators. In other words, the mere fact that a segment of the nation's top practicing arbitrators are participants in this study would seem to dictate that the results be taken seriously. Also difficult to evaluate, but probably worth reporting, are the arbitrators' evaluations of the exercises. In answer to the question: "To what extent do you feel that these exercises capture the key features of actual arbitration cases?" the distribution of arbitrator responses was as follows: "not at all," 6 percent; "to some extent," 16 percent; "reasonably well," 59 percent; "very well," 14 percent; and "almost entirely," 5 percent. In addition, the average evaluation score and the response rate varied little across the four city scenarios.

4.5 Estimation Results

The purpose of this section is to determine whether the arbitrator responses to the arbitration cases described above permit us to make inferences about whether regime 1 or regime 2 is more likely to be the true model generating conventional arbitration decisions.

Table 4.1 reports the average percent wage increase awarded by arbitrators for each of the twelve sets of semidistrict cases circulated (i.e., for each of the three pairs of final offers associated with the bargaining disputes in the four cities under consideration). The striking feature of this table is that the average arbitration award increases when the average of the employer and union final offers increases, *in each of the four cities*. Although few of the differences are statistically significant, mainly because of small cell sizes, this pattern of results does suggest the main result that the regression estimates below will confirm: the decisions of arbitrators are influenced by the parties' final offers.

Table 4.1   **Pairs of Employer and Union Final Offers and Average Arbitration Awards, by City**

	City											
	Camden			Mount Olive			Mahwah			North Bergen		
	w^e	w^u	N	w^e	w^n	N	w^e	w^u	N	w^e	w^u	N
Pair 1	6.0	8.0	3	7.4	9.8	4	8.0	10.0	3	0.0	14.0	3
(Avg. award)		(6.33)			(7.68)			(8.93)			(6.97)	
Pair 2	4.0	8.0	4	6.8	9.2	5	6.0	10.0	6	3.5	9.0	5
(Avg. award)		(6.00)			(7.60)			(7.50)			(5.70)	
Pair 3	2.0	10.0	3	6.0	8.4	6	7.0	9.0	7	0.0	9.0	6
(Avg. award)		(4.93)			(7.18)			(7.60)			(4.30)	

Note: w^e = employer's final offer in percent.

w^u = union's final offer in percent.

N = number of observations with each pair of final offers (total number of observations equals 55).

Table 4.2 reports least-squares estimates of the parameters of the two models of conventional arbitrator behavior set out in section 4.2. The first model corresponds to equation (1) and represents a regression of conventional arbitration decisions on the facts of the case (i.e., on a vector of city dummy variables). The second model corresponds to equation (2) and represents regressions of conventional arbitration decisions on both the facts and the final offers in each case. The first of the estimated forms of equation (2) is simply a reduced-form regression in which the facts and final offers are entered as right-hand-side variables. The next two columns report estimates of the structural parameters of equation (2) (i.e., β, σ, and γ); these estimates are computed from regressions in which the weights associated with the facts and the final offers are not scaled by the estimate(s) of γ.

Table 4.2 indicates that the average arbitration award in the fifty-five cases being analyzed was 6.72 percent with a standard deviation of 1.82 percent. When the arbitration awards are regressed on a vector of city dummy variables, the standard deviation of the residuals drops to 1.52 percent. In addition, the coefficient estimates for the city dummy variables indicate significant differences among arbitration decisions in the different cities ($F[5,51] = 8.88$, compared to a critical value of 2.41 for a test constructed at the 5 percent level). Since there were literally no differences in the facts presented for individual cities, these dummy variables may be viewed as completely characterizing those facts. Thus, under the maintained hypothesis that conventional arbitrators render decisions without reference to the parties' final offers, the estimates of equation (1) suggest that arbitrators are able to discern differences between the cases that are reflected in their decisions.

It is, of course, possible that the significance attributed to the facts results from omission of the final offers from the regression. In other words, since the offers are correlated with the underlying facts of the case by design, misspecifying the regression by omitting the offers might result in the coefficients of the city dummies picking up their own effect plus some of the effect of the offers. The first column of estimates of equation (2), which simply adds in the average of the parties' final offers as a regressor, is informative about this possibility. Indeed, there are three noteworthy features of these estimates. First, the city dummies are no longer significant in this equation, either singly or jointly. In addition, the coefficients of the city dummies all become quite small in magnitude when the average final offer enters the equation. Second, the average final offer explains significantly more of the total variation in the arbitration decisions than do the facts of the cases.[2] Third, the coefficient on the mean of the final offers (i.e., .880) is significantly greater than zero, but not significantly different from one. Thus, a clear winner seems to emerge when the facts and the final

Table 4.2   **Ordinary Least-Squares Estimates of Equation (1) and Alternative Specifications of Equation (2)**[a]

Parameter/ RHS Variable	Descriptive Statistics	Eq. (1)	Equation (2) Reduced-Form Coefficients	Equation (2) Structural Coefficients Constrained	Equation (2) Structural Coefficients Unconstrained
Constant	6.724	5.371 (0.406)	0.387 (1.645)	3.225 (11.401)	2.823 (15.782)
Camden dummy[b]	—	0.408 (0.629)	-0.154 (0.609)	-1.283 (4.069)	-1.092 (5.656)
Mt. Olive dummy[b]	—	2.082 (0.564)	0.163 (0.808)	1.358 (5.920)	1.681 (7.668)
Mahwah dummy[b]	—	2.441 (0.556)	0.216 (0.880)	1.800 (5.981)	2.109 (7.431)
$(w^e + w^a)/2$	—	—	0.880 (0.283)	0.880 (0.283)	—
w^a	—	—	—	—	0.435 (0.173)
w^e	—	—	—	—	0.446 (0.174)
σ	1.822	1.519	1.404	11.740	11.920
R^2	—	0.343	0.450	—	—

[a]Estimated standard errors reported in parentheses below coefficient estimates. The standard errors of the structural estimates of the constant and the coefficients of the city dummies in equations (2) were computed from the asymptotic distribution of the ratio of two coefficients (e.g., the regression constant ($\gamma\beta_0$) and the estimate of γ implied by the regression coefficient on $(w^e + w^a)/2$).
[b]North Bergen is the reference category for the city dummies.

offers are permitted to "fight it out" in the regression. Nevertheless, it is worth noting that there is still a considerable amount of random variation in the decisions of the arbitrators even after the inclusion of both the facts and the final offers (e.g., the standard error of the regression is 1.4 percent).

The first column of structural coefficients reports parameter estimates that are not scaled by γ. Note that the point estimates of the structural constant and the city coefficients are reasonably large in magnitude, although none are significantly different from zero. Thus, the data seem to contain little information about the arbitrators' underlying preferences vis-à-vis the facts of the cases. Alternatively, the data may be indicating that there is considerable variation in the structure of different arbitrators' preference functions. In addition, since none of the intercepts are significantly different from zero and since the estimate of $1 - \gamma$ (the weight on the final offers) is not significantly different from one, it appears that the relationship between the arbitration decisions and the average of the final offers is well described by a 45-degree line that goes through the origin. In other words, it appears that arbitrators *tend to* engage in mechanical compromise behavior that can literally be described as "splitting the difference."

The final column of estimates in table 4.2 differs from the preceding column in that it does not constrain the weights attached to employer final offers and union final offers to be equal. As with the previous model, none of the coefficients of the facts are significantly different from zero. In addition, it is most remarkable that the estimated weights associated with the union and employer final offers are extremely close in magnitude and estimated with almost identical precision. Thus, the simpler model in which arbitrators weigh the final offers symmetrically appears to provide a very satisfactory fit to the data.

Because of the built-in correlation between the facts and final offers in this experiment, these results do not demonstrate that arbitrator decisions are completely independent of case facts. However, they do indicate that arbitrators pay little systematic attention to the case facts beyond the information they extract from the final offers. If one views the final offers in this experiment as representing some function of the facts plus random noise, the results in table 4.2 indicate that the arbitration decisions do vary positively with the noise. This result can be further verified by fitting separate regressions of the arbitration decisions on the average of the final offers for each city. Although there are relatively few observations per city, these models provide the fullest possible set of controls for the case facts and provide a very strong test of whether arbitrators respond to the "noise component" of the parties' final offers.

Table 4.3   **City-Specific Ordinary Least-Squares Estimates of Equation (2)[a]**

Parameter/ RHS Variable	City			
	Camden	Mount Olive	Mahweh	North Bergen
Constant	0.800	4.526	−3.482	−0.155
	(5.121)	(1.077)	(5.028)	(3.603)
$(W^e + W^u)/2$	0.791	0.373	1.380	0.976
	(0.811)	(0.137)	(0.613)	(0.626)
R^2	0.110	0.360	0.270	0.170
N	10	15	16	14

[a]Estimated standard errors are reported in parentheses below coefficient estimates.

Table 4.3 reports the results of these city-specific regressions. It is worth noting that the regression lines for Camden, Mahwah, and North Bergen are all well-approximated by a 45-degree line that passes through the origin. In contrast, the estimated line for Mount Olive is flatter, although the slope is significantly greater than zero. Overall, this pattern of results indicates that arbitrator decisions tend to split the difference between the parties' final offers, albeit with a good deal of unexplained variation (as indicated by the relatively low values of R^2.

Finally, following Bazerman and Farber (1985), one additional model was estimated in which the weights associated with the facts (i.e., γ) was itself modeled as a linear function of the difference between the union and employer final offers. This is a reasonable model to estimate to test whether arbitrators look more closely at the facts of a case when the final offers are far apart. However, unlike the results reported by Bazerman and Farber, the estimates of this model provide no evidence that γ varies with the difference between the parties' final offers.

4.6 Discussion and Conclusion

The growing reliance on conventional arbitration mechanisms for resolving pay disputes arising in labor-management relations has been accompanied by numerous debates over the nature and operation of such mechanisms. A basic point in contention is whether or not conventional arbitrators make decisions by mechanically compromising between the disputants' final offers. If this is indeed the way arbitrators tend to make decisions, then conventional arbitration may provide disincentives for bargainers to engage in concessionary behavior in the negotiation process that precedes arbitration. As a result, conventional arbitration will tend to increase the fraction of disputes that are settled by a third party. This contradicts a fundamental tenet of the American system of industrial relations—the principle of voluntarism—according to which it is desirable for bargaining outcomes to be determined by the individual parties to the greatest extent possible. It seems especially worthwhile to research the extent of mechanical compromise behavior in view of: 1) the popular perception by labor relations practitioners that conventional arbitrators often do "split the difference," and 2) the growing use of final-offer arbitration, which creates a whole new set of theoretical and practical difficulties just to prevent arbitrators from compromising between the parties' final positions.

Unlike previous studies that apply sophisticated econometric techniques to relatively weak data (and report finding little evidence of compromise behavior), this study seeks to generate somewhat richer data and to apply a simple econometric technique. Ultimately, it is impossible to determine the extent to which conclusions drawn from these data generalize to behavior in an actual arbitration system. Nonetheless, the fact is that all of the arbitrators who provided decisions for this study are members of the National Academy of Arbitrators, an organization of the most experienced arbitrators in North America. In addition, 78 percent of the participating arbitrators indicated that the arbitration exercises captured the main features of interest arbitration "reasonably well" or better. Finally, since all of the arbitration awards analyzed were accompanied by a one-paragraph arbitration decision in which arbitrators almost always justified their decision in terms of the facts of the case, it is hard to argue that arbitrators decided these cases in a substantially different manner than they would decide an actual case (i.e., that because they were not being paid to arbitrate the experimental cases and presumably had no incentive to be asked to arbitrate such cases again, they took the easy way out by splitting the difference). Indeed, the variability of arbitrator decisions in the experimental data analyzed in this study is similar in magnitude to estimates of cross-arbitrator variability derived from actual arbitration decisions in New Jersey (see Ashenfelter and Bloom 1984, table 3). Nonetheless, the fact that the arbitrators had no financial incentives to respond carefully to the cases they decided must surely be viewed as a potentially important limitation of this study.

Taken at face value, the results of this study are remarkably clear: conventional arbitrators tend to split the difference between the parties' final offers with little additional systematic reference to the facts of the case. However, because of the substantial amount of unexplained variance in arbitration awards, this characterization of arbitrator behavior should not be regarded as applying to any particular case. Rather, it reflects a systematic tendency of arbitrators across some population of cases. Indeed, of the fifty-five decisions analyzed in this study, only eight were exactly equal to the average of the parties' final offers.

The results of this study do not necessarily imply that arbitrators ignore the facts in the cases they hear. Indeed, the nature of the written arbitration decisions analyzed in this study supports the view that arbitrators do pay attention to the facts. Thus, the statistical results seem to be indicating that arbitrators do not share a common preference function. In other words, arbitrators do give weight to the facts, but different arbitrators do it so differently that the weight tends to show up as random noise. This conclusion is supported by estimates of significant interarbitrator differences in behavior presented in Ashenfelter and Bloom (1984) and Bazerman (1985), and in research on Iowa's system of tri-offer arbitration discussed in Ashenfelter (1985, 1987).

The results of this study provide evidence that arbitration decisions are not invariant to the individual who is hired to be the arbitrator. In the context of public adjudication or under a grievance arbitration mechanism, this conclusion might be disturbing since the notion of justice seems to require such an invariance property, at least at a particular point in time. Wage arbitration is, however, fundamentally different from the adjudication of these other types of disputes, since there is no absolute standard for a "fair" wage. Moreover, the randomness introduced into the system by interarbitrator differences may have additional benefits insofar as uncertainty about the individual who will arbitrate a dispute will provide risk-averse bargainers with an incentive to settle their disputes both voluntarily and expeditiously (Bloom and Cavanagh 1986).

The estimates presented in this study suggest that the standard deviation of the underlying distribution of arbitral preferences, controlling for the facts of a case, is 11.75 percent. Put another way, if arbitrators were asked to decide the cases in this study without having any knowledge of the parties' final offers, roughly two-thirds of the awards would be in the range -8.5 percent to 15.0 percent, and one-third of the awards would lie outside that range. Perhaps arbitration systems provide arbitrators with knowledge of the parties' final positions to lower this grossly high variance. Alternatively, it might be that arbitrators would be able to lower the variance themselves by studying the facts of the case more closely in situations in which final offers were not available. One might even conjecture that final-offer arbitration is just the type of mechanism that can induce arbitrators to extract relatively more information from the exogenous facts of a case.

The results of this study are consistent with the view that conventional arbitrators use the parties' final offers to provide information about the range of settlements that bargainers are likely to view as acceptable. Since this task could probably be accomplished more inexpensively by averaging the parties' final offers and adding on some noise using a computer's random number generator, the findings of this study raise important questions about arbitration's raison d'être. Undoubtedly, the answer to this question has something to do with the superior ability of a human arbitrator to fine-tune arbitration decisions, to endow them with legitimacy in the eyes of disputants, and to induce bargainers to reveal true reflections of their underlying preferences. But this is surely an incomplete answer to a question that seems most worthy of deeper consideration.

Notes

1. Although the focus of this paper is on conventional arbitration, models of arbitrator behavior under final-offer arbitration are also reviewed in this section since they can play an important role in identifying the parameters of conventional arbitrator behavior.

2. The R^2 from a regression that just includes the average of the final offers is .447.

References

Ashenfelter, Orley. 1985. Evidence on U.S. experience with dispute resolution systems. Princeton University Industrial Relations Section, Working Paper no. 185.

———. 1987. Arbitrator behavior. *American Economic Association Papers and Proceedings* 77:342–46.

Ashenfelter, Orley, and David E. Bloom. 1984. Models of arbitrator behavior: Theory and evidence. *American Economic Review* 74:111–24.

Bazerman, Max H. 1985. Norms of distributive justice in interest arbitration. *Industrial and Labor Relations Review* 38:558–70.

Bazerman, Max H., and Henry S. Farber. 1985. Arbitrator decision making: When are final offers important? *Industrial and Labor Relations Review* 39:76–89.

Bloom, David E., and Christopher L. Cavanagh. 1986. An analysis of alternative mechanisms for selecting arbitrators. Harvard Institute of Economic Research Discussion Paper no. 1224.

———. 1987. Negotiator behavior under arbitration. *American Economic Review Papers and Proceedings* 77:353–58.

Farber, Henry S. 1981. Splitting the difference in interest arbitration. *Industrial and Labor Relations Review* 35:70–77.

Farber, Henry S., and Max H. Bazerman. 1986. The general basis of arbitrator behavior: An empirical analysis of conventional and final-offer arbitration. *Econometrica* 54:1503–28.

Gibbons, Robert. 1987. An equilibrium model of arbitration. Department of Economics, MIT. Mimeo.

Stevens, Carl M. 1966. Is compulsory arbitration compatible with bargaining? *Industrial Relations* 5:38–52.

Comment   Morris A. Horowitz

As an academician who has devoted a considerable amount of time over many years doing labor arbitration, I feel that some real-world experience may contribute to a better understanding of the arbitration process. Professor Bloom's paper is a significant advance in the research on arbitrators' behavior. However, real-world issues make it exceedingly difficult to do research in this area. In commenting on Professor Bloom's research I will take this opportunity to elaborate on a number of these issues that arbitrators face. Professor Bloom's research is focused on arbitrator behavior in public sector wage disputes, specifically municipal police collective bargaining. I will direct my principal comments to police disputes, based upon my experience in Massachusetts.

As background, I should note that arbitrators are not in a profession with prescribed education and training. While most arbitrators are either lawyers or academicians, those from academia come from many different academic areas; those who are not lawyers or academics come from a wide variety of professions with a variety of types of experience. A significant percentage of arbitrators are full-time, while many others, such as professors or lawyers, are involved in arbitration on a part-time basis. Further, the vast majority of arbitrators are engaged in grievance arbitration, not the interest arbitration studied by Professor Bloom. Relatively few arbitrators have had any experience in the arbitration of wage disputes.

Arbitrators are generally selected through a process involving the parties through a selection by ranking names from a list prepared by the American Arbitration Association (AAA) or the Federal Mediation and Conciliation Services (FMCS). Occasionally, arbitrators are selected by agreement of the parties. Frequently, arbitrators of wage disputes have had experience as mediators and fact finders.

Professor Bloom's main goal is to draw inferences about the extent arbitration decisions are "mechanical compromises of the parties' final offers." After analyzing his data, he concludes that ". . . arbitrators *tend to* engage in mechanical compromise behavior that can literally be described as 'splitting the difference,' " and that ". . . arbitrators pay little systematic attention to the case facts beyond the information they extract from the final offers." I do not question the accuracy of his analysis of the information and data he collected. However, real-world issues complicate and raise serious questions about such research.

Morris A. Horowitz is professor and chairman, Department of Economics, Northeastern University, vice-chairman of the Massachusetts Joint Labor-Management Committee for Municipal Police and Fire, and ad hoc labor arbitrator on AAA panel, FMCS panel, and Fact Finder Panel of the Massachusetts Board of Conciliation and Arbitration.

Last year I received six such surveys where I was asked to "decide" sample arbitration cases. They came from graduate students writing Ph.D. dissertations as well as academic researchers. As an academic I felt an obligation to respond, and I did in each case. However, depending upon my time pressure, I readily admit I did not devote the same serious thought to each questionnaire. I wonder if busy arbitrators respond in the same way I did—in some cases more seriously than in others?

One factor that concerned me in responding to each of these arbitration surveys was the inability to look into the eyes of the participants in the arbitration proceedings and to get a sense of intensity of feeling. Listening to the parties present their cases and argue their causes gives the arbitrator a better understanding of the real positions of the parties. And in the real world the arbitrator has the opportunity to ask questions and to quiz the parties for clarity.

In public sector wage disputes, especially at the local level, local politics is often a background issue that impinges on the positions of the parties. The negotiators for the community must take into account the interests and needs of the electorate, and the union negotiators must take into account the interests and needs of the union membership. As a result, the so-called case facts are sometimes ignored by the parties themselves. And when the parties ignore them, what should the arbitrator do?

In this same vein, I must note that in many cases the arbitration award, issued and signed by the arbitrator, is, in reality, the terms agreed to by the parties. When parties feel they cannot disclose to their respective constituencies a negotiated settlement because of possible political "fallout," the arbitrator becomes the dispensable person in the process. Each party can then blame the arbitrator for the award without acknowledging to its constituency its acquiescence to the terms of the award. Should arbitrators go along with such a process? The answer is "yes" if arbitrators view their role as furthering the collective bargaining process and improving the labor relations between the parties.

In such instances of "agreed upon" or "stipulated" arbitration awards, the parties' final positions are generally wrapped neatly around the terms that are to be in the award. The award, when rendered, appears to be "splitting the difference," although only those privy to the arrangement know that the so-called final positions were not really final. Arbitrators with such experiences may not hesitate to split the difference between final positions, especially when responding to an academic exercise in arbitration.

Surveys and questionnaires on the process of wage dispute arbitration inevitably focus on the issue of wage. From the perspective of the researcher, this makes a good deal of sense. Frequently, the wage increase is, or appears to be, the major issue in the negotiations over the terms and conditions of employment. Also, the wage change proposals by the parties and the final settlement of the wage change can be readily quantified. However, in the real world many other issues may be involved in the negotiations, some of which cannot be quantified or monetized, and as a group may be more important than the wage changes to one or both of the parties.

In a recent contract negotiation between a Massachusetts community and its police officers' union the following items, in addition to a wage change, were at issue:

1. Clothing allowance increase
2. Longevity pay increase
3. Night differential—new article
4. New proposals on:
   a. drug testing
   b. sick leave incentive
   c. schooling and training
   d. personal days

With such a mix of issues in a real-world situation it is understandable why research in this area is difficult and sometimes appears to be far from reality. And only an experienced arbitrator might be able to ascertain the importance of each of these nonwage issues to the parties.

I should note that the above list of issues came from a single case. Additional issues that could arise in negotiations between municipalities and police unions include many that are unique to public safety employees. A listing of some of the more common issues would include the following:

1. Paid detail rates
2. Paid court time
3. Weapons training allowance
4. Light duty when injured
5. Issuance of bulletproof vests for all officers
6. Air-conditioning in all cruisers
7. Physical fitness rules
8. Nonsmoking on duty and off duty

Such a listing is an additional indication of the complexities of real-life situations. These complexities undoubtedly make it difficult to do research on arbitrator behavior. Researchers such as Professor Bloom must take up the challenge and must bring more of these issues into the universe of their research.

5 The Evolution of Public Sector Bargaining Laws

Henry S. Farber

5.1 Introduction

It has been argued that the tremendous increase in collective bargaining among state and local government employees is largely the result of the passage of laws by states sanctioning and regulating the process of collective bargaining by government employees.[1] In 1955 less than a handful of states had laws defining the collective bargaining rights of public employees and virtually all of these prohibited bargaining. By 1984 all but a few states had adopted a policy in this area, and only a handful of states prohibited bargaining. Table 5.1 contains a breakdown of state laws governing the collective bargaining rights of public sector employees in 1955 and 1984 derived from the National Bureau of Economic Research (NBER) public sector bargaining law data set (Valletta and Freeman this volume, appendix B). While there are serious problems of causal inference in concluding that the emergence of public policy caused the increase in unionization, the emergence of public policy in this area along with public sector unionization represents an important puzzle for industrial relations scholars. If the public policy did cause the increase in unionization, then the problem is to explain the emergence of the public policy. If unionization (or the pressure for unionization) resulted in public policy to deal with it, then the problem is to explain the emergence of the unionization.

Henry S. Farber is professor of economics at Massachusetts Institute of Technology and a research associate of the National Bureau of Economic Research.

Gregory Leonard and Robin Maury provided research assistance. The author thanks John Abowd for very helpful discussions and Robert Valletta for help with the NBER public sector bargaining law data set. Useful comments on an earlier draft were provided by Casey Ichniowski and Edward Lazear.

Table 5.1   Number of States with Laws Governing Collective Bargaining
                   Rights

	1955[a]		1984	
	No Law	Law	No Law	Law
State Employees	44	4	8	42
Police	45	3	8	42
Teachers	45	3	3	47

Source: Valletta and Freeman (this volume, appendix B).
[a]There were only forty-eight states in 1955.

The ideal would be to specify and estimate a full structural model of the determination of public sector legislation and unionization that afforded the opportunity to determine the direction of causality directly. However, estimation of such a model would strain the limits of the available data and econometric techniques. A difficult, if somewhat less ambitious, task is undertaken in this study: the specification and estimation of a reduced form model of the determination of state laws governing public sector bargaining.[2] The analysis is reduced form in that the direct effect of public sector unionization on public policy is not analyzed, and it is argued that public policy is a function of the combined sets of factors that affect public policy indirectly through their effect on public sector unionization as well as the factors that affect public policy directly.

The empirical analysis relies on the NBER public sector bargaining law data set (Valletta and Freeman, this volume, appendix B), which contains information on each state's laws governing collective bargaining by public sector employees for each year in the 1955–84 period. Information is available separately for laws governing each of five classes of employees (state employees, local police, fire, teachers, and other local employees). The analysis here deals with state employees, police, and school teachers as groups that are representative of public employees more generally and capture the important variation in laws across employee groups.[3] While a number of different aspects of each law are summarized in the data (e.g., collective bargaining rights, union security provisions, policy regarding strikes, alternative dispute settlement mechanisms), the analysis focuses on the fundamental policy regarding collective bargaining rights. This can range from a prohibition on bargaining to a requirement that public sector employers bargain with their employees. These data are described more fully in section 5.2.

In section 5.3 a model of the determination of the passage of legislation governing public sector collective bargaining is developed. This model describes the process that governs states' decisions regarding:

1) whether or not to enact a law governing public sector bargaining rights, 2) what type of policy to enact if a law is passed, 3) whether or not to change an existing policy, and 4) what type of policy to change to if a change is passed. The model is based on two central constructs: the first is intensity of preferences for or against public sector unionization; the second is the cost (ease or difficulty) of enacting or changing public policy in this area. Essentially, it is argued that a state will enact a policy or change its existing policy if its preferences differ from the value of the current policy (or no policy) by enough to outweigh the costs of the change.

The econometric framework is outlined in section 5.4. A Markov model of transitions from one category of law to another (or from no law to a particular type of law) *conditional* on the initial category is specified. The transition probabilities are derived directly from the theoretical framework developed in section 5.3.

An important part of the estimation of the model is to identify the factors that influence the intensity of preferences for public sector unionization and the costs of policy change. Section 5.5 contains descriptions of the explanatory variables used to measure variation in the costs associated with the legislative process. These include the number of days the state legislature meets, a measure of general legislative activity, an indicator of whether or not the legislature and the governorship are controlled by the same party, and a time trend. Section 5.6 contains descriptions of the explanatory variables used to measure variation in intensity of preferences. These include congressional voting records on labor issues, private sector unionization, income per capita, the relative size of the government sector, a time trend, and regional factors. The same set of variables is argued to measure variation in the value to a state of having no explicit policy.

The empirical results are presented in section 5.7. The most important factors found to be influencing the intensity of preferences for public sector unionization are the congressional voting records, southern region, income per capita, and the size of the government sector. Nothing measured in this study is found to influence the costs of legislative change in a systematic fashion. Section 5.8 contains an investigation of how well the model fits the data. It is found that the model can explain the overall distribution of laws at various points in time rather well. However, the model is less successful in explaining *which* states have laws of a particular kind at each point in time. In section 5.9 the results are summarized, and it is concluded that the model of legislative change developed in this study has some explanatory power but that more work needs to be done in defining and measuring variables that affect the costs of legislative change and the preferences for public sector collective bargaining.

5.2 Description of Bargaining Law Data

The NBER public sector bargaining law data set, described in detail in appendix B of this volume, contains a record of the legislative history of each state's policy regarding public sector collective bargaining. In constructing these data, a serious attempt was also made to incorporate policies toward public sector collective bargaining that originated from judicial decisions. However, because most existing policy in this area has a legislative foundation and because the measurement of judicially made policy is likely to be incomplete, the data can be thought of as representing a largely legislative history.[4] On this basis the analysis that follows is developed in terms of policy as being derived through a legislative process.

Overall, these data represent the best available comprehensive source of quantitative information on policy regarding public sector collective bargaining. The data are compiled separately for laws covering the three employee groups focused on here: state employees, police, and school teachers, and for each group information is collected regarding public policy governing their collective bargaining rights.

Since it is not possible to characterize parsimoniously the specifics of every law with respect to collective bargaining rights, the laws are categorized with regard to their general content. Four types of laws are defined, ranging from the least favorable for bargaining to the most favorable. The categories are defined in table 5.2. In the least favorable category, bargaining is prohibited, while in the most favorable category the employer is obligated to bargain with the union. In the two intermediate categories bargaining is more-or-less optional.

The evolution of laws governing collective bargaining rights of public sector employees is quite dramatic. Table 5.3 contains a breakdown of laws governing collective bargaining rights by state for each of the three employee groups in 1955 and 1984. It is clear that in the mid-1950s very few states had any policy at all regarding collective bargaining rights for public sector employees, and the laws in those states that did have a policy were not favorable to collective bargaining. By 1984 the large majority of states had adopted a policy, and these policies were largely

Table 5.2   **Categories of Laws Governing Collective Bargaining Rights**

Type	Definition
0	No legislative policy
1	Bargaining prohibited
2	Employer permitted but not obligated to negotiate with union
3	Union has right to present proposals and/or meet with employer
4	Employer has duty to bargain with union

Table 5.3   Breakdown of Laws Governing Collective Bargaining Rights by Category[a]

	State Employees		Police		Teachers	
Type of Law	1955	1984	1955	1984	1955	1984
No Law	44	8	45	8	45	3
1	3	8	2	4	2	4
2	1	6	1	9	1	12
3	0	4	0	2	0	1
4	0	24	0	27	0	30

Source: Valletta and Freeman (this volume, appendix B).
[a]There were only forty-eight states in 1955. See table 5.2 for law category definitions.

favorable to collective bargaining. For all three employee groups, approximately half of the fifty states had adopted a policy of requiring employers to bargain with their employees' unions. While the frequency distributions of type of policy in 1984 are relatively close for the three employee groups, public policy is more favorable for bargaining, on average, for teachers than for the other two groups, and somewhat more favorable for police than for state employees. In 1984 more states had laws requiring bargaining and fewer laws prohibiting bargaining with teachers than with the other two groups. Similarly, more states had laws requiring bargaining with police than with state employees.

If we consider each year in a given state to be an opportunity for the state to modify its public policy, then there are a total of 1,490 observations on the evolutionary process for each of the three employee groups.[5] Table 5.4 contains breakdowns of these processes in the form of cross-tabulations by employee group of the current year's legislative category by the previous year's legislative category. What is obvious is that for all groups most of the 1,490 observations are on the diagonals, meaning that there is generally no change in policy. In fact, of the 1,490 opportunities to change policy, changes occurred only 52 times for state employees, 52 times for police, and 61 times for teachers.

Of the 52 changes in policy regarding state employees, 39 of these were initial enactments of a policy, 6 of which prohibited bargaining. Of the 13 changes in an existing policy, all involved a change to a more favorable law.[6] Of the 52 changes in policy regarding police, 40 of these were initial enactments of a policy, 4 of which prohibited bargaining. Of the 12 changes in an existing policy, all but one involved a change to a more favorable law. Of the 61 changes in policy regarding teachers, 45 of these were initial enactments of a policy, 3 of which prohibited bargaining. Of the 16 changes in an existing policy, all but 2 involved a change to a more favorable law.

Table 5.4   **Cross-Tabulation of Current Collective Bargaining Policy by Previous Year's Policy[a]**

Lagged Policy	Current Policy				
	0	1	2	3	4
A. State Employees					
0	748	6	13	8	12
1	0	169	0	0	1
2	0	0	127	1	6
3	0	0	0	96	5
4	0	0	0	0	298
B. Police					
0	742	4	14	5	17
1	0	89	1	0	2
2	0	1	191	0	5
3	0	0	0	47	3
4	0	0	0	0	369
C. Teachers					
0	657	3	18	5	19
1	0	89	2	0	1
2	0	2	233	1	5
3	0	0	0	50	5
4	0	0	0	0	400

[a]See table 5.2 for category definitions.

Since most of the "action" is in the initial implementation of a public policy regarding bargaining, an important focus of the analysis is on the pattern of emergence of these policies, both across states and over time. There is also a significant amount of change to existing policy that must be accounted for. However, the dominant set of observations consists of those where policy is unchanged, and the theoretical and empirical framework must be able to accommodate this fact.

5.3   Theoretical Framework

A simple model of the passage of legislation governing public sector collective bargaining relies on two factors. First, the intensity of preferences for or against public sector unionism is an important determinant both of the passage of any law and the particular type of law passed. Where preferences in a state are very favorable toward unionization, the state will be more likely to have a pro-union bargaining law. Similarly, where preferences in a state are very unfavorable toward unions, the state will be more likely to have an anti-union bargaining law. The second factor is the difficulty of passing legislation independent of the intensity of preferences for or against unionization. This difficulty level is termed the costs of enacting legislation, and it is argued to be largely a function of the structure of the legislative process. A key feature of the model is the independent nature of the intensity and the costs. Any factors that affect the difficulty of passing legislation in a way that is related to intensity are subsumed in the intensity measure.[7]

Suppose that a law governing the collective bargaining rights of public sector employees can be characterized along a single dimension and that the optimal value of a law (intensity of preference) in this dimension is denoted by R_{it} in state i and year t. A higher value for R_{it} denotes preferences that are more favorable toward bargaining. Suppose further that a loss function, L_{it}, with regard to collective bargaining policy can be defined simply as the absolute value of the deviation of the value, V, of the current policy, j, from the optimal value R_{it}. This loss function is

$$(1) \qquad L_{it} = |R_{it} - V_j|.$$

If it was costless to enact a policy or change an existing policy, then in each period each state would minimize L_{it} by choosing j such that $V_j = R_{it}$. In other words, the policy each period would reflect the currently optimal policy. However, it is generally costly to introduce a new policy or to change an existing policy due to friction in the political process.

Consider first the case where a state has no policy in place. How will that state decide whether to introduce a policy or to remain without a policy? Denote the value of no policy by V_{0it}, so that the loss function evaluated at no policy is simply

$$(2) \qquad L_{it,0} = |R_{it} - V_{0it}|.$$

If the cost of introducing a policy is C_{it}, then the state will find it optimal to introduce a policy only if the loss from introducing the law (C_{it}) is smaller than the benefit derived from elimination of the loss from no policy. This condition is

$$(3) \qquad |R_{it} - V_{0it}| > C_{it},$$

assuming that the state is able to introduce a policy that has a zero loss associated with it ($V_j = R_{it}$).[8]

Note that this formulation does not impose a particular value to "no policy" relative to the actual policies. The value of no policy has state and time subscripts because there is generally a *de facto* policy implicit in no official policy that is likely to be state specific and change over time. For example, no official policy in a generally pro-union state will have a different value than no official policy in a generally anti-union state.

The available data group the laws into the discrete categories defined in table 5.2. In order to derive the decision rules for states that have an existing policy, define V_j as the value of a law in category j. Given the definition of the four categories (excluding no policy) in table 5.2, it is natural to assume that $V_1 < V_2 < V_3 < V_4$.

Once a state has a policy in place, it is assumed that this policy can be maintained costlessly, but that a change in policy entails incurring some level of cost, C_{it}, that is independent of the particular policy in place. In this case a state will decide to change its old policy if and only if the loss associated with the current policy is greater than the loss associated with the best alternative policy plus the cost of change. It is further assumed that a state cannot retreat to having no explicit policy regarding public sector collective bargaining once a policy is enacted.[9]

Using the same notation as above, a state with a category 1 law (prohibiting bargaining) will want to change that law if

$$(4) \qquad\qquad R_{it} > K_1 + C_{it}.$$

where $K_1 = (V_1 + V_2)/2$. The value K_1 can be interpreted as the point of indifference (in R) between category 1 and category 2, and as long as preferences exceed this indifference point by enough to outweigh the cost of the change, then the state will change its policy. It is not necessarily true that the state will adopt policy 2 if this condition holds. This condition is simply necessary and sufficient for the state to desire a change to one of the other (higher) categories.

The conditions to move from each of the policy categories are derived similarly and are:

$(5) \qquad$ Start with #1: $R_{it} > K_1 + C_{it}$,

$\qquad\qquad$ Start with #2: $R_{it} < K_1 - C_{it}$ or $R_{it} > K_2 + C_{it}$,

$\qquad\qquad$ Start with #3: $R_{it} < K_2 - C_{it}$ or $R_{it} > K_3 + C_{it}$, and

$\qquad\qquad$ Start with #4: $R_{it} < K_3 - C_{it}$,

where

$$(6) \qquad\qquad K_1 = (V_1 + V_2)/2,$$

$$K_2 = (V_2 + V_3)/2, \text{ and}$$

$$K_3 = (V_3 + V_4)/2.$$

If the appropriate inequality conditional on the initial policy is not satisfied, then the state will retain its existing policy. If the appropriate inequality is satisfied so that the state decides to change its policy, the state will move to the category that yields the lowest value for the loss function.

Given that a state decides to enact a new policy or to change its existing policy, the state will use a similar decision rule in selecting the optimal category of law. The loss function is minimized by selecting the category of law whose value is closest to R_{it}. The category of law that minimizes the loss function is defined by the interval on the real line delimited by the K_1 that R_{it} falls in. For example, the lowest value law (category 1) will be chosen if $R_{it} < K_1$, where $K_1 = (V_1 + V_2)/2$. Similarly, they will choose category 2 if $K_1 < R_{it} < K_2$, where $K_2 = (V_2 + V_3)/2$. The complete set of conditions is

(7)   Choose 1 if: $R_{it} < K_1$,

              Choose 2 if: $K_1 < R_{it} < K_2$,

              Choose 3 if: $K_2 < R_{it} < K_3$, and

              Choose 4 if: $R_{it} > K_3$,

where the breakpoints are defined in equation (6).

There are two key features of this model from the standpoint of the empirical analysis carried out in succeeding sections. First is that the model allows the central construct of intensity of preferences (R_{it}) to affect three important elements of the evolution of public policy regarding collective bargaining in the public sector: 1) the process that determines whether a state has a policy at all, 2) the process that determines whether the state adjusts its law to reflect current conditions, and 3) the particular kind of law that is adopted in an ordered response context. The second key feature of the model is that the central construct of costs of adjustment (C_{it}) makes it possible for changes in policy to be relatively rare events. This is because the costs of policy change will provide a disincentive to change policy in response to small changes in preferences.

5.4 Econometric Specification

The basic approach taken to the econometric specification is to assume that there are 1,490 (48 states × 30 years + 2 states × 25 years) observations for each employee group on the current state of policy regarding public sector collective bargaining rights conditional on the policy that prevailed at the end of the previous year. Thus, the probabilities of having a particular policy in a given state-year are specified *conditional* on the previous policy, and these probabilities are used to form a likelihood function that is maximized with respect to a set of underlying parameters that are common to the various conditioning events.

The econometric framework used for this task is an extension of a standard ordered probit model. Conditional on the previous policy (or no policy), the specification will indicate the probability of the joint event of 1) change or no change in that policy and 2) choice of the particular policy that was implemented where there was a change. This is essentially a Markov model of the transition probabilities based on the frequencies in table 5.4. The contribution of the theory is that it provides a way to specify each of the transition probabilities in this matrix as a function of the same set of underlying parameters and in terms of a coherent model.

Equations (5)–(7) define the decision rules that determine whether or not a state will enact or change policy and what sort of policy will be enacted if there is a change. These depend on the values of the cost of changing policy (C_{it}), the intensity of preference (R_{it}), the value of no policy (V_{0it}), and the threshold values (K_1, K_2, and K_3).

The cost of changing policy (C_{it}) is a fundamentally unmeasurable quantity that is modeled empirically as the latent variable Y_1 for a given observation where[10]

$$(8) \qquad\qquad Y_1 = X_1\beta_1 + \epsilon_1.$$

The vector X_1 represents observable variables that affect the cost of policy change; β_1 is a vector of parameters; and ϵ_1 is a random component. Similarly, intensity of preferences (R_{it}) is a fundamentally unobservable quantity that is modeled empirically as the latent variable Y_2 for a given observation where

$$(9) \qquad\qquad Y_2 = X_2\beta_2 + \epsilon_2.$$

The vector X_2 represents observable variables that affect the intensity of preferences; β_2 is a vector of parameters; and ϵ_2 is a random component. A third underlying construct is the value of no policy (V_{0it}). This is specified simply as

$$(10) \qquad\qquad Y_3 = X_3\beta_3 ,$$

where the vector X_3 represents observable variables that affect the value of no policy, and β_3 is a vector of parameters. There is no stochastic element in this construct.

The particular variables in the X vectors are discussed in section 5.5. It is assumed that ϵ_1 and ϵ_2 have independent standard normal distributions. Given the qualitative nature of the outcomes, it is not possible to identify the variances ϵ_1 or ϵ_2 together with the scale of β_1, β_2, and β_3. Thus, the variances are normalized to one. The means of ϵ_1 and ϵ_2 are normalized to zero, because systematic unobservable factors are subsumed in the constant terms in $X_1\beta_1$, $X_2\beta_2$, and $X_3\beta_3$. The zero correlation restriction is imposed for analytical convenience, but it is consistent with the argument made in section 5.3 that the factors affecting intensity of preferences and costs of policy change are independent by construction.

Given these specifications for the costs of policy change, the intensity of preferences, and the value of no policy, along with the model outlined in the previous section, it is possible to write the probabilities of all possible outcomes for each of the conditioning sets (initial policies). Let J_t represent the type of law in place in state i in year t. The index J_t can take on any of the five values 0, 1, 2, 3, 4, where 0 represents no policy and 1 through 4 represent the four categories of collective bargaining rights law described in table 5.2. These are the five conditioning events that define the five rows of the Markov transition matrix. The transition probabilities are defined as

(11) $P_{mnt} = Pr(J_t = n | J_{t-1} = m)$ for n, $m = 1 \ldots 5$,

where P_{mnt} represents the probability that a state with law category m in year $t - 1$ has law category n in year t. These probabilities sum to one for each conditioning event such that

(12) $$\sum_{n=0}^{4} P_{mnt} = 1 \qquad \forall m = 0, 1, 2, 3, 4.$$

The various P_{mnt} depend on the same set of parameters and are defined in detail in this chapter's appendix.[11]

It is straightforward to formulate the likelihood function for this model based on the probabilities for the various events outlined in this section and presented in the appendix. The associated log-likelihood function is

(13) $$\ln(L) = \sum_{t=55}^{84} \sum_{i=1}^{50} \sum_{m=0}^{4} \sum_{n=0}^{4} I_{mnit} \ln(P_{mnt}),$$

where I_{mnit} is an indicator variable that equals one if state i had law m in year $t - 1$ and law n in year t. The variable I_{mnit} equals zero otherwise.[12] Computation of this likelihood function involves evaluation of nothing more complex than bivariate normal cumulative distribution functions (CDFs), and these are readily computable using numerical approximations. The empirical analysis consists of maximization of this likelihood function with respect to the free parameters of the model (β_1, β_2, β_3, K_1, K_2, and K_3).

One shortcoming of the Markov approach used here and implicit in the likelihood function is that it assumes there is no correlation across time and within states in the errors ϵ_1 and ϵ_2. It is certainly likely to be true that there are persistent unmeasured factors that affect the intensity of preferences and the costs of policy change within states. However, the appropriate technique for dealing with this problem is not clear. A fixed effect estimator, which includes a separate intercept for each state (perhaps in Y_1, Y_2, and Y_3) imposes too high a computational burden in a nonlinear model such as this. It also strains the limits of the information in the data. There are also difficult computational problems in using a random effects estimator.

While this section in conjunction with the appendix contains much tedious specification of probabilities, the overall structure of the two-equation model is clear. States will change their policy if their preference/cost structure changes so that a different policy is optimal net of the costs of the change. The policy that states will select if they do opt to change will be the option closet to their most preferred position. In the next two sections the observable variables that determine the cost of policy change, the intensity of preference, and the value of no policy are described.

5.5   The Costs of a Change in Public Policy

The costs of a change in public policy is a construct designed to capture how difficult it is to make a legislative change in policy. An important determinant of this is the structural makeup of the state government. While it is unclear exactly what organizational or political factors lead to higher or lower difficulty in implementing legislative change, three measures that are likely to reflect these underlying factors are used in this study.

The first is the number of days the state legislature is in session. The argument is that a legislature in session more days has a greater chance of passing a given piece of legislation. In addition, a legislature that meets frequently is argued to exhibit more professionalism. It should also be noted that a number of states had legislative sessions only every other year or had only perfunctory sessions every other year until recently. It is clear that these states are unlikely to pass important legislation in the "off" years, and a variable representing days in session will capture this phenomenon. The measure of legislative days was not available for 1983 and 1984, and the 1982 figure for each state was used for these years. The mean and standard deviation of this variable and the others discussed in this and the next section are contained in table 5.5.

The second variable used is the number of bills enacted by the state government (passed by the legislature and signed by the governor). The arguments used to justify this variable are similar to those for the number of days the legislature is in session. The data on the number

Table 5.5   **Descriptions, Means, and Standard Deviations (s.d.) of Explanatory Variables**

Variable	Mean (s.d.)	Description
COPE	0.504 (0.241)	Fraction of votes by state's delegation to U.S. House of Representatives consistent with AFL-CIO approved position on issues of interest to organized labor. (Source: AFL-CIO Department of Legislation, Congressional Voting Records.)
Union	0.231 (0.094)	Fraction of private sector work force in state unionized. (Source: U.S. BLS, Directory of Union Membership, 1964–80, See text for source prior to 1964 and after 1980.)
South	0.322	= 1 if southern census region.
Inc/Pop	3.10 (0.778)	Real income per capita in state in thousands of 1967 dollars. (Source: U.S. Regional Data Bank, Data Resources, Inc.)
Govexp/Inc	0.209 (0.0492)	Ratio of state and local government expenditures to total income. (Source: U.S. Regional Data Bank, Data Resources Inc.)
Year	69.6 (8.63)	Time trend has values equal to year 1955–84.
Legday	115.5 (101.6)	Number of days stated legislature met. (Source: *Book of the States*, various years.)
Nenact	494.4 (494.1)	Number of legislative enactments by state government. (Source: *Book of the States*, various years.)
Unified	0.622	= 1 if legislature and governorship controlled by same party. (Source: *Book of the States*, various years.)

of enactments were missing for a few observations, and values for these observations were imputed by interpolation from adjacent years.[13]

The final legislative structure variable used is a dummy variable that reflects whether or not the state legislature and the governorship are controlled by the same party. It is argued that where there is this unified control, the government will be able to achieve whatever it wants more easily. This could be favorable or unfavorable bargaining legislation.[14]

A time trend measured by year is included in the cost function in order to capture any secular change in the difficulty of legislative change in this area. One argument for such a change is that as the public sector grew over this period and/or as public sector workers became more interested in unionization, the general pressure to articulate some policy with regard to public sector collective bargaining grew. That the pressure is not particularly for a positive or a negative policy, but simply for some policy, suggests that this factor belongs in the cost equation where a negative coefficient would indicate an increase over time in the likelihood of a change in policy.

5.6   Intensity of Preferences for Public Sector Collective Bargaining and the Value of No Policy

Perhaps the most important factor that would influence a state with regard to policy toward collective bargaining by public sector employees is the general attitude toward unions in the state. Three variables are used here to reflect these attitudes. The first is a measure of the "liberalness" on labor issues of the congressional delegation of the state. This is likely to be important to the extent that 1) legislators reflect the preferences of the voters in their states on labor issues and 2) these voters elect state legislators who also reflect these same attitudes. The measure used is the "COPE score" of the congressional delegation of the state. The Committee on Political Education (COPE) and the legislative department of the AFL–CIO regularly tabulate the voting records of individual legislators on issues of interest to the labor movement. On each issue, the legislative department defines a "right" vote and a "wrong" vote where, obviously, a right vote is favorable to unions and a wrong vote is unfavorable. The COPE score is calculated as the fraction of votes cast "right" by members of the state's delegation to the U.S. House of Representatives.[15]

The second measure of the state's general attitude toward unions is the extent of private sector unionization in the state. This may be an important determinant of the intensity of preferences for public sector bargaining laws for at least two reasons. First, where the extent of unionization is high, there is also likely to be more general pro-union sentiment. Second, a strong union movement may be able to lobby more effectively for legislation it wants, and favorable public sector bargaining legislation is likely to fall into that category. It proved very difficult to find a consistent time series for unionization by state, and what is used is not entirely satisfactory. Available from the U.S. Bureau of Labor Statistics (BLS) are state level figures on union membership for the even years from 1964 through 1980. These data were interpolated for the odd years to yield a consistent series for these seventeen years. While other series are available for selected years (e.g., Troy and Sheflin 1985, for 1960, 1975, 1980, and 1982), they were not collected on a basis consistent with the BLS data, so they were not used here. A series from 1955 through 1963 was derived using data from the BLS on the aggregate extent of unionization for each year in conjunction with the state-level data available for 1964. Specifically, the interstate distribution of unionization was assumed to be the same over the 1955– 63 period as it was in 1964. However, the level in each state was adjusted proportionally so that the employment-weighted average extent of unionization in each year from 1955 to 1963 agreed with the available annual aggregate BLS data. In other words, the 1964 state-level data were used to fix the relative unionization across states and the annual aggregate data were used to fix the overall level of unionization. An analogous technique was used to derive state-level data for 1981–84 using the 1980 relative unionization across states and the annual aggregate BLS data.

The third measure of general attitudes toward unionization is a dummy variable for states that are in the south. While it is well known that unionization is lower in the south, there may be negative attitudes regarding unions in the south that go beyond the lower extent of unionization. Evidence is provided by Farber (1983, 1984) not only that workers in the south are less interested in unionization than workers outside that region but also that workers in the south who do want union jobs are less likely to be able to find union jobs, perhaps for institutional reasons. He also finds that the existence of right-to-work laws in many states in the south does not account for this inability to find union jobs.

Three other measures that may be related to the intensity of preferences for public sector unionization are also used. The first is the level of per capita income in the state. Where per capita income is higher, it may be that the citizenry demands more public services and values them more highly so that public employees have more power that they can use to create an environment favorable to unionization. Alternatively, the citizenry may view unionization of public employees as a normal good, so they create an environment favorable to public sector unionization where incomes are high. The precise measure used is real per capita income in 1967 dollars.

The second measure is designed to reflect the size of the government sector. Where the government sector is larger, public sector employees are likely to have more power and influence that they can use to promote legislation favorable to public sector collective bargaining. The measure used is the ratio of state and local government expenditures to income in the state.

The final measure used is a time trend measured by the year (1955– 80). This measure is included to capture a secular increase in preferences for public sector unionization. It reflects the hypothesis that the reason for the implementation of many favorable public sector bargaining laws over this period is simply a secular improvement in public attitudes regarding public sector unionization and/or a secular increase in public employees' demands for unionization.

The value of no explicit policy toward public sector bargaining depends heavily on the underlying attitudes toward unionization in the state. For example, attempts to unionize by public sector employees in a state very hostile to collective bargaining are likely to meet with strong resistance from employers, the populace, and possibly the courts. The result is a de facto unfavorable public policy toward unionization. Similarly, attempts to unionize by public sector employees in a state that is sympathetic to collective bargaining are likely to meet with less resistance (and perhaps implicit acceptance) from employers, the populace, and the courts. The result is a de facto favorable public policy toward unionization. On this basis, the same set of variables argued to determine the intensity of preference for unionization are argued to determine the value of no policy.

5.7   Empirical Results

The econometric specification derived in section 5.4 was estimated by maximum likelihood using the data from the NBER public sector bargaining law data set described in section 5.2.[16] The first panel of table 5.6 contains the definitions of three vectors of explanatory variables that are used in the estimation: 1) Z_1 contains only a constant, 2) Z_2 contains the full set of five explanatory variables described in section 5.5 for the cost of policy change, and 3) Z_3 contains the full set of seven explanatory variables described in section 5.6 for the intensity of preference and the value of no policy.

The second panel of table 5.6 contains a summary of eight specifications (various combinations of the Z's) used to estimate the model for each of the three employee groups. The first specification is a baseline with only constants in the three vectors (cost of policy change, intensity of preference, value of no policy). This model has a total of six parameters: three constants and three breakpoints. The second specification is fully unconstrained in that the full set of variables for each of the three vectors is included: 1) Z_2 for the cost of policy change vector, 2) Z_3 for the intensity of preference vector, and 3) Z_3 for the value of no policy vector. This specification has a total of twenty-two parameters. The next three specifications in turn have only a constant in one of the three vectors. The final three specifications have only a constant in two of the three vectors.

The last panel in table 5.6 contains maximized log-likelihood values for each of the eight specifications for each of the three employee groups. These are used to evaluate the various specifications.

Table 5.6   **Model Summary**

A. Vector Definitions[a]

	Z_1	Z_2	Z_3
	Constant	Constant Legday Nenact Unified Year	Constant COPE Union South Inc/Pop Govexp/Inc

B. Model Specifications

	1	2	3	4	5	6	7	8
Cost of Policy Change	Z_1	Z_2	Z_2	Z_2	Z_1	Z_2	Z_1	Z_1
Intensity of Preference	Z_1	Z_3	Z_3	Z_1	Z_3	Z_1	Z_3	Z_1
Value of No Policy	Z_1	Z_3	Z_1	Z_3	Z_3	Z_1	Z_1	Z_3
# of Parameters	6	22	16	16	18	10	12	12

C. Log-Likelihood Values

Employee Group	1	2	3	4	5	6	7	8
State Employees	−280.0	−250.4	−254.7	−265.8	−252.2	−276.6	−256.0	−266.8
Police	−272.7	−242.9	−247.1	−258.8	−243.6	−270.4	−247.4	−259.5
Teachers	−316.3	−270.0	−281.5	−294.2	−273.5	−311.0	−284.1	−296.7

[a]See table 5.5 for variable definitions.

Before comparing the different specifications, it is useful to examine the estimates of the unconstrained model (specification 2).

The results are not encouraging with regard to the determinants of the cost of policy change. For state employees, (table 5.7A), none of the variables seem to affect the cost of policy change significantly in the hypothesized direction. Only the number of bill enacted (Nenact) has a coefficient that is significantly different from zero at conventional levels, and that has the wrong sign. The results are no better for police (table 5.7B) or teachers (table 5.7C). Again, none of the variables hypothesized to affect the cost of policy change have coefficients that are significantly different from zero in the appropriate direction. In addition, the hypothesis that all of the coefficients in the cost of policy change vector except the constant term are zero cannot be rejected using a likelihood-ratio test at any reasonable level of significance for any of the three employee groups. These tests are based on comparisons of the log-likelihoods for specification 5 with those for specification 2. The conclusion is that the set of variables used to determine the cost of policy change is not appropriate for any of the three employee groups.

The intensity of preference function performs better. For state employees, the COPE scores are significantly positively related to preference while in the south preferences are significantly lower. It is interesting that after controlling for the COPE scores and for South, the extent of private sector unionization is not a significant determinant of preference for public sector collective bargaining for state employees, and it has the wrong sign. The value of per capita income is marginally significantly positively related to preference, but the size of the government sector, as proxied by the ratio of state and local government expenditures to total income, is not significantly related. There is no significant time trend in preferences. The estimates of the determinants of intensity are similar but somewhat less well determined for police and teachers. In all three cases the hypothesis that all of the coefficients in the intensity of preference vector except the constant term are zero *can* be rejected using a likelihood-ratio test at any reasonable level of significance. These tests are based on comparisons of the log-likelihoods for specification 4 with those for specification 2. The conclusion is that the set of variables used to determine the intensity of preference has significant explanatory power for all three groups.

The value of no policy function is not very well determined for any of the three employee groups. None of the estimated coefficients are significantly different from zero for any of the groups. For both state employees and police, the hypothesis that all of the coefficients in the value of no policy vector except the constant term are zero cannot be rejected using a likelihood-ratio test at any reasonable level of

Table 5.7   **Markov Model of Public Sector Bargaining Laws[a]**

A. State Employees

Variable	Cost of Policy Change	Variable	Intensity of Preference	Value of No Policy
Constant	3.60	Constant	3.60	−7.54
	(2.28)		(4.09)	(4.31)
Legday	0.000298	COPE	2.50	−1.55
	(0.00137)		(1.16)	(1.25)
Nenact	0.000695	Union	−4.95	6.89
	(0.000244)		(3.80)	(4.19)
Unified	−0.324	South	−1.32	0.731
	(0.237)		(0.661)	(0.749)
Year	0.00221	Inc/Pop	0.945	−0.758
	(0.0343)		(0.658)	(0.741)
		Govexp/Inc	0.922	2.05
			(3.93)	(5.88)
		Year	−0.0429	0.0911
			(0.0598)	(0.0665)

	Summary Statistics		*Breakpoints*	
	LLF = −250.4		$\hat{K}_1$	2.00
				(0.487)
	N = 1,490		$\hat{K}_2$	2.71
				(0.393)
	χ^2 statistic = 59.2[b]		$\hat{K}_3$	3.20
				(0.471)

B. Police

Variable	Cost of Policy Change	Variable	Intensity of Preference	Value of No Policy
Constant	2.87	Constant	2.69	−5.82
	(1.37)		(7.87)	(0.841)
Legday	0.000686	COPE	2.08	−0.889
	(0.00143)		(1.63)	(1.71)
Nenact	0.000112	Union	−3.36	3.78
	(0.000254)		(5.36)	(5.64)
Unified	0.00581	South	−1.36	1.09
	(0.00232)		(0.779)	(0.829)
Year	0.00681	Inc/Pop	1.01	−0.541
	(0.0204)		(0.921)	(0.949)
		Govexp/Inc	1.17	0.194
			(5.15)	(6.24)
		Year	−0.0432	0.0705
			(0.115)	(0.124)

	Summary Statistics		*Breakpoints*	
	LLF = −242.9		$\hat{K}_1$	1.35
				(0.502)
	N = 1,490		$\hat{K}_2$	2.53
				(0.361)
	χ^2 statistic = 59.2[b]		$\hat{K}_3$	2.77
				(0.369)

Table 5.7   (continued)

		C. Teachers		
Variable	Cost of Policy Change	Variable	Intensity of Preference	Value of No Policy
Constant	3.16	Constant	1.47	−5.92
	(1.47)		(5.08)	(5.39)
Legday	0.00252	COPE	1.76	−0.846
	(0.00150)		(1.29)	(1.38)
Nenact	0.0000210	Union	−1.29	1.79
	(0.000292)		(3.94)	(4.28)
Unified	−0.0432	South	−1.89	1.85
	(0.194)		(0.965)	(1.02)
Year	−0.00158	Inc/Pop	0.727	−0.0958
	(0.0220)		(0.645)	(0.690)
		Govexp/Inc	1.99	−1.18
			(4.76)	(6.24)
		Year	−0.0174	0.0640
			(0.0805)	(0.0868)

	Summary Statistics		Breakpoints	
	LLF = −269.9		$\hat{K}_1$	1.09
				(0.44)
	N = 1,490		$\hat{K}_2$	2.60
				(0.288)
	χ^2 statistic = 92.8[b]		$\hat{K}_3$	2.81
				(0.307)

[a]See table 5.5 for definitions and summary statistics of variables. Specification 2 is used from table 5.6. The numbers in parentheses are asymptotic standard errors.
[b]The χ^2 statistic is the likelihood ratio test statistic of a constrained model with constants only (six parameters).

significance. However, for teachers this hypothesis *can* be rejected, suggesting that the value of no policy does vary systematically in the measured dimensions for teachers. These tests are based on comparisons of the log-likelihoods for specification 3 with those for specification 2. The conclusion is that the set of variables used to determine the value of no policy has significant explanatory power only for teachers.

Overall, the estimates in table 5.7 are not terribly encouraging with regard to the model. It is true that for all three employee groups the hypothesis that all parameters except the three constant terms and the three breakpoints are zero (specification 1) can be rejected against specification 2 at conventional levels of significance using a likelihood ratio test. However, as is clear from the above discussion, only the coefficients of the variables determining the intensity of preference are consistently significantly different from zero as a group. In no case are the parameters of the cost of policy change function significantly different from zero, and only for teachers are the parameters of the value of no policy function significantly different from zero.

It may be that the estimation of three vectors of parameters for each group is putting an excessive burden on the data. Using the likelihood values in table 5.6 as a guide, more parsimonious specifications for each of the employee groups can be derived. For state employees and police a reasonable specification has only constants in the cost of policy change and value of no policy vectors but with the full set of parameters in the intensity of preference vector. This is specification 7, and it is nested in specifications 2, 3, and 5. Specification 7 cannot be rejected at conventional levels against any of these three alternatives for either state employees or police. For teachers a reasonable specification has only a constant in the cost of policy change vector but with the full set of parameters in the intensity of preference and the value of no policy vectors. This is specification 5, and it is nested in specification 2. As noted above, specification 5 cannot be rejected against specification 2 at conventional levels for teachers. On this basis the discussion of results proceeds using as preferred specification 7 for state employees and police and specification 5 for teachers.

Table 5.8A–B contains estimates of specification 7 for state employees and police. It is clear that the restrictions embodied in these specifications improve the precision of the parameter estimates considerably. For state employees (table 5.8A) the estimates suggest that intensity of preferences are significantly positively related to the COPE score and negatively related to being in the southern region. In addition, intensity of preferences is marginally significantly positively related to per capita income and per capita government expenditures. The results are similar for police (table 5.8B). Intensity of preferences are significantly positively related to the COPE score and marginally significantly negatively related to being in the southern region. In addition, intensity of preferences is significantly positively related to per capita income and marginally significantly positively related to per capita government expenditures.

Table 8C contains estimates of specification 5 for teachers, and the results are somewhat weaker with regard to specific parameters. The intensity of preferences are marginally significantly positively related to the COPE score and significantly negatively related to being in the southern region. However, the coefficients of per capita income and per capita government expenditures in the intensity of preference equation are small relative to their standard errors. The value of no policy is significantly positively related to union status and significantly negatively related to being in the southern region. However, the remainder of the estimated coefficients are small relative to their standard errors.

Table 5.8   **Markov Model of Public Sector Bargaining Laws[a]**

A. State Employees

Variable	Cost of Policy Change	Variable	Intensity of Preference	Value of No Policy
Constant	3.41	Constant	−0.178	−1.95
	(0.186)		(1.69)	(0.351)
Legday	—	COPE	1.18	—
			(0.459)	
Nenact	—	Union	0.300	—
			(1.31)	
Unified	—	South	−0.821	—
			(0.313)	
Year	—	Inc/Pop	0.359	—
			(0.248)	
		Govexp/Inc	3.95	—
			(2.64)	
		Year	0.0116	—
			(0.0307)	

Summary Statistics	Breakpoints	
LLF = −256.0	$\hat{K}_1$	1.68
		(0.460)
N = 1,490	$\hat{K}_2$	2.40
		(0.322)
χ^2 statistic = −48.0[b]	$\hat{K}_3$	2.90
		(0.354)

B. Police

Variable	Cost of Policy Change	Variable	Intensity of Preference	Value of No Policy
Constant	3.36	Constant	−0.274	−1.69
	(0.163)		(1.70)	(0.303)
Legday	—	COPE	1.31	—
			(0.448)	
Nenact	—	Union	−0.279	—
			(1.43)	
Unified	—	South	−0.497	—
			(0.260)	
Year	—	Inc/Pop	0.604	—
			(0.256)	
		Govexp/Inc	3.93	—
			(2.55)	
		Year	−0.00104	—
			(0.0308)	

Summary Statistics	Breakpoints	
LLF = −247.4	$\hat{K}_1$	1.31
		(0.356)
N = 1,490	$\hat{K}_2$	2.41
		(0.270)
χ^2 statistic = 50.6[b]	$\hat{K}_3$	2.63
		(0.267)

Table 5.8   (continued)

	C. Teachers			
Variable	Cost of Policy Change	Variable	Intensity of Preference	Value of No Policy
Constant	3.23	Constant	1.60	−6.02
	(0.151)		(5.00)	(5.31)
Legday	—	COPE	1.67	−0.751
			(1.29)	(1.38)
Nenact	—	Union	−1.62	1.94
			(3.62)	(0.396)
Unified	—	South	−1.78	1.72
			(0.778)	(0.805)
Year	—	Inc/Pop	0.630	−0.0404
			(0.610)	(0.668)
		Govexp/Inc	3.19	−0.894
			(4.79)	(6.22)
		Year	−0.0192	−0.0623
			(0.0773)	(0.0849)

Summary Statistics	Breakpoints	
LLF = −273.5	$\hat{K}_1$	1.01
		(0.429)
N = 1,490	$\hat{K}_2$	2.51
		(0.240)
χ^2 statistic = 85.6[b]	$\hat{K}_3$	2.73
		(0.264)

[a]See table 5.5 for definitions and summary statistics of variables. Specification 7 (state employees and police) and specification 5 (teachers) are used from table 5.6. The numbers in parentheses are asymptotic standard errors.

[b]The χ^2 statistic is the likelihood ratio test statistic of a constrained model with constants only (six parameters).

The estimates presented in this section do not provide strong support for the model. The cost of policy change, while it may be an important concept, is not measured adequately by the variables used here. Similarly, variation in the value of no policy is not explained by the data. The only systematic relationships found are for the variables that determine the intensity of preference. In particular, states with high COPE scores and states outside the south have preferences that are more probargaining. However, there is no evidence that state/years with a high level of private sector unionization, after controlling for COPE scores and the other measures, are significantly different in their preference for public sector bargaining laws. There is weaker evidence that state/years with higher levels of per capita income and per capita government expenditure are more favorably disposed toward public sector collective bargaining.

5.8 How Well Does the Model Fit the Data?

At this point, it is important to ask how well the model fits the data. While there is no consensus on an appropriate test of goodness-of-fit in a model such as this, two related concepts are used. The first asks how well the model can mimic the aggregate distribution of laws by category at five-year intervals. The second asks how well the model can differentiate the states that have a given category of law from those that do not at five-year intervals.

The parameter estimates for any given specification can be used to compute a predicted Markov transition matrix for any state i in any year t using the probabilities defined in the appendix. Denote this one-period transition matrix by $\hat{M}_{it}$ whose jkth element is the predicted probability that state i with law category j in year $t - 1$ will have law category k in year t. On this basis the estimated transition matrix for state i over a n-year period from 1955 to $1955 + n$ is

$$(14) \qquad \hat{C}_{in} = \prod_{t=55}^{55+n} \hat{M}_{it} ,$$

where π represents the matrix product. The average n-period transition matrix over m states is

$$(15) \qquad \tilde{C}_n = \frac{1}{m} \cdot \sum_{i=1}^{m} \hat{C}_{in} ,$$

where Σ represents the matrix sum. The jkth element of this matrix represents the average predicted probability that a state with category j law in 1954 will have category k law in year $1955 + n$.

The average transition matrix was computed for $n = 4, 9, 14, 19, 24, 29$ (corresponding to the years 1959, 1964, 1969, 1974, 1979, and 1984) for each of the three employee groups. The preferred specifications were used for each of the employee groups. These are based on the estimates in table 5.8 for state employees, police, and teachers. First-order approximations to the standard errors of the elements of these matrices were computed using the "delta method."[17]

The first row of the transition matrix, $\tilde{C}_n$, contains the average probabilities that a state will have a law in each of the categories in year $1955 + n$ conditional having no law in 1954. Since fewer than a handful of states had any explicit policy regarding public sector collective bargaining in 1954, it is appropriate to focus on this row of the matrix. If the model fits the data well, it ought to be true that at each of the five-year intervals these transition probabilities ought to closely reflect the actual distribution of laws at that point in time. The underlying conceptual experiment is to assume that there were no laws in 1954 in any state and to start the process of evolution of laws according to the estimated Markov process. The interesting questions are: 1) the extent to which the estimated Markov process can explain the movements over time in the fraction of states with a law in a given category, and 2) the extent to which by 1984 the cross-sectional distribution implied by the Markov process is similar to the actual distribution. The average estimated transition probabilities along with their asymptotic standard errors, as well as the actual distribution of laws for the six selected years, are contained in table 5.9 for the three employee groups. The estimated probabilities sum to one by now.

It is clear from the actual distribution of laws for state employees (table 5.9A) that most of the action in the enactment of laws was in the period from 1964 through 1979. This is indicated by the sharp rate of decline over this period in the proportion of states with no law. The predicted proportion with no law declined steadily from 1959 to 1984, but the model was not able to fully capture the steeper decline between 1964 and 1979. The model consistently underpredicted the fraction of

Table 5.9   **Actual and Predicted Distribution of Laws by Category[a], All Fifty States**

A. State Employees					
Year	No Law	Category 1	Category 2	Category 3	Category 4
1959					
Actual	0.854	0.0625	0.0417	0.0417	0.0
Predicted	0.849	0.0472	0.0376	0.0284	0.0380
(s.e.)	(0.0379)	(0.0200)	(0.0141)	(0.0123)	(0.0247)
1964					
Actual	0.740	0.0800	0.100	0.0800	0.0
Predicted	0.697	0.0756	0.0703	0.0582	0.0995
(s.e.)	(0.0564)	(0.0318)	(0.0218)	(0.0198)	(0.0445)
1969					
Actual	0.540	0.120	0.120	0.0800	0.140
Predicted	0.539	0.0896	0.0929	0.0858	0.193
(s.e.)	(0.0572)	(0.0375)	(0.0273)	(0.0261)	(0.0530)
1974					
Actual	0.280	0.160	0.100	0.0800	0.380
Predicted	0.395	0.0864	0.0996	0.103	0.317
(s.e.)	(0.0484)	(0.0364)	(0.0304)	(0.0322)	(0.0494)
1979					
Actual	0.180	0.140	0.120	0.100	0.460
Predicted	0.288	0.0778	0.0953	0.108	0.431
(s.e.)	(0.0451)	(0.0337)	(0.0309)	(0.0357)	(0.0492)
1984					
Actual	0.160	0.160	0.120	0.080	0.480
Predicted	0.220	0.0712	0.0900	0.106	0.512
(s.e.)	(0.0497)	(0.0337)	(0.0312)	(0.0369)	(0.0634)

Table 5.9 (continued)

Year	No Law	Category 1	Category 2	Category 3	Category 4
			B. Police		
1959					
Actual	0.896	0.0625	0.0208	0.0208	0.0
Predicted	0.848	0.0365	0.0523	0.0138	0.0495
(s.e.)	(0.0349)	(0.0180)	(0.0161)	(0.00737)	(0.0269)
1964					
Actual	0.740	0.0600	0.140	0.0400	0.200
Predicted	0.689	0.0581	0.0994	0.0279	0.125
(s.e.)	(0.0510)	(0.0270)	(0.0247)	(0.0131)	(0.0458)
1969					
Actual	0.480	0.0800	0.200	0.0400	0.200
Predicted	0.519	0.0658	0.135	0.0410	0.238
(s.e.)	(0.0511)	(0.0292)	(0.0321)	(0.0186)	(0.0530)
1974					
Actual	0.260	0.0400	0.160	0.0400	0.500
Predicted	0.362	0.0576	0.151	0.0487	0.381
(s.e.)	(0.0434)	(0.0249)	(0.0379)	(0.0227)	(0.0501)
1979					
Actual	0.180	0.0600	0.180	0.0400	0.540
Predicted	0.248	0.0465	0.150	0.0504	0.505
(s.e.)	(0.0412)	(0.0207)	(0.0407)	(0.0244)	(0.0533)
1984					
Actual	0.160	0.0800	0.180	0.0400	0.540
Predicted	0.180	0.0397	0.146	0.0496	0.585
(s.e.)	(0.0453)	(0.0204)	(0.0425)	(0.0247)	(0.0690)
			C. Teachers		
1959					
Actual	0.896	0.0625	0.0208	0.0208	0.0
Predicted	0.858	0.0367	0.0608	0.00909	0.0375
(s.e.)	(0.0331)	(0.0184)	(0.0203)	(0.00479)	(0.0166)
1964					
Actual	0.740	0.0600	0.120	0.0600	0.200
Predicted	0.685	0.0483	0.130	0.0227	0.115
(s.e.)	(0.0538)	(0.0231)	(0.0341)	(0.0101)	(0.0381)
1969					
Actual	0.440	0.0600	0.240	0.0800	0.180
Predicted	0.460	0.0544	0.188	0.0381	0.259
(s.e.)	(0.0536)	(0.0219)	(0.0452)	(0.0169)	(0.0535)
1974					
Actual	0.160	0.0400	0.200	0.0400	0.500
Predicted	0.237	0.0592	0.213	0.0474	0.443
(s.e.)	(0.0421)	(0.0201)	(0.0485)	(0.0227)	(0.0561)
1979					
Actual	0.0600	0.0800	0.240	0.0200	0.600
Predicted	0.0962	0.0697	0.209	0.0470	0.578
(s.e.)	(0.0337)	(0.0267)	(0.0466)	(0.0242)	(0.0590)
1984					
Actual	0.0600	0.0800	0.240	0.0200	0.600
Predicted	0.0334	0.0836	0.202	0.0426	0.639
(s.e.)	(0.0237)	(0.0478)	(0.0484)	(0.0233)	(0.0813)

[a]Predicted probabilities based on estimates of specification 7 for state employees and police and specification 5 for teachers contained in table 5.8. The numbers in parentheses are estimated asymptotic standard errors.

states with category 1 laws (prohibiting bargaining) after 1964. Roughly speaking, the model predicted that this fraction remained constant at approximately 7.5 percent after 1964, while the actual distribution stabilized at approximately 15 percent after 1974. At the other extreme, the model did a slightly better job capturing the emergence of category 4 laws (requiring bargaining). The observed fraction of states with this type of law increased dramatically from 0 percent in 1964 to 46 percent by 1979. The model did not predict quite so rapid an increase, but the predicted probabilities of category 4 laws did increase more rapidly over the 1964 to 1979 period than either earlier or later. The cross-sectional 1984 distribution differs somewhat from the actual distribution in predicting too high a fraction with no law and too low a fraction with a category 1 law.

Examination of the actual and predicted distribution of laws for police (table 5.9B) yields similar conclusions to those for state employees, though the model does seem to fit somewhat better. The timing of the enactment of laws governing collective bargaining for police was concentrated between 1964 and 1979, and the model was not able to pick this up as well as it might have. The model did a better job fitting the fairly constant low probability of having a category 1 law. The model was also able to capture a large share of the rapid increase in the introduction of category 4 laws between 1964 and 1979. The predicted cross-sectional distribution for 1984 is quite close to the actual 1984 distribution.

Table 5.9C contains the actual and predicted distributions for laws governing teachers. The overall pattern of movement of the actual distribution of laws over time is quite similar to the two other groups. The model fits the data relatively well with the exception (common to the other two groups) that the rapid decline between 1964 and 1979 in the fraction with no law is not fully captured by the model. However the relative stability in the fraction with a category 1 law, the rapid increase in the fraction with a category 4 law, and the 1984 cross-sectional distribution are all captured quite closely.

Overall, the model seems to do a reasonable job in explaining the aggregate distribution of laws at given five-year intervals. A more difficult task for the model is to predict *which* states have laws of a given type at any point in time. One way to examine the ability of the model to predict which states will have laws of a given type is to examine the average predicted probabilities that a state will have a law of a given type in a given year *where the average is taken only over states with a law of that type*. For example, it is useful to examine the average predicted probability for states that have a category 1 law in a given year that those states will, in fact, have a category 1 law.

The average *n*-period transition matrix required for this exercise is defined similarly to that in equation (15) as

(16)
$$\tilde{C}_{nk} = \frac{1}{m_{nk}} \cdot \sum_{i \in S_{nk}} \hat{C}_{in} ,$$

where S_{nk} is the set of states with category k law in year 1955 + n, m_{nk} is the number of elements in S_{nk}, and $\hat{C}_{in}$ is defined in equation (14). The conceptual experiment is the same as that underlying table 5.9 in the sense that it is assumed that no states have laws in 1954 and that the process of evolution of laws is governed by the estimated Markov process. If the model predicted perfectly, then the estimated probability that a state with category j law in fact has a category j law would equal one. The estimated probability that the state has a law in any other category would equal zero. While there is no chance that the model will do this well, the interesting question that can be answered by this analysis is whether the estimated probabilities for a state with a given category law are skewed toward the type of law that the state, in fact, has.

Table 5.10 contains estimated transition probabilities and standard errors for the three employee groups. The calculations are presented for the three selected years 1964, 1974, and 1984 (corresponding to $n = 9, 19, 29$). Three subsets of states in each year are used: 1) states with no law, 2) states with category 1 laws, and 3) states with category 4 laws. The estimated probabilities sum to one by now.

The estimates in tables 5.10A for laws governing state employees are not very encouraging. For states with no law, the estimated probability that the state, in fact, has no law is substantially different from one even in 1964 and declines dramatically by 1984. Even worse, the estimated probabilities are virtually indistinguishable from those contained in table 5.9A computed using all fifty states. For states with type 1 laws, the model does a bit better. The estimated probabilities are still dramatically smaller than one, but they are substantially larger than those contained in table 5.9A computed using all fifty states. For states with type 4 laws, the estimated probabilities are again dramatically smaller than one, and they are again larger than those contained in table 5.9A computed using all fifty states.

The results contained in table 5.10B for laws governing police are qualitatively identical to those for laws governing state employees. The model does a poor job distinguishing states that have no law, but it does a somewhat better job identifying states that have anti-bargaining or pro-bargaining laws. The estimates contained in table 5.10C suggest that the model performs even more poorly for laws governing teachers. The model can neither distinguish states that have no law, nor distinguish states that have anti-bargaining or pro-bargaining laws. Basically, the probabilities presented in table 5.10C computed using only the states with specific categories of laws are not very different at all from the probabilities presented in table 5.9C computed using all fifty states.

Table 5.10 **Predicted Distribution of Laws by Category,[a] Sets of States with Selected Category Law**

A. State Employees

Year	No. of States	No Law	Category 1	Category 2	Category 3	Category 4
		States with No Law (category 0):				
1964	37	0.704	0.0736	0.0711	0.0573	0.0939
		(0.0573)	(0.0314)	(0.0225)	(0.0200)	(0.0439)
1974	14	0.417	0.0994	0.102	0.101	0.280
		(0.0531)	(0.0414)	(0.0306)	(0.0311)	(0.0498)
1984	8	0.246	0.0751	0.108	0.118	0.454
		(0.0594)	(0.0374)	(0.035)	(0.0400)	(0.0679)
		States with Law Prohibiting Bargaining (category 1):				
1964	4	0.810	0.166	0.0128	0.00507	0.00652
		(0.0884)	(0.0933)	(0.0101)	(0.00490)	(0.00580)
1974	8	0.623	0.194	0.0515	0.0371	0.0951
		(0.0867)	(0.0901)	(0.0199)	(0.0151)	(0.0284)
1984	8	0.474	0.182	0.0826	0.0599	0.201
		(0.0956)	(0.0830)	(0.0303)	(0.0314)	(0.0640)
		States with Law Requiring Bargaining (category 4):				
1964	0	—	—	—	—	—
1974	19	0.256	0.0344	0.112	0.132	0.465
		(0.0524)	(0.0279)	(0.0383)	(0.0423)	(0.0662)
1984	24	0.105	0.0244	0.0781	0.114	0.678
		(0.0356)	(0.0173)	(0.0334)	(0.0406)	(0.0655)

B. Police

Year	No. of States	No Law	Category 1	Category 2	Category 3	Category 4
		States with No Law (category 0):				
1964	37	0.697	0.0574	0.100	0.0274	0.117
		(0.0525)	(0.0268)	(0.0252)	(0.0131)	(0.0453)
1974	13	0.459	0.0921	0.145	0.0419	0.262
		(0.0520)	(0.0403)	(0.0347)	(0.0194)	(0.0435)
1984	8	0.175	0.0462	0.150	0.0533	0.575
		(0.0482)	(0.0244)	(0.0458)	(0.0266)	(0.0741)
		States with Law Prohibiting Bargaining (category 1):				
1964	3	0.826	0.118	0.0351	0.00528	0.0157
		(0.0545)	(0.0623)	(0.0199)	(0.00456)	(0.0212)
1974	2	0.667	0.186	0.0750	0.0126	0.0591
		(0.0842)	(0.0844)	(0.0304)	(0.00831)	(0.0297)
1984	4	0.464	0.128	0.158	0.0351	0.215
		(0.101)	(0.0597)	(0.0421)	(0.0197)	(0.0857)
		States with Law Requiring Bargaining (category 4):				
1964	1	0.482	0.0159	0.159	0.0558	0.287
		(0.114)	(0.0140)	(0.0420)	(0.0260)	(0.115)
1974	25	0.260	0.0267	0.152	0.0547	0.507
		(0.0417)	(0.0135)	(0.0421)	(0.0260)	(0.0589)
1984	27	0.113	0.0175	0.125	0.0468	0.698
		(0.0341)	(0.105)	(0.0412)	(0.0242)	(0.0625)

Table 5.10   (continued)

		C. Teachers			
Year	No. of States	No Law	Category 1	Category 2	Category 3	Category 4

States with No Law (category 0):

Year	No. of States	No Law	Category 1	Category 2	Category 3	Category 4
1964	37	0.685	0.0473	0.131	0.0230	0.114
		(0.0542)	(0.0233)	(0.0347)	(0.102)	(0.0385)
1974	8	0.311	0.109	0.214	0.043	0.323
		(0.0508)	(0.0360)	(0.0476)	(0.0210)	(0.0493)
1984	3	0.0597	0.124	0.176	0.0374	0.603
		(0.0386)	(0.0684)	(0.0568)	(0.0219)	(0.0857)

States with Law Prohibiting Bargaining (category 1):

1964	3	0.783	0.114	0.0796	0.00724	0.0160
		(0.0495)	(0.0523)	(0.0367)	(0.00594)	(0.0152)
1974	2	0.482	0.203	0.213	0.0248	0.0774
		(0.0851)	(0.0686)	(0.0580)	(0.0155)	(0.0421)
1984	4	0.0842	0.288	0.360	0.0482	0.220
		(0.0620)	(0.129)	(0.0735)	(0.0281)	(0.115)

States with Law Requiring Bargaining (category 4):

1964	1	0.677	0.0170	0.157	0.0273	0.122
		(0.0797)	(0.0162)	(0.0466)	(0.0138)	(0.0502)
1974	25	0.153	0.0173	0.193	0.0509	0.586
		(0.0375)	(0.0101)	(0.0546)	(0.0247)	(0.0670)
1984	30	0.0173	0.0346	0.151	0.0380	0.759
		(0.0143)	(0.0210)	(0.0480)	(0.0226)	(0.0713)

[a]Predicted probabilities based on estimates of specification 7 for state employees and police and specification 5 for teachers contained in table 5.8. The numbers in parentheses are estimated asymptotic standard errors.

5.9   Conclusions

The character of both the parameter estimates presented in section 5.7 and the estimated transition probabilities presented in section 5.8 lead to the inescapable conclusion that the model, as estimated, does not adequately explain the evolution of public sector bargaining laws. However, the model was successful in some dimensions. A number of variables (COPE, South, Inc/Pop, Govexp/Inc) were found to be systematically related to the intensity of preference for public sector collective bargaining. In addition, the model seems to perform adequately in explaining the aggregate distribution of bargaining laws at a point in time. It did particularly well explaining the 1984 cross section.

On the negative side, virtually nothing was found that was systematically related to the cost of policy change. Whether this is due to having chosen the wrong set of variables to explain these costs or to the concept itself being misguided is difficult to know. However, one piece of evidence in support of the concept is that when the cost of policy change is estimated as a constant alone plus a stochastic term, the constant term is estimated to be significantly different from zero. Were there no rigidity in policy determination, the estimate of this constant would be insignificantly different from zero.

Another important negative for the model is its failure to be able to predict *which* states (as opposed to how many) had laws of a given category in a given year. This is clearly a difficult test, but it is something of a litmus test of our ability to explain and predict policy change.

Overall, the problem of modeling the evolution of public policy is a difficult one. The basic model developed here is a potentially fruitful approach toward modeling the evolution of public sector bargaining laws specifically and public policy more generally. At the same time, the results are disappointing with regard to the costs of legislative change and the ability of the model to predict the dynamics of public policy in a particular state. More work needs to be done in defining appropriate explanatory variables as well as in refining and testing the econometric structure.

Appendix
Specification of Transition Probabilities

In this appendix, the twenty-five elements of the Markov transition matrix are defined. The four elements associated with movement from an existing policy to no policy are assumed to equal zero by definition. These are

$$(A1) \quad P_{m0} = Pr(J_t = 0|J_{t-1} = m) = 0 \quad \forall m = 1, 2, 3, 4.$$

The remaining twenty-one elements are described in the remainder of this appendix as functions of the latent variables defined in section 5.4.

Row 1: No Preexisting Policy ($J_{t-1} = 0$)

In this case a state will remain without a policy if the absolute value of the deviation of the intensity of preference from the value of no policy is less than the cost of change. In terms of the latent variables, the probability of this event is

$$(A2) \quad Pr(J_t = 0|J_{t-1} = 0) = Pr(-Y_1 < Y_2 - Y_3 < Y_1)$$

$$= Pr(Y_1 + Y_2 - Y_3 > 0, Y_2 - Y_3 - Y_1 < 0)$$

$$= Pr(-\epsilon_1 - \epsilon_2 < X_1\beta_1 + X_2\beta_2 - X_3\beta_3,$$

$$\epsilon_2 - \epsilon_1 < X_1\beta_1 - X_3\beta_3 - X_2\beta_2)$$

$$= Pr(-\epsilon_1 - \epsilon_2 < X_1\beta_1 - X_3\beta_3 + X_2\beta_2)$$
$$\cdot Pr(\epsilon_2 - \epsilon_1 < X_1\beta_1 - X_3\beta_3 - X_2\beta_2).$$

This bivariate normal probability reduces to the product of two univariate normal CDF's because the correlation of $\epsilon_1 + \epsilon_2$ and $\epsilon_2 - \epsilon_1$ is zero under the assumption of equal variances for ϵ_1 and ϵ_2.

The detail of presentation of $Pr(J_t = 0|J_{t-1} = 0)$ is to illustrate how the elements of the specification are tied together. This level of detail will not be continued for all of the probabilities in this section.

When a state with no policy enacts a law in the most unfavorable category (1), it is known that the absolute value of the deviation of the intensity of preference from the value of no policy is greater than the cost of change *and* that intensity of preference is lower than the bottom threshold (K_1). The probability of this event is:

(A3) $Pr(J_t = 1|J_{t-1} = 0) = Pr[(Y_2 - Y_3$
$$< -Y_1 \text{ or } Y_2 - Y_3 > Y_1), Y_2 < K_1],$$

which can be expressed as sums of bivariate normal CDFs that are easily approximated numerically.

When a state with no policy enacts a law in an intermediate category m (2 or 3), it is known that the absolute value of the deviation of the intensity of preference from the value of no policy is greater than the cost of change *and* that intensity of preference is bounded by the thresholds K_{m-1} and K_m. The probability of this event is:

(A4) $Pr(J_t = m|J_{t-1} = 0)$
$$= Pr[(Y_2 - Y_3 < -Y_1 \text{ or } Y_2 - Y_3 > Y_1), K_{m-1} < Y_2 < K_m],$$

for $m = 2, 3$. Once again, this can be expressed in terms of sums of bivariate normal CDFs.

Finally, when a state with no policy enacts a law in the highest category (4), it is known that the absolute value of the deviation of the intensity of preference from the value of no policy is greater than the cost of change *and* that intensity of preference is greater than the threshold K_3. The probability of this event is:

(A5) $Pr(J_t = 4|J_{t-1} = 0)$
$$= Pr[(Y_2 - Y_3 < -Y_1 \text{ or } Y_2 - Y_3 > Y_1), Y_2 > K_3],$$

which again can be expressed in terms of bivariate normal CDFs.

Taken together these probabilities completely specify the likelihood of all possible events for the cases where no policy had existed. It is straightforward to demonstrate that these probabilities sum to one. The parameters of this specification include β_1, β_2, β_3, and the three thresholds K_1, K_2, and K_3.

Row 2: A Preexisting Policy in the Lowest Category ($J_{t-1} = 1$)

The first possibility is that no change in the law was made. In this case it is known that the intensity of preference is not high enough to warrant a change. Specifically, it is known that the intensity of preference is less than the bottom threshold plus the cost of making a change. The probability of this event is:

(A6) $\qquad Pr(J_t = 1 | J_{t-1} = 1) = Pr(Y_2 < K_1 + Y_1)$
$\qquad\qquad\qquad\qquad\qquad = Pr(\epsilon_2 - \epsilon_1 < K_1 - X_2\beta_2 + X_1\beta_1),$

which is simply a univariate normal CDF.

While it was relatively rare (see table 5.4) for a state to change its policy from one that prohibited bargaining to a more favorable category, it did happen. If a state were to change its policy from one of prohibiting bargaining to an intermediate category, m, it would be known that the intensity of preference exceeds the lower threshold (K_1) by more than the cost of change and that the intensity of preference lies in the appropriate interval (between K_{m-1} and K_m). The probability of this event is:

(A7) $\qquad Pr(J_t = m | J_{t-1} = 1) = Pr(Y_2 > K_1 + Y_1, K_{m-1} < Y_2 < K_m)$
$\qquad\qquad\qquad\qquad\qquad = Pr(Y_1 - Y_2 < -K_1, K_{m-1} < Y_2 < K_m),$

which can be expressed in terms of bivariate normal CDFs.

The final possibility for a state with a policy of prohibiting bargaining is to enact a policy in the most favorable category (4, requiring bargaining). In this case, it would be known that the intensity of preference exceeds the lower threshold (K_1) by more than the cost of change and that the intensity of preference also exceeds the highest threshold (K_3). The probability of this event is:

(A8) $\qquad Pr(J_t = 4 | J_{t-1} = 1) = Pr(Y_2 > K_1 + Y_1, Y_2 > K_3)$
$\qquad\qquad\qquad\qquad\qquad = Pr(Y_1 - Y_2 < -K_1, Y_2 > K_3),$

which can be expressed in terms of bivariate normal CDFs.

Equations (A6)–(A8) define the probabilities of all possible events for the case where there existed a policy in the lowest category. It is straightforward to demonstrate that these probabilities sum to one. The parameters of these probabilities include β_1, β_2, and the three thresholds K_1, K_2, and K_3. Note that these probabilities are *not* a function of β_3, which determines the value of no policy.

Row 3: Preexisting Policy in Category 2 ($J_{t-1} = 2$)

The first possibility is that no change in the law was made. In this case it is known that the intensity of preference is not high enough or low enough to warrant a change. More specifically, it is known that the intensity of preference is both greater than the lower threshold (K_1) minus the cost of making a change and less than K_2 plus the cost of making a change. The probability of this event is:

(A9) $Pr(J_t = 2|J_{t-1} = 2) = Pr(K_1 - Y_1 < Y_2 < K_2 + Y_1)$,

which can be expressed as sums of bivariate normal CDFs.

If a state were to change its policy from category 2 to the lowest category it would be known that the intensity of preference is less than the lower threshold by an amount at least as large as the cost of change. The probability of this event is:

(A10) $Pr(J_t = 1|J_{t-1} = 2) = Pr(Y_2 < K_1 - Y_1)$,

which is simply a univariate normal CDF.

Movement from category 2 to category 3 occurs when the intensity of preference exceeds K_2 by more than the cost of a policy change and the intensity of preference is in the interval from K_2 to K_3. The probability of this event is:

(A11) $Pr(J_t = 3|J_{t-1} = 2) = Pr(Y_2 > K_2 + Y_1, K_2 < Y_2 < K_3)$,

which again can be computed from sums of bivariate normal CDFs.

Finally, if a state were to change its policy from category 2 to the highest category (4, requiring bargaining), it would be known that the intensity of preference exceeds K_2 by more than the cost of a policy change and that the intensity of preference is greater than the highest threshold (K_3). The probability of this event is:

(A12) $Pr(J_t = 4|J_{t-1} = 2) = Pr(Y_2 > K_2 + Y_1, Y_2 > K_3)$,

which can be computed from sums of bivariate normal CDFs.

Equations (A9)–(A12) define the probabilities of all possible events for the case where there existed a category 2 policy. It is straightforward to demonstrate that these probabilities sum to one. The parameters of these probabilities include β_1, β_2, and the three thresholds K_1, K_2, and K_3.

Row 4: Preexisting Policy in Category 3 (J_{t-1}) = 3)

The first possibility is that no change in the law was made. In this case it is known that the intensity of preference is not high enough or low enough to warrant a change. More specifically, it is known that the intensity of preference is both greater than K_2 minus the cost of making a change and less than the upper threshold (K_3) plus the cost of making a change. The probability of this event is:

(A13) $Pr(J_t = 3|J_{t-1} = 3) = Pr(K_2 - Y_1 < Y_2 < K_3 + Y_1)$,

which can be expressed as sums of bivariate normal CDFs.

If a state were to change its policy from category 3 to the lowest category, it would be known that the intensity of preference is less than K_2 by an amount at least as large as the cost of change and that the intensity of preference is less than the lowest threshold. The probability of this event is:

$$(A14) \quad Pr(J_t = 1|J_{t-1} = 3) = Pr(Y_2 < K_2 - Y_1, Y_2 < K_1),$$

which can be expressed as sums of bivariate normal CDFs.

Movement from category 3 to category 2 occurs when the intensity of preference is less than K_2 by an amount at least as large as the cost of change, and the intensity of preference is greater than the lowest threshold. The probability of this event is:

$$(A15) \quad Pr(J_t = 2|J_{t-1} = 3) = Pr(Y_2 < K_2 - Y_1, Y_2 > K_1),$$

which again can be computed from sums of bivariate normal CDFs.

Finally, if a state were to change its policy from category 3 to the highest category (4, requiring bargaining), it would be known that the intensity of preference exceeds K_3 by more than the cost of a policy change. The probability of this event is:

$$(A16) \quad Pr(J_t = 4|J_{t-1} = 3) = Pr(Y_2 > K_3 + Y_1),$$

which is a univariate normal CDF.

Equations (A13)–(A16) define the probabilities of all possible events for the case where there existed a category 3 policy. It is straightforward to demonstrate that these probabilities sum to one. The parameters of these probabilities include β_1, β_2, and the three thresholds K_1, K_2, and K_3.

Row 5: Preexisting Policy in the Highest Category ($J_{t-1} = 4$)

Finally, consider the case where the state had a law requiring bargaining (category 4). While it is conceptually possible for a state to move to a less favorable policy (if intensity of preference becomes less than the highest threshold, K_3, by more than the cost of change), this was never observed for the three employee groups over the thirty-year period covered (see table 5.4). Nonetheless, the probabilities of these events will be required when the parameter estimates are used to compute predicted legal status at various points in time.

In the case where there is no change in policy (all of the observed cases), it is known that the intensity of preference exceeds the highest threshold minus the cost of a policy change. This probability is:

$$(A17) \quad Pr(J_t = 4|J_{t-1} = 4) = Pr(Y_2 > K_3 - Y_1),$$

which is a univariate normal CDF.

If the policy were to change to the lowest category, it would be known that the intensity of preference is less than the highest threshold minus the cost of a policy change and that the intensity of preference is less than the lowest threshold. The probability of this event is:

$$(A18) \quad Pr(J_t = 1|J_{t-1} = 4) = Pr(Y_2 < K_3 - Y_1, Y_2 < K_1),$$

which can be evaluated as a bivariate normal CDF.

If the policy were to change to category 2, it would be known that the intensity of preference is less than the highest threshold minus the cost of a policy change and that the intensity of preference lies between K_1 and K_2. The probability of this event is:

$$(A19) \quad Pr(J_t = 2|J_{t-1} = 4) = Pr(Y_2 < K_3 - Y_1, K_1 < Y_2 < K_2),$$

which can be evaluated as sums of bivariate normal CDFs.

Finally, if the policy were to change to category 3, it would be known that the intensity of preference is less than the highest threshold minus the cost of a policy change and the intensity of preference lies between K_2 and K_3. The probability of this event is:

$$(A20) \quad Pr(J_t = 3|J_{t-1} = 4) = Pr(Y_2 < K_3 - Y_1, K_2 < Y_2 < K_3),$$

which can be evaluated as sums of bivariate normal CDFs.

Equations (A17)–(A20) define the probabilities of all possible events for the case where there existed a category 4 policy. It is straightforward to demonstrate that these probabilities sum to one. The parameters of these probabilities include β_1, β_2, and the three thresholds K_1, K_2, and K_3.

Notes

1. Freeman (1986) makes this argument directly in the context of an interesting survey of the growth of unionism in the public sector. See also the work of Reid and Kurth (1983), Dalton (1982), Moore (1977), Ichniowski (this volume, chap. 1), and Lauer (1979).

2. Kochan (1973), Faber and Martin (1979), and Saltzman (1985) present studies of the determinants of public sector bargaining laws.

3. For example, both police and fire fighters are viewed as critical local government employees, and the public policy issues raised by unionization of these two groups are similar.

4. Incomplete measurement of judicially based policy should be more of a problem in the early years prior to the passage of legislation because, at that time, the courts could exercise discretion without reference to specific legislation.

5. There are not $30 \times 50 = 1,500$ observations because Alaska and Hawaii did not become states until 1959 and 1960. Thus, these states do not contribute

observations for the five-year period from 1955 to 1959, resulting in ten fewer observations.

6. For state employees, only Florida first prohibited bargaining (category 1) then moved to a policy requiring bargaining (category 4). For police, only Nevada and Texas had such a reversal of policy. For teachers, only Nevada had such a reversal of policy.

7. It is clear that the empirical analysis of outcomes will not support any other interpretation. For example, anything that makes it more likely that a favorable law is passed cannot be classified unambiguously as more favorable preferences as opposed to lower costs of passing *favorable* legislation. The analogous argument can be made for unfavorable legislation.

8. This is not a terribly realistic assumption, and it is not consistent with the empirical analysis that follows. However, it simplifies the analysis quite a bit without changing its fundamental nature.

9. Such a retreat is never observed.

10. The "*it*" subscripts are suppressed in this presentation, except where necessary for clarity, to keep the notation uncluttered.

11. While the derivations of the probabilities are straightforward, they make rather tedious reading. The reader may find it useful to examine the derivation of a few of the probabilities in the appendix in order to be clear about their nature.

12. The variable $I_{mnit} = 0$ for all values of m and n for Alaska and Hawaii prior to 1960.

13. Data for 1955 and 1957 for New Jersey and for 1955 for New York were missing.

14. There were nonpartisan elections in Nebraska for the entire period and in Minnesota for part of the period. Given the absence of a party structure, the concept of unified control has little meaning, so the dummy variable was assigned a value of zero in these cases.

15. The voting records were available only for congresses (pairs of years) from 1955 through 1958. For these years, the two-year record is used. For example, the 1955–56 COPE score is used for both 1955 and 1956.

16. The numerical optimization was carried out using the algorithm described by Berndt, Hall, Hall, and Hausman (1974).

17. The standard error of an element of the transition matrix is computed as the square root of $g'Vg$, where g is the gradient vector of the particular element of the matrix with respect to the parameter vector, and V is the estimated asymptotic covariance matrix of the estimated parameters. The gradient vectors were computed numerically.

References

Berndt, E. K., B. H. Hall, R. E. Hall, and J. A. Hausman. 1974. Estimation and inference in nonlinear structural models. *Annals of Economic and Social Measurement* 3/4:653–65.

Dalton, Amy. 1982. A theory of the organization of state and local government employees. *Journal of Labor Research* 3(2):163–77.

Faber, Charles F., and Donald L. Martin, Jr. 1979. Two factors affecting enactment of collective bargaining legislation in public education. *Journal of Collective Negotiations* 8(2):151–59.

Farber, Henry S. 1983. The determination of the union status of workers. *Econometrica* 51 (September):1417–37.

———. 1984. Right to work laws and the extent of unionization. *Journal of Labor Economics* 2 (July):319–52.

Freeman, Richard B. 1986. Unionism comes to the public sector. *Journal of Economic Literature* 24 (March):41–86.

Kochan, Thomas A. 1973. Correlates of state public employee bargaining laws. *Industrial Relations* 12(3):322–37.

Lauer, Harrison S. 1979. The effect of collective bargaining in municipal police forces on wages, salaries, and fringe benefits. Undergraduate thesis, Department of Economics, Harvard University.

Moore, William J. 1977. Factors affecting growth in public and private sector unions. *Journal of Collective Negotiations* 6(1):37–43.

Reid, Joseph D., Jr., and M. Kurth. 1983. The importance of union security to the growth of unionism. Center for Study of Public Choice Working Paper. George Mason University.

Saltzman, Gregory M. 1985. Bargaining laws as a cause and consequence of the growth of teacher unionism. *Industrial and Labor Relations Review* 38(3):335–51.

Troy, Leo, and Niel Sheflin. 1985. *Union sourcebook: Membership, structure, finance, directory.* West Orange, N.J.: Industrial Relations and Data Information Services.

II The Effects of Public Sector Bargaining on Wages

6   Union/Nonunion Wage Gaps in the Public Sector

H. Gregg Lewis

This paper presents the results of a survey of micro, ordinary least squares, cross-section studies of the union/nonunion wage gap in the public sector with the aim of providing mean gap estimates for that sector that are more or less comparable to those for the economy as a whole.[1] The survey covers seventy-five studies[2] and deals with several estimation problems involved with interpreting those studies.[3]

6.1 Conceptual Issues

Suppose that the concept of union status for a worker at his job is the following dichotomy: if he is unionized, his wages and working conditions are negotiated for him by a union recognized by his employer and he is covered by the negotiated collective bargaining contract; otherwise, he is nonunion and none of these, not even representation by a union, is present. Furthermore, for the moment, I do not divide the unionized category into subcategories by type of union, whether the worker is a member of the union, and so on.

Hence, denote union status by a single dummy variable $U = 1$ if unionized and zero otherwise. Let W_i be the natural logarithm of the worker's wage where $i = u$ if $U = 1$ and $i = n$ if $U = 0$, and his "wage" is his *hourly* compensation including fringe benefit costs. Then the union/nonunion wage gap for the worker is $W_u - W_n$ and the *mean* gap for a group of workers is $\bar{W}_u - \bar{W}_n$, where $\bar{W}_i$ $(i = u,n)$ denotes the mean of W_i for the group. The estimation problem is obvious: for each worker only W_u or W_n is observed; the other must be estimated.

H. Gregg Lewis is Professor Emeritus, Duke University, and a research associate of the National Bureau of Economic Research.

The most common method of estimation is to fit wage equations by ordinary least squares (OLS) to cross-section (CS) data for a sample of individual workers on their wages, union status, and variables controlling for some of the characteristics of workers and their jobs. Let the wage equation have the following form:

(1) $W = a_n + \Sigma a_{ni}X_i + U[a_u - a_n + \Sigma(a_{ui} - a_{ni})X_i] + e,$

where the a's are the estimated coefficients, the X's are control variables characterizing the worker (sex, race, age, schooling, etc.) and his job (industry, occupation, locality, etc.), and e is the residual. I use the term micro/OLS/CS to describe such equations. Then an estimate of the mean union/nonunion wage gap $\bar{M}$ for the sample of workers is:

(2) $\bar{M} = a_u - a_n + \Sigma(a_{ui} - a_{ni})\bar{X}_i,$

where $\bar{X}_i$ is the sample mean of X_i. (Of course, if the interactions UX_i are all omitted in fitting (1), the mean wage gap estimate $\bar{M}$ is simply the coefficient $a_u - a_n$ of U in the wage equation.)

This micro/OLS/CS wage gap estimate (2), however, may be seriously biased for any of the following reasons:

1. Important wage-explanatory variables that are correlated with the union status variable U have been omitted in fitting (1). This is the union status selectivity problem which has been the subject of numerous empirical studies.

Public sector union/nonunion wage gap estimates are often fitted to data obtained by surveying *establishments*—hospitals, school districts, police and fire departments, and the like—rather than households. Establishment data tend to be more informative of employment or job characteristics than of the worker characteristics in which household surveys are rich, and often pertain to groups of workers (such as police) who are homogeneous by occupation and industry. It is by no means obvious to me that these differences between establishment and household data produce greater rather than smaller selectivity bias in establishment-based gap estimates than in those from household data.[4] In any case, I will make no adjustment of public sector wage gap estimates for selectivity bias, whether the estimates are based on household or on establishment data.

2. The wage and union status variables may be inaccurately measured. Commonly, fringe benefit costs are omitted from the measured wage, and often weekly, monthly, or annual (instead of hourly) wage measures have been used. And sometimes the dependent wage variable is expressed in its natural arithmetic unit rather than in a logarithmic unit. Furthermore, even when union status is dichotomous, workers may be misclassified by union status. In addition, in some contexts,

especially in the public sector, accurate description of union status may require more than the two categories, union and nonunion.

Specifically, in the private sector, with few exceptions, unionized status ($U = 1$) implies that a worker is represented by a union, the union is recognized by the employer as the exclusive bargaining agent for the employee's bargaining unit, the employer is obliged to bargain with the union agent, and the outcome of bargaining is a written collective bargaining agreement or contract.[5] In contrast, in the public sector, unionized status, as I use the term, need not imply the entire complement of union representation, union recognition, bargaining, and a collective bargaining contract. A worker may be represented by a union that the employer has not recognized, will not bargain with, and with whom he will not enter into a contract. Or the employer may send an underling to "meet and confer" with the union representatives. Or he may agree to bargain with the union, but not to enter into a written contract. Or he may recognize the union as exclusive bargaining agent, bargain with it, and enter into a written contract. Thus much more for the public than for the private sector, union status cannot be accurately described by a single union status dummy variable based on union membership or contract coverage.

For example, Ehrenberg, in his study of fire fighters (1973), distinguished between three categories of city fire departments: those with written contracts with the fire fighter's union (IAFF), those in which an IAFF local was present but did not have a contract, and all other cities. Let $U_1 = 1$ if an IAFF local was present (with or without a contract) and zero otherwise; $U_2 = 1$ if the IAFF local had a contract and zero otherwise; and write the fitted micro/OLS/CS wage equation as

(3) $$W = a + \Sigma\, a_i x_i + M_1 U_1 + (M_2 - M_1) U_2.$$

Then M_1 estimates the union/nonunion wage gap for cities in which the IAFF local was present but had no contract, and M_2 estimates the corresponding gap for IAFF cities with a contract. Furthermore the estimated mean gap $\bar{M}$ for both categories of IAFF cities is:

$$\bar{M} = M_1 + \frac{\bar{U}_2}{\bar{U}_1} (M_2 - M_1),$$

where $\bar{U}_i$ ($i = 1,2$) is the mean of U_i over the city observations.

3. The sample may not be a random (self-weighting) sample of the population it purports to represent. For example, in two of the data sets (*National Longitudinal Surveys* [NLS] of older men and the *Panel Study of Income Dynamics* [PSID] sets that include the so-called "nonrandom half") commonly used in wage gap estimation, the sampling design resulted in heavy over-representation of black workers. This

would not matter if the observations were properly weighted or if wage gap estimates were made separately by race and then averaged with proper weights. But if the wage gap for black workers exceeds that for white workers, as it appears to in these data, and if no steps are taken to overcome the oversampling of blacks, the wage gap estimates for the two races combined will tend to be biased upward. In Lewis (1986, 159–61), I made the following adjustment for such bias in the pertinent all-sectors wage gap estimates:

$$\text{Adjustment} = 0.21 \, (\bar{M}_B - \bar{M}_W),$$

where $\bar{M}_B - \bar{M}_W$ was my estimate of the excess of the mean wage gap for black workers over that for white workers. For the NLS data I put $\bar{M}_B - \bar{M}_W$ at almost 0.12 and for the PSID data at about 0.06. Thus the resulting adjustments were -0.024 for the NLS-based estimates and -0.012 for the PSID. Unfortunately, we have very little evidence on which to base corresponding adjustments to wage gap estimates for public sector workers: Shapiro's study (1978) using NLS data and studies by Moore and Raisian (1981; 1982; 1983) using PSID data. However, these studies show much smaller values of $\bar{M}_B - \bar{M}_W$ for the public sector than for the private sector. Therefore, where appropriate, I will make the following adjustments for oversampling of blacks:

NLS data, all sectors: -0.02; public sector: zero
PSID data, all sectors: -0.01; public sector: zero

4. A common comment on union wage effect estimates is that they do not take into account spillover effects from unionized workers to nonunion workers. It is surely true that in the general equilibrium of the economy in the presence of unionism the wages of nonunion workers are affected by what happens in the unionized sector. In that sense there are spillovers from the unionized to the nonunion sector. In what respect do wage gap estimates fail to take these spillovers into account?

Imagine a U.S. economy differing from the actual one only in that antitrust laws have made unions powerless to affect wages. In this economy a worker paid a wage W_i ($i = u$ if $U = 1$, $i = n$ if $U = 0$) in the actual economy would be paid a wage V. The wage *gap* for the worker is $M = W_u - W_n$. His pair of union-induced wage *gains*, however, is $A_i = W_i - V$ where $i = u,n$. Of course, $M = A_u - A_n$. Let $\bar{M}$, $\bar{A}_u$, and $\bar{A}_n$ be the means of M, A_u, and A_n for a group of workers. Then for this group $\bar{M} = \bar{A}_u - \bar{A}_n$ where $\bar{A}_n$ in general will not be zero because of spillovers from the unionized sector of the economy. Hence if M is used as an estimate of the *gain* $\bar{A}_u$, the *gap* estimate $\bar{M}$ can be said to fail to take the spillovers $\bar{A}_n$ into account.[6]

Consider now a special class of spillover effects that I term *parity* effects. For example, a city government whose fire fighters (or police officers, teachers, nurses, etc.) are nonunion has a policy of paying them the "same" wages, conditional on some comparability criteria, as are paid to some "comparable" group of *unionized* workers in the same city or some other city. The reason for the parity policy may be fear that without it the fire fighters will become unionized. Parity effects stemming from such a policy are commonly termed threat effects. The reason for the policy, however, is not critical. What is critical is pursuit of wage parity between a group of nonunion workers and a "comparable" group of unionized workers.

Suppose that in a cross-section study of, say, city fire fighters, the cities practicing such wage parity for their nonunion fire fighters have been identified. Let $U_p = 1$ for a parity city and zero otherwise. Then it is straightforward to make wage gap estimates that take parity effects into account, provided that there are some cities whose fire departments are classified as nonunion *and* nonparity. Return to equation (3). For present purposes modify it by adding U_p as a righthand variable, suppressing U_2, and writing U_1 simply as U.

$$(4) \qquad W = d + \Sigma d_i X_i + P U_p + M_a U.$$

The coefficient P of U_p, expected to be positive, estimates the parity effect—i.e., the wage gap between parity cities and other nonunion cities. Similarly, the coefficient M_a of U estimates the wage gap between union cities and *nonunion, nonparity* cities. Thus M_a takes parity effects into account. The corresponding gap estimate, M_b, that does not take parity effects into account is $M_b = M_a - \bar{U}_p P / (1 - \bar{U})$. Clearly, if $U_p = 1 - U$, U_p and U are perfectly negatively correlated and P and M_a cannot be estimated.

In a cross-section study of fire fighters (or police officers, teachers, etc.) covering a substantial number of cities in which the fire departments were nonunion, positive identification city by city of the parity cities would be tedious and expensive. Indeed, I know of no wage gap studies that have attempted such identification. Instead, students of the subject have used what they regarded as plausible proxies for U_p. I think that it is fair to say that the notion underlying all of these proxies is that parity is practiced if and only if the environment is favorable to collective bargaining by the reference group of workers, here fire fighters. Denote the criterion variable by F where $F = 1$ if the environment is judged to be favorable and zero otherwise. In the Zax study (1985) of city workers by department (fire, police, etc.), $F = 1$ if and only if the city bargained with at least one union that was recognized by the city as the bargaining agent for some group of city workers. In the Freeman, Ichniowski, Lauer study (1985) of city police departments, $F = 1$ if and only if state or local law permitted collective bargaining between the city and a union or unions representing its police officers. In numerous other studies, $F = 1$ for the *reference* group if and only if the extent of unionism (fraction unionized) y of some *comparison* group of workers exceeded some threshold level $y_T \geq 0$.

For any specification of F, the city fire departments may be divided into four mutually exclusive and exhaustive classes as follows:

Parity: $U_p = 1$ if and only if $U = 0$, $F = 1$;

Weak union: $U_w = 1$ if and only if $U = 1$, $F = 0$;

Strong union: $U_s = 1$ if and only if $U = F = 1$;

Nonunion, nonparity: if and only if $U = F = 0$.

(The weak union class may be empty, $\bar{U}_w = 0$. In that event, $U_s = U$. But none of the other three classes may be empty; if any of the three is an empty class, P and M_a cannot be estimated from the data.) Then the parity effect and the union/nonunion wage gap M_a that takes the parity effect into account may be estimated from either of the following fitted equations:

(5a) $$W = d + \Sigma d_i X_i + P U_p + M_w U_w + M_s U_s,$$

(5b) $$W = d + \Sigma d_i X_i + PF + M_w U + (M_s - M_w - P) I,$$

where $I \equiv UF$ is the interaction of U and F. In these equations P is the parity effect estimate and M_w (weak union) and M_s (strong union) are union/nonunion wage gap estimates that take parity into account. $M_a \equiv (\bar{U}_w M_w + \bar{U}_s M_s)/\bar{U}$ is the mean gap estimate taking account of parity and $M_b = M_a - \bar{U}_p P /(1 - \bar{U})$ is the corresponding estimate that does not take account of parity. If the weak union class is empty ($\bar{U}_w = 0$), then (5a) and (5b) become:

(6a) $$W = d + \Sigma d_i X_i + P U_p + M_a U,$$

(6b) $$W = d + \Sigma d_i X_i + PF + (M_a - P) U.$$

Suppose that the weak union class is not empty and that the fitted wage equation is like (5b) except that the interaction variable $I \equiv UF$ is omitted. Let b_U and b_F be the estimated coefficients of U and F in such an equation. Then b_F is a biased estimate of P and b_U is a biased estimate of $M_a - P$. In order to estimate the size of the biases by the omitted variable theorem I assume that $0 \leq M_w \leq M_s$ and I ignore correlations of U, F, and I with the control X's. Then

$$b_F - \frac{b_U B_{IF}}{B_{IU}} \leq P \leq \frac{b_F}{1 - B_{IF}},$$

(7) $$\frac{\bar{U}_s}{\bar{U}} \left[b_F + \frac{b_U (1 - B_{IF})}{B_{IU}} \right] \leq M_a \leq b_U + \frac{b_F B_{IU}}{1 - B_{IF}},$$

$$DB_{IF} = \bar{U}_w \bar{U}_s (1 - \bar{U}); \quad DB_{IU} = \bar{U}_p \bar{U}_s (1 - \bar{F}), \text{ where}$$

$$D = \bar{U}\bar{F}(1 - \bar{U}_p - \bar{U}_w) - (\bar{U}_s)^2 > 0; \quad M_b = M_a - \frac{\bar{U}_p P}{1 - \bar{U}},$$

where the overhead bars denote means and $\bar{U} = \bar{U}_w + \bar{U}_s$ and $\bar{F} = \bar{U}_p + \bar{U}_s$. As $\bar{U}_w/\bar{U} = (\bar{U} - \bar{U}_s)/\bar{U}$ goes to zero, B_{IF} goes to zero and B_{IU} to unity.

In going from equation (3) to equations (5a), (5b), (6a) and (6b) I suppressed the distinction in equation (3) between union cities with a written collective bargaining contract ($U_2 = 1$ in equation [3]) and other union cities ($U_1 - U_2 = 1$ in equation [3]). In what follows in this paragraph I maintain rather than suppress this distinction. Write U_0 for $U_1 - U_2$ and assume for simplicity in the analysis that $F = 1$ whenever U_0 or U_1 is unity. Then (6b) with the following modification is applicable:

$$(8) \qquad W = d + \Sigma d_i X_i + PF + (M_0 - P)U_0 + (M_2 - P)U_2,$$

$$M_a = (\bar{U}_0 M_0 + \bar{U}_2 M_2)/\bar{U}; \quad \bar{U} = \bar{U}_0 + \bar{U}_2,$$

where M_0, M_2, and M_a are union/nonunion wage gap estimates that take account of parity. Suppose, however, that in fitting (8) the variable U_0 is omitted. Denote the resulting coefficients of F and U_2 by b_F and b_2, respectively. It seems reasonable to assume that $P < M_0 < M_2$. Then if correlations of U_0, U_2, and F with the X's are ignored, it follows from the omitted variable theorem that $M_2 = b_F + b_2$ and $b_F - \bar{U}_0 b_2/\bar{U}_p < P < b_F$. That is, the coefficient b_F of F in the fitted equation is an overestimate of the parity effect. This is to be expected (if $M_0 > P$) since the effect of omitting U_0 is to classify union cities without a written contract as parity cities. With the above reasoning, however, the estimate $M_2 = b_F + b_2$ is not biased and takes parity into account. I presume that $M_a < b_F + b_2$.

Return now to equation (6b) and assume that in fitting this equation F, but not U or $I = UF$, has been omitted. Then it is impossible to derive an estimate of the parity effect from the fitted equation. However, $M_b = b_U + \bar{U}_s b_I/\bar{U}$ where b_U and b_I are the coefficients of U and I, respectively.

I mentioned earlier that in some studies $F = 1$ if and only if the extent of unionism y of some specified comparison group of workers exceeded a threshold level $y_T \geq 0$. To simplify what follows assume that $\bar{U}_w = 0$ so that equation (5b) is applicable. In (5b) let P and M_a be linear functions of the chosen y-variable on $y > y_T$: $P = g + g_y y$; $M_a - P = h + h_y y$. Then (5b) becomes

$$(9) \qquad W = d + \Sigma d_i X_i + gF + g_y Fy + hU + h_y Uy.$$

A substantial number of studies reported wage equations resembling (9) in that they included U, a y-variable, and sometimes its interaction Uy with union status U, but differing from (9) in omitting F and Fy. According to (9) the expected wage in a nonunion, nonparity city is $W_n = d + \Sigma d_i X_i$, in a parity city it is $W_p = W_n + g + g_y y$, and in a union city it is $W_u = W_p + h + h_y y$. But suppose that in (9) F is set equal to unity so that the equation reads

(10) $W = (d + g) + \Sigma d_i X_i + g_y y + hU + h_y Uy.$

Then because the coefficient g of F in (9) disappears into the intercept term $d + g$ in (10), W_n, W_p, and, therefore, $P = W_p - W_n$ and $M_a = P + h + h_y y$ cannot be estimated from (10). In effect (10) implicitly assumes that $F = 1$, i.e., there are no nonunion, nonparity cities. But then, as I remarked early on in this section, parity effects cannot be estimated.

The Zax study (1985), is the only study, to the best of my knowledge, of either private sector or public sector union/nonunion wage gaps in which the wage equations were modeled so as to permit straightforward estimation of the parity effects. His study covered a nationwide sample of 889 cities in the years 1975, 1977, and 1979 and, within each city and year, four departments (or department groups): police, fire, sanitation, and other noneducational groups. The city*year*department observations were pooled and the wage equations included dummy variables for year and department.

Within each city and year the four departments were classified by union status as follows:

$U0 = 1$ if and only if some workers in the department were union members, but the union was not recognized by the city for bargaining purposes.

$UR = 1$ if and only if some workers in the department were union members *and* the union was legally recognized by the city for bargaining purposes.

$NU = 1$ if and only if $U0 = UR = 0$.

In addition the cities in each year were classified into two categories (favorable or unfavorable to collective bargaining with its employees) by the dummy variable: $F = 1$ if and only if the city has legally recognized at least one union as bargaining agent for some of its employees. Then in each year the city*department observations were divided into five mutually exclusive union status classes as follows:

Parity: $U_p = 1$ if $U0 = UR = 1 - F = 0$;
Weak union: $U_w = 1$ if $F = 1 - U0 = 0$;
Medium union: $U_m = 1$ if $U0 = F = 1$;
Strong union: $U_s = 1$ if $UR = 1$;
Nonunion, nonparity: if $U0 = UR = F = 0$, the omitted base group in the wage equations.

In addition to the dummy variables for year (2), department (4), and union status (4), the fitted wage equation included region, city-size, income, alternative wage, and demographic variables. Two wage measures, the conventional hourly wage (HW) and hourly total compensation (HC) were used.

The estimated coefficients (in logarithmic units) of the union status variables were:

Line	Union Status	Dependent Variable	
		HW	HC
1	Parity (U_p)	.032	.048
2	Weak union (U_w)	.037	.041
3	Medium union (U_m)	.060	.082
4	Strong union (U_s)	.081	.107
5	Mean, parity adjusted (M_a)	.073	.097
6	Mean, not so adjusted (M_b)	.066	.086

The wage gap estimates on lines 1–4 take parity effects into account in the sense that the base of the wage comparisons is the nonunion, nonparity observation. The parity effect itself, on line 1, though small, is roughly as large as the "weak union" gap on line 2. The parity adjusted mean (M_a) is the weighted mean of the corresponding figures on lines 2–4. The parity unadjusted mean (M_b) is the estimated (weighted) mean wage gap between the three unionized groups (weak, medium, and strong) and *all* nonunion observations including the parity observations. The excess of M_a over M_b is a quite modest 0.01. This is the best estimate that I have of the adjustment of public sector wage gap estimates to take parity effects into account.

6.2 Survey of Broad Coverage Wage Gap Estimates

In this section I summarize the wage gap estimates that I have drawn from micro/OLS/CS wage equations and related data reported in (or obtained from the authors of) studies with moderately broad to broad coverage of public sector workers. All of the wage equations were fitted to household survey data for individual workers.

Table 6.1 briefly describes these twenty-two studies. Column 2 identifies each study by author and date of publication; column 3 gives the source of the household survey data that were used; column 4 gives the year or years to which the wage gap estimates pertain; while column 5 is a short and somewhat incomplete description of the *worker* coverage of the wage gap estimates. (All of the studies exclude workers with missing data, the self-employed, and unpaid family workers. Most of them also exclude farm and private household workers.) In the nine studies listed on the first eleven lines of the table, the wage gap estimates for the public sector pertain to the whole of that sector as indicated by "All" in column 6. In the remaining thirteen studies the public sector gap estimates pertain only to the parts of the public sector identified in column 6. For example, the public sector gap estimates from Antos (1980), line 13, are for workers employed in the public

Table 6.1   Estimates of Public Sector and All-Sector Wage Gaps of Broad Coverage Studies

(1) Line No.	(2) Study	(3) Data Source	(4) Year	(5) Worker Coverage	(6) Public Sector	(7) Wage Gap Estimate Public	(8) Wage Gap Estimate All	(9) Gap Difference Unadjusted	(10) Gap Difference Adjusted
1	Freeman & Leonard (1985)	CPS	1973	All	All	.12	.17	.05	.05
2		CPS	1983	All	All	.08	.15	.07	.07
3		CPS	1984	All	All	.11	.18	.07	.07
4	Johnson & Solon (1984)	CPS	1978	All	All	.13	.20	.07	.07
5	Smith (1976, 1977a)	CPS	1973	All	All	.10/.12	.21/.22	.10/.11	.10/.11
6	Smith (1977b)	CPS	1975	All	All	.09/.11	.19/.19	.08/.10	.08/.10
7	Ashenfelter (1978)	CPS	1973	BC	All	.18	.22	.04	.01
8		CPS	1975	BC	All	.18	.23	.05	.02
9	Hirsch & Rufolo (1982)	NLS	1971	M 50—64	All	−.04	.09	.13	.08
10	Johnson (1983)	CPS	1973–76	34 SMSAs	All	.09	.11	.02	.02
11	Shapiro (1978)	NLS	1971	M 50—64	All	.03	.12	.09	.06
12	Antos (1983)	CPS	1979	WC	Pub	.09/.12	.05/.07	−.05/−.04	−.02/−.01
13	Antos (1980)	CPS	1976	All	Pub	.19	.19	.00	.00
14	Asher & Popkin (1984)	CPS	1979	All	Pub	.07	.09	.02	.02
15	Holzer (1982)	CPS	1978	M 16—64	Pub	.11	.14	.03	.00
16	Mellow (1983)	CPS	1978	All	Pub	.18	.19	.01	.01
17	Perloff & Wachter (1984)	CPS	1979	All	Pub	.10/.12	.08/.10	−.02/−.02	−.02/−.02
18		CPS	1978	All	Pub	.12	.16	.04	.04
19	Hamermesh (1975)	SCF	1968	WM HH	GME	.06	.15	.09	.07
20	Kalachek & Raines (1976)	NLS	1969	M 48–62	Gov	.04	.10	.15	.10
21	Mincer (1983)	PSID	1968–78	WM	GE	.14	.13	−.01	−.03
22	Moore (1980)	PSID	1970	FT HH	GE	.23	.19	−.04	−.05

23	Moore & Raisian (1981)	PSID	1967–77	M HH	GE	.11	.21	.09	.05
24	Moore & Raisian (1982, 1983)	PSID	1967	M HH	Gov	.17	.22	.05	.01
25		PSID	1968	M HH	Gov	.10	.21	.11	.07
26		PSID	1969	M HH	Gov	.06	.18	.12	.08
27		PSID	1970	M HH	Gov	.11	.19	.08	.04
28		PSID	1971	M HH	Gov	.05	.23	.18	.14
29		PSID	1972	M HH	Gov	.00	.19	.19	.15
30		PSID	1973	M HH	Gov	.16	.19	.05	.01
31		PSID	1974	M HH	Gov	.14	.21	.07	.03
32		PSID	1975	M HH	Gov	.17	.23	.06	.02
33		PSID	1976	M HH	Gov	.15	.25	.10	.06
34		PSID	1977	M HH	Gov	.12	.23	.11	.07
35		PSID	1967–77	M HH	Gov	.11	.21	.10	.06

Notes:

Column 3: Lines 1–8, 10, 12–18: data source is *Current Population Survey*.
Lines 9, 11, 20: data source is *National Longitudinal Survey*.
Line 19: data source is *Survey of Consumer Finances*.
Lines 21–35: data source is *Panel Study of Income Dynamics*.

Column 5: BC = blue-collar
WC = white-collar
M = male
WM = white male
HH = household head
M HH = male, household head
WM HH = white male, household head
FT HH = full-time, household head
M 50–64 = male, 50–64 years old
M 16–64 = male, 16–64 years old
M 48–62 = male, 48–62 years old
SMSA = Standard Metropolitan Statistical Area

Column 6: Pub = public administration industry
Gov = government industry
GE = government industry and educational services industry
GME = government industry, medical services industry and educational services industry

administration industry in the *Current Population Survey* (CPS) industry classification. The public sector and matching all-sector wage gap estimates that I have retrieved from these twenty-two studies are summarized in columns 7 and 8, while the differences in the gap estimates between the public sector and the all-sector are given in columns 9 and 10.

The table presents the studies in four groupings. Lines 1–6 are studies in which the coverage of wage and salary workers has few major exclusions and gap estimates are available for the whole of the public sector as well as the private sector. In this respect these studies provide the most complete picture of recent differences between the public and private sector in the union/nonunion wage gap. Lines 7–11 give wage gap estimates for the public sector that pertain to the whole of that sector but where the coverage of wage and salary workers is incomplete: Ashenfelter (1978), blue-collar workers; Hirsch and Rufolo (1982) and Shapiro (1978), males 50–64 years of age; and Hirsch and Rufolo (1982), workers in large standard metropolitan areas. The six studies on lines 12–18 pertain only to public administration, which covers about one-third of the whole public sector. In addition, Antos (1983) on line 12 covers only white-collar workers and Holzer (1982) on line 15 only male workers. The seven studies listed on lines 19–35 have wage gap estimates that pertain to less than the whole of the public sector and the coverage of wage and salary workers is incomplete: Hamermesh (1975) and Mincer (1983), white males; Kalachek and Raines (1976), and Moore and Raisian (1981; 1982; 1983), males; and Moore (1980), full-time household heads.

I turn now to the central question of this paper: Is the mean wage gap in the public sector as large or larger than that in all sectors of the economy? To answer this, turn to the estimates in columns 9 and 10 of the all-sector minus public sector gap differences for the broadest coverage of wage and salary workers and of public sector workers. The adjusted gap differences in column 10 incorporate the following adjustments to those in column 9 for exclusions of worker coverage and for overweighting of black workers. (See section 6.3 below for a discussion of wage gaps for the different groups that underlie these adjustments):

1. Overweighting of blacks: NLS data: subtract 0.02 (lines 9 and 20)
   PSID data: subtract 0.01 (lines 22–35)
2. Exclusion of white-collar workers: Subtract 0.03 (lines 7 and 8)
3. Exclusion of blue-collar workers: Add 0.03 (line 12)
4. Exclusion of females: Subtract 0.03 (lines 9, 11, 15, 19–21, 23–35)
5. Exclusion of black males: Add 0.01 (lines 19 and 20)

I have too little information to adjust lines 9, 11, and 20 for their age exclusions; lines 9 and 10 for excluding workers outside of large SMSA's; lines 19 and 22–35 for excluding those who are not household heads; and line 22 for the restriction to full-time workers.

The adjusted gap differences in column 10 range from −0.05 to 0.15 and show little or no trend. Therefore, in judging the magnitude of the mean gap difference I will ignore date differences. The mean of the column 10 figures (using midpoints of estimate ranges) on lines 1–35 is 0.044 and the standard deviation is 0.045. (This mean, 0.044, gives disproportional weight to authorships providing estimates for more than one date. When figures are first averaged within each authorship and each authorship is represented by this average, the mean is 0.033.)

The best of the estimates in terms of worker and public sector coverage are those on lines 1–6. The adjusted gap differences on these lines average 0.077 (counting each authorship once). Next best in this respect are those on lines 7–11 which average 0.044. (The corresponding average of the *unadjusted* figures, however, is 0.071.)

The all-sector minus public sector gap differences on lines 12–35 may be seriously flawed, in my judgment, by incomplete coverage of the public sector. As I mentioned, on lines 12–18 the gap estimates for the public sector pertain only to the public administration industry which employs only about one-third of the public sector work force. The column 10 figures on lines 12–18 average 0.008. Similarly, the public sector wage gap estimates on lines 19–35 all cover the government industry which I presume is mainly public administration. Those on lines 19 and 21–23 also cover educational services, and on line 19 medical services are included. I strongly suspect that both the educational services and medical services industries include private as well as public workers. The mean of the column 10 figures on lines 19–35 is 0.029 (counting each authorship only once). The corresponding mean of the unadjusted figures in column 9 is 0.057. Thus, on the basis of the adjusted estimates in column 10 of Table 6.1, I put the excess of the mean wage gap in all sectors over that in the public sector in the range 0.04 to 0.08. This gives rather greater weight to lines 1–11 than to lines 12–35.

Six studies in table 6.1 (namely, Smith [1976, 1977a, 1977b] on lines 5 and 6; Asher and Popkin [1984] on line 14; and Perloff and Wachter [1984] on line 20) and one study not covered in the table (Freeman, 1984) reported public sector wage gap estimates by level of government—federal, state, and local. (In Kalachek and Raines [1976], state and local were combined.) All of the studies showed that the wage gap for the federal government was below the average gap for all levels of government. The five studies that reported separate estimates for local governments all placed the wage gap for local governments above the average for all levels of government. Estimates drawn from these five studies of the excess of the mean gap for local governments over that for all government levels are shown below.

Study	Year	Coverage	Excess
Smith (1976; 1977a)	1973	All	.00/.02
Smith (1977b)	1975	All	.02/.03
Asher and Popkin (1984)	1979	Public Admin.	.04
Perloff and Wachter (1984)	1978	Public Admin.	.06
Freeman (1984)	1973	Public Admin.	.05
Freeman (1984)	1981	Public Admin.	.02

These estimates average 0.03 to 0.04. They suggest that the adjusted mean wage gap for local government workers was in the range 0.10 to 0.15 in 1967–79. Thus I cannot rule out the possibility that the mean union/nonunion wage gap for the local government sector was as great as that for all U.S. wage and salary workers.

6.3   Differences in Union/Nonunion Wage Gaps by Worker and Employment Characteristics

I turn next to the question: Does the union/nonunion wage gap vary in the same way in the public sector as in the private sector with respect to such worker and employment characteristics as sex, race, and occupation? Eight of the studies in table 6.1 provide information on the wage gap difference by sex (male minus female). Table 6.2 is a tabulation of this information. For white-collar workers (line 4), clerks (line 11), and salaried workers in SMSA's (line 23) the estimated male minus female gap difference on the average is negative and of about the same numerical size in both the public and private sectors. In contrast, for blue-collar workers (lines 5, 19, and 20) and hourly-rated workers (line 22) this gap difference on the average is positive in the private sector, negative in the public sector, and the between-sector difference is substantial. For both white- and blue-collar workers taken together (lines 1–3, 6, 7, 15, 21, and 24) the male minus female gap difference in the public sector ranges from −0.10 to −0.01 and averages about −0.05, while for all-sectors the range is −0.01 to 0.03 and the average is about 0.01. Thus Table 6.2 provides substantial evidence that the gap difference by sex varies considerably with collar color and sector (public vs. private). There is also a somewhat weak suggestion in the table that the gap difference by sex varies with the "level" of government within the public sector.

Consider now the estimates of the wage gap difference by race (white minus black) summarized in table 6.3. In Lewis (1986, 119–25), I observed that the estimates of the white minus black gap difference (for

Table 6.2   Wage Gap Differences by Sex (Male minus Female) (Public Sector and All-Sector)

(1) Line No.	(2) Study	(3) Year	(4) Worker Coverage	(5) Public Sector	(6) Gap Difference Public	(7) Gap Difference All
1	Freeman & Leonard (1985)	1973	All	All	−.01	.02
2		1983	All	All	−.03	.03
3		1984	All	All	−.04	.00
4		1984	White-collar	All	−.07	−.06
5		1984	Blue-collar	All	−.04	.02
6	Johnson & Solon (1984)	1978	All	All	−.04	.02
7	Smith (1976, 1977a)	1973	All	All	−.02	.03
8		1973	All	Federal	−.07/−.03	.03
9		1973	All	State	.00/.04	.03
10		1973	All	Local	−.03/.01	.03
11	Smith (1976)	1973	Clerks	All	−.02	−.04
12		1973	Clerks	Federal	.00/.01	−.04
13		1973	Clerks	State	.22	−.04
14		1973	Clerks	Local	−.05	−.04
15	Smith (1977b)	1975	All	All	−.08/−.06	−.01/.00
16		1975	All	Federal	−.17/−.11	−.01/.00
17		1975	All	State	−.13/−.09	−.01/.00
18		1975	All	Local	−.03/.00	−.01/.00
19	Ashenfelter (1978)	1973	Blue-collar	All	.05	.06
20		1975	Blue-collar	All	−.13	.04
21	Johnson (1983)	1973–76	SMSA's	All	−.07	.00
22		1973–76	SMSA's, hourly	All	−.13	.01
23		1973–76	SMSA's, salaried	All	−.03	−.01
24	Antos et.al. (1980)	1976	All	Pubad	−.10	.00

Notes: Column 4: SMSA = Standard Metropolitan Statistical Area.
Column 5: Pubad = public administration industry.
Line 8: The range in column 6 covers three estimates.
Lines 9, 10, 12, 15–19: The ranges in columns 6 and 7 cover two estimates.

Table 6.3   **Wage Gap Differences by Race (White minus Black) (Public Sector and All-Sector)**

(1)	(2)	(3)	(4)	(5)	(6)	(7)
					Gap Difference	
Line No.	Study	Year	Worker Coverage	Public Sector	Public	All
1	Ashenfelter (1978)	1973	BC	All	-.12	.01
2		1973	Male BC	All	-.11	-.01
3		1973	Male craftsmen	All	-.16	.04
4		1973	Male operatives	All	-.10	-.06
5		1973	Male laborers	All	-.09	.06
6		1975	BC	All	-.02	-.01
7		1975	Male BC	All	-.01	-.02
8		1975	Male craftsmen	All	.01	.02
9		1975	Male operatives	All	-.05	-.03
10		1975	Male laborers	All	.02	-.01
11	Shapiro (1978)	1971	Male, 50-64	All	-.05	-.15
12		1971	Male, 50-64, BC	All	.10	-.04
13		1971	Male, 50-64, WC	All	-.18	-.29
14	Moore & Raisian (1982;1983)	1967-77	Male HH	Gov	-.05	-.09
15	Moore & Raisian (1981)	1967-77	Male HH	Gov & Ed	-.02	-.08
16		1967-77	Male HH	Ed	-.05	-.08
17		1967-77	Male HH	Gov	.02	-.08

Notes: Column 4: BC = blue-collar, WC = white-collar, HH = household head.
Column 5: Gov = government industry, Ed = educational services industry.
Lines 1-10: data source is *Current Population Survey*.
Lines 11-13: data source is *National Longitudinal Survey*.
Lines 14-17: data source is *Panel Study of Income Dynamics*.

all sectors) tended to differ substantially by data source. According to the CPS data the estimated mean difference was close to zero, while other data sources pointed to a mean gap difference of -0.05 to -0.10. The white minus black gap difference estimates in Table 6.3 also differ by data source. The estimates on lines 1–10 come from CPS data. The all-sector figures on lines 1 and 2 (for 1973) and lines 6 and 7 (1975) are close to zero. The corresponding figures for the public sector for 1973, however, are -0.12 and -0.11, but those for 1975 are close to zero.

The estimates on lines 11–17, based on other sources of data and only for males tell a rather different story. For all sectors the white minus black gap difference estimates on lines 11, 14, and 15 average about -0.11 in all sectors and about -0.04 in the public sector. That is, the estimated black wage gap exceeds that for whites by considerably less in the public than in the private sector, according to data from the NLS and the PSID.

I turn now to wage gap differences by collar-color (white-collar minus blue-collar). Table 6.4 summarizes the pertinent estimates. I have included Holzer's study (1982) though the gap differences in this study are for salaried vs. hourly-rated workers. First note that all of the figures in columns 6 and 7 are negative. In both the public and private sectors the estimated white-collar wage gap is smaller than that for blue-collar workers, for both males and females, blacks and whites. Furthermore, the excess of the blue-collar gap over the white-collar gap in the public sector is less than or equal to that in all sectors except on lines 7–9 from Shapiro's study (1978). Indeed, the figures for that study are clearly outliers and in what follows I ignore them.

Freeman and Leonard (1985) and Johnson (1983) agree that for females the occupational gap difference is about the same in the public and private sectors, but for male workers the blue-collar minus white-collar gap difference is smaller in the public than in the private sector. On lines 2, 5, 10, 13, 14, 16, and 18, all pertaining to male workers, the figures in column 6 for the public sector range from -0.15 to -0.02 and average about -0.08, while those in column 7 for all sectors range from -0.25 to -0.15 and average about -0.22 or about 0.14 larger numerically than in the public sector. Thus there is some evidence that at least for males, the blue-collar minus white-collar gap difference is substantially larger in the private than in the public sector.

In addition to analyzing union/nonunion wage gaps by sex, race, and collar-color, I have also examined estimates of gaps for several detailed occupations, including fire fighters, police, hospital workers, and teachers. My conclusions from this analysis (presented in the longer conference paper from which this chapter is drawn) can be summarized briefly:

Table 6.4   Wage Gap Differences by Occupation (White-collar minus Blue-collar) (Public Sector and All-Sectors)

(1) Line No.	(2) Study	(3) Year	(4) Worker Coverage	(5) Public Sector	(6) Gap Difference Public	(7) Gap Difference All
1	Freeman & Leonard (1985)	1984	All	All	−.07	−.10
2		1984	Male	All	−.10	−.15
3		1984	Female	All	−.07	−.07
4	Johnson (1983)	1973–76	SMSA's	All	−.08	−.16
5		1973–76	SMSA's, male	All	−.04	−.16
6		1973–76	SMSA's, female	All	−.14	−.14
7	Shapiro (1978)	1971	Male, 50–64	All	−.39	−.35
8		1971	M 50–64, white	All	−.42	−.35
9		1971	M 50–64, black	All	−.14	−.10
10	Holzer (1982)	1978	Male, 16–64	Pubad	−.02	−.22
11		1978	Male, 16–24	Pubad	−.06	−.16
12		1978	Male, 25–64	Pubad	−.01	−.20
13	Moore & Raisian (1982;1983)	1967–77	Male HH	Gov	−.15	−.23
14	Moore & Raisian (1981)	1967–77	Male HH	Gov & Ed	−.10	−.25
15		1967–77	Male HH, white	Gov & Ed	−.09	−.23
16		1967–77	Male HH	Ed	−.09	−.25
17		1967–77	Male HH, white	Ed	−.03	−.23
18		1967–77	Male HH	Gov	−.09	−.25
19		1967–77	Male HH, white	Gov	−.12	−.23

Notes: Column 4: SMSA = Standard Metropolitan Statistical Area, M 50–64 = males 50–64 years old, HH = household head.

Column 5: Pubad = public administration industry, Gov = government industry, Ed = educational services industry.

Lines 4–6: Gap differences in columns 6 and 7 are salaried minus hourly rated.

1. Studies of fire fighters indicate that in the decade 1966–76, the union/nonunion wage gap may have trended upward, but even in 1976 it was probably below the corresponding average gap for all U.S. wage and salary workers. For police, wage gap estimates drawn from nine studies put the mean gap throughout the decade 1971–81 at roughly .05 below the all-worker gap. But are fire fighters and police officers really average U.S. workers? In particular, if the more apt comparison is with blue-collar rather than white-collar workers, the mean wage gaps for both police and fire fighters are even lower, relative to the more apt comparison group, than the above figures put it.

2. For public sector hospital workers, I estimate that the mean gap is about two-thirds as large as the corresponding mean for all U.S. wage and salary workers in the same period. However, the public-sector mean wage gaps for LPN's, technicians, and nonprofessionals exceeded their private sector counterparts.

3. For teachers, wage gap estimates drawn from nineteen studies indicate that until the middle 1970's, the mean gap for teachers was below that for all U.S. wage and salary workers, by about 0.05. In terms of work force mix, however, comparing the average teacher to the average U.S. wage and salary worker is misleading. Teachers are skilled white-collar workers. In Lewis (1986, 128 and 164) I estimated that the mean wage gap for all white-collar workers was about 0.05 *below* that for all workers. Thus even before 1976 the mean wage gap for teachers may have been roughly as high as that for private sector *white-collar* workers.

6.4 Conclusion

In terms of worker coverage in the public sector, the best of the public sector gap estimates are those drawn from the twenty-two studies covered in table 6.1. These studies indicate that the mean wage gap (after adjustments for fringes and work force mix) in the public sector in 1973–84 moved approximately parallel to that in all sectors, but at a level lower by about 0.03 to 0.07. I estimate that the public sector gap in this period averaged about 0.08 to 0.12, which is surely not negligible.

In terms of union/nonunion wage gaps for different groups of workers, there is, I judge, much variation in the union/nonunion wage gap across groups of workers within each of the two sectors, public and private. Furthermore, the variation in the public sector does not parallel in all of its detail that in the private sector. Thus, though the public sector gaps are typically somewhat below their private sector counterparts, there are important exceptions to this difference especially among employees of local governments: public school teachers, clerical workers, refuse collectors, local transit bus drivers, licensed practical nurses, hospital technicians, nonprofessional hospital workers, and undoubtedly some others.

Notes

1. For reasons explained in Lewis (1986), I believe that neither simultaneous equations nor panel data estimates of union wage effects are sufficiently reliable to be included in a survey of this type.

2. There have been several earlier surveys of public sector wage gap estimates: Lewin 1977; Lewin, Horton, and Kuhn 1979; Honadle 1981; Mitchell 1983; Ehrenberg and Schwarz 1983; and Freeman 1984. None of the first four of these surveys covered as many as twenty public sector wage gap studies. Ehrenberg and Schwarz covered thirty-five such studies and Freeman forty. The six surveys taken together cited public sector wage gap estimates drawn from fifty studies. For reasons stated in section 6.1, I have ignored seventeen of these fifty studies while adding forty-two studies that I presume were not covered in these earlier surveys either because of their newness or because their public sector wage gap estimates were well hidden.

The general tenor of the conclusions drawn by the authors of these six studies from the wage gap estimates surveyed was that the average wage gap in the public sector, though positive, was smaller than that in the private sector. For example, Ehrenberg and Schwarz (1983, 10) commented that: "The estimated relative wage differentials associated with union membership or collective bargaining coverage are typically smaller than 10 percent and rarely exceed 20 percent. These estimates are considerably lower than the estimates obtained from private sector studies and they suggest that the relative wage effects of unions have been less in the public sector than the private sector." And Freeman (1984, 31–33), referring to the public sector, stated that: "In the absence of a comprehensive study of various data sets, definitions of government employees, and different models, the safest conclusions are that the union effects differ significantly over time and are generally smaller than those in the private sector (for any of the reasons given earlier) but are far from negligible."

3. In the longer conference paper from which this is taken I consider several estimation problems that I do not deal with in this chapter. These include fringe benefit costs omitted from most studies, public sector hours gaps, and the skill mix of work forces. Detailed consideration of these problems shows that their resolution does not substantively affect the results given here.

4. Pages 183 and 185 of Lewis (1986) provide some support for this view.

5. Of course, a worker may be *covered* by a contract and *not* be a *member* of the covering union, but there are relatively so few *covered nonmembers,* except among young workers, that it makes little differences in wage gap estimates whether the union status dichotomy is for contract coverage or union membership. For evidence see Lewis (1986, 109–11).

6. In Lewis (1986, 16–18) I discuss several studies that I read as claiming to estimate wage gains $\bar{A}_n$ from the same cross-sectional wage equations that

were used to estimate wage gaps $\bar{M}$. In these studies the fitted wage equations were of the form:

$$\hat{W} = a_n + \Sigma a_{ni}X_i + \Sigma b_{nj}y_j + U[(a_u - a_n) + \Sigma(a_{ui} - a_{ni})X_i + \Sigma(b_{uj} - b_{nj})y_j],$$

where $\hat{W}$ is the estimated value of W and the y variables are extent of unionism (fraction unionized) variables by industry and/or occupation and/or locality, etc. I interpret these studies as implicitly estimating $\hat{V}$ by setting U and the y's equal to zero in the equation for $\hat{W}$ above, so that:

$$\hat{V} = a_n + \Sigma a_{ni}X_i; \; \hat{A}_n = \Sigma b_{nj}y_j.$$

This procedure assumes that, conditional on the control variable X's, *all* workers in the hypothetical economy would be paid a wage V equal to the wage W that is paid in the actual economy to nonunion workers ($U = 0$) in nonunion sectors (y's $= 0$). I know of no compelling analytical reasons or convincing empirical evidence supporting this assumption. Furthermore, in Lewis (1986, 38–44, 147–53), I present evidence that the estimated coefficients b_{nj} on the y variables in the above equations for W and A are quite sensitive to the choices of the set of y variables, the specification of the control X's, and the worker coverage in the W equation. I am not arguing that A_n cannot be estimated; however, I know of no estimates of A_n that command widespread confidence among students of U.S. unionism.

References

Adamache, Killard W., and Frank A. Sloan. 1982. Unions and hospitals: Some unresolved issues. *Journal of Health Economics* 1:81–108.

Antos, Joseph R. 1983. Union effects on white-collar compensation. *Industrial and Labor Relations Review* 36:461–79.

Antos, Joseph R., Mark Chandler, and Wesley Mellow. 1980. Sex differences in union membership. *Industrial and Labor Relations Review* 33:162–69.

Ashenfelter, Orley. 1971. The effect of unionization on wages in the public sector: The case of fire fighters. *Industrial and Labor Relations Review* 24:191–202.

———. 1978. Union relative wage effects: New evidence and a survey of their implications for wage inflation. In *Econometric contributions to public policy,* ed. R. Stone and W. Peterson. New York: St. Martins Press.

Asher, Martin, and Joel Popkin. 1984. The effect of gender and race differentials on public-private wage comparisons: A study of postal workers. *Industrial and Labor Relations Review* 38:16–25.

Baird, Robert N., and John H. Landon. 1972. The effects of collective bargaining on public school teachers' salaries: Comment. *Industrial and Labor Relations Review* 25:410–17.

Balkin, David B. 1984. The effect of unions on the compensation of secretaries in municipal government. *Journal of Collective Negotiations in the Public Sector* 13:29–37.

Bartel, Ann, and David Lewin. 1981. Wages and unionism in the public sector: The case of police. *Review of Economics and Statistics* 63:53–59.

Baugh, William H., and Joe A. Stone. 1982. Teachers, unions, and wages in the 1970s: Unionism now pays. *Industrial and Labor Relations Review* 35:368–76.

Becker, Brian E. 1979. Union impact on wages and fringe benefits of hospital nonprofessionals. *Quarterly Review of Economics and Business* 19:27–44.

Cain, Glen G., Brian E. Becker, Catherine G. McLaughlin, and Albert E. Schwenk. 1981. The effect of unions on wages in hospitals. *Research in Labor Economics* 4:191–320.

Chambers, Jay G. 1977. The impact of collective bargaining for teachers on resource allocation in public school districts. *Journal of Urban Economics* 4:324–39.

———. 1981. The impact of bargaining and bargaining statutes on the earnings of public school teachers: A comparison in California and Missouri. *Economics of Education Review* 1:467–81.

Cole, Raymond E. 1977. Some salary effects on Arkansas teachers of professional negotiations occurring in the absence of statutory sanctions. *Journal of Collective Negotiations in the Public Sector* 6:63–72.

Delaney, John Thomas, and Peter Feuille. 1983. Bargaining, arbitration, and public wages. In *Proceedings of the thirty-fifth annual meeting.* Madison: Industrial Relations Research Association.

Edwards, Linda N., and Franklin R. Edwards. 1982a. Wellington-Winter revisited: The case of municipal sanitation collection. *Industrial and Labor Relations Review* 35:307–17.

———. 1982b. Public unions, local government structure and the compensation of municipal sanitation workers. *Economic Inquiry* 20:405–25.

Ehrenberg, Ronald G. 1973. Municipal government structure, unionization, and the wages of fire fighters. *Industrial and Labor Relations Review* 27:36–48.

———. 1980. Retirement system characteristics and compensating wage differentials in the public sector. *Industrial and Labor Relations Review* 33:470–83.

Ehrenberg, Ronald G., and Joshua L. Schwarz. 1983. Public sector labor markets. NBER Working Paper no. 1179. Cambridge, Mass.: National Bureau of Economic Research.

Ehrenberg, Ronald G., Daniel R. Sherman, and Joshua L. Schwarz. 1983. Unions and productivity in the public sector: A study of municipal libraries. *Industrial and Labor Relations Review* 36:199–213.

Feldman, Roger, Lung-Fei Lee, and Richard Hoffbeck. 1980. Hospital employees' wages and labor union organization. Final report, grant no. 1-R03-HS03649-01, National Center for Health Services Research (November).

———. 1981. An empirical study of irreversible choices: Unionism and wages revisited. Mimeo (November). Minneapolis: University of Minnesota.

Feldman, Roger, and Richard Scheffler. 1982. Union impact on hospital wages and fringe benefits. *Industrial and Labor Relations Review* 35:196–206.

Feuille, Peter, and John Thomas Delaney. 1986. Collective bargaining, interest arbitration, and police salaries. *Industrial and Labor Relations Review* 39:228–40.

Feuille, Peter, Wallace Hendricks, and John Thomas Delaney. 1983. The impact of collective bargaining and interest arbitration on policing. Final report, grant no. 81-IJ-CX-0074, National Institute of Justice, U.S. Department of Justice (December).

————. 1985. Police bargaining, arbitration, and fringe benefits. *Journal of Labor Research* 6:1–20.

Freeman, Richard B. 1984. Unionism comes to the public sector. NBER Working Paper no. 1452. Cambridge, Mass.: National Bureau of Economic Research.

Freeman, Richard B., C. Ichniowski, and H. Lauer. 1985. Collective bargaining laws and threat effects of unionism in the determination of police compensation. NBER Working Paper no. 1578. Cambridge, Mass.: National Bureau of Economic Research.

Freeman, Richard B., and J. Leonard. 1985. Union maids: Unions and the female workforce. NBER Working Paper no. 1652. Cambridge, Mass.: National Bureau of Economic Research.

Frey, Donald E. 1975. Wage determination in public schools and the effects of unionization. In *Labor in the public and nonprofit sectors,* ed. Daniel S. Hamermesh. Princeton: Princeton University Press.

Gallagher, Daniel G. 1978. De facto bargaining and teacher salary levels: The Illinois experience. *Journal of Collective Negotiations in the Public Sector* 7:243–54.

Gomez-Mejia, Luis R., and David B. Balkin. 1984. Union impacts on secretarial earnings: A public sector case. *Industrial Relations* 23:97–102.

Gustman, Alan L., and M. O. Clement. 1977. Teachers' salary differentials and equality of educational opportunity. *Industrial and Labor Relations Review* 31:61–70.

Gustman, Alan L., and Martin Segal. 1976. The impact of teachers' unions. Final report, project no. 4-0136, National Institute of Education (September).

Hall, W. Clayton, and Norman E. Carroll. 1973. The effect of teachers' organizations on salaries and class size. *Industrial and Labor Relations Review* 26:834–41.

Hall, W. Clayton, and Bruce Vanderporten. 1977. Unionization, monopsony power, and police salaries, *Industrial Relations* 16:94–100.

Hamermesh, Daniel S. 1975. The effects of government ownership on union wages. In *Labor in the public and nonprofit sectors,* ed. Daniel S. Hamermesh. Princeton: Princeton University Press.

Hirsch, Werner Z., and Anthony M. Rufolo. 1982. Determinants of municipal wages: Some tests of the competitive wage hypothesis. *Research in Urban Economics* 2:309–27.

Holmes, Alexander B. 1976. Effects of union activity on teacher earnings. *Industrial Relations* 15:328–32.

————. 1979. Union activity and teacher salary structures. *Industrial Relations* 18:79–85.

Holzer, Harry J. 1982. Unions and the labor market status of white and minority youth. *Industrial and Labor Relations Review* 35:392–405.

Honadle, Beth Walter. 1981. Wage determination in the public sector: A critical review of the literature. *Journal of Collective Negotiations in the Public Sector* 10:309–25.

Ichniowski, Casey. 1980. Economic effects of the firefighters' union. *Industrial and Labor Relations Review* 33:198–211.

Johnson, George E. 1983. Inter-metropolitan wage differentials in the U.S. In *The measurement of labor cost,* ed. Jack E. Triplett. Chicago: University of Chicago Press.

Johnson, George E., and Gary Solon. 1984. Pay differences between women's and men's jobs: The empirical foundations of comparable worth legislation. NBER Working Paper no. 1472. Cambridge, Mass.: National Bureau of Economic Research.

Kalachek, Edward, and Fredric Raines. 1976. The structure of wage differences among mature male workers. *Journal of Human Resources* 11:484–506.

Lewin, David. 1977. Public sector labor relations. *Labor History* 18:133–44.

———. 1983. The effects of civil service systems and unionism on pay outcomes in the public sector. *Advances in Industrial and Labor Relations* 1:131–61.

Lewin, David, Raymond D. Horton, and James W. Kuhn. 1979. *Collective bargaining and manpower utilization in big city governments*. Montclair, NJ: Allanheld, Osmun and Co.

Lewin, David, and John H. Keith, Jr. 1976. Managerial responses to perceived labor shortages. *Criminology* 14:65–92.

Lewis, H. Gregg. 1983. Union Relative Wage Effects: A Survey of Macro Estimates," *Journal of Labor Economics* 1:1–27.

———. 1986. *Union relative wage effects: A survey*. Chicago: University of Chicago Press.

Link, Charles R., and John H. Landon. 1975. Monopsony and union power in the market for nurses. *Southern Economic Journal* 41:649–59.

Lipsky, David B., and John E. Drotning. 1973. The influence of collective bargaining on teachers' salaries in New York state. *Industrial and Labor Relations Review* 27:18–35.

McLaughlin, Catherine G. 1980. The impact of unions on hospital wages. Ph.D. diss., University of Wisconsin, Madison.

Mellow, Wesley. 1983. Employer size, unionism, and wages. *Research in Labor Economics* Supplement 2:253–82.

Mincer, Jacob. 1983. Union effects: Wages, turnover, and job training. *Research in Labor Economics* Supplement 2:217–52.

Mitchell, Daniel J. B. 1983. Unions and wages in the public sector: A review of recent evidence. *Journal of Collective Negotiations in the Public Sector* 12:337–53.

Moore, Gary A. 1976. The effect of collective bargaining on internal salary structure in the public schools. *Industrial and Labor Relations Review* 29:352–62.

Moore, William J. 1980. Membership and wage impact of right-to-work laws. *Journal of Labor Research* 1:349–68.

Moore, William J., and John Raisian. 1981. Unionism and wage rates in the public and private sectors: A comparative time series analysis. Mimeo (October). Washington, D.C.: U.S. Bureau of Labor Statistics.

———. 1982. A times series analysis of union/nonunion relative wage effects in the public sector. In *Proceedings of the thirty-fourth annual meeting*. Madison: Industrial Relations Research Association.

———. 1983. The level and growth of union/nonunion relative wage effects, 1967–77. *Journal of Labor Research* 4:65–79.

Noam, Eli M. 1983. The effect of unionization and civil service on the salaries and productivity of regulators. *Research in Labor Economics* Supplement 2:157–70.

Perloff, Jeffrey M., and Michael L. Wachter. 1984. Wage comparability in the U.S. Postal Service. *Industrial and Labor Relations Review* 38:26–35.

Schmenner, Roger W. 1973. The determination of municipal employee wages. *Review of Economics and Statistics* 55:83–90.

Shapiro, David. 1978. Relative wage effects of unions in the public and private sectors. *Industrial and Labor Relations Review* 31:193–203.

Sloan, Frank A., and Killard W. Adamache. 1984. The role of unions in hospital cost inflation. *Industrial and Labor Relations Review* 37:252–62.

Sloan, Frank A., and Richard A. Elnicki. 1978. Professional nurse wage-setting in hospitals. In *Equalizing access to nursing services: The geographic dimension,* ed. Frank A. Sloan. Washington, D.C.: U.S. Department of Health, Education, and Welfare (publication no. HRA 78-51).

―――. 1979. Determinants of professional nurses wages. *Research in Health Economics* 1:217–54.

Sloan, Frank A., and Bruce Steinwald. 1980. *Hospital labor markets.* Lexington, MA: Lexington Books.

Smith, Sharon P. 1976. Are postal workers over- or underpaid? *Industrial Relations* 15:168–76.

―――. 1977a. Government wage differentials. *Journal of Urban Economics* 4:248–71.

―――. 1977b. *Equal pay in the public sector: Fact or fantasy?* Princeton Industrial Relations Section, Princeton University.

Thornton, Robert J. 1971. The effects of collective negotiations on teachers' salaries. *Quarterly Review of Economics and Business* 11:37–46.

―――. 1975. Monopsony and teachers' salaries: Some contrary evidence. *Industrial and Labor Relations Review* 28:574–75.

Victor, Richard B. 1979. Municipal unions and wage patterns. In *Proceedings of the thirty-second annual meeting.* Madison: Industrial Relations Research Association.

Zax, Jeffrey S. 1985. Labor relations, wages, and nonwage compensation in municipal employment. NBER Working Paper no. 1582. Cambridge, Mass.: National Bureau of Economic Research.

Comment   Zvi Griliches

As always, Gregg Lewis has provided a valuable contribution to the profession by organizing a mass of studies into a coherent whole. I have two comments. First, all the studies Lewis cites (as well as those on private sector union wage effects) measure the union impact in terms of the geometric mean (i.e., in ln units). Does it make sense to use *geometric* means or might arithmetic means be more appropriate? If I believed that arithmetic means were more relevant, the fact that the variance of ln earnings in the union sector is *smaller* than the variance of ln earnings in the nonunion sector (Freeman 1980, 1986) implies that the union/nonunion gap would be smaller if arithmetic means were used rather than geometric. Indeed, with a lognormal distribution, the

Zvi Griliches is Paul M. Warburg Professor of Economics at Harvard University and Director of the National Bureau of Economic Research's Program in Productivity and Technical Change.

ln of the arithmetic mean equals the geometric mean plus one-half the variance of ln earnings. As it is likely that unions have a bigger impact in reducing dispersion in the private sector, my guess is that, when measured in arithmetic units, the difference between the union/non-union wage gaps between the sectors will diminish somewhat compared to the results reported by Lewis.

My second comment relates to the interpretation of all these estimates. What are we to make of them? Do we really believe that there is *one* "gap" to be found, or ought we to concentrate more on the range of gaps? It reminds me of my own earlier work on the return to schooling and the search for "the" estimate of ability bias. It is interesting, but ultimately one convinces oneself that it all depends on the particular set of data and circumstances in the labor market.

What we have here is a valuable array of the results of different studies made as comparable as is possible at the moment. In principle, they should be the input for theorists, who will take them as stylized facts, use them in constructing a model of sectoral wage determination, and try to *explain* the differences among them as the result of different supply, demand, and technology of union control, bargaining, and political context variables. For laying the groundwork for such future studies, we owe Gregg Lewis a great debt.

References

Freeman, R. 1980. Unionism and the dispersion of wages. *Industrial and Labor Relations Review* 34(October):3–23.
_____. 1986. Unionism comes to the public sector. *Journal of Economic Literature* 24(March):41–86.

7

Employer Size, Pay, and the Ability to Pay in the Public Sector

Charles C. Brown and James L. Medoff

There is much evidence that private sector employers categorized as "large" pay more than employers categorized as "small," even when their union status is the same (Brown and Medoff 1986). There is, however, much less information that can help us answer two key questions about this wage differential: How can larger private sector employers pay more and still survive? Why do they do so?

In this paper we move from the private sector to the public sector, while still focusing on the employer size–wage differential. Published tabulations of Census of Governments data (U.S. Census Bureau 1979b) suggest that larger government units *do* pay substantially higher wages than smaller ones. For example, average full-time earnings are 13 percent higher for special districts with more than 100 employees than for districts with less than 10 workers. A similar relationship holds when one divides the districts according to function and for other types of local government.[1] Moreover, the size-wage relationship is close to monotonic across the size distribution. When we investigate the magnitude of this differential more carefully in both union and nonunion settings, we find size-wage effects comparable to those found in the private sector. After this foray, we deal with the more difficult questions of how the larger employers can afford to pay more and why they do so.

Charles C. Brown is professor of economics and program director at the Institute for Social Research, University of Michigan, and a research associate of the National Bureau of Economic Research. James L. Medoff is Meyer Kestnbaum Professor of Labor and Industry at Harvard University, and a research associate of the National Bureau of Economic Research.

We have benefited significantly from the insights of David Bloom, John Dunlop, and Arnold Zack. We also wish to acknowledge the valuable assistance provided by David Carney, Jeannette Darling, Robert Valletta, Martin VanDenburgh, and Daniel Hamermesh.

One assumption made implicitly or explicitly in most discussions of size-wage differentials in the private sector is that larger employers have a greater "ability to pay." This is because employer size is thought to be positively related to product market power and to the actual and, presumably, potential rate of return on capital. The primary problem with testing whether monopoly power or above average profitability are necessary conditions for the existence of a size-wage differential is that product market power and profitability are two of the most difficult concepts in economics to measure. Moreover, in the case of profitability we have a very serious "endogeneity" problem, since the magnitude of the wage rate will most certainly be a determinant of the rate of return on capital.

Does "ability to pay" lie behind the size-wage effect in the public sector? While this question has not been addressed empirically to date, an informed response can be based on the outcomes of two statistical analyses. The first would determine whether the size of fiscs is positively related to the affluence of their citizens. The second would assess whether the remuneration a community pays is related to its economic well-being, other things, in particular the prevailing wage, held constant.

If ability to pay does in fact matter for the generation of size-wage differentials, the detection of its role should be greatly enhanced with data for public units. First of all, the ability of a state or local government to pay a given wage can be assessed quite well with truly exogenous variables, such as the average family income of the area's residents or the value of the property stock per resident. In addition, where collective bargaining occurs, arbitrators making rulings about public sector wage settlements generally make reference to an area's ability to pay. This fact is consistent with the guidance offered in legislation concerning public sector dispute resolution. To be more precise, in sixteen out of the twenty-six states with laws providing for binding arbitration, ability to pay is mentioned in the guidelines for the arbitrator. Moreover, managements and unions bargaining in the public sector also appear to pay close attention to an area's inability or ability to afford wage increases.

If ability to pay plays a key role in the size-wage effect story, we should certainly be able to view its performance in the unionized portion of the public sector. If this import is not conditional on the presence of collective bargaining, we should be able to observe it with data for public units where there is no union coverage. If ability to pay is closely associated with the magnitude of the size-wage differential among non-union public employees, one would have good reason for believing that it operated in a similar fashion throughout the private economy.

Section 7.1 of this study presents evidence supporting the belief that ability to pay should matter in the wage determination process, especially among public sector employees covered by collective bargaining. Section 7.2 presents econometric results based on two data files which indicate that there is a sizeable positive relationship between employer size and pay in the public sector, as was the case among private employers. Section 7.3 first asks whether the size of public employers is positively related to their ability to pay and then, in light of an affirmative response, asks about the importance of this relationship in the generation of the one between size and pay.[2]

Our primary findings concerning the relationships between employer size, pay, and the ability to pay in the public sector are as follows:

1. Larger public employers pay substantially more for workers with given characteristics than do those who are smaller, regardless of whether the workers are covered by collective bargaining.
2. Larger public employers are found in areas where family income and the value of property are above average.
3. The ability of an area to pay higher wages, as measured by mean family income or property value per resident, is a key determinant of whether the area does in fact pay more.
4. Measured ability to pay "explains" only about 15 percent of the public sector size-wage effect.
5. Controlling for employer size and measured ability to pay usually reduces the measured impact of collective bargaining on wage rates, but the changes are uniformly less than 20 percent of the union effect before these controls are added.

7.1 Ability to Pay and Wage Determination

The belief that the ability of an employer to pay higher wages will condition whether or not it does so can be supported by examining several sources: the writings of knowledgeable observers of the wage determination process, the decisions of arbitrators in arbitrations concerning wages, and the language of state statutes providing for the resolution of wage disputes involving public sector employees.

Those who closely watch wages being set in the U.S. public sector list an employer's ability to pay as a relevant criterion for the final settlements observed. However, while these scholars and practitioners believe that ability to pay matters, they do not regard it as the primary criterion in the wage determination process.

Only a small percentage of wage settlements throughout the U.S. economy involve arbitration. While the percentage is larger in the public sector, even here interest arbitration is the exception not the rule. Nevertheless, it is instructive to examine the wage-setting criteria chosen by arbitrators and the weight given to each, since this choice and weighting are likely to reflect what happens in the absence of an arbitrator.

In his 1982 address to the National Academy of Arbitrators, R. Theodore Clark, Jr. said:

Substantially all the public-sector interest arbitration statutes require—either explicitly or implicitly—that financial limitations on a public employer's ability to pay must be considered by the interest arbitrator. That was the specific holding of the New Jersey Supreme Court in "New Jersey State Policemen's Benevolent Association Local 29 vs. Town of Irvington." The court ruled that an interest arbitrator must "take account of a municipality's cap law constraints prior to the rendition of an award." Nevertheless, I get the very definite impression that many interest arbitrators wish that ability-to-pay arguments would simply disappear. Russell Smith at the 1971 meeting of the National Academy of Arbitrators, after commenting on the serious problems confronting arbitrators in attempting to assess an inability-to-pay argument, candidly observed that the inability-to-pay criterion, "if deemed to be relevant or required by law to be taken into consideration, is likely to be taken less seriously than others, such as comparison data." My own impression is that the attitude of many arbitrators toward the inability-to-pay criterion ranges from indifference to hostility. I also have the feeling in some cases that while a public employer's ability to pay is considered, it is considered in form only and not in substance (Clark 1982, 249–50).

The lawyer Charles C. Mulcahy (1976, 92) adds that while the financial ability of a government to meet a new wage bill is generally accepted as a legitimate factor in making an arbitration award, it too "has been sorely neglected in many instances because local government officials did not adequately and professionally present" evidence concerning their ability or inability to meet certain wage demands.

An examination of these statutes brings into focus the criteria that most arbitrators consider in ruling in wage arbitrations. In the preponderance of the laws explicit reference is made to an employer's ability to pay. However, the list of relevant criteria is generally not short. A sense of what the typical list looks like can be gained by considering the following one from the Illinois statute:

1. The lawful authority of the employer.
2. Stipulations of the parties.
3. The interests and welfare of the public and the financial ability of the unit of government to meet those costs.
4. Comparison of the wages, hours, and conditions of employment of the employees involved in the arbitration proceedings with the wages, hours, and conditions of employment of other employees performing similar services and with other employees generally:
   a. in public employment in comparable communities;
   b. in private employment in comparable communities.

5. The average consumer prices for goods and services, commonly known as the cost of living.

6. The overall compensation presently received by the employees, including direct wage compensation, vacation, holidays, and other excused time, insurance and pensions, medical and hospitalization benefits, the continuity and stability of employment, and all other benefits received.

7. Changes in any of the foregoing circumstances during the pendency of the arbitration proceedings.

8. Such other factors, not confined to the foregoing, which are normally or traditionally taken into consideration in the determination of wages, hours, and conditions of employment through voluntary collective bargaining, mediation, fact-finding, arbitration or otherwise between the parties, in the public service or in private employment (Mulcahy 1976, 91–92).

While most arbitrators will have considered the ability or inability of employers to pay, the weight attached to this criterion is likely to vary significantly. The nature of this variation was delineated clearly in a 1948 arbitration involving the Twin City Rapid Transit Company by the board's chairman John T. Dunlop, who wrote:

(1) In the case of properties which have been highly profitable over a period of years, the wage rate would normally be increased slightly over the levels indicated by other standards; (2) in the case of persistently unprofitable firms, the wage rate would normally be reduced slightly from the levels indicated by other standards; (3) in the case of the companies whose financial record over a period of years falls between these extremes, the wage rate level would be determined largely by other standards (Elkouri and Elkouri 1985, 826).

In sum, the opinions of arbitrators and the language of statutes referring to dispute resolution in the public sector both lend credence to the position that in wage determination ability to pay matters, but it is certainly not all that matters. Similar institutional evidence is not available for public sector workers not covered by collective bargaining. Despite this gap, we believe the importance of ability to pay in the public sector needs to be assessed empirically for three reasons. First, according to the Current Population Survey data we analyze below, the percentage of state and local employees covered by collective bargaining is quite high: 48 percent of those labeled "white collar" and 44 percent of those labeled "blue collar" or "service". Second, much of what we observe under collective bargaining differs only in degree from what happens in nonunion settings; while the codification embodied in a collective agreement and a formal agent clearly matter, it is wrong to believe that most groups of employees that are not represented by a union are not organized in other ways. And finally, the belief that the ability-to-pay criterion is more important in the presence of collective bargaining is testable. As we will see later, the importance of this criterion seems to be as great among employees who are not covered by a collective agreement as among those who are, at least in the public sector.

7.2   The Public Employer Size–Wage Effect

This section provides evidence of the relationship between employer size and pay in the public sector. Employer size can mean either the number of workers employed at the individual's worksite or the number employed by the individual's employer at all worksites. For private sector workers, these are usually called "establishment" and "company" size. For government employees, the second concept is less well defined; dictated largely by data availability, we define it to equal the total employment of a governmental unit and refer to it as "government size."

7.2.1   Evidence from Current Population Surveys

The only data files containing both size measures for government employees[3] are the May 1979 and May 1983 Current Population Surveys (CPS). We pooled these two files. Our analysis is based on the sample of 5,723 state and local government workers for whom data on wage rates and the other variables we use were available.

We estimated wage equations with the usual explanatory variables: education, tenure, experience, race, sex, location, and industry and occupation dummy variables. We also used a dummy variable to distinguish 1979 from 1983 observations and state from local government workers. Finally, we analyzed the variables of interest: employment at worksite, employment of the government unit, and coverage by a union or employee association contract. Our results are reported in table 7.1.

The first four lines of table 7.1 suggest two conclusions.[4] First, both worksite employment and government employment matter: those working for larger employers by either measure earn higher wages. Second, the estimated impact of collective bargaining coverage is reduced, *but not dramatically,* when we control for employer size.

When the sample is split by collar color and unionization, the main finding is that government size matters a great deal for covered blue-collar workers but not at all for uncovered blue-collar workers. Given the nontrivial standard errors for subgroup size effects, the similarity of the site-size premia are striking.

Table 7.1   **Effects of Employer Size and Union Coverage on ln(Wage), State and Local Government Workers, Current Population Survey, 1979 and 1983**

Sample	ln(Site Employment)	ln(Government Employment)	Covered
All Workers	—	—	0.069
(N = 5,723)	—	—	(0.010)
	0.016	—	0.067
	(0.003)	—	(0.010)
	—	0.021	0.056
	—	(0.003)	(0.011)
	0.010	0.018	0.057
	(0.003)	(0.003)	(0.010)
Union White-Collar Workers	0.015	—	—
(N = 1,956)	(0.005)	—	—
	—	0.022	—
	—	(0.005)	—
	0.010	0.019	—
	(0.005)	(0.006)	—
Nonunion White-Collar Workers	0.016	—	—
(N = 2,077)	(0.005)	—	—
	—	0.027	—
	—	(0.005)	—
	0.009	0.024	—
	(0.005)	(0.005)	—
Union Blue-Collar Workers	0.025	—	—
(N = 749)	(0.007)	—	—
	—	0.035	—
	—	(0.007)	—
	0.015	0.030	—
	(0.007)	(0.007)	—
Nonunion Blue-Collar Workers	0.014	—	—
(N = 941)	(0.007)	—	—
	—	−0.004	—
	—	(0.007)	—
	0.018	−0.011	—
	(0.008)	(0.008)	—

Note: Other variables held constant in the estimation are: education, tenure, tenure squared, experience, experience squared; dummy variables for race, sex, metropolitan location, region (3), industry (27), occupation (8), local government, and year.

It is natural to compare these findings to those we obtained for the private sector (Brown and Medoff 1986). Table 7.2, which is based on May 1979 CPS private sector workers, provides a basis for such a comparison.[5]

While union coverage matters less in the public sector than in the private sector, the employer size effects are, in the aggregate, broadly similar. This is particularly evident when one focuses on the sum of site and company coefficients—the effect of making the company (or government) larger by expanding each worksite. The effect of employer size on the wages of white-collar workers is very similar to the all-worker results. Among blue-collar workers a different pattern appears. In the public sector, the impact of employer size is greater among union than among nonunion workers, while in the private sector the reverse is true. However, one probably should not make too much of this last

Table 7.2   **Effects of Employer Size and Union Coverage on ln(Wage), Private Sector Workers, Current Population Survey, 1979**

Sample	ln(Site Employment)	ln(Company Employment)	Covered
All Workers	0.028	—	0.123
(N = 13,829)	(0.002)	—	(0.009)
	—	0.020	0.116
	—	(0.001)	(0.009)
	0.015	0.013	0.113
	(0.002)	(0.002)	(0.009)
White-Collar Workers	0.029	—	0.049
(N = 6,901)	(0.003)	—	(0.015)
	—	0.020	0.044
	—	(0.002)	(0.015)
	0.019	0.012	0.043
	(0.003)	(0.002)	(0.015)
Union Blue-Collar Workers	0.014	—	—
(N = 2,337)	(0.004)	—	—
	—	0.017	—
	—	(0.003)	—
	0.002	0.016	—
	(0.005)	(0.004)	—
Nonunion Blue-Collar Workers	0.026	—	—
(N = 4,591)	(0.003)	—	—
	—	0.018	—
	—	(0.002)	—
	0.011	0.013	—
	(0.005)	(0.003)	—

Note: Other variables held constant in the estimation are: same as table 7.1, except for local government and year dummies.

result, since the pattern for private sector workers shown in table 7.2 is not always confirmed in other data sets (Brown and Medoff 1986).

7.2.2 Evidence from the Census of Governments

The CPS has the advantage of reporting number of workers at the individual's worksite and the individual's schooling, and so forth. As is typical of surveys of individuals, there is little information about their employer apart from the size variables, and the fact that these are coded as categories is undesirable. The Census of Governments file, in contrast, has no information about the characteristics of the workers (apart from the functional category they work in) but does have accurate measures of government size and better information about labor relations characteristics. It also identifies the governments involved, a fact essential to (eventually) measuring ability to pay.

We began with 82,973 governments included in the 1982 Census of Governments file. After deleting those with data reported for a year prior to 1982 and any zero-employment "governments," the sample size fell to 31,267.[6]

Our dependent variable is the logarithm of the average wage, defined as monthly payroll divided by full-time plus half of part-time employment. We control for the proportion of workers who are part-time, so errors in estimating the appropriate average weight to part-time workers in computing full-time equivalent employment should be dealt with by that variable. We also control for the shares of employment devoted to each of twenty-nine governmental functions and for region and metropolitan or nonmetropolitan location.

The explanatory variables of primary interest are government size and the labor relations variables. Our size measure is the logarithm of the number of individuals employed by the government in question.[7] The Census of Governments file includes several labor relations variables; our strategy is to try the various alternatives in a fairly agnostic way. The first set of labor relations variables are dummy variables that capture the type of labor relations policy, if any, of the government in question. One dummy variable distinguishes governments that have a labor relations policy from those that do not. As defined in the Census of Governments file, there are two types of policy: a collective bargaining policy or a meet and confer policy.[8] We include additional dummy variables for each of these. It is possible for a government to have *both* types of policies, so the first dummy is not the exact sum of the other two. Second, three alternative measures of the degree of organization are available: the proportion of workers covered by contracts, in bargaining units, and unionized.

Each of these labor relations variables is reported separately for school and nonschool employers: we have aggregated them. Thus, for example, a government that has a "bargaining policy" for its school employees only would have a value equal to the ratio of (full-time equivalent) school to total employment.

Our results are presented in the first six regressions in table 7.3. The main finding here is a large and statistically significant effect of government size on wages, controlling for differences among different-sized governments in the distribution of employment across functions. To get a sense of the importance of the 0.039 coefficient for ln(government size), we calculated the difference in wages by governments one standard deviation above and below the mean of ln(government size). Since that standard deviation is 1.83, the implied proportional wage difference is 2(1.83)(0.039) = 0.125. The size premium does not depend on which measure of worker organization we utilize. Controlling for size has little effect on the coefficients of the labor relations dummies or the proportions organized.

The coefficients of the collective bargaining variables suggest that each of the labor-management policies are associated with higher wages compared to the no-policy alternative. According to the first line of table 7.3, a meet and confer policy raises ln(wage) by 0.12 (= 0.125 − 0.005), a collective bargaining policy by 0.17 (= 0.125 + 0.047), and a combination of policies by about the same amount. This general pattern holds for the other specifications as well. The major puzzle is the lack of the expected positive coefficient for the degree of unionization variable.

We also estimate similar equations with the logarithm of monthly wages plus fringes as a dependent variable. Perhaps because of incomplete reporting on the tape (U.S. Census Bureau, 1985, 15), these fringes amounted to only about 7 percent of payroll, and their inclusion in the wage measure did not qualitatively change our earlier findings.

Disaggregation by collar color as in tables 7.1 and 7.2 is not possible with the Census of Governments data, and the contract coverage data refer to the proportion of the government's workers covered by a contract rather than an individual worker's status. We divided the sample by proportion covered, with the groups being none, a minority, and a majority. The size coefficient is essentially the same for all three groups. Unlike table 7.1, size matters here regardless of coverage, though, if anything, the impact rises with coverage.

The labor relations coefficients now tell a generally plausible if complicated story. Even for governments with no union contracts, having a labor relations policy—especially a collective bargaining policy—is associated with higher wages.[9] For governments with some workers

Table 7.3   Effects of Employer Size and Union Coverage on ln(Wage), Census of Governments (1982)

Sample	Dummy Variables for:				Proportion of Workers:		
	ln(Government Size)	Labor Relations Policy	Collective Bargaining	Meet & Confer	Covered by Contracts	In Barg. Units	Organized
All Local Governments (N = 31,267)	—	0.125 (0.017)	0.047 (0.017)	-0.005 (0.010)	-0.022 (0.017)	—	—
	0.039 (0.002)	0.089 (0.017)	0.045 (0.017)	-0.005 (0.010)	-0.047 (0.017)	—	—
	—	0.127 (0.018)	0.037 (0.015)	-0.004 (0.010)	—	-0.004 (0.017)	—
	0.039 (0.002)	0.101 (0.018)	0.027 (0.015)	-0.004 (0.010)	—	-0.033 (0.017)	—
	—	0.125 (0.017)	0.036 (0.015)	-0.004 (0.010)	—	—	0.001 (0.001)
	0.039 (0.002)	0.089 (0.017)	0.021 (0.015)	-0.004 (0.010)	—	—	0.001 (0.001)
Local Governments with Cov. = 0 (N = 21,309)	—	0.078 (0.061)	0.040 (0.043)	0.032 (0.059)	—	—	—
	0.039 (0.003)	0.056 (0.060)	0.029 (0.043)	0.017 (0.058)	—	—	—

(continued)

Table 7.3 (continued)

Sample	ln(Government Size)	Labor Relations Policy	Collective Bargaining	Meet & Confer	Covered by Contracts	In Barg. Units	Organized
			Dummy Variables for:		Proportion of Workers:		
Local Governments with 0 < Cov. < 50 (N = 3,844)	—	0.162	−0.134	−0.011	0.238	—	—
	—	(0.048)	(0.037)	(0.006)	(0.027)	—	—
	0.040	0.172	−0.128	−0.013	0.241	—	—
	(0.003)	(0.047)	(0.036)	(0.006)	(0.027)	—	—
Local Governments with Cov. ≥ 0.50 (N = 6,114)	—	0.005	0.013	0.002	0.096	—	—
	—	(0.063)	(0.049)	(0.004)	(0.010)	—	—
	0.043	0.050	−0.045	0.002	0.078	—	—
	(0.002)	(0.061)	(0.047)	(0.004)	(0.010)	—	—

Note: Other variables held constant in the estimation are: shares of employment devoted to individual functions (29), proportion of workers who are part-time; dummy varables for region (3) and SMSA.

covered, the extent of coverage matters, though at a decreasing rate, as might be expected if initial contract inroads had spillover effects.

7.3   The Role of Ability to Pay

Because the governments in the Census of Governments file are separately identified, we can match data on the characteristics of those who live in that government's jurisdiction or in the surrounding area from the 1980 Census of Population. Unfortunately, this proved possible only for 4,775 larger governments (counties, municipalities, and townships) for whom matching Census of Population data were available.

The equations in the first two lines of table 7.4 are the same as those in table 7.3, except for the smaller sample. The size effect is unaffected. The collective bargaining policy dummy is no longer important, but the proportion covered by contracts now has the expected positive effect. Using the proportion in bargaining units or the proportion who are members of employer organizations as the union coverage variable produced quite similar results.

The main result in table 7.4 is contained in lines 3 and 4. The two control variables, which appear for the first time at this point, are the logarithm of the average wage in the county (defined as aggregate household wage and salary and self-employment earnings divided by aggregate weeks worked) and the logarithm of median family income in the jurisdiction. The former is intended to capture the effect of variations in wage rates in the government's local labor market, and the latter the wealth or "ability to pay" of its residents. The message of lines 3 and 4 is simple and clear: controlling for ability to pay explains little (12 percent) of the wage premium paid by larger local governments and marginally *increases* the estimated union premium.

The estimated coefficients of the ln(average wage) variable are implausibly small. One might expect a coefficient near one, if local governments pay a fixed proportional markup (or markdown) on wages in their area. Constraining the coefficient of ln(average wage) to equal one left the government size variable virtually unaffected but reduced the coefficient of ln(median income) to -0.416(s.e. $= 0.013$). Thus, the constrained results might lead one to question the importance of ability to pay or to interpret our average wage measure as capturing both the going wage and ability to pay. But the conclusion that size matters remains secure. We have not emphasized these "constrained" results because the constraint is so severe—it is hard to imagine measurement error in ln(average wage) severe enough to produce an unconstrained coefficient estimate of 0.03 when the true coefficient is close to 1.0.

Table 7.4   Effects of Employer Size, Unionization, and Ability to Pay on ln(Wages), Census of Government, Large-Unit Subsample, 1982

Sample	ln(Govt. Size)	Dummy Variables for: Labor Relations Policy	Collective Bargaining	Meet & Confer	Proportion of Workers Covered by Contracts	ln(Avg. Wage in County)	ln(Median Family Income in Jurisdiction)
All "Large" Local Governments (N = 4,775)	—	0.104 (0.013)	−0.001 (0.012)	0.002 (0.007)	0.051 (0.010)	—	—
	0.040 (0.003)	0.096 (0.012)	−0.004 (0.011)	0.002 (0.007)	0.043 (0.009)	—	—
	—	0.107 (0.012)	−0.012 (0.011)	0.005 (0.007)	0.057 (0.009)	0.030 (0.020)	0.305 (0.018)
	0.035 (0.003)	0.100 (0.011)	−0.014 (0.010)	0.004 (0.007)	0.051 (0.009)	0.034 (0.019)	0.295 (0.018)
"Large" Local Governments with Cov. = 0 (N = 2,950)	0.038 (0.004)	−0.004 (0.034)	0.022 (0.024)	0.098 (0.033)	—	—	—
	0.026 (0.004)	0.016 (0.031)	0.012 (0.022)	0.093 (0.030)	—	0.038 (0.026)	0.310 (0.023)
"Large" Local Governments with 0 < Cov. <0.50 (N = 956)	0.035 (0.007)	−0.055 (0.066)	−0.109 (0.047)	−0.009 (0.009)	0.185 (0.037)	—	—
	0.035 (0.006)	−0.046 (0.062)	−0.100 (0.044)	−0.002 (0.009)	0.193 (0.035)	−0.018 (0.039)	0.290 (0.038)
"Large" Local Governments with Cov. ≥ 0.50 (N = 869)	0.048 (0.006)	−0.003 (0.471)	−0.038 (0.423)	0.005 (0.009)	0.014 (0.010)	—	—
	0.052 (0.005)	−0.068 (0.421)	0.011 (0.379)	0.005 (0.008)	0.014 (0.009)	0.068 (0.042)	0.255 (0.041)

Note: Other variables held constant: see table 7.3.

We also used the matched government-population file to test another conjecture—that the wage premium paid by larger local governments is because they are large relative to their labor market. Adding the logarithm of the ratio of government employment to *county* population produced a significant *negative* coefficient (-0.032) for the added variable (and a coefficient of 0.055 for the government size variable), so the large-demand model does not explain the size-wage effect. This result implies, however, that if we enter ln(government size) and ln(county population) separately, the coefficient of the former falls to $0.055 - 0.032 = 0.023.$[10]

The remainder of table 7.4 separates the sample into three parts, where the proportion of the work force covered by collective bargaining is zero, between zero and one-half, or greater than or equal to one-half. These results indicate that the importance of ability to pay in explaining either cross-unit wage rates or the cross-unit, size-wage effect does *not* increase with the extent of collective bargaining coverage. In fact, ability to pay is of somewhat greater importance in the units with no collective bargaining than in the units with the most in terms of both its direct effect on wages and its capacity to explain the size-wage effect. As in the earlier tables, size effects are also larger in organized jurisdictions.

While median family income is a widely used measure of the economic status of a jurisdiction's residents, it neglects the taxable wealth represented by commercial enterprises in the jurisdiction. For a smaller sample of jurisdictions, property values (which count residential and nonresidential wealth) can be used to fill this gap.

The Census of Governments collects assessed property values from over 13,500 assessing units. Unfortunately, the ratio of assessed to market value is known to vary widely across jurisdictions. However, the census collected the assessed and market values of 55,300 property sales in a sample of jurisdictions, from which estimates of the market value of all locally assessed property by jurisdiction are calculated (U.S. Census Bureau 1984, 118–22).

By matching jurisdictions where that data on property values attained census standards for publication to those with Census of Population data on family income and average wages (and the Census of Government data on payroll, employment, and labor relations) we arrived at a final sample of 669 observations. We then added ln(market value of property per capita) to the equations in table 7.4. Results are presented in table 7.5. Comparison of the first two equations of table 7.5 with analogous table 7.4 entries shows that, in this smaller sample, both government size and the proportion organized have larger coefficients than in the larger (table 7.4) sample. The last three equations in table 7.5 demonstrate that neither of these coefficients is greatly affected by

Table 7.5 Effects of Employer Size, Unionization, and Ability to Pay on ln(Wages), Census of Government, Large-Unit Subsample with Property Value Data ($N = 669$)

ln(Government Size)	Dummy Variables for:				ln(Average Wage in County)	ln(Median Family Income in Jurisdiction)	ln(Property Value per Capita)
	Labor Relations Policy	Collective Bargaining	Meet & Confer	Proportion of Workers Covered by Contracts			
0.066	0.103	-0.059	-0.004	0.143	—	—	—
(0.007)	(0.027)	(0.027)	(0.016)	(0.031)			
0.057	0.097	-0.051	-0.011	0.128	-0.019	0.376	—
(0.006)	(0.025)	(0.025)	(0.014)	(0.028)	(0.064)	(0.057)	
0.059	0.104	-0.054	-0.007	0.135	—	—	0.082
(0.006)	(0.026)	(0.026)	(0.015)	(0.029)			(0.011)
0.055	0.098	-0.049	-0.12	0.126	-0.032	0.341	0.040
(0.006)	(0.025)	(0.024)	(0.014)	(0.028)	(0.064)	(0.057)	(0.011)

Note: Other variables held constant: see table 7.3.

adding family income and property value as controls. While there is evidence that both ability-to-pay measures affect wages, both are loosely enough related to government size that their inclusion reduces the estimated size effect by at most one-sixth of its original value. The impact of the proportion organized is even less sensitive to the inclusion of the ability-to-pay variables.

7.4 Conclusion

Larger public employers pay substantially more for a given quality of labor than do public employers who are smaller, even when their collective bargaining status is the same. Despite the fact that ability to pay is positively related to wage rates in the public sector and that larger fiscs are richer, financial capacity can explain very little of the public employer size–wage differential.

Thus, ability to pay plays a very small role in explaining the fact that larger employers pay more in the sector where we would expect this role to be the largest. As a result, we must turn to other actors in trying to explain why size-wage differentials exist and how they can persist.

Notes

1. The published tabulations measure size by jurisdiction population rather than number of employees for counties, municipalities, and townships, and by enrollment for school districts.

2. We sampled the public sector wage studies surveyed by Freeman (1986). Size of government receives surprisingly little attention in these studies. Often it is not included; sometimes it is included as a "control" whose coefficient is not reported. In any case, the minority of studies that include both size and ability to pay as wage determinants (e.g., Frey 1975; Ehrenberg, Chaykowski, and Ehrenberg 1986) do not report size coefficients with and without ability to pay variables, as would be needed to judge whether ability to pay was an important part of the size-wage relationship.

3. Our "government employment" variable is based on a CPS question for which interviewers received the following instruction: "The employer of Federal, State, and local government employees . . . is the *highest* appropriate governmental level. For example, if a person works for the county circuit court, the employer is the county government, not the circuit court." (U.S. Census Bureau 1983, 7) Our "site employment" is employment at "the person's work-site, the place where the person performs his/her major activities or duties."

The CPS reports both size variables as categories (1–24, 25–99, 100–499, 500–999, and 1,000 or more). Our continuous size measures use category means. For local government workers, we measure "government size" as the average level of full-time equivalent employment in the reported size class in the individual's state, using 1977 Census of Government tabulations (U.S.

Census Bureau 1979a, 428–35). For state government workers, "government size" is the number of full-time equivalent workers employed by the state (U.S. Census Bureau 1978c, 317). Our "site size" variable is defined as the average level of employment of establishments in the individual's site-class, using *County Business Patterns* data (U.S. Census Bureau 1978a, 3). These data relate to private sector establishments, but we know of no comparable series for public sector workers.

4. We obtained similar results with the subsample of 4,008 local government workers.

5. Because so few private sector white-collar workers are unionized (less than 11 percent in our CPS file), we did not separate white-collar workers by union status.

6. The proportions of cases deleted by type of government were: counties, 18 percent; municipalities, 62 percent; townships, 73 percent; special districts, 81 percent; school districts, 23 percent. Zero employment accounted for most of the special-district deletions, while noncurrent data accounted for the majority of deletions for other government types. We decided not to use the noncurrent data because the labor relations variables were current values, and because we know of no a priori reason to expect nonreporting to be correlated with the error term in the equation that determines the wage rate.

7. "Government" is defined as an "organization which, in addition to governmental character, has sufficient discretion in the management of its own affairs to distinguish it as separate from the administrative structure of any other governmental unit" (U.S. Census Bureau 1978b, 14). In addition to counties, municipalities, and townships, school districts and special districts are counted as separate governments if they are sufficiently independent. Only 8 percent of all school systems (with 19 percent of all public school enrollment) are classified as separate, independent school districts rather than part of a larger government. Independent "special districts," often organized for single functions, accounted for 26,000 of the 80,000 local governments in 1977. For example, the Massachusetts Bay Transit Authority and the Boston Housing Authority are separate governments, but the Boston School Committee is not.

8. Collective bargaining refers to "negotiations in which both management and employee representatives are equal legal parties in the bargaining process and . . . the end result . . . is a mutually binding contractual agreement." "Meet and confer discussions" refers to "the process by which the public employer consents to discuss conditions of employment with representatives of an employee organization. . . . The employer is, however, not legally bound to enter into these discussions, nor to abide by any resulting memorandum of understanding" (U.S. Census Bureau 1979b, 2).

9. For governments with some workers covered, the various types of labor relations policies have small estimated effects; the exception is meet and confer policies when a minority of workers are covered, where the effect is 0.16 ($= 0.172 - 0.013$) when size is included. At first, a government with workers covered by collective bargaining would seem to necessarily have labor relations policy (indeed, a collective bargaining policy). But recall that these "dummies" are in fact weighted averages of separated dummies for education and other workers. Thus, if the teachers are covered but other workers are not, the labor relations and collective bargaining "dummies" take on fractional values.

10. We also considered the possibility that it is the population of the jurisdiction rather than its number of employees per se which influences wages. When the logarithm of jurisdiction population was added as an additional con-

trol variable to the second equation in table 7.4, it was significant (with a coefficient of 0.021) and the size of government coefficient fell to 0.022(s.e. = 0.005). However, when jurisdiction population was added to the fourth equation in table 7.4 (i.e., county population and median income held constant), its coefficient was a statistically insignificant 0.006, the government employment coefficient was 0.030 (s.e. = 0.005), and the remaining coefficients were not appreciably affected by its inclusion.

References

Brown, Charles, and James L. Medoff. 1986. The employer size–wage effect. Harvard Institute of Economics Research Discussion Paper no. 1202. Harvard University.

Clark, R. Theodore, Jr. 1982. A management perspective. In Interest arbitration: Can the public sector afford it? Developing limitations on the process, Wayne Minami, R. Theodore Clark, Jr., and William J. Fallon, *Proceedings of the 34th Annual Meeting of the National Academy of Arbitrators*, pp. 241–72.

Ehrenberg, Ronald, Richard Chaykowski, and Randy Ehrenberg. 1986. Merit pay for school superintendents. NBER Working Paper no. 1954. Cambridge, Mass.: National Bureau of Economic Research.

Elkouri, Frank, and Edna Asper Elkouri. 1985. *How arbitration works*, 4th ed. Washington, D.C.: Bureau of National Affairs, Inc.

Freeman, Richard B. 1986. Unionism comes to the public sector. *Journal of Economic Literature* 24(1):41–86.

Frey, Donald E. 1975. Wage determination in public schools and the effects of unionization. In *Labor in the public and nonprofit sectors*, ed. Daniel Hamermesh, 183–219. Princeton, N.J.: Princeton University Press.

Lester, Richard A. 1984. *Labor arbitration in state and local government*. Princeton, N.J.: Industrial Relations Section, Princeton University.

Mulcahy, Charles C. 1976. Ability to pay: The public employee dilemma. *Arbitration Journal* 31: 90–96.

U.S. Census Bureau. 1978a. *County business patterns, 1977*. Washington, D.C.: Government Printing Office.

———. 1978b. Governmental organization. *1977 Census of Governments*, vol. 1, no. 1. Washington, D.C.: Government Printing Office.

———. 1978c. *Statistical abstract of the United States, 1978*. Washington, D.C.: Government Printing Office.

———. 1979a. Compendium of public employment. *1977 Census of Governments*, vol. 3, no. 2. Washington, D.C.: Government Printing Office.

———. 1979b. Labor management relations in state and local government. *1977 Census of Governments*, vol. 3, no. 3. Washington, D.C.: Government Printing Office.

———. 1983. Interviewers' Memorandum no. 83–6.

———. 1984. Taxable property values and assessment—Sales price ratios. *1982 Census of Governments*, vol. 2. Washington, D.C.: Government Printing Office.

———. 1985. Census of Governments, 1982 Employment Statistics, Technical Documentation. Photocopy.

Comment   Daniel S. Hamermesh

Brown and Medoff have replicated their work on the private sector and have demonstrated that larger employers (in the public sector) pay higher wages to observationally identical workers. It is quite doubtful that measuring compensation more broadly would affect the result appreciably or that adding any additional, imaginable, obtainable control variables would overturn the finding. Nonetheless, a number of extensions seem worthwhile.

First among these is an examination of whether larger jurisdictions offer greater promotion opportunities and more jurisdiction-specific training. One might expect this to occur and, if it does, to affect the measured size–*lifetime earnings* relationship. To circumvent this potential problem by following workers over time, the authors, or other interested researchers, should obtain longitudinal data on workers and their characteristics that can be linked to data on the governments for which they work. Such data are not readily available in the United States, but foreign alternatives may be useful for this purpose. Data on job changers could also be used, as in Krueger (chap. 8, this volume), to analyze whether unmeasured individual characteristics are producing a spurious size-wage effect.

There is a general belief that government employment became less secure in the 1970s than it had been previously. Layoffs of government workers, due in some cases to reductions in demand (e.g., because of declines in the size of the school-age population) and in others to union-imposed wage increases that move governments up the demand schedule, increased the risk of job loss in the public sector relative to private employment. If markets work at all, this should have reduced the compensating wage differential for such risk between the private and public sectors. More important for our purposes, if the risk of layoff increased especially in larger jurisdictions, it could account for part of the size-wage differential in public employment in the late 1970s and early 1980s. It is not easy to discover the importance of this potential cause of the differential; at the least, though, one could examine whether the risk of job losses in public employment is greater in larger jurisdictions or at larger sites.

While Brown and Medoff make some effort to account for differences in occupation in the estimates using the CPS samples, the occupations are defined very broadly. If there is a compensating differential for positions of responsibility, the average differential will be greater in

Daniel S. Hamermesh is professor and chairperson at the Department of Economics, Michigan State University, and a research associate of the National Bureau of Economic Research.

larger jurisdictions and at larger sites. Thus part of the size-wage relationship may be accounted for by a failure to hold constant satisfactorily for occupational level. This possibility could be easily examined if the authors were to use readily available data on salaries in a narrowly defined occupation, for example, classroom teachers or bus drivers, and relate them to site or jurisdiction size.

All of these extensions are worth pursuing and should be pursued. I doubt, though, that they will obliterate the size-wage effect the authors have found. We should accept their findings in both the public and private sectors as "true facts," though relatively unsurprising ones, and endeavor to explain why they arise. In the context of the private sector, this means rationalizing the simultaneous existence of firms in the same market having different labor costs; in the public sector it requires the more difficult task of explaining why voters in larger jurisdictions want higher-paid public servants, or, alternatively, why taxpayers remain in those jurisdictions. Such rationalization requires more than the careful presentation of data that constitutes this study.

The authors show that union coverage has less effect on wage differentials than do public policies that encourage bargaining. This result suggests that the major cause of higher wages under collective bargaining is not union coverage but rather public leniency toward workers' exercising their rights collectively. This accords with the conservative view that unionism expanded in the United States in the 1930s mainly because of encourgement provided by federal policy. It indicates, though it by no means proves, that union successes depend crucially more on their political clout than on their ability to attract members or to extract rents from firms. It is not a very happy conclusion for those who see public attitudes, and their reflection in public policy, as becoming increasingly negative toward unionism.

8

Are Public Sector Workers Paid More Than Their Alternative Wage? Evidence from Longitudinal Data and Job Queues

Alan B. Krueger

Several academic researchers have addressed the issue of whether federal government workers are paid more than comparable private sector workers. In general, these studies use cross-sectional data to estimate the differential in wages between federal and private sector workers, controlling for observed worker characteristics such as age and education. (Examples are Smith 1976, 1977 and Quinn 1979.) This literature typically finds that wages are 10–20 percent greater for federal workers than private sector workers, all else constant. In conflict with the findings of academic studies, the Bureau of Labor Statistics's official wage comparability survey consistently finds that federal workers are paid less than private sector workers who perform similar jobs.[1] Moreover, the government's findings have been confirmed by an independent study by Hay Associates (1984). Additional research is needed to resolve this conflict.

When the focus turns to state and local governments, insignificant differences in pay are generally found between state and local government employees and private sector employees. One important difference, however, is the varying effect of unions on compensation in the two sectors. An overwhelming amount of evidence suggests that the union-nonunion wage gap is substantially smaller in the state and local government sector than in the private sector.[2]

Alan B. Krueger is assistant professor of economics and public affairs in the Economics Department and Woodrow Wilson School at Princeton University, and a faculty research fellow of the National Bureau of Economic Research.

Without implicating them for any of the results or interpretations, the author thanks David Bloom, John Dunlop, Richard Freeman, Robert Hartman, James Medoff, Larry Summers, John Bound, Harry Holzer, Joe Tracy, and Steve Venti for helpful comments. The author was a graduate student in the Department of Economics at Harvard University when this paper was completed.

This chapter extends the literature on public sector/private sector wage differentials by examining two new types of evidence, namely longitudinal data and job queues.[3] With longitudinal data I examine the change in a worker's pay as he or she moves from the private to the public sector, or vice versa. This analysis has the advantage of reflecting the government's relevant external labor market because it is based on the actual transitions of workers, and of controlling for worker characteristics that remain fixed as workers change jobs. The data on job queues are used to compare the number of individuals who apply for jobs in the federal government to the number who apply for jobs in the private sector. If prospective employees consider government employment (e.g., wage and nonwage benefits) more attractive than private sector employment, we would expect to find a longer queue of applicants for government jobs than private sector jobs, all else constant.

The major result of this chapter is that longitudinal and cross-sectional analyses yield broadly similar estimates of the differential in pay between public and private sector workers, and similar estimates of the union-nonunion wage gap in the public sector. Furthermore, the comparison of job application rates suggests that for the average job opening the federal government receives more applications than the average private sector firm. For certain occupations such as engineers, however, it appears that the government has a shortage of job applicants. The findings are generally consistent with the previous academic literature.

Finally, this chapter explores several possible rationales that might explain why the federal government appears to consistently pay higher wages than the private sector for comparable employees. The specific focus is on issues relating to turnover, morale, motivation, supervision, employee transfers, employer size, and unions.

8.1 Pay Determination in the Federal Government

Federal employees are covered by a number of different wage schedules.[4] However, the General Schedule (GS) for white-collar workers and the Federal Wage System (FWS) for blue-collar workers are the two major wage schedules for civilian federal employees. Since federal employees are overwhelmingly white-collar workers, the GS is the predominant wage schedule used by the U.S. government—nearly 1.5 million full-time federal employees were covered by the GS as of March 1985.

The GS consists of eighteen grades, GS-1 through GS-15, with GS-1 the lowest grade.[5] A grade corresponds to a salary range. Each work level of each occupation is assigned to one of the grades. For example, nearly all nurses are classified between GS-4 and GS-9. Within a grade, employees may advance through ten salary steps, depending on length of service and completion of sufficiently competent work. Some additional flexibility is introduced into the system because agencies may apply to the Office of Personnel Management's Special Rates and Analysis Division for higher step classifications (up to the tenth step of the grade) if they encounter difficulty in recruiting or retaining employees in certain occupations (e.g., engineering) or regions (e.g., Los Angeles).

The Federal Pay Comparability Act of 1970 is the statutory basis of the GS. The Act requires that federal workers receive wages equivalent to private sector workers performing the same level of work. To this end, each year in March the U.S. Bureau of Labor Statistics (BLS) conducts a survey of private sector wages of professional, administrative, technical, and clerical jobs (the PATC survey). Based on this survey, the BLS recommends to Congress and the president salary increases for each grade to take effect the following October. The president, in turn, has the option to submit an alternative proposal for white-collar pay increases to Congress. Each year since 1976 the president has elected this option and proposed wage increases that were less than the amount called for by the PATC survey.

In the early 1970s the PATC comparability survey found that wages were virtually equal between GS and private sector workers in similar occupations, but by 1980 the GS fell behind the private sector by 14 percent, and by 1986 the GS trailed the private sector by 23.8 percent.

The PATC survey has been criticized on several grounds. First, many jobs in the public sector are not directly comparable to private sector jobs, and jobs that are equivalent may have inaccurate job descriptions. Second, the PATC survey neglects nonwage compensation. Finally, the survey has been unduly criticized because it oversamples large establishments. In 1985, the minimum establishment size requirement for the PATC survey ranged from 50 to 250 employees depending on the industry. Although larger establishments appear to pay higher wages for workers of equal quality (e.g., Brown and Medoff 1985), the following calculation suggests that it is unlikely that the sampling design of the PATC survey produces a sizeable bias on the estimated pay differential. A wage regression with 1979 CPS data shows that white-collar employees in establishments with fewer than 100 employees earn about 7 percent lower wages than employees in larger establishments. Since less than half of private sector employees work in establishments with fewer than 100 employees, neglecting employees in small establishments will upwardly bias the estimated wage of private sector workers by less than 3.5 percent.

It should be noted, however, that an independent study by Hay Associates (1984) for the House Committee on Post Office and Civil Service reached conclusions similar to the PATC survey. The Hay

Associates applied the same compensation analyses it uses to evaluate the pay scales of major private sector employers: jobs in both sectors were assigned points by managers according to their degree of difficulty, and comparisons were made between the GS and the wages of a sample of private sector employers who had previously used Hay Associates' services. The study found that GS pay was 10.3 percent less than the pay of private sector employees performing similar jobs in 1984. Although the Hay Associates' study can be easily criticized for its non-random sample of private employers, the results are qualitatively similar to the PATC survey.

8.2. Methodology

Studies of public sector wages that estimate human capital earnings functions with cross-sectional data cannot control for unobserved differences in worker productivity, such as innate ability and motivation. This can be seen in equation (1), where w_{it} is the hourly wage rate, X_{it} is a vector of observed productivity and demographic characteristics, β is a vector of returns to those characteristics, P_{it} is a dummy variable that takes on the value of one if the worker is employed in the public sector and zero if employed in the private sector, δ is the public sector wage differential, μ_i represents unobserved, time invariant worker characteristics, and ϵ_{it} is a white noise error term.[6] The subscript i refers to individuals and t to time.

$$(1) \qquad \ln(w_{it}) = X_{it}\beta + P_{it}\delta + \mu_i + \epsilon_{it}.$$

If public sector workers are more productive than their private sector counterparts in terms of unobserved characteristics and if workers are positively rewarded for these unobserved characteristics, the unobserved factors will "load on" the public sector dummy variable and thus upwardly bias the estimated public sector wage differential.

Longitudinal data provide a means to control for time-invariant, unobserved variables. The approach taken here is to estimate first differenced regressions to control for unobserved variables.[7] As can be seen in equation (2), first differencing the data (denoted by Δ) nets out the constant unobserved factors that bias cross-sectional analyses. Since the panel data set only includes two years of data on each individual, the first differenced regression is equivalent to a fixed-effects estimator. However, controlling for fixed effects is not without costs, since first differencing typically exacerbates measurement error bias and raises issues about the selectivity of job switchers. These potential biases are considered in the empirical analysis.

$$(2) \qquad \Delta\ln(w_{it}) = \Delta X_{it}\beta + \Delta P_{it}\delta + \Delta\epsilon_{it}.$$

Finally, it should be noted that equation (2) can be generalized to allow different changes in employment to have different effects on wages. Because of the voluntary mobility of many job changers, the wage growth, W, of workers who join the government relative to those who remain in the private sector, $(W_{pg} - W_{pp})$, may not equal the relative wage change of workers who leave the government, $(W_{gp} - W_{gg})$, in absolute value. The consequences of voluntary job changes for the longitudinal analysis is discussed further in the empirical section below.

8.2.1 Data Sets

A longitudinal data set that follows individuals over time is necessary to estimate equation (2). Two longitudinal data sets are used. The first is a series of matched May Current Population Surveys (CPS). The rotation group design of the CPS allows for the creation of a large longitudinal data set because half of the households surveyed in a given month are reinterviewed the following year, and thus may be matched from one year to the next.

This study uses matched May CPS data from 1979–80, 1977–78, and 1974–75. Each individual is observed in two consecutive years. The data from all three matched data sets are pooled together to create a large sample of public sector/private sector switchers, and year dummy variables are included in the regressions to control for wage inflation. CPS reports that about 70 percent of eligible observations are typically matched from one year to the next. Even with this large data set, there is only a relatively small sample of workers who move between the public and private sectors, and it is necessary to pool together observations on men and women to estimate the public sector wage differential more precisely.

Since CPS cannot match individuals who change their address during the course of the year, the sample is not completely representative of all workers. However, this sample selection rule is not likely to produce an important bias in the estimated wage differentials because both joiners and leavers who move to a new location are eliminated from the sample.[8] On the other hand, this feature of the data has the virtue of assuring that wage changes do not represent cost-of-living adjustments for workers who move to relatively high-wage areas (e.g., Washington, D.C.), because all workers remain in the same area both time periods.

Following most previous studies, government employees are identified from their reported industry status. (In recent years CPS identifies the level of government in the class of worker variable.) Unfortunately, this procedure only identifies government employees involved in public administration, which consists of employees engaged in legislative, judicial, administrative, and regulatory activities. At the federal level, this includes workers employed by most agencies and bureaus, the courts, and the secret service. The Army Corp of Engineers and Government Printing Office are examples of exclusions from public administration. At the state and local government level, policemen, fire fighters and tax collectors are examples of workers classified in public administration, while other employees such as public school teachers and librarians are classified in private sector industries. In total, 51 percent of federal workers, 35 percent of state government workers, and 20 percent of local government workers are classified in public administration.[9]

The sample contains full-time and part-time civilian nonagricultural employees sixteen years old or older. The earnings variable is usual weekly earnings divided by usual weekly hours. All individuals whose derived wage rate is less than $1 per hour or more than $200 per hour are eliminated from the sample.[10] Furthermore, workers who are categorized as government employees according to the class of worker variable but who are not categorized in a public administration industry are eliminated from the sample. Finally, workers who move from one branch of government service to another (e.g., state government to local government) are eliminated from the sample in order to compare public sector workers to private sector workers.

8.2.2   Displaced Workers Survey

The second longitudinal data set is drawn from the CPS supplemental surveys of displaced workers. In January of 1984 and 1986 the U.S. Census Bureau asked a sequence of retrospective questions of workers who lost a job in the preceding five years because of a plant closing, permanent layoff, or unforeseen job abolishment. Responses from both surveys are pooled together to create a sample of more than 4,000 workers who were displaced from private sector jobs. Almost 10 percent of these workers joined the public sector.

This data set (hereafter referred to as the Displaced Workers Survey) helps solve the problem of selective job changers because only workers who were involuntarily displaced from their jobs are in the sample. Since the notion of a job displacement from the public sector is questionable, workers who are initially in the public sector are eliminated from the sample. Furthermore, construction workers are eliminated from the sample because of the temporary, discontinuous nature of their work.

One disadvantage of the Displaced Workers Survey is that hourly wage rates and weekly hours are not available. Instead, the usual weekly wage is used as the dependent variable and the sample is restricted to full-time (at least thirty-five hours per week) workers. On the other hand, the data set has the advantages of following workers who moved to a new location, contains tenure on the initial job, and identifies government workers on the basis of the class of worker variable rather than the industry variable.[11] Furthermore, the sample covers a recent time period.

8.3 Empirical Results

Longitudinal and cross-sectional estimates of the public sector wage differential are considered below. The results for federal, postal, state and local government employees are considered in turn, with most attention devoted to the federal sector.

8.3.1 The Federal Wage Differential

Before proceeding to the multivariate analysis, it is useful to consider some summary statistics. Table 8.1 focuses on differences between federal and private sector workers who move between sectors or remain in the same sector using the matched CPS data set, which includes voluntary and involuntary movers. The table contains means of several variables for four subgroups: 1) joiners to the federal government (from the private sector, 2) stayers in the private sector, 3) stayers in the federal government, and 4) leavers from the federal government (to the private sector).

Several conclusions can be drawn from table 8.1. One striking difference between switchers and stayers is that labor mobility is disproportionately large between the federal sector and the service industry. Of workers who joined the public sector, 55 percent left jobs in the service industry, while 38 percent of the workers who left federal employment for private employment joined the service industry. In comparison, only about 20 percent of private sector workers are employed in the service sector at a point in time.

It is also apparent from table 8.1 that workers who join the federal government are more likely to be in white-collar jobs and to be female, white, unmarried, nonunion, and younger than workers who remain in the private sector, while workers who leave the federal government are more likely to be male, nonwhite, unmarried, nonunion, and slightly younger than those who remain in the federal sector.

Table 8.2 presents regression estimates of the public sector wage differential for each level of government, holding constant the occupation, human capital, and demographic controls listed at the bottom of the table.[12] Column (1) of the table reports results of regressions on first differences (eq. 2) and, for comparison, column (2) reports cross-sectional results (eq. 1). Each coefficient reported in the table is estimated from a separate regression. A puzzling result is that the longi-

Table 8.1   Characteristics of Sector Changers and Stayers

Variable	(1) Joiners (to federal)	(2) Stayers (private)	(3) Stayers (federal)	(4) Leavers (from federal)
Change Log Wage				
Males	0.192	0.093	0.080	0.083
Females	0.262	0.106	0.076	0.226
Initial Occupation				
Professional	0.161	0.103	0.327	0.143
Management	0.065	0.097	0.148	0.238
Clerical	0.484	0.185	0.337	0.286
Sales	0.032	0.067	0.000	0.000
Crafts	0.097	0.170	0.097	0.143
Operatives	0.032	0.212	0.092	0.095
Laborers	0.000	0.049	0.026	0.048
Service Workers	0.129	0.117	0.047	0.048
Industry				
Construction	0.000	0.058	NA	0.048
Manufacturing	0.129	0.346	NA	0.048
Transportation	0.032	0.082	NA	0.095
Wholesale & Retail Trade	0.226	0.240	NA	0.143
Finance, Insurance, and Real Estate	0.065	0.064	NA	0.238
Service	0.548	0.193	NA	0.381
Mining	0.000	0.016	NA	0.048
Demographic				
Age	32.7	38.5	41.9	37.7
Education	12.5	11.9	13.6	12.9
Nonwhite	0.065	0.091	0.162	0.190
Female	0.677	0.397	0.339	0.286
Married	0.774	0.836	0.899	0.714
Union Status				
Period One	0.032	0.257	0.176	0.143
Period Two	0.097	0.259	0.203	0.191

Note: Sample sizes for columns (1)–(4) are 31, 18, 348, 493, and 21, respectively. Data set is matched May CPS, 1974–75, 1977–78, and 1979–80. NA means not applicable.

tudinal analysis finds a statistically insignificant 6 percent wage differential for federal workers relative to private sector workers, while the cross-sectional estimate with the same data set is nearly 25 percent and highly statistically significant. Furthermore, the cross-sectional finding is similar in magnitude to the results of studies surveyed earlier.

Estimation of a more flexible specification that allows the wage differential to vary for joiners and leavers helps resolve this puzzle. The estimated wage change (standard error) of workers who join the federal sector from the private sector as opposed to remaining in the private sector ($Wpg - Wpp$) is 0.12 (0.05), while workers who move from the

Table 8.2   Public Sector/Private Sector Wage Differentials, Fixed-Effects and Cross-Sectional Estimates[a]

	Estimation Technique	
Sample	(1) Fixed-Effects[b]	(2) Cross-Section[c]
Federal and Private [18,893]	0.058	0.247
	(0.042)	(0.017)
Postal and Private [18,603]	0.312	0.113
	(0.088)	(0.024)
State and Private [18,600]	0.051	0.062
	(0.054)	(0.025)
Local and Private [18,920]	−0.038	0.042
	(0.037)	(0.017)

[a]Data set for fixed-effects models is CPS matched May 1979–80, 1978–79, and 1974–75. Sample size is in brackets. Cross-section is 1974, 1977, and 1979 CPS samples pooled together. Results were qualitatively similar with the second-period data sample. Standard errors are in parentheses.

[b]Controls column (1): change in occupation dummies (8), change in education, change in union status, change in marital status, age, and year dummies (2).

[c]Controls column (2): occupation dummies (8), education, union status, marital status, nonwhite, age group dummies (6), sex, region dummies (3), and year dummies (2).

federal government to the private sector ($Wgp - Wgg$) experience a 0.05 (0.07) wage gain over those who remain federal employees.[13] Unfortunately, these wage differentials are not estimated very precisely because of the limited number of transitions between the private sector and the federal government in this data set.

Consideration of the selection forces that affect job changers suggests that the relative wage gains for workers who join the federal government are more representative of the "true" average difference in wages between the federal government and private sector.[14] If employees face a distribution of jobs with different wages (i.e., due to job matches or imperfect information), optimal search behavior would lead employees to voluntarily change jobs only if the new job offered better wage and nonwage benefits than the current job. In addition, the large pension losses imposed on workers who leave the federal government discourage federal workers from moving to the private sector unless they receive large wage gains (Ippolito 1987).

On the other hand, focusing on workers who join the federal government obviates many of the selectivity problems. First, if wages in the federal sector truly exceed private sector wages in comparable jobs, private sector workers would have an incentive to queue for federal jobs. The "lucky" private sector workers who were selected for federal jobs would reap large wage gains. Furthermore, private sector workers are less constrained by pension rules.

Results of Displaced Workers Survey

The issue of selectivity of job changers is dealt with in perhaps a more satisfactory manner in our analysis of displaced workers. In the ideal longitudinal experiment, workers would be randomly assigned to move between the government and the private sector. The Displaced Workers Survey is a better approximation to the ideal experimental design because only workers who were involuntarily displaced from their original private sector jobs are included in the sample.[15]

Table 8.3 compares the wage growth of workers who joined the government after being displaced from their initial jobs in the private sector to the wage growth of workers who accepted private sector jobs after being displaced from their initial private sector jobs. The regressions control for the year the worker was displaced and the survey year, as well as tenure on the initial job, geographic mobility, and changes in eight major occupations. For comparison, the second column of the table presents cross-sectional regression estimates of the various public sector wage differentials using the May 1984 CPS.

The results indicate that earnings growth of displaced private sector workers who join the federal government exceeds the earnings growth

Table 8.3   Longitudinal Analysis of Displaced Workers Survey

	Estimation Technique	
Sample	(1) Fixed-Effects[a]	(2) Cross-Section[b]
Federal and Private	0.107 (0.055)	0.126 (0.020)
Postal and Private	0.126 (0.097)	0.065 (0.038)
State and Private	−0.037 (0.045)	−0.100 (0.018)
Local and Private	−0.044 (0.033)	−0.096 (0.013)

[a]Data set for fixed-effects models is the January 1984 and January 1986 CPS supplemental displaced worker surveys. The sample consists of 3,844 workers who remained in the private sector, 59 who joined the federal government, 19 who joined the postal service, 91 who joined state governments, and 174 who joined local governments. Controls are change in major occupation dummies (8), tenure on previous job, age, a dummy variable indicating whether the worker moved to a new location, year of displacement dummies (4), and a dummy variable indicating whether the observation is taken from the 1984 or 1986 survey. Standard errors are in parentheses.

[b]Cross-section estimates are based on the May 1984 CPS survey. Dependent variable is log usual weekly wage and sample is restricted to full-time workers. Sample sizes for rows 1 through 3 are 9,740, 9,896, and 10,521, respectively. Controls are occupation dummies (8), education, union status, marital status, nonwhite, age group dummies (6), sex, central city dummy, and region dummies (3). Standard errors are in parentheses.

of displaced workers who remain in the private sector by a statistically significant 10.7 percent. This estimate is similar in magnitude to the 12.6 percent federal earnings differential obtained from the cross-sectional regression with the May 1984 CPS. Because of changes in relative federal-private compensation over time, these results vary from table 8.2.

The initial industry that workers are employed in does not appear to have an important effect on these findings. When the sample is divided into subsamples of manufacturing and nonmanufacturing workers, the first difference estimate of the federal wage premium (standard error) is 0.11 (0.08) for nonmanufacturing workers and 0.10 (0.07) for manufacturing workers.

Measurement Error

Estimation using both longitudinal data sets finds that the federal wage differential is smaller in the longitudinal analysis than in the corresponding cross-sectional analysis. It is well known that measurement error biases regression coefficients downward in absolute value, and Freeman (1984) proves that under plausible assumptions measurement error produces a greater bias in longitudinal analyses than cross-sectional analyses. Since Mellow and Sider (1983) report evidence that misclassification in the reporting of industry status at a point in time is a pervasive problem in CPS data, measurement error bias may be responsible for the smaller estimate of the federal wage differential in the longitudinal analysis.

What effect does measurement error have on the longitudinal estimation? If half of the observed transitions between the federal government and private sector in the matched CPS data set are the result of random misclassification errors, the first difference estimate would be biased downward by about 50 percent. This would be large enough to account for the entire difference between the longitudinal and cross-sectional results in the matched CPS data set.

There is likely to be a smaller bias from measurement error in the Displaced Workers Surveys than in the matched CPS data set for two reasons. First, there are relatively more true sectoral transitions in this data set because all of the workers changed jobs. As a result, the signal in the data increases relative to the noise. Second, government workers are identified by the class of worker variable instead of the industry variable, which is likely to reduce measurement error.

Unfortunately, given the small sample of switchers in the data sets and the potentially large effect of measurement error bias, it is difficult to precisely estimate the federal wage differential from the longitudinal analyses. Nonetheless, it appears that longitudinal estimates of the federal wage differential in both data sets are less than the corresponding cross-sectional estimates. The difference between the longitudinal and cross-sectional estimates may stem from measurement errors and/or unobserved worker-specific characteristics. Since Freeman (1984) has shown that cross-sectional and longitudinal estimates of wage differentials probably bound the true wage differential, it would appear that the federal wage premium was between 12 percent and 25 percent in the 1970s and between 11 percent and 13 percent in the mid-1980s.

Who Gains from Federal Employment?

Lastly, I examine how the federal wage premium varies across different types of workers, different regions of the United States, and over time. Table 8.4 examines these issues for separate samples of men and women. The federal wage premium is estimated for various groups of workers by interacting several independent variables with a dummy variable that equals one if the worker is employed by the federal government. Cross-sectional data are analyzed because there are too few job changers in the longitudinal data set to make accurate comparisons, and because the previous results suggest that unobserved heterogeneity may not be a serious problem in cross-sectional studies of the federal wage premium.

Consistent with the findings of previous researchers, the results indicate that the federal wage premium is greater for female workers (especially nonwhite female workers) than for male workers. This may reflect less discrimination in the federal government than in the private sector (Asher and Popkin 1984; Freeman 1987) or, alternatively, that the compressed government wage structure benefits female-dominated occupations relative to male-dominated occupations.

Along occupational lines, white-collar workers appear to receive a larger wage premium from federal employment than blue-collar workers. In addition, older workers and workers in the South appear to benefit more from federal employment than younger workers and workers in other regions of the country. The regional differences may result from inherent rigidities caused by a national nominal wage scale.

Finally, an analysis of the federal wage premium over time shows that the wage gap between male federal workers and private sector workers fell quite dramatically in the latter part of the 1970s, although a trend for women is much less pronounced. Freeman (1987) notes a similar decline in the relative pay of federal workers in several data sets.

8.3.2   Postal Workers

Turning next to postal workers, the longitudinal and cross-sectional analyses in tables 8.2 and 8.3 both find that the wage of postal workers exceeds the wage of private sector workers, although the magnitude

Table 8.4   **The Federal Wage Premium for Different Types of Workers and Over Time**

	Sample	
	Male	Female
Race		
White	0.210	0.299
	(0.023)	(0.030)
Nonwhite	0.181	0.369
	(0.056)	(0.059)
Age		
25	0.140	0.246
	(0.037)	(0.033)
50	0.232	0.363
	(0.026)	(0.127)
Occupation		
White Collar	0.215	0.317
	(0.024)	(0.026)
Blue Collar	0.184	0.178
	(0.039)	(0.154)
Region		
North East	0.051	0.285
	(0.062)	(0.070)
South	0.279	0.373
	(0.030)	(0.036)
West	0.176	0.252
	(0.042)	(0.060)
North Central	0.140	0.199
	(0.053)	(0.072)
Year		
1974	0.240	0.348
	(0.033)	(0.043)
1977	0.202	0.267
	(0.030)	(0.036)
1979	0.115	0.385
	(0.059)	(0.074)
Sample Size	11,410	7,483

Notes: Coefficients are estimated from cross-section regressions interacting each variable with a dummy variable for federal employment. Controls are year dummies, occupation dummies (8), union status, marital status, age group dummies (6), education, and race. Data set is pooled CPS data from 1974, 1977, and 1979.

of the differential appears to have diminished over time. Given the small sample of postal workers, however, the estimated wage differentials are extremely imprecise. Nonetheless, these results support Perloff and Wachter's (1984) claim that postal workers are paid more than comparable private sector workers.

8.3.3   State and Local Government Workers

The estimated wage differential between state and local government employees and private sector employees is similar in the longitudinal and cross-sectional analyses using both data sets. Furthermore, a decline in the wages of state and local workers relative to private sector workers is evident in the Displaced Workers Survey, which covers the years 1980 through 1986, and in the matched CPS data set, which covers the years 1974 through 1980.

The first difference regression using the matched CPS data reported in table 8.2 indicates that state government employees earn 5.1 percent higher wages than private sector workers, while the cross-sectional regression finds a 6.2 percent wage advantage for state government employees over private sector employees. The longitudinal estimate, however, is statistically insignificant. Analysis of the second data set reported in table 8.3 finds that displaced private workers who take employment in state governments experience 3.7 percent less earnings growth than displaced workers who remain in the private sector. And a cross-sectional regression using the May 1984 CPS finds that earnings are 10 percent less among state government employees than private sector employees.

Lastly, on the local government level, the first difference regression using the matched CPS data finds a statistically insignificant −3.8 percent public sector wage differential, while the cross-sectional regression shows a statistically significant positive 4.2 percent public sector wage differential. The Displaced Workers Survey, on the other hand, shows a −4.4 percent earnings differential for workers who join local governments, and the cross-sectional regression with the May 1984 CPS shows a statistically significant −9.6 percent earnings differential for local government employees.

As noted earlier in the case of federal workers, reporting errors in the state and local government variable would bias the public sector wage differentials toward zero.

8.4   Queues for Federal Jobs

Long (1982), Utgoff (1983), and others turn to evidence on the quit rate in the federal government and the private sector to infer conclusions about pay comparability. Since the quit rate is substantially lower among federal workers, this is often cited as support of the view that federal workers receive economic rents. Ippolito (1987), however, challenges this interpretation. He argues that the abnormally low quit rate in the federal sector is due to the substantial pension losses imposed on workers who quit the government early because federal pension benefits are based on nominal wages at the time of departure, and because pension benefits make up a larger share of compensation in the public sector than in the private sector.

An alternative form of evidence—the application rate for federal government and private sector jobs—is examined here.[16] In a textbook competitive labor market, firms pay a wage that is just high enough to attract, motivate, and retain a sufficient number of qualified workers. Consequently, the number of workers who queue for a job opening at a particular firm reflects the relative attractiveness of working for that firm. A longer job queue signals that workers perceive the firm to offer relatively high pecuniary and nonpecuniary benefits. It should be noted that a comparison of job application rates overcomes a major limitation of the quit rate studies because workers who are applying for a job consider the expected discounted value of future earnings and are not seriously influenced by the "lock-in" effects of pensions.

In addition to the overall attractiveness of the job, the direct and indirect costs of the application process will affect the number of applicants for a given job opening. More costly and difficult application procedures will discourage applicants. Included in the application cost are the psychic and time costs of obtaining information about job openings, filling out an application, being interviewed, and possibly taking an exam. If the cost of applying for a job does not differ substantially between two employers that draw from the same labor market, it is reasonable to expect that the employer with the longer job queue offers relatively more desirable employment.

There are three major limitations to judging federal pay comparability by comparing the length of queues for federal and private sector jobs. First, the cost of applying for federal jobs and private sector jobs is not equal. For instance, the federal government requires a competitive entrance exam of many job applicants, while this procedure may be less common in private sector firms. In addition, the cost and process of obtaining information about federal jobs differ from private sector jobs. To the extent that it is more (less) costly to apply for federal jobs than private sector jobs, there will be relatively fewer (more) applicants for available jobs in the federal sector at a given level of wages and working conditions.

The second limitation is that analyzing raw data on the number of applicants per selection does not control for the quality of the applicant pool.[17] Krueger (1988) finds evidence that an increase in the wage of federal workers relative to private sector workers increases both the number and average quality of applicants for federal jobs. The third limitation is that the number of actual applicants is an imperfect measure of the number of workers who would be willing to work for a given firm.

Controlling for the different application costs and the quality of applicants in the federal and private sectors is beyond the scope of available data, but a comparison between the number of applicants for federal and private jobs provides a crude indication of wage comparability. Table 8.5 presents data on the length of the queue for federal jobs, measured by the number of outside job applicants per new worker hired. Column (1) contains the number of applicants from outside the government (excluding the postal service), and column (2) contains the number of workers hired from these applicants during fiscal year 1982.[18] Column (3) contains the ratio of applicants to new hires. The data are broken down for several occupations.

The length of the queue for federal jobs varies considerably across occupations, ranging from a high of 38.4 applicants per new hire in the field of life science to a low of 4.5 applicants per new hire for engineers. The varying length of occupational job queues probably reflects the relative scarcity of certain skills (e.g., engineers) as well as the varying federal wage premium among occupations. On average, 10.5 candidates applied per new hire in the federal government in 1982.

How does this compare with the typical job application rate in the private sector? Unfortunately, only scant data on applications for private sector jobs are available. The most suitable data set for our purposes is the Employment Opportunities Pilot Project (EOPP) survey conducted by Gallup in 1982. The EOPP survey contains establishment-level information on three relevant items: 1) the number of applicants who applied for the last position filled; 2) the number of applications

Table 8.5   **Queues for Jobs in the Federal Government in Fiscal Year 1982**

Occupation/Field	(1) Applications Processed	(2) New Hires	(1)/(2) Applications per New Hire
Blue Collar	127,783	12,673	10.1
Steno/Typist	162,164	20,720	7.8
Life Science	5,370	140	38.4
Engineers	19,025	4,273	4.5
Mathematician	4,803	634	7.6
Physical Science	13,356	1,057	12.6
Computer Specialist	8,958	864	10.4
Nurse	4,257	826	5.2
Accountant/Auditor	10,930	340	32.1
All Jobs	1,132,260	107,967	10.5

Source: Unpublished data provided by the Office of Personnel Management. Total for all jobs does not equal the sum of occupations because of unclassified occupations and because delegations to agencies are not recorded by occupation.

received and job offers made in the preceding ten days; and 3) the average number of job offers made per worker hired. Although these questions are not identical to the application data collected for federal government jobs, they provide a rough indication of the number of applicants for private sector jobs.

According to tabulations using the EOPP data set, on average private sector establishments receive 8.37 applications for the most recently filled position, and 7.60 applications for each accepted job offer.[19] Unfortunately, these data are not available by occupation.

Although there are severe data limitations, a comparison of the length of private sector and federal sector job queues is suggestive. On average, openings for federal government jobs appear to attract more applicants than openings for private sector jobs. Depending on the survey question used, the results indicate that on average there is a 25 percent to 38 percent higher application rate in the federal government than in the private sector. These findings suggest that the positive federal wage differential is not a compensating differential for undesirable work in the federal government.

However, extreme caution should be taken in interpreting these findings given the differences in the occupational composition of the work forces in the federal government and private sector and the paucity of private sector data.

8.5   Why Does the Federal Government Pay High Wages?

A variety of evidence suggests that the federal government pays at least some workers more than their alternative wage in the private sector. Why does such a policy exist? Are there any possible benefits of this policy that might offset the cost of higher wages? Can the government wage structure be reorganized in a more efficient way?

Undoubtedly, political constraints and motivations have an important influence on public sector wages. (See Fogel and Lewin 1974 and Borjas 1980 for evidence on the political aspects of wage setting in the public sector.) My purpose here is not to examine the political forces that affect the determination of public sector wages, but instead to consider the possible benefits to the government of pursuing a "high wage" policy and to suggest alternative, less costly, means to achieve some of these benefits.

The so-called efficiency wage theories of the labor market surveyed in Stiglitz (1986) emphasize the potential benefits to employers of paying workers a greater wage than their alternative wage. According to these theories, possible benefits to the firm that result from paying relatively high wages can at least partially offset the cost of paying above market-clearing wages. These benefits include reduced turnover, reduced absenteeism, improved morale, less worker malfeasance, lower supervision costs, and improved employee selection.[20]

Evidence suggests that the federal government does reap at least some return from its compensation policy. For instance, Long (1982), Utgoff (1983), and others find that the turnover rate of federal workers is unusually low. And Krueger (1988) demonstrates that an increase in the wages of federal workers relative to private sector workers increases both the number and average quality of applicants for federal jobs. The quantitative economic importance of these benefits, however, is uncertain.

Another element of the government wage structure that is relevant to this discussion is that white-collar federal workers have a uniform nationwide wage schedule. A secretary in New York City earns the same wage as a secretary in Omaha, Nebraska, even though the cost of living and labor market conditions differ considerably between the two regions. Proponents of this system justify nominal regional wage rigidity on the basis of efficiency; they allege that employee morale would be damaged if workers are forced to take a cut in *nominal* pay when they are transferred from one area of the country to another.

It is instructive that many large private sector firms, such as IBM, resolve this problem by maintaining a uniform *real* wage schedule across different regions of the country. Regional cost-of-living adjustments are provided to workers who transfer from one region of the country to another. Introducing regional wage flexibility to the government wage structure (at least for jobs with low transfer rates) would improve the efficiency of providing government compensation. Additionally, this policy would improve equity in the sense that all federal workers regardless of their region of employment would receive the same real wage compensation.

Finally, it should be noted that some large private sector firms pay wages that are at least as high as the federal government and that wages appear to rise with employer size (see Brown and Medoff 1985). The federal government, it should be remembered, is the single largest employer in the United States. Although the reasons for the employer-size wage effect are far from clear, the federal wage premium may be closely related to the size of the government.

8.6 The Union Wage Gap in the Public and Private Sectors

Since unions in the federal sector are usually prohibited from bargaining over wages, the analysis of the effect of public sector unions focuses on state and local government employees. Nonetheless, it is reassuring to note that we do not find evidence of a differential in pay between union and nonunion federal workers.

Most studies of union wage differences at the state and local government level analyze cross-sectional data, and the unit of observation is typically the bargaining unit or municipality.[21] By analyzing a longitudinal sample of individual workers it is possible to control for unchanging, unobserved worker characteristics. Furthermore, first difference estimation controls for the possible endogeneity of unionization, since the effect of time-invariant, unobserved variables that might be correlated with public sector union membership and wages net out.

Table 8.6 presents longitudinal and cross-sectional estimates of the public sector union wage differential. The samples are limited to workers who remain in the same sector each year and are drawn from the matched CPS data set, since initial union status is not available in the Displaced Workers Survey.

The major finding is that union membership does not have a statistically or economically significant effect on the wages of state and local government employees in either the longitudinal or the cross-sectional estimation. Although the union variable is likely to be fraught with reporting errors because workers remained in the public sector (and probably the same job) each period, the magnitude of the union wage gaps in the longitudinal estimation are so small that it is unlikely that measurement error is responsible for these results. Furthermore, the growth in public sector union membership during this period creates true transitions between union and nonunion status even for workers who remain on the same job.

It should be stressed that our inability to find a statistically significant difference in pay between union members and nonmembers in the public sector does not necessarily imply that unions have no effect on

Table 8.6   Union/Nonunion Wage Differentials by Sector, Fixed-Effects and Cross-Sectional Estimates

	Estimation Technique	
Sample	(1) Fixed Effects	(2) Cross Section
Private Sector [22,042]	0.087	0.204
	(0.009)	(0.007)
State Government [220]	0.002	−0.010
	(0.044)	(0.058)
Local Government [502]	0.002	0.055
	(0.038)	(0.039)

Notes: Reported wage differentials are coefficients of the union membership dummy variable in a log-wage regression. Each sample contains workers who remained in the same sector both periods. Controls are the same as in table 8.2, except industry dummies were included in the regressions for private sector employees. See table 8.2 for other notes. Standard errors are in parentheses.

public sector compensation. It is possible that unions raise wages for all public sector workers (i.e., through lobbying) and not just union members. Furthermore, unions may have a substantial effect on fringe benefits and working conditions (Mitchell 1979).

In contrast to the insignificant union wage effect in the public sector, the union wage effect in the private sector is substantial during the same time period. The longitudinal estimate of the union wage differential is about 9 percent and the cross-sectional estimate is about 20 percent. When separate wage changes are estimated for workers who join unions and leave unions, the change in wages from going nonunion to union as opposed to remaining union is 8.4 percent, while the change in wages from going union to nonunion as opposed to remaining a union member is − 7.9 percent. These results are typical of this type of research. (See Freeman and Medoff 1983 and Lewis 1986b for surveys.)

It is interesting to compare the estimates of the private sector union wage differential to the federal wage differential. The estimated federal wage differential and the private sector union wage gap are about equal in magnitude. In addition, evidence suggests that a greater share of total compensation is composed of fringe benefits in both the federal government and the union private sector than in the nonunion private sector (see Mitchell 1979). A high proportion of federal workers are unionized (Burton 1979). Although federal unions are generally precluded from bargaining over compensation, the wage gap between federal workers and private sector workers and the composition of compensation in the federal sector closely parallel the unionized private sector. These findings are consistent with Levitan and Noden's (1983) view that unions legislatively influence the determination of compensation in the federal sector.

8.6 Conclusion

This chapter asks whether public sector workers are paid more than their alternative wage. Although the longitudinal analysis and evidence from job queues are by no means definitive, the results suggest that the average federal worker received a higher wage than his or her alternative private sector wage in the late 1970s and mid-1980s. The major results are summarized below.

The average worker who joins the federal government appears to experience greater wage gains than the average worker who remains in the private sector, while at the same time workers who leave the federal government do not have a statistically significant change in their wages. These results appear to hold for men and women and for a sample of displaced private sector workers who join the federal government. However, in two data sets the cross-sectional estimate of the federal wage differential exceeds the longitudinal estimate. A large share of the difference between the longitudinal and cross-sectional estimates is probably due to measurement errors, although it is possible that unobserved worker-specific quality differentials account for much of the difference.

In addition, evidence on the length of job queues as measured by the number of outside job applicants per new hire was considered. The analysis suggests that for the average job opening the federal government receives more outside applicants than the average private sector firm, which supports a conclusion that the positive federal wage differential is not a compensating differential for disagreeable work.

Why does the federal government pay higher wages on average than the private sector? The chapter conjectures that the answer to this question lies in the political nature of public sector wage determination, the size of the government, possible efficiency benefits of high wages, and the rigid federal wage schedule.

At the state and local government level, both the longitudinal and cross-sectional analyses suggest that the differential in earnings between public and private sector workers was small and positive in the 1970s, but became negative by the mid-1980s. Furthermore, the empirical analysis finds no evidence of a difference in pay between union and nonunion members in the public sector.

Notes

1. Results of the government survey are reported annually in U.S. Bureau of Labor Statistics, *National Survey of Professional, Administrative, Technical, and Clerical Pay.*

2. See Lewis (1986a) for a thorough review of studies of the effects of unions in the public sector.

3. Moore and Raisian (1986) and Venti (1987) have carried out longitudinal studies of public sector pay that are similar in many respects to this one. The analysis presented here differs from theirs primarily in that I separately examine wage comparability for each level of government (i.e., federal, postal, state, and local) and analyze a sample of involuntarily "displaced" private sector workers.

4. See Smith (1976), Hartman (1983), and Ehrenberg and Schwarz (1986) for an overview of wage determination in the public sector.

5. The GS actually extends through GS-18, but almost all of the positions above GS-15 have been reclassified into the Senior Executive Service.

6. For simplicity, we abstract from differences in wages across industries in the private sector and treat the entire private sector as a homogeneous group. This procedure gives a weighted average of the difference in wages between the government and private industries.

7. This approach has been used to examine the union wage effect (Mellow 1981), compensating wage differentials (Brown 1980), the employer-size wage effect (Brown and Medoff 1985) and interindustry wage differences (Krueger and Summers 1988).

8. This will not produce a bias in the estimated wage effects when the wage change for joiners is constrained to equal the negative of the wage change for leavers (i.e., when the change dummy variable is 1 for joiners, 0 for stayers, and −1 for leavers) because the "move premium" will have an equal effect on leavers and joiners. However, when we estimate wage differentials for joiners and leavers separately, the coefficients will probably be somewhat biased toward zero due to the sample selection rule of not following workers who move to a new location.

9. These tabulations are from the May 1984 CPS, which identifies public administration and nonpublic administration government workers for each level of government by the class of worker variable. In addition, wage regressions with the same data set find that wages of public and nonpublic administration workers are not statistically or economically different.

10. Results were qualitatively the same when the sample was restricted to workers whose annual log wage growth was between −0.75 and 0.75.

11. Postal workers, however, are identified from their three-digit industry.

12. Addition of a dummy variable measuring whether private sector workers changed three-digit industries to control for the possibility that private sector workers may have changed jobs did not qualitatively alter the results.

13. It should be noted that these results do not appear to be due to the pooling of men and women in the sample. Table 8.1 shows that both men and women experience substantial wage gains when they join the federal government; both also experience wage gains when they leave the government, although the latter finding occurs to a greater extent for women.

14. See Freeman (1984) and Solon (1985) for a formal treatment of selectivity bias in longitudinal analyses.

15. One possible source of nonrandomness in the sample is the selectivity of private sector firms that displace workers (e.g., because their wages exceed the competitive level). However, this selection bias affects all workers in the data set.

16. Perloff and Wachter (1984) examine accounts of excessive application rates in their analysis of pay comparability between the postal service and private sector.

17. It should be noted that analyses of the quit rate may also be biased by omitted worker quality controls.

18. An applicant remains on the register for one year. At the end of the year if the applicant is not selected for a job but wishes to remain eligible for selection in the following year, he or she must formally notify the Office of Personnel Management. In addition, an applicant may apply for multiple jobs. See Krueger (1987) for a further description of the application process and an analysis of the determinants of applications for government jobs.

19. These averages are weighted by sample weights to reflect the general population of employers. I thank Harry Holzer for generously carrying out these tabulations.

20. The notion that a firm's compensation policy influences organizational performance has long been stressed in the personnel and economics literature. See Katz (1986) and Ehrenberg and Milkovich (1987) for a survey.

21. One exception is Ichniowski (1980), who performs before-union and after-union comparison of fire fighters' wages in different municipalities and con-

cludes that the longitudinal and cross-sectional analyses both show a small union wage differential.

References

Asher, M ., and J. Popkin. 1984. The effect of gender and race differentials on public-private wage comparisons: A study of postal workers. *Industrial and Labor Relations Review* 38:16–25.

Borjas, George. 1980. Wage determination in the federal government: The role of constituents and bureaucrats. *Journal of Political Economy* 88:1110–47.

Brown, Charles. 1980. Equalizing differences in the labor market. *Quarterly Journal of Economics* 94:113–34.

Brown, Charles, and James Medoff. 1985. The employer size-wage effect. Harvard University. Mimeo.

Burton, John F. 1979. The extent of collective bargaining in the public sector. In *Public sector bargaining*, ed. B. Aaron, J. Grodin, and R. Stern. Washington, D.C.: Bureau of National Affairs, Industrial Relations Research Association Series.

Ehrenberg, Ronald, and Joshua Schwarz. 1986. Public sector labor markets. In *Handbook of labor economics*, ed. O. Ashenfelter and R. Layard. Amsterdam: North-Holland.

Ehrenberg, Ronald, and George Milkovich. 1987. Compensation and firm performance. NBER working paper no. 2145, February.

Fogel, Walter, and David Lewin. 1974. Wage determination in the public sector. *Industrial and Labor Relations Review* 27:410–31.

Freeman, Richard. 1984. Longitudinal analyses of the effects of trade unions. *Journal of Labor Economics* 2:1–26.

———. 1987. How do public sector wages and employment respond to economic conditions? In *Public sector payrolls*, ed. David Wise. Chicago: University of Chicago Press.

Freeman, Richard, and James Medoff. 1983. The impact of collective bargaining: Can the new facts be explained by monopoly unionism? In *Research in labor economics*, supplement 2, ed. R. Ehrenberg, 293–332. Greenwich, C.: JAI Press.

Hartman, Robert. 1983. Pay and pensions for federal workers. Washington, D.C.: The Brookings Institution.

Hay Associates. 1984. Study of total compensation in the federal, state, and private sectors. Washington, D.C.: Government Printing Office.

Ichniowski, Casey. 1980. Economic effects of the firefighters' union. *Industrial and Labor Relations Review* 33:198–211.

Ippolito, Richard. 1987. Why federal workers don't quit. *Journal of Human Resources* 22:281–99.

Katz, Lawrence. 1986. Efficiency wage theories: A partial evaluation. In *NBER macroeconomics annual 1986*, ed. S. Fischer, 235–75. Cambridge, Mass.: MIT Press.

Krueger, Alan. 1988. The determinants of queues for federal jobs. *Industrial and Labor Relations Review* 42. Forthcoming.

Krueger, Alan, and Lawrence Summers. 1988. Efficiency wages and the wage structure. *Econometrica* 56(2).

Levitan, Sar, and Alexandra Noden. 1983. *Working for the sovereign.* Baltimore, Md.: The Johns Hopkins University Press.
Lewis, H. G. 1986a. Union/nonunion wage gaps in the public sector. Duke University. Mimeo.
———. 1986b. *Union relative wage effects: A survey.* Chicago: University of Chicago Press.
Long, James. 1982. Are government workers overpaid? Alternative evidence. *Journal of Human Resources* 17:123–31.
Mellow, Wesley. 1981. Unionism and wages: A longitudinal analysis. *Review of Economics and Statistics* 63:43–52.
Mellow, Wesley, and Hal Sider. 1983. Accuracy of response in labor market surveys: Evidence and implications. *Journal of Labor Economics* 1:331–44.
Mitchell, Daniel. 1979. The impact of collective bargaining on compensation in the public sector. In *Public sector bargaining,* ed. B. Aaron, R. Grodin, and J. Stern. Washington, D.C.: The Bureau of National Affairs, IRRA Series.
Moore, William, and John Raisian. 1986. Government wage differentials revisited. Mimeo.
Perloff, J., and M. Wachter. 1984. Wage comparability in the U.S. Postal Service. *Industrial and Labor Relations Review* 38:26–35.
Quinn, Joseph. 1979. Wage differentials among older workers in the public sector. *Journal of Human Resources* 14:41–62.
Solon, Gary. 1985. Bias in longitudinal estimation of compensating wage differences. University of Michigan. Mimeo.
Smith, Sharon, 1976. Pay differentials between federal government and private sector workers. *Industrial and Labor Relations Review* 29:179–97.
———. 1977. *Equal pay in the public sector: Fact or fantasy?* Princeton, N.J.: Princeton University Press.
Stiglitz, Joseph. 1986. Theories of wage rigidities. In *Keynes' economic legacy: Contemporary economic theories,* ed. J. Butkiewicz, et al. New York: Praeger.
Utgoff, Kathleen. 1983. Compensation levels and quit rates in the public sector. *Journal of Human Resources* 18:394–406.
Venti, Steven. 1987. Wages in the federal and private sectors. In *Public sector payrolls,* ed. David Wise, 147–76. Chicago: University of Chicago Press.

Comment   Lisa M. Lynch

Alan Krueger's paper tries to provide the answer to the provocative question, "Are public sector workers really overpaid?" Krueger is concerned with understanding why cross-sectional studies of federal workers indicate that their wages are significantly greater than those of private sector workers with similar observed characteristics, while the government's pay comparability studies claim that federal workers

Lisa M. Lynch is assistant professor of industrial relations, Sloan School of Management, Massachusetts Institute of Technology, and a faculty research fellow of the National Bureau of Economic Research.

earn less than their private sector counterparts. One of the criticisms of previous studies using cross-sectional data has been that if public sector workers are more productive than their private sector counterparts in some unobserved characteristic that is rewarded by employers, there will be an upward bias in the estimated public sector wage differential. Krueger attempts to control for this problem by using two longitudinal data sets of public sector/private sector job switchers and stayers. The first data set was created by matching Current Population Surveys from 1974–75, 1977–78, and 1979–80. At first glance this appears to be a wealth of data, but unfortunately this is not the case. In this data set not that many workers actually switch sectors—only thirty-one workers from the private to federal sector and only twenty-one workers from the federal to private sector. In an attempt to obtain a larger sample size, Krueger also examines data from the two CPS supplemental surveys of displaced workers in January 1984 and 1986. The total sample is over 4,000 workers; however, the number of workers who actually switch into the federal sector is only 59. Consequently, Krueger is forced to pool the data for the male and female respondents when estimating the public sector wage differential. Given that one of the findings from cross-sectional studies has been the higher earnings of women employed in government, this pooling of observations potentially masks one of the most interesting findings on public sector wage differentials. In fact, an interesting question to have examined might have been, "Why are private sector women paid less than comparable public sector women?" Nevertheless, using longitudinal data rather than cross-sectional data, Krueger claims that workers in the federal government seem to receive a wage premium on the order of 6–12 percent (aggregating across males and females). But this conclusion is drawn from a longitudinal estimate of 6 percent that is not statistically significant and a cross-sectional estimate of 25 percent, with its associated problem of unobserved heterogeneity.

A second issue that Krueger addresses is that if there are errors in the data due to mistakes in the measurement of actual transitions between sectors, the public sector wage differential estimated from the longitudinal data will be biased downward. This measurement problem, as shown in Freeman (1984),[1] may be a serious problem when using longitudinal data. Krueger suggests that the bias of his longitudinal estimates may be as large as 50 percent, which might reconcile the difference between the cross-sectional and longitudinal estimates. However, given the extremely small sample size of switchers, it is very

1. Richard Freeman, "Longitudinal analyses of the effects of trade unions", *Journal of Labor Economics* 2(1984):1–26.

difficult to pin down the actual size of this bias. All of the above problems are present again in Krueger's analysis of wages of postal workers and state and local government workers.

Given these problems, Krueger examines the length of queues for federal jobs assuming that evidence of longer queues indicates that an employer is paying relatively higher wages. Krueger does this by using data for the private sector from the Employment Opportunities Pilot Project (EOPP) of 1982 and data for the public sector from the number of applicants listed in the federal applicant registers. He suggests that each federal job appears to attract many more applicants than each private sector job. However, if one examines the largest government job (in terms of number employed) listed in table 8.5, the queue for steno/typists in the federal government is shorter than the average number of applicants in private sector establishments reported in the EOPP data. Ideally one would want to have data on similar occupations across the public and private sectors to have a better understanding of the lengths of queues for public and private sector jobs, but this is not the case here.

Finally, Krueger examines the impact of public sector unions on the pay of public sector workers. He finds with both longitudinal data and cross-sectional data that union membership does not have a statistically significant effect on the wages of state and local government employees. However, as he notes, this result may mean that public sector unions are successful not only for their own members but for all state and local employees in their area regardless of their union status.

Krueger concludes his paper by stating that there is strong evidence that federal workers are paid more than comparable private sector workers. However, while I think that Krueger has done a fine job of addressing the issue of wage determination in the public sector from a variety of perspectives, the quality and the quantity of the data currently available should make him much more cautious in his interpretation of his results. I hope that as better data become available he will examine this fascinating issue further.

III Effects on Nonwage Outcomes

9 On Estimating the Effects of Increased Aid to Education

Ronald G. Ehrenberg and Richard P. Chaykowski

9.1 Introduction

The 1983 report, *A Nation at Risk,* of the National Commission on Excellence in Education decried the state of public education in the United States and suggested a number of reforms. Among their recommendations was increased federal aid for education. The view was that this would lead to desirable outcomes such as reduced class sizes and higher teacher salaries, with the latter aiding in the recruitment and retention of high-quality teachers.

Somewhat surprisingly, previous research on the economics of education provides us with very few insights about what the effects of such proposals might be. For example, while there is an extensive literature on the determinants of cross-section variations in teachers' salaries and teacher/student ratios, virtually nothing has been written on how changes in aid levels influence changes in salaries, teacher/student ratios, other expenditure levels, and local tax rates.[1] Similarly, while there are many studies of how grants-in-aid affect overall expenditure levels and some studies of the determinants of cross-section variations in the share of expenditures spent on various categories (e.g., instructional and administrative), virtually nothing has been written on how changes in aid affect the various expenditure shares.[2]

Ronald G. Ehrenberg is Irving M. Ives Professor of Industrial and Labor Relations and Economics, Cornell University, and research associate of the National Bureau of Economic Research. Richard P. Chaykowski is assistant professor, Department of Economics and School of Industrial Relations, Queen's University, Canada.

This research was partially supported by the NBER's Public Sector Labor Relations project. However, the authors alone are responsible for the contents of this paper. Without implicating him for what remains, the authors are extremely grateful to Richard Murnane for his detailed comments on an earlier draft.

To provide answers to some of these questions, our paper examines data from a panel of approximately 700 school districts in New York State over a five-year period (1978–79 to 1982–83) and tries to infer how school districts will respond to future changes in aid from how they responded to changes in state aid during the period. We focus on how past aid changes have influenced teacher salaries, tax rates, teacher/student ratios, and other staff/student ratios. The analyses exploit the fact that although school aid formulas change frequently in New York State, each district is usually guaranteed at least the same aid level as the previous year ("save harmless" provisions). As a result, over any given two-year period, the percentage increase in aid varies widely across districts. This provides a convenient form of natural experiment.

The organization of our paper is as follows. Section 9.2 discusses how state aid to education in New York State was allocated to school districts in 1978–79 and then how the allocation formulas changed during the sample period. Section 9.3 describes our methodological approach and the data base we have collected. Empirical results are presented in section 9.4, which is then followed by some brief concluding remarks.

9.2   State Aid to Education in New York State

By far the largest form of state aid to education in New York State[3] is general operating aid; this category ranged between 68 and 75 percent of total state aid during the sample years. Operating aid is based on an aid-ratio formulation in which low "wealth" districts receive more aid than high "wealth" districts. Specifically, the state establishes two expenditure/pupil levels, E_L and E_H, and then for average "wealth" districts pays 49 percent of district operating expenditures up to E_L and 20 percent of any district operating expenditures between E_L and E_H. For other districts, the share paid by the state of expenditures up to E_L is

(1) $$r_{i1} = (1 - (W_i/\bar{W}) * .51),$$

and the share paid by the state of expenditures between E_L and E_H is

(2) $$r_{i2} = (1 - (Y_i/\bar{Y}) * .8).$$

In these equations W_i and Y_i are measures of the district's wealth relative to the number of "aidable pupil units" in the district, while $\bar{W}$ and $\bar{Y}$ are comparable statewide average measures. "Aidable pupil units" depend upon average daily attendance in the district, with extra weight being given for secondary school pupils, handicapped pupils, and pupils with special needs (those who scored low on standardized tests). Throughout the sample period, W_i and $\bar{W}$ were always based on the full value of property, and Y_i and $\bar{Y}$ were similarly defined through 1980–81. However, in 1981–82 and 1982–83 the latter were redefined in terms of 1979 and 1980 community income, respectively (as reported from Internal Revenue Service records).

The level of general operating aid received by a district changes over time because of changes in E_L and E_H (these grew from \$1,450 and \$1,500 in 1978–79 to \$1,885 and \$2,155 by 1982–83, with the magnitude of the increase varying widely across years), changes in district wealth and school enrollment (both relative to statewide changes), and changes in the definition of wealth (in eq. [2]) in the latter two years.[4] In addition, "save harmless" provisions were always in effect. They stated that general operating aid could never be reduced, typically either on a total or per pupil basis, with the school district allowed to choose the option that was most beneficial to it. As a result school districts in which wealth was increasing rapidly or enrollments declining did not have to face a loss of general aid. These "save harmless" provisions substantially influenced the distribution of state aid; for example in 1979–80 over 35 percent (249) of the districts received aid under them.

In principle, the level of general operating aid received by a district might also increase simply because the district had increased its per pupil expenditures. That is, as long as the district was spending less than E_H, increases in expenditures (up to E_H) would induce increases in state aid through the matching formulas (eqs. [1] and [2]). In such a situation, it would not be meaningful to refer to an increase in aid "causing" the expenditure increase. However, the majority of districts appeared to have spent more than E_H each year, so this concern is probably not relevant for our data.

Although general operating aid is by far the largest component of state aid to education in New York, numerous other forms of aid exist. Some, like transportation aid (which comprises typically 10 percent of total aid), are based on formulas in which the state pays a specified share of mandated costs. Others, like construction aid, are based on a sharing of actual expenses. These latter categories, however, represent only a small share of total aid.

Of special interest to us are two other forms of aid that existed during at least part of the period. First, in 1979–80, prior to the inclusion of income as a measure of wealth in the general operating aid formula, the state instituted a "low-income aid" component of school aid; this provided between \$1.76 (highest income district) and \$27.50 (lowest income district) on a per pupil basis. This type of aid represented roughly 10 percent of the increase in state aid that occurred that year.

Second, each year the state provided special aid programs for "city" school districts. In most school districts in New York State the voters implicitly set the tax rate each year via budget referenda. In city districts, however, the tax rate is set by local school boards, subject to the rate not exceeding a state constitutionally determined maximum. The special aid programs for these city districts were designed to help out those districts that were near their constitutional maximum tax rate and to help other city school systems meet special needs that their districts faced.

Because of all of the above provisions and other types of aid to education, the percentage change in total aid varied widely across school districts in any given year. As mentioned above, this provides a convenient form of natural experiment in which we can try to infer how districts would respond to changes in federal aid in the future from observations on how they have responded to changes in state aid in the past. In much of what follows we shall treat these aid changes as exogenous; however, our discussion suggests that a district's percentage changes in full value of property, in enrollment, in level of income, and whether the district is a city school district, all influenced the district's percentage change in state aid in a highly nonlinear manner that both varied from year to year and depended upon whether a "save harmless" provision was an effective constraint on a district in a given year. As a consequence, in places below we have attempted to obtain instrumental variable estimates for changes in aid and have used these in our analyses.

9.3 Methodological Framework and Data

The outcomes we focus on are percentage changes in teachers' salaries—minimum salary with a bachelor's degree ($P1$), maximum with a bachelor's degree ($P2$), minimum with a master's degree ($P3$), and maximum with a master's degree ($P4$)—percentage changes in the property tax rate on the full value of property in the district ($P5$), and percentage changes in staff per pupil ratios—teacher/pupil ($P6$), nonprofessional staff/pupil ($P7$), other professional staff/pupil ($P8$), and paraprofessional staff/student ($P9$).[5] Given the initial level of these outcomes that prevail in a school district in a period, their percentage changes are determined by a complex process that involves bargaining between a school board and a union and, in the case of small districts in New York State, a voter referendum on the proposed school district budget. Rather than attempting to model this process formally, we pursue a strategy of estimating reduced-form equations of the form:

$$(3) \quad P_i = F^i(Gg, Y, A, N, Z, CB, d, B_i), \quad i = 1, 2, \ldots 9 .$$

Here G is the annual percentage change in state aid received by the school district; this is multiplied by the base-year share of state aid in the district's budget (g) to allow the effects of percentage changes in aid to depend upon aid's initial "importance" to the district. Y and A are the percentage changes in income and the full value of property in the district, respectively; they are measures of changes in the district's ability to pay for education.[6] N is the percentage change in student enrollment in the district. Z is a vector of sociodemographic variables expected to influence the community's "taste" for education and hence the various outcomes (e.g., community education level, student test scores, percent of households with children). CB is a vector of collective bargaining contract provisions (to be discussed below), while d is a dummy variable that indicates whether the school district is a "city" school district where tax rates are set by the school board (subject to constitutional tax limitations) rather than by the voters in an annual budget referendum. Finally, B_i, which differs for each outcome, is a measure of the base-period position of the district on a variable relating to the outcome.

A description of the specific variables included in each equation and their sources are found in the notes to table 9.1 As indicated there, we have collected data from a variety of sources for over 700 school districts in New York State for a five-year period (1978–79 to 1982–83). Since the outcome variables are expressed as changes, a maximum sample size of roughly 2,800 observations exists. However, due to missing data and problems, described below, actual sample sizes are much smaller.

The teacher salary variables were available only for school districts represented by the New York State United Teachers, an AFL–CIO affiliate, and hence districts represented by National Education Association (NEA) locals were excluded from the wage equations. These salary data had to be hand-coded from printed material, and many gaps in the data further reduced sample sizes. In addition, one might argue that since teacher contracts are often multiyear in nature, the process governing the outcomes may differ in years when collective bargaining negotiations took place. Consequently, results are presented below for both year-district observations when negotiations took place (table 9.1) and all observations (table 9.2) In the latter case, a dummy variable for whether negotiations took place in the year is included as a separate explanatory variable.[7]

Three collective bargaining contract provision variables are included in the analyses.[8] The first two capture the presence of employment-related provisions in the agreement, while the third represents a measure of bargaining strength. The first variable indicates the presence or absence of a provision governing staff reductions. The second variable indicates the presence or absence of a provision affecting the determination of class size. Together, the presence of these variables capture the extent to which the collective bargaining agreement constrains employer discretion over the determination of employment levels: staff reduction procedures affect the level of employment directly, while class size provisions affect employment levels indirectly. The third variable is a contract strength index that is meant to capture the relative bargaining power of the union. It is the sum of the number of times that other provisions that unions might want in a contract appear (with a maximum score of 58). Ceteris paribus, the higher the contract index the more bargaining power the union has and thus the more favorably the outcomes in equation (3) will be to the union.

The city school district dummy variable is included to test whether the way tax rates are set influences the growth rate of taxes and/or the other outcome variables. One's intuition is that when voters directly vote on tax increases that the rate of increase is likely to be lower.

The measure of the base period salary positions of teachers (B_i) is taken to be the initial category (BAmin, BAmax, MAmin, MAmax) salary in the district relative to the comparable category's salary average across districts in the county. For all other outcomes, the base period variable is taken to be the initial level of the variable. We expect that the phenomenon of "regression to the mean" will cause each of these base period variables to be negatively related to the percentage change in the outcome.

Finally, among the sociodemographic variables included in the analyses was an index of student test scores in the district relative to the statewide average during the 1979–80 to 1981–82 period. In each of the three years covered by this period, all third and sixth graders in New York State were given standardized math and reading tests. A "state reference point" was established for each test in each year; students who scored below this point were deemed to have special needs and to require remedial help. Letting $S(i, j, t)$ be the proportion of students in district i who scored below the state reference point on test j in year t and $S(A, j, t)$ the comparable proportion statewide for test j in year t, we define a district's relative test score index as

$$(4) \qquad R_i = \sum_t \sum_j [S(i, j, t)/S(A, j, t)] \, ,$$

where t = 79–80, 80–81, 81–82 and j = 3R,3M,6R,6M.

Low scores for R_i indicate districts whose students performed better on the standardized tests.

9.4 Empirical Results

Table 9.1 presents estimates of the change in outcome equations, with the sample restricted to year-observation combinations in which

Table 9.1   Change in Outcome Equations: Restricted to Observations Where Negotiations Took Place in Year (absolute value t statistic)

	P_1	P_2	P_3	P_4	P_5	P_6	P_7	P_8	P_9
C	0.070 (2.2)	0.082 (2.1)	0.043 (1.8)	0.216 (5.5)	−0.009 (0.2)	0.119 (3.5)	0.012 (0.3)	0.021 (0.3)	0.076 (0.7)
X1	−0.045 (1.7)								
X2		−0.034 (1.4)							
X3			−0.010 (0.6)						
X4				−0.102 (3.5)					
X5					−0.034 (5.1)				
X6						−2.003 (7.2)			
X7							−0.947 (2.5)		
X8								−21.616 (7.7)	
X9									−7.060 (3.6)
X10	0.001 (0.3)	0.008 (1.0)	−0.001 (0.3)	−0.000 (0.0)	−0.012 (1.3)	−0.010 (1.5)	0.012 (1.1)	−0.005 (0.2)	−0.017 (0.6)
X11	−0.040 (1.4)	−0.154 (3.0)	−0.053 (1.9)	−0.141 (3.0)	0.077 (1.3)	0.118 (2.5)	0.093 (1.3)	0.539 (3.2)	−0.277 (1.5)
X12	0.010 (0.4)	−0.072 (1.8)	0.003 (0.1)	−0.102 (3.0)	0.130 (2.7)	0.003 (0.1)	0.004 (0.1)	−0.194 (1.5)	−0.154 (1.1)
X13	0.000 (1.3)	0.000 (0.5)	0.000 (1.1)	0.001 (2.1)	0.000 (0.2)	0.000 (0.4)	−0.001 (1.9)	0.005 (2.5)	0.006 (2.9)
X14	0.011 (2.0)	0.007 (0.7)	0.014 (2.6)	−0.002 (0.3)	−0.027 (2.2)	−0.006 (0.6)	−0.020 (1.4)	0.001 (0.0)	0.006 (0.2)
X15	0.046 (0.6)	0.210 (1.5)	0.041 (0.6)	−0.103 (0.9)	0.228 (1.3)	0.201 (1.5)	0.377 (1.8)	−0.769 (1.6)	0.299 (0.6)
X16	0.014 (3.9)	0.044 (7.2)	0.015 (4.3)	0.021 (3.7)	0.037 (5.4)	−0.006 (1.1)	−0.000 (0.0)	0.007 (0.4)	−0.071 (3.4)
X17	0.020 (5.2)	0.035 (5.9)	0.019 (5.3)	0.033 (5.8)	0.012 (1.8)	−0.012 (2.1)	−0.017 (1.9)	0.008 (0.4)	−0.074 (3.3)
X18	0.017 (3.5)	0.085 (10.4)	0.017 (3.7)	0.057 (7.5)	−0.005 (0.5)	0.003 (0.5)	0.016 (1.3)	−0.020 (0.7)	−0.010 (0.3)
X19	−0.001 (0.5)	−0.003 (0.7)	−0.001 (0.2)	0.004 (1.1)	0.009 (1.8)	0.002 (0.5)	−0.006 (0.9)	−0.005 (0.3)	−0.012 (0.8)
X20	−0.000 (0.5)	−0.000 (0.1)	−0.004 (1.5)	0.003 (0.9)	−0.004 (0.9)	−0.001 (0.4)	0.005 (0.7)	0.005 (0.3)	0.007 (0.4)
X21	0.000 (0.7)	−0.000 (0.1)	−0.000 (0.9)	−0.000 (0.7)	0.000 (0.4)	−0.000 (0.9)	0.000 (0.0)	0.000 (0.4)	−0.001 (0.6)
X22	0.004 (0.7)	0.004 (0.4)	0.005 (0.9)	0.011 (1.2)	0.019 (1.7)	−0.001 (0.5)	0.009 (0.7)	0.015 (0.4)	0.033 (1.0)
X23	−0.014 (0.3)	0.106 (1.4)	−0.033 (0.8)	0.087 (1.2)	−0.145 (1.8)	−0.693 (10.4)	−0.776 (7.7)	−0.737 (3.1)	−0.494 (2.0)
X24	−0.051 (1.4)	−0.052 (0.8)	−0.039 (1.1)	−0.069 (1.1)	−0.145 (2.0)	−0.115 (2.0)	−0.116 (1.3)	0.415 (1.9)	−0.165 (0.8)
X25	0.025 (1.0)	0.028 (0.6)	0.021 (0.9)	−0.009 (0.2)	−0.820 (14.3)	−0.011 (0.3)	0.058 (0.9)	0.124 (0.9)	0.278 (1.8)
$\bar{R}^2/N$	0.068/424	0.228/598	0.070/412	0.271/419	0.314/718	0.180/800	0.090/751	0.096/734	0.058/675

Table 9.1 (continued)

Sources: New York State Education Department, "Basic Educational Data System" (BEDS), school district tapes for 1978–79, 1979–80, 1980–81, 1981–82, and 1982–83 ($P_6, P_7, P_8, P_9, X6, X7, X8, X9, X23$).

New York State Education Department, "Financial Data System" (ST3), school district tapes for 1978–79, 1979–80, 1980–81, 1981–82, and 1982–83 ($P_5, X5, X14, X24, X25$).

New York State Education Department, "New York State Pupil Evaluation Program" (PEP), test scores for 1978–79, 1979–80, 1980–81, 1981–82, and 1982–83 ($X22$).

New York State United Teachers, *Salary Schedule Rankings*, 1978–79, 1980–81, 1981–82; *Salary Schedules*, 1979–80; unpublished computer printouts, 1982–83 ($P_1, P_2, P_3, P_4, X1, X2, X3, X4, n$). Information on the latter variable also came from contracts on file in the Labor-Management Documentation Center at the New York State School of Industrial and Labor Relations.

U.S. Bureau of the Census, *1980 Census of Population*, school district data file for New York State ($X10, X11, X12, X13$).

U.S. Department of Commerce, Bureau of Economic Analysis, unpublished tabulations, 1978, 1979, 1980, 1981, 1982 ($X15$).

New York State United Teachers, "Contract Provisions," tape for 1976–77 ($X21$).

Notes: P_1 = percentage change in the bachelor's-level minimum salary.

P_2 = percentage change in the bachelor's-level maximum salary.

P_3 = percentage change in the master's-level minimum salary.

P_4 = percentage change in the master's-level maximum salary.

P_5 = percentage change in the school district's property tax rate on full value.

P_6 = percentage change in the teacher/student ratio.

P_7 = percentage change in the nonprofessional/student ratio (nonprofessionals include secretaries, maintenance, bus drivers, school lunch workers).

P_8 = percentage change in the other professional staff/student ratio (other professionals include administrators, psychologists, guidance counselors, librarians).

P_9 = percentage change in the paraprofessional/student ratio (paraprofessionals include teaching assistants, teacher aides, pupil personnel service aides, library aides, health aides).

$X1$, $X2$, $X3$, $X4$ = district salary level/average salary level in the country: $X1$ (bachelor's minimum), $X2$ (bachelor's minimum), $X3$ (master's minimum), $X4$ (master's maximum).

$X5$, $X6$, $X7$, $X8$, $X9$ = level at the start of the period of the outcome variable: $X5$ (school district's tax on full value), $X6$ (teacher/student ratio), $X7$ (nonprofessional/student ratio), $X8$ (other professional staff/student ratio), $X9$ (paraprofessional/student ratio).

$X10$ = percent urban residents of the school district in 1979.

$X11$ = percent nonwhite residents of the school district in 1979.

$X12$ = percent of households in the school district with children at home in 1979.

$X13$ = median family income in the school district in 1979 (in thousands).

$X14$ = 1 = city school district where school board sets tax rate; 0 = voters vote on tax rate in annual referendum.

$X15$ = percentage change in per capita personal income in the county between the calendar years.

$X16$ = 1 = 1980–81 academic year; 0 = otherwise

$X17$ = 1 = 1981–82 academic year; 0 = otherwise } 1979–80 is the reference year.

$X18$ = 1 = 1982–83 academic year; 0 = otherwise

$X19$ = 1 = class size provision is in the teachers' contract; 0 = no provision.

$X20$ = 1 = reduction-in-force provision is in the teachers' contract; 0 = no provision.

$X21$ = index of number of provisions present in the teachers' contract (mean = 20, variance = 24 in the sample).

$X22$ = index of student test scores in the district relative to statewide average during the 1979–80 to 1981–82 period (1 = mean, low index equals higher test scores; see text).

$X23$ = percentage change in enrollment in the district.

$X24$ = percentage change in state aid received by the district multiplied by the initial share of state aid in the district's budget.

$X25$ = percentage change in the full value of property in the school district.

n = 1 = negotiations with teachers over salary took place in the year; 0 = no negotiations.

contract negotiations took place. Table 9.2 presents similar estimates without this restriction on the sample; not surprisingly, sample sizes in the latter table are typically twice as large (many teachers' contracts in New York State were for two years during the period). The estimates in the latter table do contain a dummy variable (n) for whether negotiations took place in the year, and both tables also include year dummy variables to control for omitted year-specific factors like the average growth of wages and prices in the state. The inclusion of these year dummies is not an innocuous modification; in principle they may capture the effects of year-to-year variations in the average rate of change of other included variables, leaving the coefficients of these variables (e.g., state aid) to capture only within-year variations of rates of change across districts. However, as we shall indicate later, excluding the year dummies rarely significantly altered the coefficients of other variables of interest (e.g., state aid).

The results in tables 9.1 and 9.2 are not particularly impressive; statistically insignificant coefficients predominate and the explanatory power of the models is not high. Nonetheless, there are a few results worth noting. First, we are much more successful in explaining salary increases for experienced teachers than we are in explaining salary increases for newly hired teachers. This is not surprising as during the period enrollments were not expanding and there was little hiring of new teachers. As such, teachers' unions paid relatively little attention to starting salaries, and in a number of cases no increases were given at that level.

Second, at the maximum salary level there did tend to be a policy of "regression to the mean," in the sense that the higher a district's salary relative to the county average, the smaller the district's increase would be. This effect was quite small though; a district whose salary level was 10 percent above the county average would moderate its increase by no more than 1 percent. Similar results hold for the tax rate outcome; districts with high initial tax rates have smaller rates of growth of tax rates, ceteris paribus.[9]

Third, the growth of "ability to pay" measures, such as county income ($X15$) and the full value of property in a district ($X25$), appeared to rarely influence the outcome variables. The only exception was the district's tax rate on full value ($P5$); indeed one cannot reject the hypothesis that a 10 percent increase in property values was associated with an equivalent percent decrease in the tax rate.

Fourth, contrary to our expectations, city school districts ($X14$) in which the school board sets the tax rate tended to have lower rates of tax rate increase than districts in which voters approved the tax rate at an annual budget referendum. Quantitatively, however, this effect was very small, less than 0.03 percent a year.

Table 9.2　　　Change in Outcome Equations: All Observations[a] (absolute value t statistic)

	P_1	P_2	P_3	P_4	P_5	P_6	P_7	P_8	P_9
C	0.036 (1.8)	0.030 (1.2)	0.052 (3.1)	0.142 (5.8)	0.019 (0.8)	0.121 (5.1)	0.055 (1.8)	0.227 (3.1)	−0.010 (0.1)
n	−0.003 (2.6)	−0.002 (0.8)	−0.004 (2.8)	−0.006 (2.5)	−0.001 (0.2)	−0.002 (0.7)	−0.008 (2.0)	0.008 (0.9)	−0.011 (1.2)
X1	0.013 (0.8)								
X2		0.009 (0.5)							
X3			−0.005 (0.4)						
X4				−0.061 (3.4)					
X5					−0.027 (6.2)				
X6						−1.985(10.0)			
X7							−1.500 (6.1)		
X8								−21.990(11.4)	
X9									−10.009 (7.8)
X10	0.000 (0.1)	0.010 (2.1)	0.002 (0.7)	0.004 (1.0)	−0.011 (1.8)	−0.010 (2.2)	0.002 (0.2)	0.002 (0.1)	−0.037 (2.2)
X11	−0.011 (0.6)	−0.044 (1.3)	−0.026 (1.4)	−0.053 (1.9)	0.008 (0.8)	0.098 (3.0)	0.026 (0.5)	0.243 (2.1)	0.104 (0.8)
X12	−0.001 (0.0)	−0.041 (1.6)	−0.005 (0.4)	−0.031 (1.4)	0.104 (3.2)	0.005 (0.2)	0.006 (0.1)	−0.272 (3.0)	−0.047 (0.5)
X13	0.000 (1.4)	0.000 (0.4)	0.000 (1.3)	0.000 (0.4)	−0.000 (0.5)	0.000 (0.0)	0.000 (1.0)	0.005 (3.7)	0.006 (4.4)
X14	0.003 (0.9)	−0.002 (0.4)	0.005 (1.3)	0.001 (0.1)	−0.017 (2.0)	−0.007 (1.1)	−0.003 (0.3)	−0.022 (1.0)	−0.017 (0.7)
X15	−0.069 (1.3)	0.088 (0.9)	−0.011 (0.2)	−0.095 (1.2)	0.250 (2.2)	0.083 (0.9)	0.364 (2.5)	−0.040 (0.1)	0.313 (1.0)
X16	0.009 (4.2)	0.028 (7.0)	0.009 (3.6)	0.014 (4.3)	0.043 (9.3)	0.000 (0.0)	−0.000 (1.7)	0.023 (1.7)	−0.067 (4.7)
X17	0.018 (7.8)	0.027 (6.8)	0.018 (7.5)	0.032 (8.7)	0.014 (2.7)	−0.004 (1.1)	−0.026 (0.4)	−0.001 (0.1)	−0.063 (4.0)
X18	0.014 (5.2)	0.076(14.8)	0.017 (5.7)	0.065(14.7)	−0.001 (0.3)	0.008 (1.5)	0.003 (0.5)	0.000 (0.0)	−0.017 (0.8)
X19	0.001 (0.8)	0.000 (0.1)	0.001 (0.6)	0.004 (1.8)	0.004 (1.2)	0.003 (1.2)	0.002 (0.3)	0.002 (0.2)	0.007 (0.6)
X20	0.002 (1.0)	0.003 (1.2)	0.002 (1.2)	0.002 (1.0)	−0.003 (1.0)	−0.004 (1.2)	0.005 (1.0)	0.007 (0.7)	0.004 (0.4)
X21	−0.000 (1.5)	0.000 (0.2)	−0.000 (2.0)	−0.000 (0.9)	0.000 (0.0)	−0.001 (1.8)	−0.001 (2.9)	0.000 (0.3)	−0.000 (0.1)
X22	0.006 (1.5)	0.006 (0.9)	0.006 (1.6)	0.004 (0.8)	0.011 (1.5)	0.006 (0.9)	−0.001 (0.1)	0.018 (0.8)	0.024 (1.0)
X23	0.014 (0.5)	0.059 (1.3)	0.016 (0.6)	0.033 (0.8)	−0.029 (0.5)	−0.717(15.3)	−3.792(11.5)	−0.436 (2.8)	−0.723 (4.3)
X24	−0.024 (1.1)	−0.049 (1.2)	−0.007 (0.3)	−0.028 (0.7)	−0.081 (1.5)	−0.062 (1.5)	0.004 (0.1)	0.018 (0.1)	0.154 (1.0)
X25	−0.001 (0.1)	0.032 (1.1)	0.000 (0.0)	−0.015 (0.6)	−0.860(21.5)	−0.016 (0.6)	0.017 (0.3)	−0.070 (0.7)	0.088 (0.8)
$\bar{R}^2/N$	0.095/922	0.239/1,205	0.100/893	0.358/904	0.321/1,504	0.168/1,664	0.111/1,553	0.084/1,509	0.081/1,390

[a]See notes to table 9.1 for variable definitions.

Fifth, the results in table 9.2 suggest that teacher salary increases were actually marginally lower in the years that contracts were negotiated than they were in second and third years of existing contracts. This may reflect the well-known preferences of management to "backload" salary increases in multiyear contracts to reduce the present value of the cost.

Finally, we turn to the effects of changes in state aid to education—the primary focus of our study. Table 9.3 summarizes the aid coefficients from tables 9.1 and 9.2 as well as comparable coefficients that came from models that excluded the year dummy variables and, in the case of the "whole sample results" the negotiations dummy. Exclusion of the year dummies allow us to test if their presence captures some of the effects of across-year variations in increases in aid to education.

Rows A1, A2 and B1 to B4 of table 9.3 report estimates of the effects of changes in state aid when such changes are treated as exogenous. Although these coefficients are often insignificant and/or differ across specifications, some tentative conclusions can be drawn. Changes in state aid levels did *not* appear to influence teacher salary increases ($P1$, $P2$, $P3$, $P4$). There is some evidence in the specifications that include the year dummy variables that they negatively affected tax rate growth; however, this relationship was far from one to one. Unexpectedly, in some specifications increases in aid were associated with *decreases* in teacher/student ratios, but *increases* in other professional/student ratios.

Of course, as noted in section 9.2, changes in state aid to school districts in New York State were not truly exogenous during the 1978–79 to 1982–83 period. Rather they depended each year on (among other things) changes in the district's full value of property and enrollment, changes in the district's income level (after 1980–81), whether the district was a city school district, and "save harmless" provisions, with the effect of each of these variables often varying across years. Treating aid changes as being exogenous may distort our estimates, given these facts.

To address this problem, table 9.4 reports estimates of two simple specifications used by us to analyze the determinants of the percentage change in state aid. In the first, percentage changes in aid are regressed on year dummy variables and these variables interacted with the city school district dummy, the percentage change in assessed value, the percentage change in enrollment, and the 1979 income level in the community. The second attempts to approximate the existence of "save harmless" provisions by adding a dummy variable if the percentage change in enrollment in the year is negative and interacting one minus that variable with the changes in full value of district property and enrollment, and with income.[10]

Table 9.3   Effects of State Aid Changes on Outcomes: Various Specifications[a] (absolute value *t* statistics)

Specification [number of observations]	P1 [425]	P2 [599]	P3 [413]	P4 [420]	P5 [728]	P6 [801]	P7 [752]	P8 [735]	P9 [676]
A) Contracts Negotiated in the Year									
A1) Include Year Dummies	-0.051	-0.052	-0.039	-0.069	-0.145	-0.115	-0.116	0.415	-0.165
	(1.4)	(0.8)	(1.1)	(1.2)	(2.0)	(2.0)	(1.2)	(1.9)	(0.8)
A2) Exclude Year Dummies	-0.057	-0.022	-0.040	-0.113	-0.081	-0.123	-0.108	0.428	-0.241
	(1.5)	(0.3)	(1.1)	(1.8)	(1.0)	(2.2)	(1.2)	(2.0)	(1.1)
A3) Include Year Dummies (IV1)	0.066	0.071	0.119	0.007	-0.122	-0.951	-0.490	-0.156	-2.216
	(0.5)	(0.3)	(1.0)	(0.0)	(0.5)	(4.3)	(1.5)	(0.2)	(2.9)
A4) Include Year Dummies (IV2)	0.279	0.014	0.138	0.061	0.189	-0.762	-0.293	-0.474	-1.492
	(2.6)	(0.1)	(1.4)	(0.4)	(0.9)	(4.5)	(1.1)	(0.7)	(2.5)
	[923]	[1,206]	[894]	[905]	[1,504]	[1,665]	[1,554]	[151]	[1,391]
B) All Years' Data									
B1) Include Year and Negotiations Dummies	-0.024	-0.049	-0.007	-0.028	-0.081	-0.062	0.004	0.018	0.154
	(1.1)	(1.2)	(0.3)	(0.7)	(1.5)	(1.5)	(0.1)	(0.1)	(1.0)
B2) Exclude Negotiations Dummies	-0.019	-0.017	-0.005	-0.045	0.019	-0.060	-0.013	0.073	0.046
	(0.8)	(0.4)	(0.2)	(1.1)	(0.3)	(1.5)	(0.2)	(0.5)	(0.3)
B3) Exclude Year Dummies	-0.034	-0.030	-0.029	-0.023	-0.103	0.050	-0.034	0.090	0.085
	(1.6)	(0.7)	(1.3)	(0.7)	(2.1)	(1.3)	(0.5)	(0.6)	(0.6)
B4) Neither Included	-0.026	-0.004	-0.024	-0.038	-0.006	-0.049	-0.048	0.135	-0.009
	(1.1)	(0.1)	(1.0)	(1.0)	(0.1)	(1.3)	(0.8)	(0.9)	(0.9)

[a]Coefficients come from equations in tables 9.1 and 9.2 and similar equations which included the indicated dummy variables. To derive elasticities with respect to state aid, these coefficients should be divided by the share of state aid in the initial budget—approximately 40 percent in the sample—where outcomes are the percentage changes in:

P1 = minimum salary with bachelor's degree.
P2 = maximum salary with bachelor's degree.
P3 = minimum salary with master's degree.
P4 = maximum salary with master's degree.
P5 = school district property tax rate on full value.

P6 = teacher/student ratio.
P7 = nonprofessional/student ratio.
P8 = other professional/student ratio.
P9 = paraprofessional/student ratio.

IV1(IV2) = instrument for percentage change in aid obtained from columns (1) and (2) of table 9.4.

Table 9.4   **Annual Percentage Change in State Aid Equations: Observations When Negotiations Took Place (absolute value of t statistics)**

Explanatory Variables	(1)	Explanatory Variables	(2)
C	0.056 (5.6)	C	0.066 (3.3)
Y80	0.048 (2.6)	Y80	0.038 (2.7)
Y81	0.047 (2.5)	Y81	0.010 (1.7)
Y82	0.076 (3.9)	Y82	0.018 (3.0)
$X14*Y79$	0.050 (3.5)	$X14*Y79$	0.052 (3.7)
$X14*Y80$	0.039 (2.6)	$X14*Y80$	0.047 (3.3)
$X14*Y81$	-0.007 (0.4)	$X14*Y81$	-0.007 (0.5)
$X14*Y82$	-0.009 (0.5)	$X14*Y82$	0.008 (0.5)
$X25*Y79$	0.004 (0.1)	$X25*Y79*(1 - D)$	-0.141 (0.5)
$X25*Y80$	-0.097 (1.4)	$X25*Y80*(1 - D)$	-0.203 (0.6)
$X25*Y81$	-0.169 (2.0)	$X25*Y81*(1 - D)$	-1.400 (4.8)
$X25*Y82$	-0.087 (1.0)	$X25*Y82*(1 - D)$	-0.053 (1.4)
$X23*Y79$	0.270 (2.3)	$X23*Y79*(1 - D)$	-0.126 (0.2)
$X23*Y80$	0.197 (2.0)	$X23*Y80*(1 - D)$	0.498 (2.0)
$X23*Y81$	0.530 (4.1)	$X23*Y81*(1 - D)$	0.321 (0.3)
$X23*Y82$	0.198 (1.5)	$X23*Y82*(1 - D)$	0.885 (1.9)
$X13*Y80$	-0.001 (1.2)	$X13*Y80$	-0.001 (0.1)
$X13*Y81$	-0.001 (0.8)	$X13*Y81*(1 - D)$	0.011 (5.2)
	—	D	-0.020 (1.0)
$\bar{R}^2/N$	0.083/1,001		0.108/1,001

Note: C = intercept term.

$Y_j = 1$ = change from academic year $19j - 1$ to $19j$ to academic year $19j$ to $19j + 1$; 0 = other.

$D = 1$ = percentage change in enrollment was negative, 0 = not negative.

$X13$, $X14$, $X23$, $X25$ are as defined before.

The estimates in table 9.4 can then be used to obtain instruments (IV1 and IV2) for the percentage change in state aid in each district, these estimated values interacted with the initial share of state aid in the district's budget, and then the outcome equations reestimated using the instruments rather than the actual values of percentage changes in state aid. Rows A3 and A4 of table 9.3 contain the estimated state aid coefficients from equations estimated for the "negotiations only" sample when year dummies were included, along with the instruments for percentage change in state aid. Unfortunately, these results do differ substantially from the OLS ones. While in the preferred specification (IV2, row A4) there is evidence that higher state aid was associated with higher bachelor's level entry salaries, we no longer observe increased state aid displacing increases in the tax rate. Moreover, increases in state aid now appear to be negatively associated with *both* teacher/student and paraprofessional/student ratios. The magnitude of the latter relationship is sufficiently large to make one question what we have found.[11]

9.5 Concluding Remarks

Sometimes the best laid plans of mice and men (and economists) go astray. To be blunt, the results presented above shed very little light on the effects of changes in state aid and other financial variables on teacher salaries, tax rates, and staff/student ratios. While there was some evidence that aid increases moderate tax rate increases, this relationship was not sufficiently robust across different model specifications to draw firm conclusions.

There are many possible explanations for our failure to find systematic significant effects of financial variables. There were *many* errors in the underlying financial data we used, which we tried to correct but may not have always succeeded. School district residents' income was unavailable, save for 1979, so instead we had to use county income as a proxy. Parts of aid increases were often tied to specific uses (e.g., textbooks, transportation, special needs), and our use of total state aid rather than general operating aid may have distorted our findings.

More importantly, it is possible that school districts did not make major allocation decisions based on changes in financial variables that were thought to be uncertain to persist in the future. For example, granting teachers a large salary increase in a year of generous aid increases would come back to haunt a district if aid remained constant or fell in the next year. As such, we may well have performed the wrong conceptual experiment. Our quasi-experimental design may not have been appropriate to capture what the effects would be of a "permanent" federal program that mandated increased aid to education.

In fact, while year-to-year average percentage increases in state aid varied during the sample period, the average share of state aid in total school district revenue remained roughly constant at 40 percent.[12] Changes in state aid formulas during the period *did* serve to redistribute state aid across school districts each year, however the aid changes were so weakly correlated across school districts over time that for all practical purposes above, or below, average increases were probably treated as random events.[13] As such, they probably affected things like the timing of capital expenditures and the issuance and retirement of debt much more than they did the outcomes on which we have focused in this paper.

Lest we appear too pessimistic, however, we hasten to stress that our paper has found some results, primarily relating to more "institutional" variables, that are of interest. For example, teacher salary increases tended to be smaller in years when contracts were negotiated;

school districts seemed to be successful in "backloading" wage increases in multiyear contracts. Or to take another example, city school districts, where elected school boards set the tax rate, appeared to have *lower* tax rate increases than other districts. In addition, we observed a regression to the mean phenomenon as school districts whose teachers' salaries were above the county average tended to have lower rates of salary increase. The latter result is exactly what one would expect to see with a system of impasse resolution (mediation and fact finding), where neutrals place a weight on comparability in making decisions.[14] While we attempted to obtain data on whether each negotiation went to impasse in order to test whether comparability considerations mattered primarily in negotiations that went to impasse, unfortunately such data were not available.

Finally, it is interesting to note that state legislatures have begun to realize what we have found econometrically; namely, that past state aid increases to school districts (at least in New York State) have not been used to increase teachers' salaries. As a result, recently enacted laws in a number of states have provided increased state aid earmarked for specified higher minimum salaries for teachers (e.g., New Jersey) or increased aid for general teachers' salaries, with school districts and teachers' unions to negotiate how these funds are to be allocated (e.g., New York).[15] Whether these targeted programs actually serve to increase teachers' salaries above the level that would have existed in their absence, especially in the long run, is a subject worthy of future empirical investigation.

Notes

1. See Ehrenberg and Schwarz (1987) and Lipsky (1982) for surveys of the teacher compensation literature.
2. Examples of studies on the effects of grants on public school expenditure levels are Denzau (1975) and Feldstein (1975). Studies on determinants of cross-section variations in expenditure shares include Carroll (1976) and Monk (1984).
3. Much of the discussion in this section is derived from our reading of New York State Education Department (1978, 1980) and New York State Division of the Budget (1979, 1981, 1982). We are grateful to David Monk for calling this material to our attention.
4. The following table, which lists the values of E_L and E_H each year and their percentage changes from the previous year (in parentheses), illustrates the variability in the percentage changes over time.

	1978–79	1979–80		1980–81		1981–82		1982–83	
E_L	$1,450	$1,500	(3.4%)	$1,600	(6.7%)	$1,650	(3.1%)	$1,885	(14.2%)
E_H	$1,500	$1,550	(3.3%)	$1,700	(9.7%)	$1,885	(10.9%)	$2,155	(14.3%)

5. Nonprofessional staff includes secretaries, maintenance workers, bus drivers, and school lunch workers. Other professional staff include administrators, psychologists, guidance counselors, and librarians. Paraprofessionals include teaching assistants, teacher aides, pupil personnel service aides, library aides, and health aides.

6. In actuality, annual income data were available only at the county level.

7. Whether a contract negotiation took place in a year was obtained from information in the wage data sources and a search of teachers' contracts on file in the data archives of the Labor-Management Documentation Center of the New York State School of Industrial and Labor Relations.

8. These collective bargaining provision variables were available on tape only for the 1975–76 academic year and thus represent the strength of the contract prior to the first year in the sample. We are grateful to Randall Eberts of the University of Oregon for providing these data. They have previously been used in Eberts and Stone (1986).

9. The large negative coefficients of the initial level of the outcome variable in columns $P6$ to $P9$ are undoubtedly biased in a negative direction since in each case were are regressing the log $(Ot/Ot - 1)$ on $Ot - 1$ (where O represents an outcome).

10. In specification 1 district income was *not* interacted with the 1979–80 year dummy because income did *not* enter the aid allocation formula until the next year. Similarly, in specification 2 the interaction of income and the 1980–81 year dummy was not further interacted with D because the "save harmless" provisions did *not* apply to aid based on district income in 1980–81. Deflating median family income by the proportion of households with children at home (to approximate a persistent income measure) did not appreciably alter any of the estimates. Income for 1979 in the district was used throughout because it was the only year that district (as opposed to county) income data were available.

11. One further extension warrants being briefly reported here. During the period covered by the study, enrollment was declining in many school districts in New York State; indeed in roughly 80 percent of the district/year observations in our sample enrollment fell. Discussants of previous drafts of our paper have suggested that the response of school districts to changes in state aid may differ between increasing and decreasing enrollment districts. (See Calvin, Murnane, and Brown 1985 for evidence that in Michigan the response of school district expenditure levels to enrollment changes differed between increasing and decreasing enrollment districts.)

To test for this possibility, the equations that underlie rows B1 and B3 of table 9.3 were reestimated for both increasing enrollment and decreasing enrollment subsamples of school district–year observations. The patterns of results observed were very similar to those reported in table 9.3 with the vast majority of coefficients again proving statistically insignificant. The absolute magnitudes of the coefficients tended to be larger for the increasing enrollment districts, but these differences across enrollment change types were all statistically insignificant.

12. More precisely the shares of state aid in total school district revenue in New York State (excluding New York City) were 39.9, 39.9, 39.8, and 40.4, respectively, for 1979–80, 1980–81, 1981–82, and 1982–83. See New York State Office of the Comptroller (1985, table C).

13. For the roughly 700 school districts in our sample, the computed correlations of total and per student state aid changes (from the previous academic year) across school districts over time were as follows:

	Total Aid				Per Student Aid		
1980–81	0.221			1980–81	0.052		
1981–82	0.151	−0.202		1981–82	0.175	−0.096	
1982–83	−0.011	0.060	−0.102	1982–83	−0.022	−0.048	−0.053
	1979–80	1980–81	1981–82		1979–80	1980–81	1981–82

14. Previous studies of actual public sector labor markets have found that when *arbitration* statutes are present area wage differentials tend to be compressed. See Ehrenberg and Schwarz (1987) for citations to these studies.

15. For brief discussions of the New York and New Jersey programs, see David Dunlap (1986) and Alfonso Narvaez (1985), respectively. These programs raise a host of other issues including their effects on mandated and bargained fringe benefit costs, on the seniority structure of teachers' salaries, and on collective bargaining in education, per se, which we do not discuss here.

References

Calvin, Edward, Richard Murnane, and Randall Brown. 1985. School district responses to enrollment changes: The direction of change matters. *Journal of Education Finance* 10:426–40.

Carroll, Stephen. 1976. School district expenditure behavior. *Journal of Human Resources* 11:317–27.

Denzau, Arthur. 1975. An empirical survey of studies in public school spending. *National Tax Journal* 28:241–48.

Dunlop, David. 1986. City may reject state aid for teachers' raises. *New York Times* 135 (12 April):31.

Eberts, Randall, and Joe Stone. 1986. On the contract curve. *Journal of Labor Economics* 4:66–81.

Ehrenberg, Ronald, and Joshua Schwarz. 1987. Public sector labor markets. In *Handbook of labor economics,* ed. Orley Ashenfelter and Richard Layard. Amsterdam: North-Holland.

Feldstein, Martin. 1975. Wealth neutrality and local choice in public education. *American Economic Review* 65:75–89.

Lipsky, David. 1982. The effect of collective bargaining on teacher pay: A review of the evidence. *Educational Administration Quarterly* 18:14–42.

Monk, David. 1984. The conception of size and the internal allocation of school district resources. *Educational Administration Quarterly* 20:39–67.

Narvaez, Alfonso. 1985. Minimum teacher pay set at $18,500 in Jersey. *New York Times* 134 (10 September):B2.

New York State Division of the Budget. 1979. Description of New York State public school aid provisions—1979–80 school year. Albany, New York.

———. 1981. Description of the 1981–82 New York State aid programs relating to state support for public schools. Albany, New York.

———. 1982. Description of 1982–83 New York State aid programs relating to state support for public schools. Albany, New York.

New York State Education Department. 1978. *Understanding financial support of public schools, 1978–79.* Albany, New York.

———. 1980. 1980–81 state aid to school districts. Albany, New York.

New York State Office of the Comptroller. 1985. *Financial data for school districts for fiscal year ended June 30, 1984.* Albany, New York.

Comment   Richard J. Murnane

The Ehrenberg-Chaykowski (henceforth, E-C) paper examines the effects that changes in state aid to local school districts have on teachers' salaries, local property tax rates, teacher/student ratios, and other staff/ student ratios. Their data consist of information on a panel of 700 school districts in New York State over the five-year period from the 1978– 79 school year through the 1982–83 school year. The school district is the unit of analysis in their empirical work. Their methodology exploits the fact that the percentage increase in state aid going to individual school districts varied widely over the five-year period.

E-C's analysis strategy is to estimate nine reduced-form models. The dependent variables in these models include the percentage change in a school district's minimum salary, the percentage change in the district's maximum teacher's salary, the percentage change in the property tax rate, and the percentage changes in a number of staff-to-student ratios. The explanatory variables include a measure of the percentage change in state aid, demographic characteristics of each school district in the base year (1979), information about the teachers' contract (such as whether it contains a reduction-in-force clause), and 1979 values for the outcome variable (included to account for the possibility that the percentage change in the outcome variable may depend on the initial value). The models are estimated both with ordinary least squares and, for reasons that I explain below, with instrumental variables.

I will briefly summarize the state aid results and then discuss these and other results in more detail.

1. Changes in state aid levels did not influence teacher salary increases.
2. State aid increases did have a negative impact on property tax rates.
3. State aid increases were positively associated with increases in the ratio of "other professionals" (not teachers) to students, but were associated with *decreases* in teacher-student ratios. (In other words, more aid leads to larger class sizes, a result even more puzzling than the Kleiner-Petree (chap. 11, this volume) finding that unionization leads to larger classes.)

When I read an earlier version of E-C's paper six months ago, I was somewhat surprised by the lack of findings. Since then two colleagues and I have been doing similar work using longitudinal data on Michigan school districts, and now I do not find the results so surprising (cf. Murnane, Singer, and Willett 1986). In fact, in many respects our results are extremely similar to E-C's.

Richard J. Murnane, an economist, is a professor at the Harvard Graduate School of Education.

I want to start my comments by focusing on three common findings.

E-C found that increases in state aid are not associated with increases in teacher salaries in New York State school districts. I found the same thing to be true in Michigan districts. The Michigan finding is not surprising, however, given prior research indicating that local school districts in that state responded to state aid increases by reducing local property tax rates and keeping per pupil expenditures roughly constant (Carroll 1982). In other words, when state aid increased, local property tax rates decreased, but local school superintendents did not get larger school budgets. Given that school budgets did not increase when state aid increased, it is not surprising that teacher salaries did not increase.

Can E-C's finding that teachers' salaries in New York State school districts did not increase when state aid increased be explained in the same way? It is not possible to provide a precise answer to this question because, to my knowledge, no research has explored how changes in state aid formulas in New York influenced school districts' per pupil expenditures.[1] Thus, we do not know whether changes in New York State school aid formulas resulted in superintendents having larger budgets (denominated in per pupil terms) or not.

We do know from the E-C work that some part of the increases in state aid went for property tax relief. E-C's estimates reported in table 9.3 imply that a 10 percent increase in state aid is associated with a 2–5 percent reduction in property tax rates (see footnote *a* of E-C's table 9.3 for a description of the method for calculating elasticities). Is this a big enough reduction in property tax rates to absorb totally the increased state aid, leaving school districts with no more funds to spend on teachers' salaries or anything else? Apparently E-C do not think so, because they comment that although increases in state aid levels negatively affected tax rate growth, "this relationship was far from one to one." It does not need to be one to one, however. How large the elasticity of tax rate change with respect to state aid change must be to keep per pupil expenditures constant depends on the relative importance of state aid and local property taxes in supporting school expenditures. For plausible values of state aid and property tax revenues per pupil, E-C's estimates of the sensitivity of property tax rates to state aid are large enough to support the conclusion that changes in the New York State school aid formula over the early 1980s did not result in increased teacher salaries because they did not result in increased expenditures per pupil.[2]

If, in fact, the reductions in property tax rates brought on by the increase in the generosity of the New York State school aid formula were large enough to absorb the extra revenue made available to local school districts, then there is no puzzle. Teacher salaries did not increase because there was no increase in funds made available to local school districts. I believe that E-C's estimates are consistent with this hypothesis, but without longitudinal data on per pupil expenditures, we cannot know for sure.

What if the property tax rate reductions did not absorb all of the increases in state aid? What happened to the rest of the increased aid? If it did not go into higher teacher salaries and if it did not go into smaller class sizes (E-C find that more aid is associated with larger classes—a real puzzle), where did the money go? The only category of resources that E-C find to increase in response to increased state aid is "other professionals" per student (i.e., not teachers). It is puzzling that "other professionals" per student would increase in response to increased state aid, but teachers per student would decrease.

Another possible use of the resources made available through increased state aid is maintenance. Carroll (1982) found that noninstructional expenditures, including maintenance, were more sensitive to state aid than instructional expenditures were. This is a plausible finding for New York as well as Michigan. Many school districts in these two states were experiencing severe fiscal stress at the end of the 1970s. Rapid inflation—especially in the price of fuel oil—was making it difficult to balance the budget. Many communities were not willing to pay for the higher taxes needed to increase revenues. Moreover, many school expenditures, especially teacher and administrator salaries, were fixed contractual commitments. The only place school officials could save money was by skimping on maintenance. After several years of such skimping, however, roofs begin to leak, and the need for catch-up expenditures to save the physical plant is great. Meeting this need may have absorbed the increased resources that state aid in Michigan made available to some local school districts.

It is possible that maintenance may also be the category that experienced the largest expenditure increase in New York State school districts when changes in the state school aid formula led to increases in state aid. Unfortunately, we do not know whether this is true because E-C do not report results on maintenance expenditures.

One final note on state aid. The New York State school aid program is actually a closed-end matching grant program. Thus, for districts that spend less than a given expenditure level per pupil (E_H in E-C's paper), the state aid level depends on the district's expenditure level. For such districts it is not appropriate to treat the state aid level as if it were a block grant. E-C deal with the matching nature of the grant program in two ways. First, they argue that "the majority of districts appeared to have spent more than E_H each year" and, thus, it is legitimate to treat state aid as exogenous. While this is true for those districts with expenditures above E_H, what about the other districts? Might not the results be different if the statistical work took into account that these districts can influence their aid levels? In fact, the results are different when E-C adopt their second approach (instrumental variables) to estimate the impact of changes in the state aid formula on teacher salaries, tax rates, and staffing ratios. Unfortunately, however, the second set of results do not form a consistent pattern. In E-C's words,

> . . . increases in state aid now appear to be negatively associated with *both* teacher/student and paraprofessional/student ratios. The magnitude of the latter relationship is sufficiently large to make one question what we have found.

I appreciate the honesty of E-C's evaluation of their results. However, the results themselves are troubling. The second-round (instrumental variables) results are sufficiently different from the first-round OLS results to leave serious questions about what inferences should be drawn from the E-C work about the effects of state aid formula changes. I wish that E-C had adopted the strategy of modeling the changes in the matching grant formula as changes in the prices that local school districts pay for education and then had estimated the responses to these price changes. This is the strategy that public finance economists usually employ to examine the effects of matching grant programs.

What would E-C have found if they had modeled the changes in the New York State school aid formula as changes in the prices school districts pay for education? Would they have been similar to their first-round OLS results? Or to their somewhat confusing instrumental variable results? In our Michigan data, my colleagues and I found that modeling changes in the state aid matching grant formula as changes in the prices school districts face produced results almost identical to the results of modeling the aid changes as changes in block grants. With both models, the results were that increasing the generosity of the aid formula did not result in higher teacher salaries. This is E-C's result based on modeling state aid as block grants. Thus, experience with the Michigan data leads me to guess that had E-C chosen to model the formula changes as changes in the prices school districts face, their results would have been similar to their OLS results in which state aid is treated as exogenous.

Looking at E-C's other results, they are more successful in explaining the trends in the salaries of experienced teachers than they are in explaining the trends in starting salaries. I found the same pattern in Michigan. In commenting on their inability to explain changes in starting salaries, E-C state: ". . . teachers' unions paid relatively little attention to starting salaries, and in a number of cases no increases were given at that level." Should we infer from this statement that starting salaries did not change much over the time period and therefore the regression coefficient is small because there is little variation in the dependent variable? E-C do not present the data needed to answer this question. I found in Michigan, however, that there was *more* variation in the log of starting salaries in 1980 than there was in the log of 1970 starting salaries. This was not the case for minimum salaries. I also found that the structure of salary scales became steeper over the decade. In other words, the maximum salary increased at a greater rate than the starting salary did. One plausible explanation for this is union politics. The teaching staffs in most school districts in New York and Michigan aged over the 1970s because few new teachers were hired. Older teachers pushed for increases in the part of the salary scale that pertained to them, and the school districts did not resist because they were not trying to attract new teachers. This hypothesis suggests that the change in the experience distribution of the teaching staff in a school district may be a variable that would help to explain the change in the salary structure.

I also found that starting salaries and maximum salaries increased more in Michigan school districts with growing student enrollments than in districts with declining enrollments. This made sense in that teachers' unions in districts with declining enrollments may have forgone salary increases in order to protect the jobs of union members. I was curious to see whether E-C also found that student enrollment changes influence salary changes and was disappointed to learn that they did not find this pattern.

E-C and I did both find that the variable most important in explaining the salary change over time was the base year salary; the lower the base year salary the larger the change. This is quite plausible; it may just reflect a catching-up phenomenon, as E-C suggest.

One finding in the E-C paper that I did find surprising is that tax rate increases were greater in communities that voted on annual budget referenda than in communities in which the school board set the tax rate. My intuition was in the opposite direction. I wonder whether it is legitimate to interpret this finding as indicating the impact of the method by which the school budget is set. I interpet E-C's discussion of the critical variable as indicating that it is, in effect, a dichotomous variable taking on a value of one for a city school district and a value of zero for a suburban or rural district. The method of determining the school budget is only one of many things that differentiate big city school districts from other districts. I wonder whether it is the method of determining the school budget that really explains why city school districts increased their local tax rates less during the early 1980s than other school districts did.

With this caution in mind, I would support E-C's intuition that examination of the roles institutional considerations, such as how budgets are determined, play in determining tax rates and expenditure patterns is a promising line for future research.

Having expressed a number of reservations about particular findings in the E-C paper, I would like to conclude by endorsing several aspects of E-C's approach. First, their use of longitudinal data is a significant improvement over studies that use cross-sectional data. Second, their interpretation of results is informed by knowledge of collective bargaining practices, such as the tendency to "backload" salary increases to the last contract years. Third, their candor in pointing out that their results contain a number of puzzles is refreshing and all too rare.

Notes

1. Eberts and Stone (1984) reported that a $1.00 increase in state aid per pupil in New York State increased school spending by $0.88 per pupil. However, they treated state aid as block grant aid, while the formula in fact was a closed-end matching grant formula.

2. Assume that a particular school district's budget is financed exclusively from local property taxes and state block grant aid.

Let: S_i = state school aid per pupil provided to the district in year i
$S_1 = \$500$
$S_2 = \$750$
V_i = the school district tax base per pupil in year i
$V_1 = V_2 = \$100,000$
r_i = the local property tax rate in year i
$r_1 = 0.02$
$E_i = S_i + r_iV_i$ = per pupil expenditures in year i
$E_1 = 500 + (0.02)(100,000) = \$2,500$

Solve for the value of r_2 that keeps the per pupil expenditure level at $2,500 in year 2:

$$r_2 = \frac{E_2 - S_2}{V_2} = \frac{2500 - 750}{100,000} = 0.0175 .$$

Solve for the arc elasticity indicating the response of the local property tax rate to a change in state aid:

$$\begin{aligned}
\text{Elasticity} &= \frac{(r_2 - r_1)/[(r_1 + r_2)/2]}{(S_2 - S_1)/[(S_1 + S_2)/2]} \\
&= \frac{-0.0025/0.01875}{250/625} \\
&= \frac{-0.133}{0.40} \\
&= -0.33 .
\end{aligned}$$

This elasticity is within the range estimated by E-C.

References

Carroll, Stephen J. 1982. The search for equity in school finance. In *Financing education: Overcoming inefficiency and inequity,* ed. Walter W. McMahon and Terry G. Geske, 237–66. Urbana, Ill.: University of Illinois Press.

Eberts, Randall W., and Joe A. Stone. 1984. *Unions and public schools.* Lexington, Mass.: Lexington Books.

Murnane, Richard J., Judy Singer, and John Willett. 1986. How did teacher salary schedules change during the 1970s? Harvard Graduate School of Education. Mimeo.

10 Unions and Job Security in the Public Sector

Steven G. Allen

Altogether, it's one sweet deal: generous pay and benefits, lifetime job security, meaningless performance evaluation, and, last, but not least, protection from all the swings of fortune that affect workers in private industry.

Alan Crawford, *Washington Monthly*, January 1983

10.1 Introduction

The question of how public sector employers adjust employment in periods of declining demand would not have been considered a serious issue until the last half of the 1970s. Employment at both the state and local levels grew at such a rapid and sustained pace before then that this issue arose only in a few isolated cases. This all changed with the 1974–75 recession and the widespread adoption of tax and expenditure limitations such as Proposition 13 in California. Since 1975, government employment has declined as a share of total employment, and since 1980 it has stayed about constant in absolute terms. As a result, many

Steven G. Allen is professor of economics and business at North Carolina State University and research associate of the National Bureau of Economic Research.

The author thanks Richard Freeman, Charles Brown, Casey Ichniowski, Joe Altonji, Henry Farber, and participants of the North Carolina State University Labor Workshop for helpful comments; Jim Comer and Ron Holanek for computing assistance; and Myra Ragland for research assistance. This research was partially supported by the NBER's Public Sector Union project. The data utilized in this paper were made available in part by the Inter-University Consortium for Political and Social Research. The empirical results are reported in more detail in an earlier version of this paper, circulated as NBER working paper no. 2108.

governments have been forced to make hard decisions about how to trim their payrolls.

This paper examines how public sector unions have been able to influence these decisions. Studies by Medoff (1979) and Blau and Kahn (1983) on the impact of unions on labor market adjustment in the private sector have found much higher temporary and indefinite layoff rates for union than for nonunion workers. There is mixed evidence on how unions affect permanent layoff rates. Freeman and Medoff (1984) report that permanent layoff rates calculated for three-digit manufacturing industries between 1958 and 1971 and in 1981 show no difference between industries that are predominantly unionized and those that are not, but they also show that the May 1973–75 and 1977 Current Population Surveys (CPS) for manufacturing workers indicate lower permanent layoff rates for union members. Blau and Kahn find higher permanent layoff rates for union than nonunion workers in manufacturing in the National Longitudinal Survey (NLS) younger male cohort, but no union-nonunion difference for manufacturing workers in the NLS older male cohort. When they expand these samples to include all sectors except construction, they find unionism has no effect on the probability of permanent layoff for either younger or older males.

Section 10.2 compares the postwar trend in unemployment rates for private and public sector workers and reports the first estimates of layoff rates for public sector workers. These results show that although there has been some convergence of the unemployment rates of these two groups, the odds of being on layoff remain much lower in the public sector. Among public sector workers, layoff probabilities are considerably lower for union members, a marked contrast to the pattern of higher layoff rates under unionism in the private sector.

Sections 10.3 and 10.4 compare both the theoretical and institutional factors that influence employment adjustment decisions in the public and private sector and point out how the impact of unionism is likely to vary between the two sectors. The May 1973–75 and 1983 Current Population Surveys and the 1976–82 Panel Survey of Income Dynamics (PSID) are used in sections 10.5 and 10.6 to estimate public-private and union-nonunion differences in unemployment and layoff probabilities. The main results, summarized in section 10.7, are: (1) unions reduce by a substantial amount the already low layoff and unemployment probabilities in the public sector in contrast to those in the private sector, where layoff rates are much higher under unionism, and (2) nonunion public sector workers have temporary layoff rates and overall unemployment probabilities comparable to those of nonunion private sector workers.

10.2 Public Sector Layoff and Unemployment Rates

Unemployment rates for all civilian workers and for government workers are presented in figure 10.1. Both series exhibit a rising trend over time, a reflection of well-known structural changes in the labor market. What is less apparent in figure 10.1, but can be shown easily in a simple regression equation, is that the gap between these two

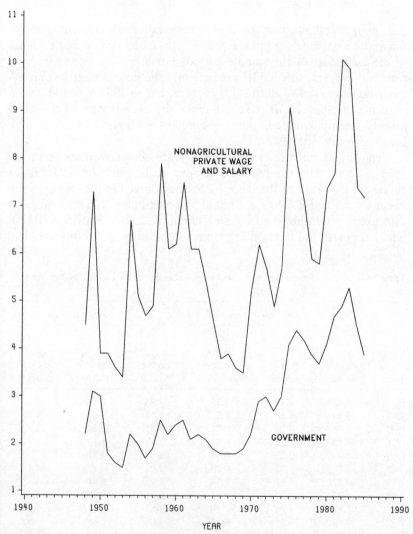

Fig. 10.1   Unemployment rates for nonagricultural private wage and salary workers and for government workers, 1948–85

unemployment rates has narrowed throughout this period. Let UGOV = unemployment rate for government workers, UTOT = unemployment rate for nonagricultural private wage and salary workers, and T = time trend (1 for 1948, . . . , 38 for 1985). These variables were used to estimate the following equation:

$$UGOV = 1.373 + 0.086*UTOT - 0.027*T + 0.0117*T*UTOT$$
$$(0.528) \quad (0.095) \qquad\qquad (0.024) \qquad (0.0037)$$
$$R^2 = 0.854$$

This equation shows that for a given national unemployment rate, the unemployment rate for government workers was considerably higher in the later part of the sample period. For a civilian unemployment rate of 6 percent, this model predicts that the government unemployment rate for 1948 would be 1.9 percent, but in 1985 it would be 3.5 percent. In other words, controlling for the overall state of the labor market, unemployment of government workers is almost twice as high today as in the late 1940s.

Mean layoff rates for public and private sector workers from the 1973–84 May CPS are reported in table 10.1. These layoff statistics represent the share of the labor force unemployed in the survey week because of a layoff. They are not at all comparable to the layoff rates that used to be published by the Bureau of Labor Statistics (BLS), which reported the fraction of workers (instead of the labor force) laid

Table 10.1   **Percentage of Experienced Labor Force on Layoff, by Year and Class of Worker**

Year	Temporary and Indefinite Layoff			Permanent Layoff		
	Private Sector	Public Sector	Public Sector Excluding Education	Private Sector	Public Sector	Public Sector Excluding Education
1973	0.63	0.17	0.25	1.45	0.51	0.67
1974	0.70	0.18	0.25	1.59	0.53	0.61
1975	2.44	0.22	0.32	3.62	1.22	1.53
1976	1.15	0.35	0.44	3.01	1.19	1.47
1977	0.93	0.27	0.37	2.62	0.85	1.12
1978	0.72	0.22	0.29	2.09	0.89	1.12
1979	0.72	0.15	0.16	1.75	0.84	1.13
1980	1.92	0.27	0.34	2.57	0.98	1.30
1981	1.42	0.36	0.36	2.82	1.40	1.91
1982	2.08	0.35	0.42	4.06	1.66	1.93
1983	2.06	0.50	0.59	4.98	1.99	2.47
1984	1.24	0.31	0.43	3.09	1.36	1.72

Source: May CPS public use tapes.

off in a particular month (rather than all previous months). The sample is restricted to the May surveys because of the availability of data on union status in that month and the computational burden of using all of the monthly tapes over a twelve-year interval. One problem with using the May survey for estimating public sector layoff rates is that educational employees are unlikely to be on layoff in that month. To adjust for this bias, separate estimates are reported for the public sector with schools, colleges, and universities excluded from the sample.

Temporary layoffs are those with recall within less than thirty days, whereas indefinite layoffs are those with recall within thirty days or more or those with no definite recall date. Because of the very small number of public sector workers experiencing either of these types of layoffs, the sum of these two layoff rates is reported in table 10.1. Both are distinguished from permanent layoffs by the expectation of recall. The permanent layoff rate is the fraction of the experienced labor force consisting of unemployed workers who said they started looking for work because they had lost their previous job.

Average temporary and indefinite layoff probabilities in May for 1973 through 1984 are about four times greater in the private than in the public sector. Between 0.6 and 2.4 percent of the experienced labor force in the private sector was on temporary or indefinite layoff during those years. The corresponding layoff probabilities for the public sector are not only much lower but their range is much narrower—between 0.2 and 0.5 percent for all public sector employees and between 0.2 and 0.6 percent for public sector employees excluding education. Although the time period under consideration is quite narrow, the patterns for 1975–76, 1980–81, and 1982–83 indicate that the peak in layoff rates for the public sector lags that for the private sector by one year. There is no evidence that the ratio of the public to the private temporary and indefinite layoff rate has changed between 1973 and 1984.

Permanent layoff rates also are much greater in the private sector, but the relative gap between public and private permanent layoff rates seems to have narrowed in recent years. Between 1973 and 1977, permanent layoff rates were about three times larger in the private sector than in the public sector (two and a half times larger when education is excluded from the public sector). This gap has narrowed to about two and a half times larger between 1978 and 1984 (two times larger when education is excluded from the public sector). This narrowing is largely attributable to upward drift in the permanent layoff rate in the public sector. The layoff rate for all public sector employees was 0.5 percent in 1973 and 1974 but never fell below 0.8 percent in later years. The pattern is more pronounced when education is excluded; the layoff rate was 0.7 and 0.6 percent in 1973 and 1974 but never fell below 1.1 percent thereafter.

Even though the average public employee is subject to a very low layoff risk, this may be attributable to differences in the type of work between the public and the private sector. To determine whether any public sector workers are subject to layoff risks comparable to those for the average private sector worker, layoff rates for public and private sector employees are reported for selected industries in table 10.2. Because of small samples in individual years, the data are summarized in three-year groups.

These results show that the risk of temporary or indefinite layoff is greatest for public sector jobs in construction, utilities, and federal and state public administration. However, these layoff rates are almost always far below those for the average private sector worker in table

Table 10.2   **Percentage of Experienced Labor Force on Layoff, by Time Period and Industry**

	Temporary and Indefinite Layoff				Permanent Layoff			
Industry	1973–75	1976–78	1979–81	1982–84	1973–75	1976–78	1979–81	1982–84
Construction								
Public	0.75	0.22	0.50	0.17	1.09	2.19	2.38	3.61
Private	3.15	2.84	3.70	4.63	5.97	5.95	5.48	9.12
Street railways, bus lines								
Public	0.22	0.00	0.20	1.30	0.45	0.55	0.55	1.17
Private	0.00	0.53	0.29	0.88	0.61	1.43	2.35	3.70
Utilities and sanitary services								
Public	0.00	0.72	0.24	0.90	0.90	1.14	1.64	2.61
Private	0.20	0.24	0.09	0.60	0.57	0.60	0.89	1.55
Hospitals								
Public	0.20	0.20	0.14	0.27	1.11	0.67	0.47	1.62
Private	0.12	0.12	0.16	0.50	0.62	0.82	0.72	0.99
Elementary and secondary schools								
Public	0.03	0.12	0.24	0.23	0.26	0.59	0.56	0.92
Private	0.16	0.08	0.19	0.14	0.30	1.29	1.31	1.50
Colleges								
Public	0.18	0.12	0.14	0.22	1.05	0.47	0.53	1.60
Private	0.26	0.26	0.00	0.37	0.60	1.12	1.06	1.35
Postal service	0.13	0.24	0.08	0.04	0.34	0.32	0.08	0.43
Federal public administration	0.26	0.38	0.40	0.29	0.71	1.21	0.95	1.42
State public administration	0.46	0.96	0.44	0.46	0.56	0.97	1.38	1.33
Local public administration	0.08	0.34	0.19	0.45	1.10	1.23	2.00	2.16

Source: May CPS public use tapes.

10.1. The only exceptions to this general trend are employees in state public administration in 1976–78 and in urban transit in 1982–84. The odds of temporary or indefinite layoffs are practically zero in education and the postal service. Permanent layoffs in the public sector are most likely to occur in construction, utilities, and local public administration. Except for construction, these layoff rates are also well below those in the private sector in table 10.1.

The public-private comparisons within particular industry groups for temporary and indefinite layoffs in table 10.2 show that layoff rates are roughly equal in the public and private sectors in transportation, utilities, hospitals, and education, but that private sector layoff rates are much higher in construction. The patterns for permanent layoffs are quite different. Although the private sector has higher permanent layoff rates in construction, transportation, and elementary and secondary schools, the public sector has higher permanent layoff rates in utilities and hospitals. These patterns suggest that careful controls for industry characteristics will be needed to estimate accurately the difference in layoff and unemployment probabilities between the public and private sectors.

Comparisons of mean layoff rates for union and nonunion workers in the public and private sectors are reported in table 10.3. These can be computed only for 1973–1975 and 1977 because in all other years unemployed workers were not asked about union membership. Within the public sector, temporary and indefinite layoff probabilities are slightly lower (0.1 percentage points) for union workers. The average gap in permanent layoff rates is also rather small in three out of the four years. However, the exception to this overall tendency is a very important one. In 1975, at the trough of a severe recession, the permanent layoff rate for nonunion public employees was twice as large (1.4 percent) as that for union workers (0.7 percent). This suggests that when the pres-

Table 10.3   **Percentage of Experienced Labor Force on Layoff, by Year, Class of Worker, and Union Status**

| | Temporary and Indefinite Layoff | | | | Permanent Layoff | | | |
| | Private Sector | | Public Sector | | Private Sector | | Public Sector | |
Year	Union	Nonunion	Union	Nonunion	Union	Nonunion	Union	Nonunion
1973	1.22	0.45	0.24	0.16	1.74	1.36	0.37	0.55
1974	1.54	0.44	0.08	0.22	1.88	1.50	0.71	0.47
1975	5.56	1.58	0.04	0.28	4.26	3.45	0.72	1.38
1977	1.80	0.69	0.20	0.30	2.98	2.52	0.67	0.93

Source: May CPS public use tapes.

sure for layoffs is greatest, union workers in the public sector have a much better chance of keeping their jobs than nonunion public employees. The exact opposite pattern is observed in the private sector, where union members have considerably higher layoff rates than nonunion workers.

10.3   Unions and Public Sector Layoffs: Theory

Demand shocks are likely to differ between the public and private sectors because of differences in technology and consumer characteristics. For instance, labor demand in agriculture and construction fluctuates a great deal over the course of a year because of the dictates of seasons and weather, whereas except for elementary and secondary education, public sector labor demand consists of services provided throughout the year. Demand for public services is also relatively insensitive to conditions in credit markets, in contrast to some goods produced in the private sector, such as construction and durable manufactures. These arguments indicate that there will be less seasonal and cyclical variability in demand for public services than for private goods, which will result in lower layoff rates in the public sector, other things equal.

Even if public and private employers had to deal with the same labor demand shocks, there are still a number of reasons to expect them to have different layoff rates. Two obvious factors are purely technological—public services cannot be produced for inventory in periods of slack demand, and they are very labor intensive. As a result, cuts in government budgets almost always require some cuts in payroll.

These cuts must be obtained by some combination of reduced wages, reduced hours, or reduced employment. Most government jobs are at the state and local levels, where wage studies such as Smith (1977) and Freeman (1985) tend to find rates equal to those in the private sector. In such a situation, wage cuts would produce savings in the short run but would eventually result in higher turnover and excessive recruiting, hiring, and training costs. Wage cuts in federal jobs would be less likely to create these problems, as all studies have found those rates to be well above those paid in comparable private sector jobs. The trade-off between hours and employment cuts will be heavily influenced by the attractive fringe benefit packages offered by most public sector employers and the relatively small amount of specific on-the-job training in many government jobs, especially in education. Both of these factors will make it more economical to use layoffs instead of hours reductions in many public sector jobs.

This assumes, however, that all downward shifts in demand are actually translated into budget cuts. Throughout the 1970s state and local governments were highly successful in obtaining federal aid under various guises (revenue sharing, CETA) to maintain programs that would have been terminated otherwise. On various occasions local governments also have received fiscal infusions from state governments. This avenue of revenue enhancement is not available to the federal government, but it does not have to meet the balanced budget constraint that most state and local governments face. All of these examples illustrate how governments can find substitutes for tax revenue (some of which are automatically tied to local unemployment rates and thus indirectly tied to the revenue of state and local governments) to maintain their budgets and thereby avoid layoffs.

Freeman (1985) has shown that public sector employment has less year-to-year variability than private sector employment. His study, along with the results on mean layoff rates in table 10.1, also suggests that the cyclical pattern in public sector employment lags that observed for private sector employment.

These patterns probably result from differences in sources of revenue between the public and private sectors. Much of the revenue of state and local governments comes from sources well insulated from cyclical behavior, such as property taxes and intergovernmental grants. (Fluctuations in revenue would arise mainly from income and sales taxes, which would vary with output and sales in a particular state, county, or city.) This dampens the impact of any shock.

Lags in making adjustments to any given shock result from the political process. If these lags are long enough, managers in the public sector have more time to plan their manpower responses to declines in demand. This allows them to make greater use of hiring freezes, which allow them to reduce their adjustment costs by 1) avoiding hiring persons who will later have to be laid off and 2) using attrition to reduce the number of employees, thereby avoiding the costs of layoffs (severance pay, unemployment benefits, reputation). An adequate planning horizon is absolutely essential for hiring freezes to be a very useful adjustment device. The incentive to use hiring freezes and attrition in the public sector in place of layoffs will be offset to some extent by low rates of voluntary turnover, which result in smaller reductions in employment levels through attrition than in the private sector.

It would be inappropriate to discuss public-private differences in layoff probabilities and completely ignore unemployment insurance (UI). Today almost all private and government employees are covered by UI, so differences in coverage are not likely to create differences in employee preferences for layoffs relative to other adjustment devices. The low unemployment rates in the public sector make it quite unlikely that any group of public sector workers will collectively receive more in benefits than they spend on payroll taxes. In fact, many governments finance UI benefits for their workers through direct reimbursement rather than using payroll tax contributions. Thus, UI will encourage layoffs to a lesser degree in the public than the private sector.

The above discussion indicates that the factors likely to influence layoff decisions in the public sector are quite distinct from those in the private sector. In the absence of collective bargaining, no unambiguous predictions can be made about how layoff and unemployment rates are likely to vary between the public and private sectors.

Under collective bargaining, median voter models predict that, in both the public and private sectors, greater weight will be given to the preferences of older, less mobile workers in the determination of personnel policies. Except in cases of drastic declines in demand, these workers will prefer a policy of layoffs based on seniority. Such a policy completely insulates them from any cutbacks in wages or hours that might otherwise be required.

Another factor behind the preference of unions in the private sector for seniority-based layoffs is the union-nonunion differential in UI subsidies. This is not likely to be important in the public sector because, as noted above, the financing mechanisms and low layoff rates result in effective self-insurance. Furthermore, supplemental unemployment benefits are rarely provided in union contracts in the public sector. These two factors suggest that the union-nonunion gap in layoff rates should at least be smaller in the public than the private sector.

In addition, there are unique aspects of unionism in the public sector that could result in lower layoff rates for union workers in that sector. Freeman (1986) argues that public sector unions have the ability to shift the demand curve for their services through political activity. Public sector union members represent a significant part of the electorate in many state and local elections. This allows them to use both political power and bargaining power to push for higher wages and membership. In addition, the utility function of public sector unions will put a higher weight on membership because additional members give them even more political leverage. Whether public sector unions are actually successful in obtaining higher wages and employment is an empirical question, however, because they can also serve as a lightning rod for attracting political opposition to the higher taxes required to fund higher payrolls.

This political dimension of union behavior in the public sector is likely to influence layoffs through two different channels. First, the observed lag of employment in the public sector suggests that unions as well as managers have the opportunity to plan strategies for avoiding layoffs. This can be done in a variety of different ways, such as moderation in wage negotiations or political pressure within the appropriate government body to keep its payrolls intact. Second, public sector unions at the local and state levels can also push for additional revenue from higher levels of government as a substitute for any drop in local or state tax revenues. For instance, in Congress public sector unions have been strong supporters of CETA which, under Titles I, II, and VI, granted sizeable sums for public employment programs. These programs prevented a number of cities from having to lay off municipal employees.

On balance, the effect of unions on layoffs in the public sector cannot be predicted ex ante. Although the most senior workers would prefer a system of layoffs based on seniority if payroll cuts are required, the potential political power of unions may enable them to prevent such cuts from taking place or make them considerably smaller than they would have been in the absence of collective bargaining.

10.4   Unions and Public Sector Layoffs: Institutions

Rules and procedures governing layoffs in the nonunion segment of the public sector, if they exist at all, are determined by legislation or regulation. There has been only one study to my knowledge of layoff policies in the public sector. A survey of state governments by the Bureau of National Affairs (1982a) found that twenty states based layoffs primarily or solely on seniority, twenty-four have policies that take both seniority and performance into account, and six states have no laws or policies on layoffs. Even in states in which layoffs are based on both seniority and performance, managers sometimes do not have much discretion in deciding who is to be laid off. For instance, in Utah layoffs are based on the sum of the employee's rankings with respect to previous performance evaluations and seniority. In many cases veterans are given special preference in layoff or recall procedures.

During the 1981–82 recession, a number of states revised their layoff procedures to ensure that recent gains in hiring women and minorities were not eradicated by "last hired, first fired" policies. The Bureau of National Affairs (1982b) identified five states in which state agencies were required to maintain a percentage of women and minorities after a layoff equal to that in the agency prior to the layoff. In many other cases, managers were instructed to take affirmative action into consideration along with other criteria in deciding which persons were to be laid off and which were to be recalled.

Under collective bargaining in the private sector, procedures for layoffs are almost always specified in the union contract. Freeman and Medoff (1984) report that seniority is the most important factor in determining who gets laid off in about 80 percent of all contracts. Five different studies by BLS of contract provisions between 1970 and 1975 indicate that these practices were not as widespread in the public sector. The percentage of employees covered by agreements containing various layoff-related provisions in these studies is reported in table 10.4. Most of the municipal agreements in cities with populations of 250,000 and over in 1970 contained no provisions regarding layoffs. This can be attributed to a combination of three factors: 1) the recentness of most collective bargaining relationships in that period, 2) layoff procedures already specified by ordinances or civil service regulations that in many cases were presumably based at least in part on seniority, and 3) the rapid growth in municipal employment that had taken place in preceding years. Given these three factors, most unions at that time apparently placed little priority on bargaining over layoff and recall provisions. Collaborating evidence for the BLS studies is found in Eberts's (forthcoming) study of over 500 New York school districts in the mid-1970s—only 20 percent of public school teachers were covered by reduction-in-force (RIF) provisions.

Even five years later, the share of union contracts containing layoff and recall provisions in the public sector, although much higher than before, was still much smaller than that in the private sector. Only 65 percent of the contracts during this period contained language pertaining to layoffs and only 35 percent specified recall rights. Both figures are considerably higher than their counterparts in 1970, which no doubt reflects the decline in the fiscal health of many cities over this period as well as increased experience with how layoffs are conducted under civil service rules. Perry's (1979) case study of nine school systems also points out a trend toward a greater percentage of teachers' union contracts containing layoff provisions. He found that in 1967 contractual provisions regarding layoffs were "virtually nonexistent." Ten years later, the contracts in eight of the nine school districts contained language regarding layoffs.

Even if union contracts in the public sector are still less likely to address layoff issues than contracts in the private sector, it seems safe to conclude that much greater weight is given to seniority in determining layoffs in governments with collective bargaining agreements than in those without collective bargaining. There is also evidence that contract provisions do affect layoff decisions in the public sector. Eberts shows that RIF provisions are correlated with much lower separation rates for teachers in school districts with declining enrollment, especially for teachers with more than nine years of experience.

Layoff provisions are far from the only mechanism that public sector unions have to influence government behavior. Levine, Rubin, and Wolohojian (1981) discuss a case in Oakland where the fire fighters union used binding arbitration to reverse a city council decision to eliminate twenty-six positions in 1975. In other cases unions have exerted political pressure to prevent cutbacks. For instance, in 1976 the police and fire fighters unions in Cincinnati petitioned for a referendum

Table 10.4   **Percentage of Workers Covered by Collective Bargaining Agreements with Selected Layoff Provisions**

	Municipal Agreements 1970	Police and Fire Agreements, 1972–73	State and County Agreements, 1972–73	State and Local Agreements, 1 Jan. 1974	State and Local Agreements, 1 July 1975
Reference to reduction in force	—	15.0	46.2	62.0	65.2
Advance notice of layoff	4.7	—	—	23.9	24.1
Union role in reduction in force	1.7	—	12.3	16.9	19.8
Bumping procedures	6.4	—	—	26.5	28.3
Recall rights	18.6	12.6	31.9	30.8	35.2

Source: BLS Bulletin, nos. 1759, 1861, 1885, 1920, 1947.

to freeze staffing at current levels (the petition did not pass). To protest the proposed transfer of a state-managed hospital in Pennsylvania, Wilburn and Worman (1980) report that five unions successfully joined forces to exert pressure, including radio, newspaper, and television advertisements telling residents in the area where the hospital was located that it was vital to their welfare.

A final factor that may be important in some of the period under study here is the endogeneity of UI coverage for many state and local employees before December 1974. Before 1972, when state employees in hospitals and higher education were brought into the system, relatively few state and local public sector employees were covered by UI. Some states had voluntarily decided to cover their own employees, and a few even had laws requiring all local employees to participate. Title II of the Emergency Jobs and Unemployment Assistance Act of 1974 (PL 93-567) brought almost all state and local workers into the system. Although this program was supposedly a temporary measure prompted by the 1974–75 recession, the Unemployment Compensation Amendments of 1976 (U.S. Congress 1976) made these changes permanent. Before these federal statutes were enacted, the political power of public sector unions could increase the odds of UI coverage in areas that were heavily unionized, which would result in somewhat higher layoff rates. However, Allen (1987) found little evidence supporting this conjecture; there is only a weak correlation between unionization and UI coverage and no correlation between UI coverage and unemployment and layoff probabilities in the CPS.

10.5   Evidence from the Current Population Survey

To identify the separate effects of unionism and public sector status on layoff probabilities, two specifications were estimated over the May 1973–75 CPS. The first includes separate dummies for union and public sector status; the second adds a union–public sector interaction term. The extremely large sample size precludes estimation of probit equations over all observations. Probit results for one-fourth of the sample, randomly selected, appear in table 10.5. Temporary layoff equations were not estimated for this sample because none of the public sector workers in the smaller sample were on temporary layoff.

10.5.1   Public-Private Comparisons

How do layoff rates for public and private sector workers compare? Once controls for union status and other job and personal characteristics are included, are the layoff probabilities for public sector workers still very small relative to those of private sector employees? The answers from the first specification largely reaffirm the results from

Table 10.5 Coefficients of Union and Public Sector Status in CPS Unemployment Probit Equations

Sample and Dependent Variable	Mean of Dependent Variable	Model 1: No Interaction		Model 2: Union–Public Section Interaction		
		Union	Public Sector	Union	Public Sector	Interaction
A. 1973–75 CPS ($N = 38,739$)						
1. Indefinite layoff	0.0086	0.178 (0.054) [0.0012]	−0.363 (0.145) [−0.0016]	0.205 (0.055) [0.0015]	−0.162 (0.158) [−0.0008]	−0.700 (0.319) [−0.0019]
2. Permanent layoff	0.0184	−0.009 (0.042) [−0.0003]	−0.233 (0.080) [−0.0066]	0.010 (0.044) [0.0003]	−0.178 (0.087) [−0.0052]	−0.210 (0.144) [−0.0056]
3. Reenter labor force	0.0184	−0.086 (0.049) [−0.0022]	0.169 (0.071) [0.0052]	−0.039 (0.053) [−0.0010]	0.219 (0.074) [0.0070]	−0.273 (0.132) [−0.0056]
4. Quit last job	0.0073	−0.053 (0.064) [−0.0007]	−0.024 (0.102) [−0.0003]	−0.044 (0.069) [−0.0006]	−0.008 (0.110) [−0.0001]	−0.065 (0.174) [−0.0008]
5. Unemployed, any reason	0.0554	0.047 (0.029) [0.0042]	−0.095 (0.051) [−0.0079]	0.095 (0.031) [0.0086]	0.007 (0.055) [0.0006]	−0.416 (0.093) [−0.0261]
B. 1983 CPS ($N = 22,803$)						
Unemployed during 1982	0.148	−0.032 (0.028) [−0.006]	−0.329 (0.048) [−0.060]	0.022 (0.032) [0.005]	−0.234 (0.053) [−0.044]	−0.255 (0.068) [−0.046]

Note: Standard errors are reported in parentheses and the partial derivative of the probability of the dependent variable at the mean values of the independent variables is reported in brackets. Each equation also contains the following variables: age and its square, years of schooling completed, and binary indicators of race (1), sex, marital status (1), region (3), occupation (11), industry (34 for 1973–75 and 37 for 1983), and year (2 in 1973–75).

table 10.1. For both types of layoffs under consideration, the results indicate that layoff rates are much lower in the public sector: 0.2 percentage points lower for indefinite layoffs, and 0.7 percentage points lower for permanent layoffs.

The second model allows these comparisons to be made separately for union and nonunion workers. The results show that the public-private difference in layoff rates for nonunion workers is smaller than the public-private difference for union and nonunion workers combined. There is no public-private difference in indefinite layoffs for nonunion workers. The public-private difference in permanent layoffs is slightly smaller for nonunion workers than for union and nonunion workers combined.

Events initiating spells of unemployment for the experienced labor force include not only layoffs, but also quits and labor force reentries. To get a complete picture of how job security compares in the public and private sectors, quits and labor force reentries should also be examined, especially the latter. Previous research by Clark and Summers (1979), among others, shows frequent transitions between the states of unemployment and out of the labor force. These transitions have raised the question of whether being unemployed is behaviorally distinct from being out of the labor force, as many transitions could arise from measurement error or temporary cessation of job search. There is a clear possibility that many of the persons who are classified as labor force reentrants were laid off before the survey period. If so, then ignoring labor force reentrants may result in a biased comparison of public and private sector job security.

The drawback with using the information on labor force reentry is the difficulty in interpreting the results. It is impossible to distinguish between persons who left their last jobs voluntarily and those who were laid off. Despite the problems with interpretation of labor force reentrant behavior, the empirical results should provide a more complete picture of relative job stability in the public and private sectors. The impact of union and public sector status on unemployment attributable to labor force reentry, along with unemployment resulting from quits and total unemployment regardless of source is reported in the last three rows of panel A of table 10.5.

In both models, workers whose last job was in the public sector are much more likely to be unemployed labor force reentrants than workers whose last job was in the private sector. The results for the second model show that this relationship holds for nonunion, but not union, public sector workers. Nonunion public sector workers are 0.7 percent more likely than nonunion private sector workers and 0.8 percent more likely than union private sector workers to be unemployed force reentrants. These results, although difficult to interpret, suggest that the lower permanent layoff rates observed in the public sector may not tell the entire story about job security in the public sector. One of two things is certain: either the public-private difference in layoff rates for nonunion workers is overstated in table 10.5 or unemployment resulting from voluntary turnover is higher in the public than the private sector for nonunion workers.

In contrast to other studies (e.g., Long 1982) that have found lower voluntary turnover in the public sector, the odds that a person will quit his last job to search for a new job are no lower for public than for private sector workers. The discrepancy between this finding and those of earlier studies is probably attributable to the narrowness of the turnover variable in the CPS, which does not report quits unless they are followed by a spell of unemployment.

Further evidence on quits from the PSID is reported in table 10.6. (Details on how the data set was constructed are reported in section 10.6.) These results show that quit rates for heads of households are lower in the public sector than private sector. In the model which allows the public sector coefficient to vary for union and nonunion workers, quit probabilities in the public sector are 2.1 percent lower for nonunion workers and 0.3 percent lower for union workers than for their counterparts in the private sector. The estimated public-private differences for wives are very imprecise, indicating that there is no pronounced quit differential for them. It is interesting to note that among both heads and wives the impact of union status on quits is smaller in the public sector.

The key issue for interpreting the labor force reentry results in table 10.5 is how quits accompanied by unemployment compare for union and nonunion workers in the public sector. To examine this question, the dependent variable was set equal to one if a person quit the job held a year ago and experienced unemployment during the past year. These results, also reported in table 10.6, show a slightly lower probability of quits followed by unemployment for union than for nonunion workers in the public sector. This evidence, along with earlier research, strongly rejects any possibility that unemployment associated with voluntary turnover for nonunion workers is higher in the public sector than in the private sector. This means that the results on layoffs in table 10.5 actually overstate the public-private difference in job security.

The last row of panel A in table 10.5 compares the odds that public and private sector workers will be unemployed for any reason. The first specification shows unemployment rates are 0.8 percent lower in the public sector. This difference vanishes in the second specification— unemployment probabilities are the same in the public and private sectors for nonunion workers. In other words, considering all possible causes of unemployment together, nonunion public sector workers are

Table 10.6   **Coefficients of Union and Public Sector Status in PSID Unemployment, Quit, and Layoff Probit Equations**

Sample and Dependent Variable	Mean of Dependent Variable	Model 1: No Interaction		Model 2: Union-Public Sector Interaction		
		Union	Public Sector	Union	Public Sector	Interaction
A. Heads (N = 13,873)						
1. Quit previous job	0.083	-0.206	-0.134	-0.235	-0.171	0.128
		(0.040)	(0.054)	(0.045)	(0.060)	(0.090)
		[-0.026]	[-0.017]	[-0.030]	[-0.021]	[0.018]
2. Quit and unemployed during year	0.023	-0.253	-0.175	-0.231	-0.141	-0.138
		(0.067)	(0.094)	(0.072)	(0.103)	(0.177)
		[-0.006]	[-0.004]	[-0.005]	[-0.003]	[-0.003]
3. Unemployed during year	0.0154	0.190	-0.176	0.242	-0.058	-0.300
		(0.033)	(0.050)	(0.036)	(0.059)	(0.083)
		[0.038]	[-0.031]	[0.048]	[-0.011]	[-0.049]
4. Job loser	0.049	-0.020	-0.300	-0.037	-0.342	0.109
		(0.046)	(0.076)	(0.050)	(0.090)	(0.121)
		[-0.001]	[-0.019]	[-0.003]	[-0.021]	[0.008]

B. Wives ($N = 3{,}796$)

1. Quit previous job	0.127	−0.295 (0.087) [−0.048]	−0.030 (0.082) [−0.006]	−0.375 (0.113) [−0.059]	−0.065 (0.088) [−0.012]	0.200 (0.173) [0.041]
2. Quit and unemployed during year	0.022	−0.214 (0.161) [−0.007]	−0.203 (0.158) [−0.007]	−0.235 (0.188) [−0.008]	−0.215 (0.169) [−0.007]	0.076 (0.352) [0.003]
3. Unemployed during year	0.140	0.149 (0.074) [0.031]	0.034 (0.083) [0.007]	0.294 (0.086) [0.064]	0.148 (0.089) [0.030]	−0.508 (0.162) [−0.076]
4. Job loser	0.046	−0.096 (0.114) [−0.007]	−0.163 (0.127) [−0.011]	−0.035 (0.124) [−0.002]	−0.103 (0.135) [−0.007]	−0.334 (0.299) [−0.019]

Note: All equations are estimated over the PSID (1976–82 for heads, 1979–82 for wives). Each equation also contains the following variables: age and its square, tenure with employers and its square, years of schooling, number of children, and binary indicators of race (2), region (3), occupation (5), industry (8), and year (5 for heads, 2 for wives). Dummies for sex and marital status (1) are also included in the equation for heads.

just as likely to be unemployed as nonunion private sector workers. The lower odds of permanent layoffs are offset by the greater odds of being an unemployed labor force reentrant.

10.5.2   The Role of Unions

The results from the second specification in table 10.5 can also be used to compare the impact of unions on job security in the public and private sectors. Whereas union members in the private sector are 0.15 percentage points more likely to be on indefinite layoff than nonunion members, this does not seem to be the case in the public sector. The coefficient implies slightly lower indefinite layoff rates in the public sector for union members, but the standard error is sufficiently large to prevent rejection of the null hypothesis of no union-nonunion difference.

The impact of unionism on permanent layoffs also is completely different in the public and private sectors. In the private sector, union members are just as likely to be laid off permanently as nonunion workers. In the public sector, permanent layoff rates are 0.5 percentage points lower for union than nonunion workers. These results on layoffs imply that public sector unions have been much more successful in promoting job security than their private sector counterparts.

The evidence on unemployment due to quits and labor force reentry as well as the evidence for all types of unemployment combined is consistent with this implication. Union members are less likely to become unemployed reentrants in both sectors, but the impact of unionism is greater in the public sector both in proportional and absolute terms. Surprisingly, there is no union-nonunion difference in quits resulting in unemployment in either the private or public sector.

Looking across all types of unemployment, the results in the last row of panel A of table 10.5 show that union members are 0.9 percentage points more likely than nonunion workers to become unemployed in the private sector, but 1.8 percentage points *less* likely in the public sector. The impact of unions on job security is completely different in the public and private sectors. Unions are associated with a higher unemployment risk in private sector jobs, but a lower risk of joblessness in the public sector.

10.5.3   Retrospective Evidence for 1982

Two key limitations of the results from the 1973–75 CPS are that 1) during that period employment in the public sector was still growing and 2) many union contracts did not contain layoff provisions. Since then, government budgets have been squeezed by legislation to limit taxes and expenditures as well as by a recession more severe than that in 1974–75. This would presumably give unions less political flexibility to maintain public sector payrolls, while at the same time make union members more sensitive to job security issues and in all likelihood increase the share of union contracts containing rules on layoffs. As a result, one would have good reason to question whether the results for 1973–75 are still pertinent today.

These results cannot be replicated for more recent years, because after 1977 the CPS stopped asking unemployed workers about union status at their previous job. One alternative approach is to use the May 1983 CPS, which reports union status for half the sample (instead of a quarter of the sample as in all other surveys since 1981) and matches these records with the March 1983 CPS, which contains retrospective data on unemployment during 1982. At the cost of restricting the sample to employed workers, union-nonunion differences in unemployment during 1982 can be estimated for both the public and private sectors.

Unemployed persons in the May 1983 sample consist of those who either were recalled to their old jobs or were successful in finding new jobs. Those who were still jobless at the time of the survey are omitted from the sample. This should be kept in mind when interpreting the results; they are not directly comparable to those reported from the 1973–75 CPS. The dependent variable is a dummy equal to one if the respondent was unemployed during 1982. The distinctions between union and nonunion as well as private and public workers are based on the job held at the time of the survey. (The models were also estimated over a data set in which these distinctions were based on the longest job held in 1982. The results were basically the same and are not reported here.)

With regard to union-nonunion differences, the probit results in panel B of table 10.5 are comparable to those in panel A. The key result of a negative union impact on unemployment probability in the public sector from the 1973–75 CPS continues to hold for the 1982 CPS. Public employees belonging to unions were 4.1 percentage points less likely to have been unemployed in 1982 than nonunion public employees. Union workers are 0.5 percentage points more likely to have been unemployed than nonunion workers in the private sector, but the difference is not statistically significant.

The only finding from the 1973–75 CPS that does not carry over to the more recent sample is that pertaining to public-private differences in unemployment probabilities for nonunion workers. Nonunion public employees were 4.4 percentage points less likely to have been unemployed in 1982 than nonunion private employees. This result is most likely attributable to either the restricted sample in the May 1983 CPS or the lagged response of public sector layoffs to downturns in economic activity documented in table 10.1; it need not be inconsistent with the findings in table 10.5.

10.6   Evidence from the Panel Survey of Income Dynamics

The PSID has reported both union status and class of worker on a continuous basis since 1976. The main advantages of exploring this data set are that it spans the period between the two CPS samples and that it can be used to estimate fixed-effects models. A possible disadvantage is that the PSID sample consists of households that have been continuously tracked for fourteen years, and such households are likely to be less than perfectly representative of the labor force.

Two different indicators of job security are examined: 1) whether the respondent is currently unemployed or was unemployed in the past year, and 2) whether the respondent lost his previous job because he was laid off or fired or because his company closed (job losses for any of these reasons will be referred to as layoffs below). Survey responses to these questions in year $t + 1$ are regressed on independent variables for year t. As in the CPS, the sample is restricted to wage and salary workers. When using the PSID, the question always arises as to whether observations from the 1967 Survey of Economic Opportunity (SEO) subsample should be included. In this case the coefficients are relatively insensitive to composition of the sample, so observations from the SEO subsample are included in the results reported below. Split-off households formed during the sample period and persons who were self-employed during any of the sample years are deleted to facilitate data-set management. Separate models are estimated for heads of households (assumed by the PSID to be the male in two-earner households) and wives.

The PSID results for heads in table 10.6 show that, just as in the CPS, the odds of being unemployed are about the same for public and private sector workers not covered by collective bargaining. In the model without any interaction between union and public sector status, union employees have a 3.8 percentage point higher probability of being unemployed; public sector employees, a 3.1 percentage point lower probability. However, this model restricts the impact of unionism to be the same in both the public and private sectors. When this restriction is removed by adding a union-public sector interaction term, there is no longer any significant difference between the odds of being unemployed in public and private sector jobs for nonunion workers. Union workers in the private sector are 4.8 percentage points more likely to have been unemployed than nonunion workers, but there is no difference in unemployment probabilities in the public sector between union and nonunion workers.

Wives who are union members working in the private sector are 6.4 percentage points more likely to experience unemployment than nonunion workers in that sector. In the public sector, union members are

1.2 percentage points less likely to have been unemployed than non-union workers. Among nonunion workers there is once again no significant public-private difference in unemployment probabilities.

Unionism has little impact on the odds that a person in the PSID will lose his job in either the public or private sector. The union and union–public sector interaction coefficients are both not significantly different from zero, in contrast to the CPS in which the interaction was negative. Household heads working in the public sector are 2.1 percentage points less likely to lose their jobs regardless of union status, but the odds of job loss for wives are equal in the public and private sectors.

A final way to establish the robustness of this result over these samples is to estimate a fixed-effects model. Although it is now widely accepted that such models are not a panacea for biases associated with unobserved heterogeneity of workers who obtain jobs in the public and private sectors, it would be difficult to be very confident in the findings in table 10.6 if they were completely inconsistent with the results from a fixed-effects specification. The fixed-effects results for heads (see table 10.7) are quite similar in terms of the signs of the coefficients to the results reported above. The decrease in the size of the coefficients and the increase in the size of the standard errors is not surprising in light of results obtained in other studies with fixed-effects estimators. However, in the wives sample, the coefficients actually tend to be somewhat larger in the fixed-effects results. There is no readily apparent reason for this unusual result. Whatever the reason, it is quite clear, even in the fixed-effects results, that the impact of unionism on the odds of becoming unemployed is quite different in the public and private sectors.

Table 10.7   Fixed Effects Estimates of PSID Unemployment Probability Equations

Sample	Model 1: No Interaction		Model 2: Union-Public Section Interaction		
	Union	Public Sector	Union	Public Sector	Interaction
A. Heads	0.014	−0.013	0.024	−0.004	−0.028
	(0.013)	(0.014)	(0.015)	(0.016)	(0.022)
B. Wives	0.017	0.020	0.078	0.050	−0.148
	(0.036)	(0.029)	(0.043)	(0.031)	(0.058)

Note: The dependent variable equals one for those who were unemployed during the year; zero, otherwise. Each equation also includes tenure with employer and its square, number of children, and binary indicators of marital status (1), region (3), occupation (5), industry (8), and year (5 for heads, 2 for wives).

10.7 Conclusion

The results of this paper show that much of the observed public-private difference in unemployment rates is attributable to the ability of unions to promote job security in the public sector. Despite the much lower observed unemployment probabilities for workers in the public sector, once one controls for differences in worker and job characteristics, the odds of being unemployed are identical in the public and private sectors for nonunion workers in the May 1973–75 CPS and the PSID. Even though public sector jobs are less subject to seasonal and cyclical shocks and their cyclical patterns lag those in the private sector, these factors seem to be exactly offset by the inability to produce for inventory and the labor intensity of the production process in the public sector. Although the May 1983 CPS indicates lower unemployment probabilities for nonunion public sector workers than for nonunion private sector workers, this could very well be attributable to the restriction of the sample to employed persons or the lag of public sector layoff rates behind those in the private sector. One important implication of this result is that failure to account for differences in job security is not likely to systematically bias the results of public-private pay comparisons.

This paper's other major conclusion is that the impact of unions on unemployment and permanent layoff probabilities varies substantially between private and government jobs. The odds of being unemployed are much higher under unionism in the private sector, but they tend to be lower for union than nonunion workers in the public sector. Previous studies have attributed the higher layoff rates for union members in the private sector to the greater weight given to the preferences of older workers under unionism, as reflected by the widespread use of layoffs by seniority in downturns, and larger benefits while unemployed (both from UI and supplemental benefit plans). The adjustment process in the public sector operates differently because the political power of public employee unions can be used in many cases to prevent budget cuts, an optimal outcome for both senior and junior employees. When cuts are necessary, the absence of any UI subsidy or supplemental benefits makes layoffs a less attractive option for members of public sector unions than other adjustment mechanisms such as wage moderation.

This paper has also reported new evidence on voluntary turnover in the public sector. The quit rate is lower in the public than the private sector for heads of households, but there is no public-private difference in quits for wives. Unions decrease voluntary turnover in both sectors, but they seem to have a greater impact on turnover in the private sector.

The evidence in table 10.1 suggests that the public-private gap in unemployment and layoff rates has narrowed over time. As Joe Altonji points out in his comments below, this is difficult to reconcile with the findings that unions promote job security in the public sector. Given the growth of public sector unionism, one would expect this gap to have widened. This seeming paradox can be resolved by noting two offsetting factors. First, employment in the public sector has been growing much more slowly than in the private sector since the mid-1970s. Second, unions have lost ground in the private sector, which should lower unemployment in that sector, other things equal. Each of these would narrow the difference in unemployment rates between the public and private sectors, and combined they could override the impact of growing public sector unionism.

References

Allen, Steven G. 1986. Unionism and job security in the public sector. NBER Working Paper no. 2108. Cambridge, Mass.: National Bureau of Economic Research.

Blau, Francine D., and Lawrence M. Kahn. 1983. Unionism, seniority, and turnover. *Industrial Relations* 22:362–73.

Bureau of National Affairs. 1982a. RIFs, layoffs, and EEO in state governments. *Government Employee Relations Report* 948:1–13.

———. 1982b. *Layoffs, RIFs, and EEO in the public sector.* BNA Special Report. Washington, D.C.: Bureau of National Affairs.

Clark, Kim B., and Lawrence H. Summers. 1979. Labor market dynamics and unemployment: A reconsideration. *Brookings Papers on Economic Activity* 1:13–72.

Crawford, Alan. 1983. Having it all: The rise of government unions and the decline of the work ethic. *Washington Monthly* 14:33–39.

Eberts, Randall W. Forthcoming. Union-negotiated employment rules and teacher quits. *Economics of Education Review.*

Freeman, Richard B. 1985. How do public sector wages and employment respond to economic conditions? NBER Working Paper no. 1653. Cambridge, Mass.: National Bureau of Economic Research.

———. 1986. Unionism comes to the public sector. *Journal of Economic Literature* 24:41–86.

Freeman, Richard B., and James L. Medoff. 1984. *What do unions do?* New York: Basic.

Levine, Charles H., Irene S. Rubin, and George G. Wolohojian. 1981. *The politics of retrenchment.* Beverly Hills, Calif.: Sage.

Long, James E. 1982. Are government workers overpaid? Alternative evidence. *Journal of Human Resources* 17:123–31.

Medoff, James L. 1979. Layoffs and alternatives under trade unions in U.S. manufacturing. *American Economic Review* 69:380–95.

Perry, Charles R. 1979. Teachers bargaining: The experience in nine systems. *Industrial and Labor Relations Review* 33:3–17.

Smith, Sharon P. 1977. *Equal pay in the public sector: Fact or fantasy?* Princeton, N.J.: Industrial Relations Section, Princeton University.

U.S. Congress, Senate Committee on Finance. 1976. *Unemployment compensation amendments of 1976: Hearings on H.R. 10210.* 94th Congress, 2d sess., 8–9.

U.S. Department of Labor. Bureau of Labor Statistics. 1972. Municipal collective bargaining agreements in large cities. *BLS Bulletin*, no. 1759. Washington, D.C.: Government Printing Office (GPO).

———. 1975. Characteristics of agreements in state and local governments January 1, 1974. *BLS Bulletin*, no. 1861. Washington, D.C.: GPO

———. 1976. Collective bargaining agreements of police and firefighters. *BLS Bulletin*, no. 1885. Washington, D.C.: GPO

———. 1976. Collective bargaining agreements for state and county government employees. *BLS Bulletin*, no. 1920. Washington, D.C.: GPO

———. 1977. Characteristics of agreements in state and local governments July 1975. *BLS Bulletin*, no. 1947. Washington, D.C.: GPO

Wilburn, Robert C., and Michael A. Worman. 1980. Overcoming the limits to personnel cut-backs: Lessons learned in Pennsylvania. *Public Administration Review* 40:609–12.

Comment   Joseph G. Altonji

Steven Allen has left few data sets unexplored in this straightforward and thorough empirical study of the effect of unions on layoff rates, quit rates, and unemployment rates of public and private sector workers. In discussing the paper, I first comment on why this topic is of interest. I then summarize the empirical analysis and suggest some extensions. In my final comments, I suggest how the main result of the paper—that union workers in the public sector have a lower probability of being on layoff than their nonunion counterparts—might be examined within a broader study of the dynamics of labor demand in the public sector.

Motivation for the Study

Historically, workers in public sector jobs have had much lower layoff and unemployment rates than private sector workers. There is also substantial evidence that in the private sector union workers experience somewhat higher layoff rates than nonunion workers. Furthermore, there are important differences in the legal and political environment faced by public and private unions and in the nature of public and private sector employers. Consequently, there are a number of reasons to expect that the effects of unionism on turnover and unemployment incidence is not the same in the public and private sector. Allen is the first to carefully investigate this issue.

Joseph G. Altonji is associate professor of economics, Northwestern University, and faculty research fellow of the National Bureau of Economic Research.

There are at least three reasons why this question deserves careful consideration. First, the public sector accounts for about 20 percent of the work force.[1] Changes in labor market structure that alter turnover behavior and unemployment in the public sector may have important effects on the unemployment rate of the economy as a whole.

Second, union effects on unemployment risk are very important in evaluating the returns to union membership for public sector workers. Most previous studies have focused on wage gains or fringe benefits.

Third, layoff behavior, wage flexibility, and hiring policies are among the factors that influence how governments respond to changes in voter preferences and to exogenous shifts in grants and revenue. Do unions alter the dynamic efficiency and the responsiveness of government? Little is known about this question. Indeed, little is known of the dynamic behavior of governments in the production of goods and services. (See Holtz-Eakin [1986] for some evidence on dynamic adjustments in municipal expenditures and references to other studies.)

Methodology and Results

The main purpose of the econometric analysis of the paper is to document union-nonunion differences and public-private differences in turnover and unemployment rather than to explain them, although Allen provides a good general discussion of how unions might affect layoff rates and unemployment incidence in the public sector and of why public-private sector differences in union effects are likely. Allen begins the empirical analysis by using CPS data files for several years to produce tables summarizing public-private sector differences in the percentage of the experienced labor force on layoff by year, type of layoff, and industry. These show that the percentage of workers on layoff is indeed much higher in the private sector than in the public sector. They also show that the union effect is positive (and strong) in the private sector.

The heart of the paper is a careful multivariate analysis of the effects of unionism on unemployment probabilities in the public and private sectors. Much of the analysis relates the probability of unemployment arising from a given cause to a set of control variables, a dummy variable for union membership, a dummy variable for public sector employment, and the product of the union membership and public sector employment dummies. Separate equations are estimated for the probability of a spell of unemployment arising from a temporary layoff (reported in Allen 1986), indefinite layoff, permanent layoff, labor force reentrance, and a quit. Using the PSID, Allen also estimates equations

---

1. Ehrenberg and Schwartz (1983).

for quits and for permanent layoffs without distinguishing separations with and without unemployment.

The most important control variables used in the analysis are occupation dummies, industry dummies, age, and schooling. When working with the PSID, Allen includes tenure with employer. The use of tenure can be defended but does reduce the comparability of the results across data sets and is likely to lead to biases in the fixed-effects estimates of the unemployment probability equations reported in table 10.7.

Allen estimates the probability of at least one spell of unemployment during 1982 using data obtained from the March 1983 CPS matched to information on union status from the May 1983 CPS. Unfortunately, the union data are available only for workers employed in May. Such workers are likely to have lower unemployment probabilities and stronger labor force attachment than a representative sample. As Allen points out, this makes it difficult to draw inferences about changes over time in the effects of public sector unionism on unemployment behavior.

The main results in the paper and the more detailed evidence in Allen (1986) may be summarized as follows.[2]

Differences between Union and Nonunion Workers in the Public Sector

Allen's most important result is that in the public sector union workers have lower unemployment probabilities and fewer weeks of unemployment during the year than nonunion workers. The overall negative differential in the unemployment probability results from a substantially smaller probability of being unemployed due to a permanent layoff as well as a smaller probability of being unemployed as a result of reentering the labor force. I suspect that a partial explanation for the higher unemployment probability associated with reentry experienced by nonunion workers is participation by disadvantaged workers in public employment programs that are classified as nonunion. In 1978 CETA accounted for 3.3 percent of total state and local employment.[3]

Public sector union members have a slightly lower overall quit rate than their nonunion counterparts. This is consistent with a union wage premium in the public sector.

2. Due to space constraints, Allen only reports estimates based on a pooled sample of public and private sector workers. In the working paper version of the study (Allen 1986), he reports separate estimates for public sector and private sector workers. Use of the separate samples permits the effects of the control variables to vary across sectors. These estimates probably provide a more reliable indication of union-nonunion differences in the two sectors, although they are qualitatively similar to those Allen does report here.

3. Ehrenberg and Schwartz (1983). However, at least some of the CETA jobs were regular government jobs reclassified to qualify for CETA funds.

Differences between Union and Nonunion Workers in the Private Sector

Results for the 1973–75 CPS indicate that in the private sector union members have somewhat higher unemployment probabilities than nonunion workers. The positive unemployment differential appears to be due primarily to differences in the incidence and duration of temporary and indefinite layoffs. The analysis of the probability of a spell of unemployment during the year using the PSID shows that the probability of at least one spell is about 25 percent higher for union workers than for nonunion. However, using the matched March and May 1983 CPS files, Allen obtains a small negative estimate of the union differential in the private sector for weeks of unemployment in 1982 (Allen 1986, table 11). It is possible that this finding is an artifact of using a sample of workers who were employed in May of the following year. Overall, Allen's results suggest that in the private sector union workers have higher unemployment probabilities than nonunion workers.

In the private sector, union workers have lower quit rates.

The Public-Private Differential among Union Workers

Union workers in the public sector have much lower probabilities of being unemployed and only about half as many weeks of unemployment during the year as their private sector counterparts (see Allen 1986). Most of the reduction may be attributed to the fact that few workers are on temporary or indefinite layoff in the public sector as well as to much lower probabilities of being on permanent layoff.

The Public-Private Differential among Nonunion Workers

The evidence on this is mixed. The results of the CPS for 1973–75 and of the PSID indicate that public and private sector nonunion workers have similar unemployment rates. The probability of unemployment due to a layoff is lower for public sector workers, but this is offset by a substantially higher probability that a public sector worker will be unemployed following labor force reentrance. I suspect the much higher probability of unemployment following reentrance to the labor force may arise in part because in the mid-1970s the nonunion public sector group may contain a disproportionate number of disadvantaged workers who held short-term, nonunion jobs through public employment programs. Furthermore, the results from the matched CPS data from 1983 indicate that the probability of at least one unemployment spell during the year and annual weeks of unemployment are both about 30 percent lower for public sector workers (see Allen 1986), although these results may be sensitive to the fact that they are for workers who were employed in May 1983. My reading of this mixed evidence is somewhat different from Allen's in that I tentatively conclude that unemployment probabilities are lower for nonunion public sector workers than for nonunion private sector workers. However, the differential clearly is much smaller than the public-private differential among union members.

With the data sources used in the study, the analysis could be improved and extended in a number of ways. First, one could use March and May CPS tapes from the mid-1970s to analyze weeks of unemployment and the probability of unemployment over the year for a sample of workers who were employed in May of the following year. Using the PSID, one could also analyze unemployment during the year for workers who were employed in March or April of the following year. The results would be more comparable to Allen's results for the March and May 1983 CPS and could be used to identify changes over time in the effects of public sector unionism. They might also shed light on the discrepancy in the findings based on the 1983 CPS data and the other results.

Second, in analyzing unemployment by cause it would be useful to focus more attention on distinguishing between effects on the incidence of layoffs and quits and the amount of unemployment conditional on a layoff or quit. The probability that a person is unemployed at the time of the CPS survey, due, for example, to an indefinite layoff reflects both the probability of an indefinite layoff and the duration of unemployment conditional on a layoff.

Third, careful consideration should be given to the effects of public employment programs, such as CETA, on the estimates of union-nonunion and public-private differentials in the 1970s.

Fourth, it would be useful to analyze the effect that growth in public sector unionism during the 1960s and early 1970s has had on the public-private sector differential in turnover rates and unemployment. Figure 10.1 and the tables of descriptive statistics in the paper suggest that the public-private unemployment rate differential has not increased or (as Allen argues) has actually narrowed during this period. The data and discussion in Freeman (1986, 44–45) suggest that the percentage of public sector workers in unions and associations acting like unions increased from about 15 percent in the early 1960s to about 40 percent in the late 1970s, although Freeman emphasizes that problems of data comparability over time and changes in the distinction between associations and unions make it difficult to provide precise estimates of the growth of public sector unionism. Taken at face value, the estimate of − 1.8 percentage points for the union-nonunion differential in the public sector (see table 10.5, row 5) implies that this increase in public sector union membership would lead to a modest reduction in the unemployment rate of 0.45 percentage points. For comparison, the unemployment probability was typically between 2 and 3 percent in the 1960s and early 1970s.

How does one explain the discrepancy between the cross-section findings and the time-series trends? First, other changes in public and private sector labor markets may have led to increases in the unemployment rate in the public sector relative to the private sector and offset the effects of the expansion of union membership. A second possibility is that the cross-section findings overstate the unionism effect. Biases might arise if unionism in the public sector is more heavily concentrated in occupations and industries or among types of workers with lower unemployment rates, and the controls for occupation, industry, and worker characteristics in Allen's analysis are not sufficiently detailed. The estimate of the public sector union differential for the PSID sample declines from − 1.8 percentage points to − 0.4 percent when a fixed-effects estimator is used to control for unobserved personal characteristics, although measurement error and other potential problems may bias the fixed-effects results toward zero.

A third explanation is the possibility that public sector unions are in fact successful in resisting budget cuts and worker force reductions affecting union members, but that as a result a larger share of work force reductions are borne by nonunion workers. One could examine this "spillover" hypothesis using methods employed in studies of union wage effects.

Research on Why Differences in Layoffs and Unemployment Risk Exist

Future empirical studies should not only follow up on Allen's analysis documenting union-nonunion and public-private differentials in turnover behavior and unemployment risk but should also address why the differentials exist. The paper provides a useful background discussion of the reasons why layoff, quit, and unemployment rates should differ between the public and private sectors. In any given year, the layoff rate is influenced by the level of demand for labor relative to demand in previous years. While the layoff rate will vary from year to year, on average the layoff rate is connected to demand variability through the following links:

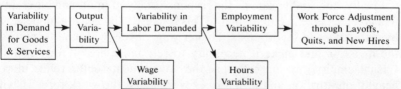

In analyzing layoff behavior one could proceed by examining variability in product demand and the strength of each of the links between product demand variability and layoffs. One could examine how they differ between union and nonunion employers in the public and private sectors.

Demand variability will depend upon seasonality, cyclical sensitivity of product demand, and the volatility of consumer preferences. There are also likely to be differences in the speed of adjustment of output and employment to changes in demand. There is evidence to suggest that in the public sector the unions have greater ability to stabilize demand than in the private sector. It would be useful to examine and compare the cyclical and seasonal variability of firm expenditures and government expenditures. One could also compare the variability of relative demand shifts within the public sector and within the private sector using techniques similar to those of Lilien (1982). In a study of employment growth by industry and province in Canada (Altonji and Ham 1986), the variability in innovations in government employment in each province was found to be lower than in all other sectors of the economy except services because government employment is less responsive to external and national shocks to the economy and less responsive to shocks to each province. Most of the response of government employment growth to these shocks occurs with a lag. We also found that the variance of shocks to employment that are specific to the public sector and common to all provinces are smaller than the variances of shocks that are specific to most other sectors. Freeman (1985) shows that employment in the public sector is less responsive to cyclical fluctuations than employment in the private sector. More work in this area is needed, particularly studies of the variability of expenditures and studies that control for union coverage.

One could examine the other links connecting demand to layoffs. Briefly, one could investigate sectoral differences in the response of man-hours to output or expenditure changes. These are likely to be affected by the degree of wage flexibility.

One could also examine public-private and union-nonunion differences in the extent that the man-hours adjustment is made through hours per week or through employment changes. Work rules concerning hours reductions, overtime provisions, the unemployment insurance system, and the ability of unions to resist work force reductions will influence how man-hours adjustments are made.

Finally, one could examine the response of layoff, quit, and hire rates to a given change in employment. This is likely to be heavily influenced by differences in layoff costs. Higher wage levels will tend to reduce the quit rate and make it necessary to rely more heavily on layoffs. Casual empiricism suggests that the government sector relies more heavily on attrition and hiring freezes to adjust the work force. Civil service rules, the ability of labor to impose political costs on governments that use layoffs, and the predictability of labor demand changes may provide a partial explanation.

In summary, this paper has uncovered some important public-private and union-nonunion differences in turnover behavior and unemployment risk. The institutional background and econometric analysis in the paper are a very good base for future researchers to build upon.

References

Allen, S. G. 1986. Unionism and job security in the public sector. NBER Working Paper no. 2108. Cambridge, Mass.: National Bureau of Economic Research.

Altonji, J. G., and J. C. Ham. 1986. Variation in employment growth in Canada: The role of external, national, regional and industrial factors. NBER Working Paper no. 1816. Cambridge, Mass.: National Bureau of Economic Research.

Ehrenberg, R. G., and J. L. Schwartz. 1983. Public sector labor markets. NBER Working Paper no. 1179. Cambridge, Mass.: National Bureau of Economic Research.

Freeman, R. B. 1986. Unionism comes to the public sector. *Journal of Economic Literature* 24(1):41–86.

———. 1985. How do public sector wages and employment respond to economic conditions? NBER Working Paper no. 1653. Cambridge, Mass.: National Bureau of Economic Research.

Holtz-Eakin, D. 1986. Short-run dynamics of municipal budgets. Discussion Paper no. 320. Department of Economics, Columbia University.

Lilien, David. 1982. Sectoral shifts and cyclical unemployment. *Journal of Political Economy* 90:773–93.

11 Unionism and Licensing of Public School Teachers: Impact on Wages and Educational Output

Morris M. Kleiner and Daniel L. Petree

Teacher union chief Albert Shanker is urging education leaders to join him in an effort to create a tough new national exam for entry to the profession. Asked if the test was really a way to help his members get higher pay and status, Shanker said: "I confess (it is). And you might also get the same quality and standards that go with (professionalism)."

Associated Press, 16 April 1985

As this statement by the leader of the American Federation of Teachers (AFT) suggests, teachers unions seek to increase the quality of the educational system as well as to raise the earnings of its members. Are they successful in improving the quality of education? How important is occupational licensure as a tool for improving the quality of education and raising wages compared to collective bargaining and the other activities of public sector unions?

To answer these questions we will examine in this paper the extent to which unionism leads to stronger licensing statutes for teachers, and

Morris M. Kleiner is professor of industrial relations and public affairs at the Hubert H. Humphrey Institute of Public Affairs and Industrial Relations Center, University of Minnesota, and a research economist of the National Bureau of Economic Research. Daniel L. Petree is instructor at Rockhurst College, Kansas City, and director of labor management relations programs for Kansas City, Missouri.

The authors wish to thank Steven Allen, John Delaney, Ronald Ehrenberg, Richard Freeman, Nancy Johnson, Richard Murnane, participants at a University of Kansas Human Resources Seminar, and the editors for comments on earlier drafts. In addition, we want to especially thank Shelley Skie for her assistance with the statistical analysis. The following organizations provided data or other helpful assistance for this study: National Education Association, American Federation of Teachers, Scholastic Aptitude Testing Service, and Richard Sawyer from the American College Testing Service.

alters teacher wages and student test scores directly and through provisions to license schoolteachers. We analyze the experience of U.S. states from 1972–82—a decade when school enrollments and the demand for teachers declined (Murnane 1985). This decline led to increased teacher layoffs, fewer opportunities to move across school districts, fewer transfers to better schools, and a decline in teachers' real earnings of over 10 percent (O'Neil 1984). As a consequence of these developments, entrance into the profession was reduced: the number of students graduating with education degrees declined from 177,000 in 1971 to 101,000 in 1982, and the number meeting minimum licensing requirements fell from 317,254 in 1971–72 to 140,639 in 1980–81. Further, the number of first-year college students planning to choose teaching as an occupation fell from 19.3 percent to 4.7 percent (Condition of Education 1983).

Comparing states with greater and lesser unionization we find that collective bargaining coverage is associated with higher salaries for public school teachers and generally, though not uniformly, higher educational performance as measured by student test scores and high graduation rates. Fixed-effects analysis of the effects of unionism on teacher wages and student performance yield greatly reduced estimated effects of unionism on wages but continue to show substantial teacher union impacts on student performance. We also find that unionization and licensure are complementary for schoolteachers in the sense that more heavily unionized states have more stringent licensing laws. With collective bargaining held fixed, however, we find no impact for rigid licensing statutes on pay and uncertain effects on student achievement scores. Hence, licensure does not appear to be an important route by which teacher unionism affects the education marketplace.

We present our analysis in three stages. First, we briefly review past findings on the relation between teacher unionism, licensure, and wage and educational performance outcomes. Then we describe our data and present our empirical results. Finally, we offer a general interpretation, with caveats, of our findings.

11.1 Past Work

There exists a substantial literature on the impact of teacher unions on wages, but relatively little analysis of the role of licensing provisions as an intervening route for the union wage effect or of the impact of teacher unions on the output of the educational system. As a prelude to our analysis it will be useful to briefly review past findings on the issues of concern.

With respect to the effect of teacher unions on pay there is a wide variation in the estimated impact, depending on the unit of analysis, which ranges from states and school districts to individual teachers, and differs in the period of time covered (see the summary in Freeman 1986). From the late 1960s through the early 1970s studies using state-level data showed a range of estimates from 2 percent to 9 percent for the impact of teachers unions on pay (Kaspar 1970; Brown 1975). Studies that used the school district as the level of analysis estimated effects that varied from 1 percent (Landon and Baird 1971) to 12–14 percent (Schmenner 1973). Analyses for the 1980s covering districts and individuals suggest a greater impact of unions on wages. For example, Baugh and Stone (1982) find union wage effects that range from 12 to 21 percent. Apparently, for reasons having to do with changes in union power and in conditions in the teaching market (union wage effects are often larger in declining rather than booming markets (Lewis 1963)), the impact of unions on wages appears to have increased for teachers in the period covered by our study.

In contrast to the well-documented impact of unions on wages, past studies have not systematically analyzed the relation between unionism and licensure or between licensure and wages. Much of the theoretical literature on the effect of licensing treats its impact on societal welfare, with ambiguous results (Leland 1980), rather than directly addressing its effect on wages or performance. In this framework licensing is seen as a means to protect the public from an inability to judge the quality of services delivered by specialists, given that it is unlikely that specialists will act strictly in the interest of the consumer (Jensen and Meckling 1976; Williamson 1964). At the same time, however, it is to the advantage of teachers (as well as other groups) to use licensing to limit supply and extract economic rents (Stigler 1975). In the education market the fact that governments employ teachers as well as determine licensing laws creates further complexities, as it is not in the government's interest to restrict supply and drive up costs. Given these considerations, we expect licensing laws for teachers to affect the teachers market in two ways: assuring the meeting of minimum quality standards that improve performance (Ehrenberg 1973; Frey 1975) and raising wages by limiting supply.

Relatively few studies have examined the impact of teacher unionism or licensing on student performance. To the extent that unions raise the quality of teaching through licensing, improve the operation of schools by forcing administrators to behave more efficiently, or improve the quality of teachers by creating professional standards and reducing turnover, unions will have positive effects on the productivity of the educational system, as has been found to occur in some parts of manufacturing (Freeman and Medoff 1984). To the extent that unions simply reduce teacher resources by raising costs, they are likely to have the opposite impact. We are aware of only two studies that provide empirical evidence on which of these effects dominates. Eberts and Stone (1986) use test scores on 14,000 fourth graders in selected school districts to evaluate the impact of unionization on performance and find that when other socioeconomic factors are controlled for, scores are 7 percent higher in union districts. In a study published after the work for this paper was completed, Kurth reports the opposite result: a negative relation between union strength and SAT scores across states and time. This finding, however, appears to be due to the absence of any trend or regional controls in the regressions, in contrast to the work that we report in this paper. As for the impact of licensing on student performance, we do not know of any studies. The few studies that have attempted to examine the impact of licensing on output in other fields, such as dentistry (Holen 1978) or medical and legal specialties (Carroll and Gaston 1981), find no systematic relation between licensing provisions and performance, suggesting that it is not easy to uncover a licensing productivity relation, if one exists.

In sum, while existing work provides us with reasonable expectations about the wage effects of teaching unions, the other issues under study—the impact of unions on licensure and the impact of unions and licensing on performance—are rarely explored, with existing studies yielding uncertain results. It is this "hole" in the literature that motivates our study.

11.2 Data and Analysis

To estimate the impact of teacher unionism on wages, licensing laws, and student performance we have obtained state-level data for the 1972–82 period. We chose states as units of observation for four reasons. First, licensing of public school teachers in the United States is implemented on a state-by-state basis, so that states are the natural unit for studying licensure. Second, we have reasonably good data on unionization and collective bargaining coverage at the state level for the entire period. Third, we are able to obtain student test scores by states for the period, providing us with a critical outcome variable. Fourth, we can use the state data to develop a longitudinal or fixed-effects analysis that examines how within-state changes in unionization produce changes in the outcomes under study. Recent work in labor economics has stressed the importance of checking cross-section findings with longitudinal data to control for potential unmeasured variables that can bias cross-section results (Freeman 1984).

Table 11.1 lists the key variables in our analysis and gives their source, mean, and standard deviation for all states in the 1972–82 period. Lines 1–3 give the independent variables reflecting unionization and licensing. We use the percent of teachers who are members of the

Table 11.1   **Means and Standard Deviations of Key Independent and**
                Dependent Variables

	Mean	(std dev)
Key Independent Variables		
1. Percent of teachers organized	.86	(.20)
2. Percent of teachers with collective bargaining contracts	.65	(.35)
3. State-set licensing statutes	.45	(.50)
Dependent Variables		
4. Average state SAT score	951	(73)
5. Average state ACT score	18.80	(1.14)
6. State graduation rate	.75	(.07)
7. Average state teacher pay	12,235	(2,175)

Sources:
Line 1: NEA membership data obtained from NEA and National Council of State Education Associations (Washington, D.C.), *Profiles of State Associations*, various editions. AFT membership provided by the union with confidential computer printout. To get the percentage organized, we divided by the number of teachers in the state.

Line 2: Calculated from U.S. Bureau of the Census, Survey and Census of Governments, various editions.

Line 3: Obtained by reading relevant state legal statutes.

Line 4: Obtained from Educational Testing Service.

Line 5: Obtained from American College Testing Service. For reasons of confidentiality, the ACT tabulated means for us and performed the various regressions reported here.

Line 6: U.S. Bureau of the Census, *U.S. Statistical Abstract*.

Line 7: National Education Association and National Council of State Education Associations (Washington, D.C.), *Profiles of State Associations*, various editions.

AFT or National Education Association (NEA) and the percent of teachers covered by a collective bargaining contract to measure the strength of unionism in a state. Because not all teacher union locals bargain collectively it is generally believed that having a contract is a more desirable measure (see Lewis, this volume, chap. 6). Still, the percent union may reflect the political power of the union in lobbying or campaigning for outcomes, leading us to examine each of these variables in our analysis. To measure the strength of state licensing of teachers we use a dummy variable that takes on the value 1 if state statutes make licensing subject to specific kinds of education, experience, and a statewide examination. The means and standard deviations in table 11.1 show an average across states of 86 percent of teachers in the AFT or the NEA with, however, considerable dispersion among states; a smaller but still high percentage covered by collective bargaining of 65 percent; and 45 percent of the states having what we categorize as a strong teacher-licensing statute.

Lines 4–7 relate to our primary dependent variables: the average earnings of schoolteachers in a state, and the average Scholastic Aptitude (SAT) and American College Testing (ACT) scores of students, which we obtained from special tabulations of test results from the Educational Testing Service in Princeton, New Jersey and from the American College Testing Service in Iowa City, Iowa. Although only about 27 percent of high school students take either of these exams, the exams are the most widely administered national measures of performance available (Dynarski 1985). To evaluate the effects of unionism and licensing on lower educational achievers, we also examine the percentage of students who graduate from high school.

In addition to these variables our calculations include diverse controls for a range of factors that might be expected to affect teacher salaries or educational performance across states: real (price-deflated) expenditures per student, nonwage expenditures per student; per capita personal income; the percentage of high school graduates in a state; the percentage of students attending private schools; the average wage in manufacturing; average public school enrollment; the percentage of minority students in a state; and the average age and experience (estimated as age − years of schooling − 5 years) of teachers in a state, calculated from the Current Population Surveys as a measure of the human capital of teachers in a state, and an indicator of the favorableness of state labor law toward teacher collective bargaining.[1]

As our analysis covers an eleven-year period (1972–82), there are 555 state-by-year observations for most variables, though there are some missing values for some states and years in several cases. In all of our empirical work we pool the cross sections for the years and include year dummy variables to allow for any year effects. In addition, in some calculations we add state dummy variables as independent variables, changing the structure of the analysis from cross-section comparisons to a fixed-effects longitudinal design. We deal first with the relation between unionism and licensing, and then analyze the impact of the two variables on outcomes.

11.2.1 Teacher Unionism and Licensing

To see whether unionization in a state is associated with stronger or weaker licensing laws we estimated a logistic equation linking the presence of a strong statewide licensing policy to the proportion of teachers who are members of organizations, or to the proportion who are covered by collective bargaining and by various control variables using our complete pooled cross-section data set.[2] The results of these calculations reveal the expected positive relation between unionization and licensing statutes. In our logit analysis of the impact of the extent of union membership on statewide licensing statutes, the membership variable obtained a positive and significant coefficient of 1.34 with a standard error of .57. This implies that an increase in union density of 10 percentage points would raise the probability of having a statewide statute by about 4 percentage points. In our logit analysis of the impact of the extent of collective bargaining coverage, we obtained a similar positive and significant coefficient for that variable: .91 with a standard error of .44. These results indicate that in states where teachers unions are stronger, legislatures pass more rigorous licensing statutes. This is consistent with the Shanker quote with which we began this paper.

11.2.2 Unionization and Wages Across States

Given that unionization appears to increase the strength of licensing provisions, the next question to investigate is whether licensing and unionism affect outcomes. We consider first their impact on wages. Our wage analysis takes two forms. First, we regress the log of teacher pay in a state on the percentage of teachers in a teacher organization or on the percentage of teachers covered by collective bargaining, the licensing dummy variable, and various controls. Second, to remove the influence of any persistent state effect over time, we add dummy variables for states and thus estimate the impact of the variables in a fixed-effects model. Table 11.2 summarizes the results of these regressions in terms of the estimated coefficients on the unionism and licensing variables. The cross-section regressions show moderate unionization effects, which are higher for the collective bargaining coverage variable than for the union membership variable. The regression

Table 11.2   **Coefficient Estimates and Standard Errors for the Effects of Unionization on Log of Teacher Wages**

Independent Variables	Cross-Section Analysis		Fixed-Effects Analysis	
Percent members	.04		−.01	
	(.01)		(.01)	
Percent covered by contracts		.07		.01
		(.01)		(.01)
State licensing	.01	.01	.003	.003
	(.02)	(.01)	(.004)	(.004)
State dummies	no	no	yes	yes
R^2	.65	.70	—	—

Notes: Cross-section regressions include the following control variables: manufacturing wage, index of legal environment in the state toward collective bargaining, age and experience of teachers, year dummies, and three-region dummies. Fixed-effect regressions include the same control variable as the cross-section regressions. The R^2 are not reported as they are extraordinarily high with the state dummy variables.

with percentage union membership also shows a modest impact for licensing laws. However, when we replace membership with collective bargaining coverage the coefficient on licensing becomes smaller and remains insignificant. The implication is that collective bargaining rather than licensing was the means by which teacher unions affected wages in the period. Note, finally, that our cross-state results are within the same range as the earlier estimates of the effect of teacher unionism on pay using states data cited in section 11.1.

The results of the fixed-effects analysis are more surprising, as they show that state dummy variables absorb any union wage effect. This does not mean that unionization has no effect on teacher wages, as longitudinal analyses tend to understate union wage effects due to measurement error (Freeman 1984). Rather, it indicates that the longitudinal test is in fact a relatively stringent one, as it eliminates all cross-state variation and general time-series variation to focus on changes within states over time. The fixed-effects wage results do, however, provide us with a measuring rod for assessing ensuing fixed-effects analyses of the relation between unionism and educational performance.

11.2.3   Unionization, Test Scores, and Graduation Rates

The most controversial issue that we address in this paper is the impact of unionism and licensing on the quality of educational performance. Is educational performance better or worse in states with stronger teacher unionization and/or licensing than in other states?

To answer this question we have regressed the average level of the SAT and ACT standardized test scores and the proportion of students who graduate high school, on the percentage of teachers who are union members and the percentage of teachers who are covered by collective bargaining and various control variables. These variables include: the percent minority in the state (because of the tendency of minorities to score lower on standardized tests); the student/teacher ratio; nonwage expenditures per student (to reflect resources for public education); and the proportion of high school graduates in the state and the per capita income (to reflect the educational and income background of students). We exclude measures of the physical capital in the state school systems because prior studies have not shown an impact of physical capital on outcomes (Brown and Saks 1975). As before we have calculated both cross-section and fixed-effects estimates of the impact of unionism and licensing on outcomes.[3]

Table 11.3 presents the results of our cross-section analysis. Columns 1 and 2 record the coefficients and standard errors on the unionization and licensing variables when the SAT is the measure of performance, columns 3 and 4 treat the ACT test scores, while columns 5 and 6 relate

Table 11.3   **Coefficients and Standard Errors for the Cross-Section Impact of Unionism and Licensing on Student Achievement Scores and Graduation Rates**

| Independent Variables | Dependent Variables | | | | | |
| | SAT | | ACT | | Graduation Rate | |
	(1)	(2)	(3)	(4)	(5)	(6)
Percent members	49.09		.35		5.67	
	(13.66)		(.25)		(1.26)	
Percent covered by		− .40		1.06		3.27
contracts		(10.92)		(.20)		(1.01)
State licensing	− 20.96	− 19.75	.33	.30	1.25	1.38
	(4.45)	(4.49)	(.08)	(.08)	(.41)	(.41)
R²	.54	.53	.58	.63	.56	.55
Sample size	490	490	446	446	490	490

Note: All regressions include the following control variables: student/teacher ratios, nonwage expenditures per student, percent minority, per capita income, percentage of population who are high school graduates, index of the legal environment for collective bargaining, experience of teachers. Estimates using selectivity bias controls also were estimated and are available from the authors (Murnane et. al., 1985).

to state graduation rates. With test scores as the dependent variables, the coefficients on union membership are positive and significant. With mean values of 951 for the SAT and of 18.8 for the ACT, the coefficients imply unionization impacts on the order of 6–8 percent for increases in unionization from 0 to 1.00 and elasticities of test scores to unionization of about 0.5 to 0.7. These are of similar magnitude to the impacts estimated by Eberts and Stone on individual students (Eberts and Stone 1986). By contrast, the coefficients on the percentage of teachers covered by union contracts are insignificant in the SAT calculations and smaller and less significant in the ACT calculations than the coefficients on the percentage of teachers who are union members. With state graduation rates as the dependent variable, both union variables are accorded significant positive effects. In sum, the general impression from the table is that unionism is associated with better performance of the school system, but varies with the measure of union strength and outcome.

The estimated coefficients on our licensing dummy variable, by contrast, present a less clear pattern. In columns 1 and 2 licensing is estimated to reduce SAT scores, whereas in columns 3 and 4 it is estimated to raise them, and in columns 5 and 6 it is estimated to raise graduation rates. Given the negative results with the SAT variable, we are reluctant to make any firm conclusion about the impact of licensing on outcomes.

To test further the impact of unionization and licensing on educational outcomes we performed a fixed-effects analysis, adding state dummy variables to our regressions. These dummy variables pick up the impact of any omitted state factor that has a constant effect on outcomes over time. Including them can greatly reduce the estimated effect of independent variables on outcomes, as we saw with our wage analysis. The results of these calculations are given in table 11.4, which follows the same format as table 11.3. The majority of the results here confirm the positive effect of teacher unionism on test scores: both the percentage of teachers who are union members and the percentage who are covered by collective bargaining contracts are estimated to raise test scores, with the difference between the coefficients on the two variables considerably less than in the cross-section regressions. Roughly, unionism has a 3 percent impact on performance in these calculations. The results with respect to graduation rates are more ambiguous, as the union membership variable is estimated to have a modest positive effect while the collective bargaining variable has a modest negative effect on graduation. As for licensing, inclusion of the state dummy variables reverses the negative relation between licensing statutes and SAT scores and the positive relation between licensing and graduation rates, while leaving the positive relation between licensing and the ACT scores virtually unchanged. As the estimated impact of licensing appears to vary with

Table 11.4   **Coefficients and Standard Errors for the Fixed-Effect Impact of Unionism and Licensing on Student Achievement Scores and Graduation Rates**

	Dependent Variables					
	SAT		ACT		Graduation Rate	
Independent Variables	(1)	(2)	(3)	(4)	(5)	(6)
Percent members	18.86		.19		1.30	
	(5.76)		(.12)		(.87)	
Percent covered by contracts		27.47		.15		−.83
		(6.92)		(.34)		(1.06)
State licensing	4.70	6.33	.28	.30	1.25	−1.18
	(3.60)	(3.57)	(.08)	(.07)	(.54)	(.54)
State dummy variables	yes	yes	yes	yes	yes	yes
Sample size	490	490	446	446	490	490

Note: All regressions include the following control variables: student/teacher ratios, nonwage expenditures per student, percent minority, per capita income, percentage of population who are high school graduates, index of the legal environment for collective bargaining, experience of teachers.

the outcome measure and estimating technique, we feel that the most sensible conclusion is that our evidence is ambiguous on the effect of licensing on outcomes.

11.2.4 Unionism and Educational Process Variables

To see whether we can delineate, at least in part, some of the ways in which unionization may affect outcomes, we examine the relation of unionism and licensing to two educational process variables likely to play a role in the performance of the system—student/teacher ratios and nonwage expenditures per student—and between those variables and outcomes. Table 11.5 shows the results of the two sets of calculations in terms of the estimated impacts of unionization and licensing on student/teacher ratios and on nonwage expenditures per student and of those variables on test scores and graduation rates. Columns 1–4 show that unionization is associated with higher student/teacher ratios and greater nonwage expenditures per student, while licensure is associated with lower student/teacher ratios and has ambiguous effects on nonwage expenditures, depending on the unionization measure. The impact of unionization on student/teacher ratios presumably reflects the standard labor demand response to higher union-induced wages: a decline in employment. Columns 5–7 show that higher student/teacher ratios are associated with lower test scores and lower graduation rates, while nonwage spending per pupil has no noticeable effect on the SAT, a positive effect on the ACT, and a negative effect on the graduation rate. Since unionization tends to raise the student/teacher ratios, the implication is that unions reduce rather than improve performance through this route. The ambiguous effects of nonwage spending on outcomes also rules out the union effect on this variable as a potential route of impact. In short, our state data are not rich enough to enable us to determine the educational process variables by which unionism improves student test scores and reduces dropout rates among states.

In order to examine further the impact of unionization and licensing on outcomes, and to help us interpret our econometric results, we conducted telephone interviews with union and government officials in ten states with varying degrees of teacher unionization, ranging from Mississippi, which has long outlawed bargaining, to New York, where unionization is strong. The general opinion of these officials was that teacher unionism increases wages through political and bargaining means. There were, by contrast, conflicting opinions on the effect of teachers unions on educational quality. Our interviews suggested that unionized school districts have lower turnover, greater teacher voice on the job, and greater standardization of work activity, which might contribute positively to productivity. With respect to licensing, some respondents suggested that the weak or ambiguous effects that we have

Table 11.5 Regression Coefficients and Standard Errors for the **Relation of Unionism and Licensing to "Educational Resource Variables"** and of the Resource Variables to Outcomes

	Dependent Variables						
	Student/Teacher Ratio		NonWage Expenditures Per Student		SAT	ACT	Graduation Rate
Independent Variables	(1)	(2)	(3)	(4)	(5)	(6)	(7)
Percent members	1.22 (.48)						
Percent covered by contracts		1.48 (.38)	93.97 (52.42)	158.41 (40.85)			
State licensing	−.35 (.16)	−.33 (.16)	−37.38 (17.07)	35.54 (16.81)			
Student/Teacher Ratio					−7.62 (1.33)	−.04 (.03)	−.90 (.12)
Non-wage expenditure per pupil					.001 (.012)	.0005 (.0002)	−.004 (.001)
R^2	.53	.54	.54	.53	.55	.47	.58

Note: All regressions include the following control variables: percent minority, relative per capita income, year and regional dummies.

found are due to differences in the market for schoolteachers across states, since state and local education officials relax licensing constraints in response to the condition of the market.

11.3 Conclusions

Our cross-state analysis suggests that greater teacher unionism is associated with better performance of students across states, consistent with the analysis of individual students by Eberts and Stone. The relatively strong relation between unionism and student performance found in the longitudinal analysis, compared to the negligible relation between unionism and wages there, is our strongest piece of evidence that teacher unionization is in fact a positive factor in education. Our inability to show empirically how unionization improved outcomes, and the sensitivity of the cross-section results to the measure of outcomes and unionization represent the major weaknesses in our findings. At a minimum, however, our study rejects any claim that unionization contributed to the decline in student achievement scores during the 1970s and early 1980s. With respect to licensing, given the modest statutes in existence during the period, it is perhaps not surprising that we obtained ambiguous effects in the statistical analysis. Recent strengthening of licensing laws and pressures to increase entry requirements for schoolteachers may result in greater and more consistent effects of licensure in the future.

Finally, while our analysis provides some evidence of the relation between unionization and education, there are several important questions that we did not address. First, from the perspective of economics, what was the effect of teacher unionization on the earnings of graduates as opposed to on their test scores? Second, how do licensing and unionization affect students who do not take college entrance exams or are on the verge of dropping out? Third, would we obtain similar longitudinal results with more disaggregate school district data over time to those reported for states? More evidence on these issues would enhance our knowledge of the role of unions in education.

Notes

1. These variables are obtained as follows: percent population graduated high school, percent students in private school, per capita income, student/teacher ratio, percent minority students. All are from the U.S. Bureau of the Census *Statistical Abstract,* various editions. Mean experience of teachers (age − education − 5 years) is tabulated from annual Current Population

Surveys. The index of labor laws for collective bargaining in education is from the NBER Public Sector Law data set.

2. In these calculations we controlled for: enrollment, percent minority, per capita income, nonwage expenditures, the legal environment, the percent of students in private schools, age of teachers, and year dummies.

3. These calculations included the same controls as in note 2.

References

Bacharach, Samuel, D. A. Lipsky, and J. B. Shedd. 1984. *Paying for better teaching.* Ithaca, N.Y.: Organizational Analysis and Practice.

Baugh, William, and Joe Stone. 1982. Teachers, unions and wages in the 1970's: Unionism now pays. *Industrial and Labor Relations Review* 35(3):368–76.

Brown, Byron W., and Daniel M. Saks. 1975. The production and distribution of cognitive skills within schools. *Journal of Political Economy* 83(3):571–95.

Brown, T. A. 1975. Have collective negotiations increased teachers' salaries? *Journal of Collective Negotiations* 4(1):53–65.

Carroll, Sydney, and Robert J. Gaston. 1981. Occupational restrictions and the quality of services received: Some evidence. *Southern Economic Journal* 47(4):959–76.

Condition of education. 1983. U.S. Department of Education, Washington, D.C.

Delaney, John T. 1986. Impasses and teacher contract outcomes. *Industrial Relations* 25(1)45–55.

Dynarski, Mark. 1985. The Scholastic Aptitude Test: Participation and performance. University of California, Davis Working Paper Series, no. 258.

Eberts, Randall, and Joe Stone. 1984. *Unions and the public schools.* Mass.: Lexington Books.

———. 1986. Unions and productivity in the public sector: The effect of teacher unions on student achievement. Mimeo.

Ehrenberg, Ronald. 1973. Heterogeneous labor, minimum hiring standards, and job vacancies in public employment. Journal of Political Economy 81:1442–50.

Freeman, Richard B. 1984. Longitudinal Analyses of the effects of trade unions. *Journal of Labor Economics* 2(1):1–26.

———. 1986. Unionism comes to the public sector. *Journal of Economic Literature* 24(1):41–134.

Freeman, Richard B., and J. Medoff. 1984. *What do unions do?* New York: Basic Books.

Frey, Donald. 1975. Wage determination in public schools and the effects of unionization. In *Labor in the public and nonprofit sectors,* ed. D. S. Hamermesh, 183–219. New Jersey: Princeton University Press.

Holen, Arlene. 1978. The economics of dental licensing. Final report submitted to the Department of Health and Human Services.

Jensen, M. C., and W. H. Meckling. 1976. Theory of the firm: Managerial behavior, agency costs and ownership structure. *Journal of Financial Economics* 3:305–60.

Kasper, Hirschel. 1970. The effects of collective bargaining on public school teachers' salaries. *Industrial and Labor Relations Review* 24(1):57–71.

Kleiner, Morris M., and C. Krider. 1979. Determinants of negotiated agreements for public school teachers. *Educational Administration Quarterly* 15 (13):66–82.

Kurth, Michael. 1987. Teacher unions and excellence in education: An analysis of the decline in SAT scores. *Journal of Labor Research* 8 (4):351–65.

Landon, J. H., and R. N. Baird. 1971. Monopsony in the market for public school teachers. *American Economic Review* 51(5):996–71.

Leland, Hayne, 1980. Minimum-quality standards and licensing in markets with asymmetric information. In *Occupational licensure and regulation,* ed. S. Rottenberg, 265–84. Washington, D.C.: American Enterprise Institute for Public Policy Research.

Lewis, H. G. 1963. *Unionism and relative wages in the United States.* Chicago: University of Chicago Press.

McFadden, Daniel. 1974. Conditional logit analysis of qualitative choice behavior. In *Frontiers in econometrics,* ed. P. Zarembka, 105–42. New York: Academic Press.

Murnane, Richard J. 1985. An economist's look at federal and state education policies. In *American domestic Priorities: An economic appraisal,* ed. John M. Quigley and Daniel Rubinfeld, 1–30. Berkeley: University of California Press.

Murnane, Richard J., S. Newstead, and R. J. Olsen. 1985. Comparing public and private schools: The puzzling role of selectivity bias. *Journal of Business and Economic Statistics* 3 (1):23–35.

O'Neil, David A. 1984. Education in the United States, 1940–1983. Washington, D.C.: U.S. Bureau of the Census.

Orazem, Peter. 1984. Black white differences in schooling investment and human capital production in segregated schools. Working paper, Iowa State University.

Schmenner, R. W. 1973. The determination of municipal employee wages. *Review of Economics and Statistics* 55(1):83–90.

Stigler, George. 1975. *The citizen and the state: Essays on regulation.* Chicago: University of Chicago Press.

U.S. Bureau of the Census. *Statistical Abstract,* various editions. Washington, D.C.

Williamson, O. E. 1964. *The economics of discretionary behavior: Managerial objectives in a theory of the firm.* Englewood Cliffs, N.J.: Prentice-Hall.

Zarkin, Gary A. 1985. Occupational choice: An application to the market for public school teachers. *Quarterly Journal of Economics* (May):409–46.

Comment   Randall W. Eberts and Joe A. Stone

Kleiner and Petree explore the effects of teacher unions and teacher licensing on various aspects of the operation of public schools: teacher wages, allocation of school resources, and student performance. Although substantial work has been done on teacher unions and public

Randall W. Eberts is assistant vice president and economist at the Federal Reserve Bank of Cleveland. Joe A. Stone is W. E. Miner Professor of Economics at the University of Oregon.

schools, very little attention has been given to the effect of licensing on school effectiveness. The authors argue that both institutions should be considered simultaneously since each potentially can raise wages and affect student achievement.

The relationship between teacher collective bargaining and licensing, on the one hand, and teacher salaries, on the other, is easy to understand. Studies of teacher unions show that collective bargaining increases teacher salaries an average of 15 percent. Kleiner and Petree's results for teacher unions support these estimates. However, they find no evidence that licensing affects wages.

The link between unions and licensing, on the one hand, and student performance, on the other, is much more subtle. While education takes place primarily in the classroom, contract negotiations and teacher certification and licensing are determined at the district or state level. For unionization and licensing to affect student achievement, they must enter the classroom. The obvious primary carrier of these effects is the teacher. To register a significant effect, these institutions must significantly affect various teacher characteristics and/or basic aspects of the classroom environment: class size; the time teachers spend on instruction and preparation; the age, experience, and educational attainment of the teaching force; classroom organization; just to name a few.

We already know something about the effect of unions on student achievement from our own work (Eberts and Stone, 1984, *Unions and Public Schools*). Although our data sets and methodology differ in various respects (most importantly, Kleiner and Petree use state-level aggregates of student test scores while we use individual student data), it is interesting to compare the two sets of results. We find that teachers covered by collective bargaining face smaller classes; they find the opposite. We find that teachers represented by unions are more experienced; they find that these teachers are less experienced, although their estimates are statistically insignificant. We find that resources are diverted away from school activities not related to teacher salaries, presumably to finance higher salaries; they find that nonwage expenditures per student go up. Finally, we both find a significant union productivity gain. However, we may also disagree here as well because of the difference in test score measures. By using SAT and ACT test scores, Kleiner and Petree's estimates tend to include only above-average achievers. Although we find a 7 percent union productivity gain for the average elementary student, holding constant school resources and teacher and student characteristics, we find the opposite effect for above-average achievers, who are typically the students taking SAT and ACT tests.

Why do our two sets of results differ so substantially? In addition to the fact that we use different data sets and look at students in different grades, there are a number of more detailed issues that may contribute to the differences. Kleiner and Petree specify a production function for student achievement with expenditures per student as an input. This equation resembles a short-run, minimum-cost function normalized on output rather than a production function. Moreover, without specifying a production function, Kleiner and Petree are unable to account for other important educational inputs.

Another significant difference between the two studies is the level of aggregation of the respective data sets. Kleiner and Petree argue that the use of aggregate state data on student achievement is appropriate because licensing is a state function and union organization in public schools is strongly conditioned by state bargaining laws. The arguments for treating licensing and union organization at the state level may be correct, but one can use disaggregate data on individual students and schools and still also use state licensing variables as explanatory variables. The appropriate level of aggregation for one independent variable should not determine the appropriate level of aggregation for the dependent and other independent variables.

We also have concern over several details of the empirical analysis. The pooling of time-series and cross-section data in the estimates with no attention to dynamics, for example, suggests that licensing, unionization, and other independent variables have immediate effects on student test scores. In reality, however, these effects are likely to accumulate over time and take place over a protracted period. There is also the issue of selection bias in the SAT and ACT test scores. These tests are taken by only a fraction of students in each state, and this fraction varies substantially from state to state. It is difficult to separate the true effect of unionization from the spurious relationship between unionization and the students who took the test. Finally, the use of union membership as a measure of unionization for teachers means that some effect of unionization is expected in states with union members but with explicit prohibitions of collective bargaining by teachers. Presumably, such teachers should be treated differently than union members in states that permit formal collective bargaining.

In short, many of the differences in results and methodologies can be traced to the problem of data collection. It is very difficult to find data that meet all the needs of a project of this magnitude. Nonetheless, Kleiner and Petree direct our attention to a neglected but important issue: the interaction of teacher unions with the legal structure of the industry and their collective influence on the operation of public schools.

12 The Effects of Public Sector Unionism on Pay, Employment, Department Budgets, and Municipal Expenditures

Jeffrey Zax and Casey Ichniowski

Several recent reviews of the research on public sector union compensation effects conclude that the effects of public sector unions on compensation, while positive, are generally smaller than the effects of unions on compensation in the private sector (Lewin 1977; Mitchell 1978; Methe and Perry 1980; Ehernberg and Schwarz 1983; Freeman 1986; Lewis, chap. 6, this volume). However, compensation is only one of the issues with which unions might be concerned. In particular, limited empirical evidence suggests that public unions, in addition to their positive effects on compensation, also have positive effects on employment (Zax 1985a). Freeman (1986, 52) believes this is characteristic: "public sector unions can be viewed as *using their political power* to raise demand for public services, as well as using their bargaining power to fight for higher wages." He goes on to argue that while his proposition "requires empirical analysis . . . what is lacking, and needed, is a consistent analysis of public sector unionism on labor costs, employment and finances" (p. 62).

In this study, we pursue these issues by examining how municipal public unions affect employment and pay levels in their own functions and in other functions in their municipality, the overall budget allocation for their particular function and for other functions in their municipality, and the overall level of general expenditures in the municipality. We analyze the effects of public unions on this broad range of economic outcomes using an extensive data set on nearly 500 municipalities that

Jeffrey Zax is assistant professor of economics at Queens College, City University of New York, and research economist of the National Bureau of Economic Research. Casey Ichniowski is associate professor of the Graduate School of Business Administration of Columbia University and faculty research fellow of the National Bureau of Economic Research.

maintain their own police, fire, sanitation, and streets and highways departments.

While we do find some function-specific exceptions to the following general pattern of the effects of public unions, our analysis generates these results:

1. The presence of a "bargaining unit" (one of two forms of public employee unionization analyzed in this study) in a function increases pay in that function significantly. Other forms of unionization that are not formally a "bargaining unit" (referred to as "organization" or "association" throughout) also raise pay levels significantly but by less than a "bargaining unit."

2. In all functions, bargaining units raise employment above what it would otherwise be given the union levels of compensation and thus increase total function expenditures. Associations, however, do not increase employment levels.

3. Despite the effect of a bargaining unit on the expenditures of its own function, total *general* expenditures of the municipality are not increased by bargaining units, implying that some other components of the expenditures of municipalities, outside of expenditures in those functions that we specifically analyze, will be lower when bargaining units are present in municipal functions.

4. The effects of bargaining units on the pay of employees in other departments are uniformly positive and frequently significant, but the estimates of bargaining-unit effects on employment levels in other departments in its municipality are consistently negative and frequently significant.

In single-equation models that do not control for function expenditures, bargaining units increase employment. In multi-equation models, unions increase function expenditures and reduce employment when function expenditures are held constant. These results suggest that the positive union-employment effects in single-equation models are attributable to positive union effects on function expenditures and to the derived effects on labor demand.

12.1   Union Influence on Public Sector Budgets and Pay Determination: Own and Cross-Departmental Effects

The central hypothesis of this research is that union power and influence manifest themselves at many levels of municipal finance. Therefore, this section briefly reviews the distinctive political, legal, and economic aspects of the public sector pay determination process. Unions intervene as voters, lobbyists, or negotiators at all accessible levels of that process. The potential effects of public employees' political power on municipal budgets have been considered theoretically. For example,

Courant, Gramlich, and Rubinfeld (1979) investigate how public employees could increase budgets through bloc voting in a model where citizens can move between jurisdictions.

The empirical investigations of public employees' political activity are primarily case studies and descriptive research. These studies contain detailed accounts of the wide range of political activity pursued by public employee labor organizations and provide persuasive evidence that the labor organizations participate vigorously in political processes.

Public employee labor organizations exert much of their political pressure through various forms of lobbying. Generally, public unions are some of the most significant lobbyists at all levels of government. For example, at the federal level, three public employee unions—the Post Office Clerks, the National Education Association, and the National Association of Letter Carriers—were among the top twenty-five spenders in lobbying activities as early as the 1960s (Moskow, Lowenberg, and Koziara 1970, 264). While there is no comprehensive listing of union expenditures at the state and local levels of government, public employee unions are again "prominent" in expenditure reports in states that require filing of lobbying expenditures (Moskow, Lowenberg, and Koziara 1970, 264–65).

This lobbying activity takes many forms. Local unions lobby at various levels of government, over a range of issues, and at various points in time relative to collective bargaining negotiations. For example, state legislatures have enacted supportive bargaining legislation and have legislated fringe benefits for municipal employees, such as pensions, insurance programs, and educational benefits. These same issues, including protective bargaining ordinances, may be legislated at the municipal level as well. Public sector unions may also lobby civil service boards to obtain pay and benefit increases they could not achieve through lobbying in legislatures or through collective bargaining.[1] One study of the political lobbying activity of public employee organizations uncovered numerous instances of direct lobbying of legislators by public unions to achieve their objectives:

> On the local level, the Los Angeles city council acknowledges that the Fire and Police Protective League . . . was instrumental in persuading the council to grant $40 million in pay increases to Los Angeles policemen and firemen. . . . Similarly, the firefighters in Syracuse, New York, were able to gain a mandatory forty-hour work week from the state legislature after failing to obtain this concession at the bargaining table. Again at the state level, Illinois fire and police organizations were . . . successful in obtaining a state-mandated minimum wage for uniformed personnel (Labor Management Relations Service 1972, 12).

The strategy of pursuing pay and benefit increases through legislation when they are denied in collective negotiations as practiced by the Syracuse fire fighters is sufficiently common to be known as "end-run" bargaining. Labor organizations can also make an end run to civil service boards to obtain benefits not obtained in bargaining.[2] Political activity of public employee labor organizations is not confined to direct lobbying in municipal councils, state legislatures, and civil service boards. It also includes activities such as letter-writing campaigns, demonstrations, and marches before seats of government, and even the use of petitions and referendum elections, sometimes referred to as "indirect lobbying," that force legislative responses (Labor Management Relations Service 1972, 7–8).

Lobbying by public employee groups in the budgetary process is designed to influence the overall size of the budget for their function and allocations across items within their function's budget. Craft (1970), for example, describes a three-tier process followed by teachers in California. He found that employee representatives first lobbied for revenue-increasing mechanisms such as tax increases, special assessments, and bond elections early in the budget-setting process. After an overall budget was set, employee representatives reviewed allocations for various items in the budget. Craft cites instances where the employees' representatives reduced line items for hiring new teachers, since they had better estimates of projected employee turnover. They were also able to restructure various educational programs to qualify for state or federal funding, thereby reducing other line-item commitments in the local budget. In all cases, any savings that became available in this "budget search" process were reallocated to the payroll expenditures of currently employed teachers.

Such a scenario suggests that this type of lobbying may not necessarily increase the overall budget, but it might lead to a relative reduction in nonpayroll items. Gallagher (1978) addresses this issue in his study of school district budgets. He finds that unionization did not decrease expenditures on any budget item that he investigated, and it increased payroll line items for bargaining unit and nonbargaining unit employees. If this result is general, it implies that union payroll gains must increase government expenditures by at least as much.

The legal framework for the budgeting process is a principal reason why employee unions devote such energy and resources to lobbying legislatures over budget size and budget allocations. Any state in which a court case specifically addresses the issue has ruled that legislatures have the final authority to appropriate funds (Henkel and Wood 1982). While the relevant court cases will often address the issue because a state or local legislature did not appropriate funds for a collective bargaining agreement between a union and a representative of the government's executive branch, the effect of the decisions may be an increase in union lobbying activity of the legislatures to avoid such a legislative veto. Interestingly, it has been argued that since state and local legislators are often part-time officials, they may have less time than members of the executive branch to assess the service needs in their community and might therefore respond more favorably than executives to requests or demands made by public employee representatives (Henkel and Wood 1982).

Furthermore, the political objectives of government officials and of public employees may often be in concert rather than in conflict. Elected officials invariably value public employee votes and may find that the political cost of those votes is small. Appointed officials and public employees may find that their objectives are mutually compatible. Niskanen (1975) and Ott (1980), in their theoretical studies, conclude that the "bureaucrat's" objective is to increase the size of his bureau. Larger departments offer, at a minimum, more employment; so this is an objective that public employees endorse as well.

These examples do not provide enough detail to determine how much public sector union members benefit from political activities pursued by their union. They also do not indicate how much political activity is engaged in by unorganized public employees. However, they are sufficiently vivid to encourage measurement of union-nonunion differentials other than the union-wage effect.

Finally, of course, public sector unions influence the pay determination process through collective negotiations at the bargaining table. While the preceding discussion highlights the multipronged lobbying efforts of public unions to influence pay, employment, and budgets, the collective bargaining process in the public sector has also been described as inherently "multilateral."

Multilateralism has been defined to exist when more than two distinct parties are involved in negotiations so that no clear dichotomy exists between employee and management organizations (Kochan 1974, 526). Stanley (1972, 2) provides an extreme example of the often fuzzy distinction between public employer and public employee organization. In Hartford, Connecticut, an American Federation of State, County, and Municipal Employees (AFSCME) business agent served as chairman of the Connecticut State Assembly Labor Committee.

We do not argue that all public unions operate in a similar fashion and with equal effect at various levels. The diversity of possible activity by public unions within budget-making and bargaining processes in different environments has already been documented (Derber et al. 1973; Horton, Lewin, and Kuhn 1976). Similarly, while our empirical models incorporate a number of the institutional aspects of the public sector "pay determination" process and union participation in those processes, we cannot account for all possible details. The preceding discussion, however, does clearly indicate that public unions may affect budgetary outcomes. To the extent they are successful, they could stimulate an increase in the demand for their services.

These considerations lead us to believe that the "monopoly" union (Dunlop 1944) characterization is not representative of union behavior in the local public sector. The objectives of public sector unions include many aspects of employment conditions in addition to compensation. Theoretically, other objectives, such as employment increases, are obtainable if the employer's demand curve is not a constraint. With appropriate cooperation from the public employer, it need not be. More recently, the "efficient contract" construct has been refined to provide another framework for considering union-employer bargains (Fellner 1947; Hall and Lilien 1979; McDonald and Solow 1981). An "efficient" contract curve lies to the right of the labor demand curve so that employment exceeds the level on the employer's demand curve at the negotiated wage.

In sum, discussion of public sector unions' involvement in lobbying and budget-setting activity suggests that public unions devote substantial energies to expanding the surplus available to them by expanding public sector budgets. Absent any immediate disciplining mechanisms in which voting and mobility of citizens force municipal compensation and employment decisions to reflect their preferences for services perfectly, unions may not operate under the assumption of a fixed labor demand schedule or a fixed surplus. If public unions do increase overall municipal or function-specific budgets through simultaneous increases in pay and employment, this could correspond to an outward shift in the labor schedule and not a "monopoly union" or "efficient contract" framework. With empirical evidence below, we assess how well these theoretical frameworks describe union behavior in the local government sector.

12.1.1   Effects of Public Sector Unions on Other Departments

To add up the effects of public unions on a municipality's general expenditures, one must also consider how union effects on one function affect expenditures on another function. Here we briefly describe a number of ways that a union-induced change in expenditures in one department might manifest itself in other departments.

Panel 1 in figure 12.1 illustrates the basic proposition that unions in the public sector may shift the labor demand curve for their own services (department 1) from D_1 to D_2, thereby increasing relative wage and employment levels. In light of past research, we expect that increases in wages and employment are more likely the result of increases in the overall demand for the particular service and not a result of

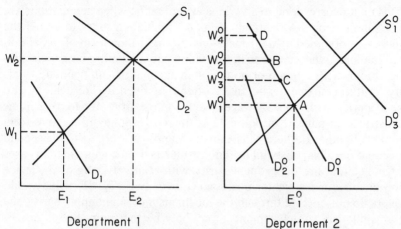

Fig. 12.1   The effects of public sector unions on pay and employment
in their own and other departments. W = wages; E = employment level; D = demand for services; S = supply of
workers. *Panel 1:* The effects of public sector unions on pay
and employment in their own department. *Panel 2:* Possible
effects of public sector unions on pay and employment in
other departments.

decreases in the capital budgets (Gallagher 1978). A decrease in capital
budgets in the face of increases in compensation would amount to a
shift away from relatively less expensive inputs in the production of a
given public service.

An increase in one function's expenditures may affect other functions' expenditures in a number of ways. First, a nonunion department,
or a department with a relatively weaker union, may not be sufficiently
protected inside the budget process and, as a result, have its own budget
reduced. That is, a second department may fund the increases in the
first department. In panel 2 of figure 12.1, a shift in department 2's
demand from D_1 to D_2 would reflect such an effect.

One should also not rule out the possibility that positive pay "spillovers" on certain departments might exist or even that positive spillovers exist on most departments. If positive spillovers dominate, one
would also be likely to observe increases in overall expenditure levels
and tax revenues.

Positive spillovers in pay rates across functions, where an increase
in pay from W_1 to W_2 in department 1 leads to an increase in department
2's pay, may occur by several mechanisms. Nonunion departments
may receive an increase in pay via the "threat" effect, as public managers try to stave off unionization of other departments. Unions will
also try to match the wage increases obtained by other departments.

This might correspond to a "whipsawing" tactic when negotiations are not simultaneous. A relatively weak union might also try to garner the increases obtained by a stronger one through some form of "coalition bargaining," where more than one union bargain jointly with their public employer. If a union or nonunion department 2 can maintain "parity" with department 1—a tactic often employed by fire fighters who seek parity with police—wages would move from W_1^0 to W_2^0. If, as illustrated in panel 2 of figure 12.1, this corresponds to a move from point A to point B, there will be an oversupply of workers to the second occupation. This "disequilibrium" result has been documented in cases of police and fire department parity with relatively long civil service job queues for fire fighter positions (Lewin 1973, 78–81). If pay spillovers do not operate through the mechanism of maintaining parity, the pay spillovers to department 2 may only be to a point like C on D_1^Q, which corresponds to a wage of W_3^0 which is less than W_2^0. If department 2 enjoyed a relative pay advantage over department 1 prior to the shift in demand from D_1 to D_2 in department 1 (shown in fig. 12.1 as $W_1^0 > W_1$), employees in department 2, following a strategy of maintaining the relative wage differential between the two departments, may try to increase pay to point D. At point D, W_4^0 in department 2 is greater than W_2 in department 1. Clearly, positive pay spillovers as described come at the expense of decreases in relative employment levels.

It is also possible that union-induced increases in wage and employment levels in department 1 may lead to wage and employment increases in department 2. For example, if the "own department" effect is achieved through wage increases and "minimum manning" contract clauses via collective bargaining (which would require the legislature to appropriate funds for a larger budget), a union in a second department might bargain for both the wage and employment contract clauses in their contract. If this kind of spillover was prevalent, one would also observe that unionized cities are associated with higher levels of overall expenditures and therefore higher tax rates to raise the necessary revenues. In panel 2 of figure 12.1, this kind of spillover effect would correspond to a shift in the department 2 demand curve from D_1^Q to D_3^Q.

Theories of the budget-setting process are not developed enough to predict which kinds of direct and indirect effects of public employee unions exist in U.S. municipalities. Previous studies have documented the diversity of arrangements among public sector unions, municipal executives, and state and local legislatures in the budget and pay determination process. While the descriptive studies provide a useful starting point for conceptualizing the budgeting process, they cannot document effects of unions without reference to some comparison group. Ultimately, discovering what direct and indirect effects the activities of unions have on economic outcomes requires empirical investigation across a broad range of functions and municipalities.

12.2   The Sample and Data

Because the data set for this study is extensive, a complete list of variables and their precise definitions is given in a separate statistical appendix. Here we briefly describe the nature of the sample, several different classes of variables, and the dimensions along which variation exists for any given variable. As indicated in the statistical appendix, these data have been collected from several annual surveys conducted by the Governments Division of the U.S. Bureau of Census (1977, 1978, 1979, 1980, 1982), by the International City Management Association, and independent data collection efforts sponsored by the National Bureau of Economic Research.

The sample for this study consists of data on 463 municipalities. Data on these municipalities cover five years: 1977, 1978, 1979, 1980, and 1982. In addition, there are data specific to four functions in the municipalities: police, fire, streets and highways, and sanitation and refuse collection. The 463 municipalities in the sample are those that report having employment in all four functions across all five years. Across the five years and four functions, the sample can consist of up to 9,260 "municipality-function-years." For any one of the four functions, the sample can consist of up to 2,315 "function-years."

The empirical models consider several dependent variables: general municipal expenditures (other than educational and public utility expenditures); total expenditures on each of the four departmental functions; average payroll per employee in a function; and employment per capita in a function.

Two measures for unionization are available for a given function: bargaining unit (U) and other nonbargaining organizations or associations (O). The survey defines "bargaining unit" as: "A group of employees recognized as appropriate for representation by an employee organization for the purpose of collective bargaining or other discussions." An employee organization is defined as: "Any organization which exists for the purposes in whole or in part of dealing with the employer concerning grievances, personnel policies and practices, labor disputes, wages, rates of pay, hours of employment, or conditions of work." In our analysis, $U = 1$ when a bargaining unit is present, while $O = 1$ when an organization is present but a bargaining unit is not.

Also describing the bargaining environment is a detailed set of mutually exclusive bargaining laws. These are: duty-to-bargain with strikes permitted; duty-to-bargain with compulsory interest arbitration; other duty-to-bargain statutes; statutes that permit bargaining but do not require employers to bargain with employee representatives, such as laws allowing employee representatives to "meet and confer with" or to "present proposals to" their employers; no explicit bargaining law; and a final category of laws that makes public employee bargaining illegal. These bargaining laws vary by function, and any amendments or new legislation during the 1977–82 period are reflected in year-to-year changes in these laws. In addition, there is a separate law variable that measures whether or not there is a right-to-work law for public employees in a given state.

While the economic effects of variables describing the bargaining environment, particularly U and $O,$ are the focus of this study, it is important to include controls for other characteristics of the municipality that might influence the demand for municipal services or the supply of workers to that service. These variables are obtained from sources other than the *Survey of Governments,* and variation in these factors is only across municipalities. For financial and demographic characteristics, these variables refer to 1970 levels of the given measure, while variables measuring government structure refer to characteristics in 1979.[3]

Some of these variables may reflect differences in the tastes of the community for different services and may therefore be systematically related to different levels of demand. Such variables include: a dummy for whether the municipality is a central city; population and population changes; median years of schooling in the population; characteristics of the housing stock; and ability-to-pay measures such as median family income and percentage of families below the poverty level. If, for example, a higher percentage of one-unit structures corresponds to relatively high (low) demand for fire services, this variable will enter positively (negatively) in reduced-form fire-fighter pay equations. If median family income corresponds to an increase in the demand for all services, this variable would enter positively in all functions' reduced-form pay equations.

Other control variables may indicate factors influencing the supply of workers to a particular service. An alternative wage variable, median earnings of male operatives in 1970, should be negatively related to the supply of workers to municipal functions, and therefore would be positively correlated with pay in such functions in a reduced-form specification.

Additionally, the statistical appendix lists a number of variables describing various characteristics of the municipal government. Since pay and employment decisions are filtered through a politically influenced budget process, characteristics of the government may affect these economic outcomes. If results in this sample parallel those found in previous research, we would expect to find governments with city managers paying relatively higher salaries (see, for example, Edwards and Edwards 1982; Ehrenberg 1973; or Zax 1985b), and when city councils are elected at large, municipal work forces will likely be both larger and better paid (Zax 1985b).

The empirical strategy of this study is as follows: First, we estimate compensation and employment as a function of all exogenous variables—city demographics and wealth, city government structure, geographic and time dummy variables, bargaining law variables, and union variables. These single-equation estimates impose relatively little structure on the data and serve as a straightforward method of describing average differences in pay and employment between union and nonunion municipal departments, ceteris paribus. We then construct a three-tier thirteen-equation budgeting model. In addition to the compensation and employment equations for each of the municipal functions, this system includes equations for total expenditures in each function and one equation for general municipal expenditures. The validity of the structure of this system depends on the validity of the a priori restrictions it imposes, but if those restrictions are accepted, it provides a much richer description of union effects on municipal finance.

12.3 Single-Equation Models

The basic proposition of this study, that public sector unions may affect pay, employment, other department expenditures, and general municipal expenditures, calls for the simultaneous estimation of a system of equations. However, as a foundation for that analysis, we estimate several cross-section pay and employment equations. Specifically, we estimate:

$$(1) \qquad \text{PAY}_{ift} = \alpha_1 + \beta_1 \vec{X}_i + \beta_0 O_{ift} + \beta_u U_{ift} + \epsilon_{ift},$$

$$(2) \qquad \text{EMP}_{ift} = \alpha_2 + \gamma_1 \vec{Y}_i + \gamma_0 O_{ift} + \gamma_u U_{ift} + \lambda_{ift}.$$

The equations vary across municipalities (i), functions (f), and years (t). The set of exogenous variables that enter the pay equation ($\vec{X}$) do not have to be the same as those that enter the employment equation ($\vec{Y}$). Since observations vary over time, X and Y include a set of five dummy variables for the year of the observation.

If bargaining units do increase the demand for their services, we expect both β_u and γ_u to be significantly positive as a preliminary indication of increased demand due to the activities of public unions. If the nonbargaining unit organizations have effects similar to the effects of bargaining units, β_0 and γ_0 will likewise be positive.

Table 12.1 reports the coefficients on the bargaining unit and organization variables in the reduced-form pay and employment equations. The sample for the table 12.1 equations is 463 municipalities pooled across four functions and five years—or 9,260 "municipality-function-year" observations. In the average monthly payroll per employee equation, a bargaining unit is associated with a significant increase of $60.26 in the average monthly pay of a municipal employee, or 4.8 percent of average compensation. Employees in departments with nonbargaining unit organizations also receive significantly higher pay than employees in nonunion departments. The increase is $10.99, or 0.87 percent of the average pay in the sample. As judged by an F-test, the coefficients on the U and O variables are significantly different from one another. The magnitude of the estimated union effects on pay are in keeping with the magnitude observed in many previous studies on this topic— generally positive and significant, but less than the compensation differentials generally associated with private sector unions.

Table 12.1   **The Effects of Public Sector Bargaining Units and Organizations on Pay and Employment; $N = 9,260$ City-Function-Years[a]**
(t-statistics in parentheses; coefficient as percentage of mean of dependent variables in brackets)

	Pay Per Full-Time Employee	Employment Per 10,000 Capita
Mean of Dependent Variable	1256.91	15.5
1. Union	60.26***	1.71***
	(9.11)	(9.06)
	[0.048]	[0.110]
2. Association	10.99*	−0.364**
	(1.81)	(2.10)
	[0.009]	[−0.023]
R^2	0.750	0.655

[a]Other controls include: three function dummy variables; four year dummy variables; eight geographic divisional dummy variables; 1970 population and population changes between 1960 and 1970 and between 1970 and 1980; the percentage of the population that is Hispanic, black, of foreign stock, has a high school education, is below the poverty level; median family income; median value of housing; percentage of housing that is one-unit structure; median education; median earnings of male operatives; the ratio of nonworking to working persons; the percentage of workers in white-collar occupations; a central city dummy variable; eight variables describing characteristics of the municipal government; six bargaining laws for public employees (arbitration, strikes permitted, duty-to-bargain, bargaining permitted, no law, and bargaining illegal); and a dummy variable for whether or not a public sector right-to-work law exists. The control variables do not include other functions' unionization.

***Significant at the 0.01 level, two-tailed test.

**Significant at the 0.05 level, two-tailed test.

*Significant at the 0.10 level, two tailed test.

In the traditional "monopoly union" framework for conceptualizing positive union wage effects, positive pay effects of unions are achieved through bargaining power that forces employers up a labor demand curve, thereby increasing pay at the expense of employment levels. In a reduced-form equation, one might therefore expect the relatively higher paid union departments in the public sector to operate with smaller departments. As suggested in section 12.2, however, the lobbying activity of public sector unions in the budgetary process might allow these employee organizations to counter this effect by increasing demand for their services.

From the coefficients in the second column of table 12.1 on the bargaining unit and organization variables in the employment-per-capita equation, one finds preliminary support for the latter framework for bargaining units. Despite the significant positive pay effects observed in the first column, bargaining units are associated with relatively larger municipal departments. The bargaining unit coefficient, 1.71, corresponds to 11 percent of the mean of the dependent variable. Other types of employee organizations significantly reduce employment by 0.364, or 2.3 percent. The magnitude of the estimated effect of bargaining units on employment is similar in magnitude to the previous estimate by Zax (1985a) using a different data set for an earlier, but overlapping, time period.

In table 12.2, the bargaining unit and organization effects are allowed to vary by function by estimating separate pay and employment equations for each of the four functions. The coefficients from the four function-specific pay equations are listed in columns (1)–(4), while coefficients from the four employment equations are listed in columns (5)–(8). The general pattern observed in table 12.1 is observed across the functions with an occasional function-specific exception: bargaining units are associated with relatively larger and better paid departments, while organizations appear to increase pay. In the function-specific equation, organizations have no significant effect on employment. The pay effect of bargaining units exceeds the effect of organizations in all functions.

The lone exceptions to this overall pattern are that neither form of unionization increases pay significantly in the sanitation function, and that police bargaining units do not have relatively larger departments. Still, police bargaining units are not associated with any significant declines in employment. Interestingly, this cross-section result concerning the union effect on police employment replicates the result obtained by Victor (1977), who found that unionized fire departments had relatively larger departments but found no employment effect for police unions.

Before exploring this initial set of results concerning the effects of "own" unionization in greater detail in a structured system of equations

Table 12.2   **The Effects of Public Sector Unions and Associations on Pay and Employment in Function-Specific Equations; N = 2,315 City-Years[a] (t-statistics in parentheses; coefficient as percentage of mean of dependent variables in brackets)**

	Monthly Pay Per Full-Time Employee				Employment Per 10,000 Capita			
	(1) Streets and Highways	(2) Police	(3) Fire	(4) Sanitation	(5) Streets and Highways	(6) Police	(7) Fire	(8) Sanitation
Mean of Dependent Variable	1130.28	1382.66	1440.49	1073.99	9.88	24.70	18.19	9.06
1. Bargaining Unit	57.51***	52.79***	64.87***	10.59	0.80**	-0.29	2.13**	1.41***
	(4.05)	(4.21)	(13.25)	(0.74)	(2.44)	(0.35)	(6.15)	(4.18)
	[0.051]	[0.038]	[0.045]	[0.009]	[0.081]	[-0.012]	[0.117]	[0.156]
2. Organization	29.14***	28.64*	48.73***	-0.42	-0.26	0.36	-0.17	-0.22
	(2.60)	(1.90)	(3.18)	(0.04)	(0.98)	(0.42)	(0.42)	(0.95)
	[0.026]	[0.021]	[0.034]	[0.001]	[0.026]	[0.015]	[0.009]	[-0.024]
R^2	0.682	0.746	0.758	0.695	0.321	0.603	0.486	0.650

[a]Other controls are those listed in footnote a of table 12.1 except that no function dummy variables can be included in the models for this table.

***Significant at the 0.01 level, two-tailed test.

**Significant at the 0.05 level, two-tailed test.

*Significant at the 0.10 level, two-tailed test.

in which union effects on general expenditures and on function expenditures are allowed to affect department-level pay and employment, we lay the foundation for the effects of public employee unions on function and total municipal expenditures by considering how unionization in one function does or does not affect pay and employment outcomes in other departments. The function-specific pay and employment equations presented in table 12.2 are therefore expanded to include the unionization measures of other functions. Table 12.3 presents the coefficients on the bargaining unit variables of the given function and the bargaining unit variables in the other three functions. Because bargaining units were shown to be associated with both higher pay and more employment, we focus on the bargaining unit effects in table 12.3. The coefficients that measure the effects of a bargaining unit on the pay and employment in the same function, listed in row 1, are similar to those presented in row 1 of table 12.2 from models without the cross-bargaining unit and cross-organization variables included. However, the magnitudes of several "own bargaining unit" effects decrease in magnitude. Still, the only "own bargaining unit" coefficient that becomes insignificantly different from zero after adding the "other unionization" variables is the police bargaining unit coefficient in the police pay equation (column 2, line 1). In this reduced-form model, police unions are not found to increase police pay levels. It should be noted that the presence of bargaining units in police departments and bargaining units in other departments, particularly in fire departments, are highly correlated. In this way, the positive effect of fire unionization on police pay will more often than not be enjoyed by a police department with a bargaining unit since fire units are usually found in municipalities with police units. In fact, of the 1,367 municipality-years in which a fire bargaining unit is present, 1,246, or 91.3 percent, occur in observations in which a police bargaining unit is also present.

The effects of bargaining units on pay and employment in other departments also reveal an interesting pattern. Except for sanitation bargaining units (which do not increase pay in their own departments), point estimates of the effects of bargaining units in other functions on pay are always positive and often significant. Streets-and-highways bargaining units are associated with higher pay for police, fire, and sanitation workers. Police bargaining units have a significant positive effect on fire-fighter pay, while fire-fighter bargaining units increase the pay of police and sanitation workers significantly. For all four functions, the three "other" bargaining unit variables add significantly to the explanatory power of the pay equations as judged by an F-test. The cause of the significant negative pay effect of sanitation bargaining units on fire-fighter pay may be related to some kind of budgetary displacement due to the "own" positive employment effect of sanitation bargaining units.

Table 12.3 The Effects of Own and Other Unionization on Pay and Employment in Function-Specific Equations; $N = 2,315$ City-Years for each function[a] (t-statistics in parentheses; coefficient as percentage of mean of dependent variables in brackets)

	Monthly Pay Per Full-Time Employee				Employment Per 10,000 Capita			
	(1) Streets and Highways	(2) Police	(3) Fire	(4) Sanitation	(5) Streets and Highways	(6) Police	(7) Fire	(8) Sanitation
Mean of Dependent Variable	1130.28	1382.66	1440.49	1073.99	9.88	24.70	18.19	9.06
1. Own Bargaining Unit	58.60*** (3.12) [0.052]	13.71 (0.74) [0.010]	31.07* (1.67) [0.022]	−24.20 (1.37) [−0.023]	0.98** (2.25) [−0.099]	0.31 (0.60) [0.013]	2.65*** (5.47) [0.146]	3.29*** (8.01) [0.363]
2. Other Functions' Bargaining Units								
a. Streets and Highways Union	— — —	55.47*** (2.95) [0.040]	34.18* (1.66) [0.024]	31.00* (1.78) [0.029]	— — —	−0.20 (0.38) [−0.008]	−0.30 (0.56) [−0.016]	−2.57*** (6.34) [−0.284]

	1	2	3	4	5	6	7	8
b. Police Union	28.58 (1.55) [0.025]	—	48.37** (2.42) [0.34]	3.56 (0.21) [0.003]	−0.63 (1.47) [−0.064]	—	−0.42 (0.81) [−0.023]	0.48 (1.20) [0.053]
c. Fire Union	25.75 (1.52) [0.023]	27.42* (1.61) [0.20]	—	47.61*** (3.04) [0.044]	−0.30 (0.76) [−0.030]	−0.87* (1.80) [0.035]	—	−1.12 (3.07) [−0.124]
d. Sanitation Union	−23.45 (1.23) [−0.021]	−26.63 (1.39) [−0.019]	−47.12** (2.25) [−0.033]	—	−0.38 (0.85) [−0.038]	−0.28 (0.52) [−0.011]	−0.61 (1.11) [−0.034]	—
3. F-test (3,2262): Do bargaining units in all other functions significantly affect dependent variable?	Yes	Yes	Yes	Yes	Yes	No	No	Yes
R^2	0.685	0.749	0.760	0.699	0.327	0.605	0.490	0.661

[a]Other controls are those listed in footnote a of table 12.1 except for the function dummy variables.

***Significant at the 0.01 level, two-tailed test.

**Significant at the 0.05 level, two-tailed test.

*Significant at the 0.10 level, two-tailed test.

While bargaining units tend to increase pay in other functions, the relatively higher pay is occasionally associated with significantly lower employment levels in other departments. In all but one case (i.e., the effect of a police bargaining unit on sanitation employment), the point estimate of the coefficients are negative but generally not significantly different from zero. The three insignificant "other" bargaining unit coefficients in the streets-and-highways employment equation, when taken as a set, are significant determinants of streets-and-highways employment as judged by an F-test. For the police and fire employment equations, bargaining units in the three other departments jointly are not significant determinants of employment, while in the sanitation employment equation, the streets-and-highways bargaining unit variable adds to the explanatory power of the model.

Absent relatively elastic demand for these services, it does not appear that bargaining units in a given function are necessarily funding the pay and employment increases in their own departments with reductions in the payroll of other departments. That is, other departments generally receive relatively higher pay as a result of a bargaining unit in another department. While the positive pay spillovers observed in these equations occasionally come at the expense of lower employment, there is no obvious evidence (given positive pay spillovers) that expenditure increases due to employment and compensation effects of a bargaining unit in a given department come from a decline in expenditures of one or more of the other three functions.

Before interpreting these results further and speculating about the mechanisms by which bargaining units increase the pay and/or employment in their own function and in other functions, we estimate a system of equations to assess the effects of public sector unions more thoroughly. General municipal expenditures and total function expenditures as well as the pay and employment in the various departments are dependent variables in this system. If a similar pattern of "own" and "other" bargaining unit effects emerges from this more complete analysis, there will be more confidence in these basic, reduced-form, cross-section equation results.

12.4 Municipal Budgeting Systems

This section develops and estimates a hierarchical model of municipal budgeting, which permits unions to affect general municipal expenditures; expenditures for streets and highways, police, fire, and sanitation; as well as employment and compensation levels in each of these functions. It identifies three stages of the budgeting process and estimates the effects of unions at each level. Importantly, results from this more elaborate model support the conclusion that bargaining units increase both employment and compensation in their own departments. The results indicate that these joint effects are made possible by the effect of bargaining units on overall expenditures in their own function. Finally, results from this model strengthen the conclusion that the spillover effects of bargaining units on other departments increase compensation, but only at the expense of reductions in employment.

All models described in this section are variations on a single structure. Each is a system of thirteen equations. Eight equations estimate the determinants of compensation and employment levels in streets and highways, police, fire, and sanitation. Four equations estimate the determinants of *total* expenditures in streets and highways, police, fire, and sanitation functions, where total function expenditures include nonpayroll as well as payroll expenditures. The last equation estimates the determinants of general expenditures in each municipality.

These endogenous variables represent outcomes determined at three levels of a municipal budgeting hierarchy: employment and compensation are the outcomes at the lowest, most disaggregate level of this hierarchy. The systems model these pay and employment outcomes as dependent upon the outcomes of municipal budgeting decisions at higher levels of aggregation. Total expenditures for streets and highways, police, fire, and sanitation per 10,000 capita represent an intermediate budgeting level. Total function expenditures include payrolls, payments to other factors of production, and service purchases from other levels of government through intergovernmental transfers. The single equation for general expenditures per 10,000 capita represents the highest, most aggregate level of the budgetary process. General expenditures include all municipal expenditures except those on education and utilities. Expenditures on streets and highways, police, fire, and sanitation are, on average, 38.9 percent of general municipal expenditures. The remainder includes expenditures on central administration, finance, and parks and recreation, for example. Both function and general expenditures are measured as dollars per year, in contrast to payrolls which are measured as dollars per month.[4]

The following analyses begin with the simplest model of interactions across the three levels of this budgeting hierarchy: outcomes at lower levels are dependent on predetermined outcomes at higher levels. This is a recursive model, in which the electorate and elected officials first determine the level of general expenditures. Then, dependent on the level of general expenditures, they allocate shares for expenditures in each function. Lastly, given function expenditures, the municipality and its workers agree on compensation and employment levels.

More sophisticated models of budgeting interactions would allow outcomes at lower levels of the budgeting process to enter into the determination of outcomes at higher levels. For example, if compensation often rises unexpectedly, function expenditures may be, in part, determined by payrolls. While this section begins by analyzing the recursive model, it goes on to compare the recursive model with other models which allow feedback from the lower levels of the budgeting process to the upper levels.

The conceptual budgeting process underlying the recursive system of endogenous variables also implies a specification for the exogenous variables: the level of general expenditures is determined by citizens' wealth, by their tastes for public as opposed to private consumption, and by institutional factors. Therefore, the exogenous variables in the equation for general expenditures include demographic and economic characteristics of city residents, structure of municipal government, year, and geographic division dummy variables. Given the level of general expenditures, its allocation among individual functions is determined again by citizens' wealth and tastes and by institutional organization. The array of exogenous variables in equations for function expenditures is the same as that appearing in the equation for general expenditures.

Citizens have two sets of concerns in this process. One, the level of taxation, is effectively determined by general expenditures.[5] The other is service levels. Given the level of taxation and the level of services provided by a function, citizens should be indifferent to compensation and employment levels; they should not care whether the services they receive are produced by a few high-paid workers or many low-paid workers. With function expenditures—as proxies for service output[6]—included among the explanatory variables in equations for compensation and employment, demographic and economic characteristics of city residents are irrelevant. However, the employment and compensation variables do depend on the range of labor relations practices that are legal in each state. Therefore, variables identifying the legal environment are included in these equations.[7] The purpose of these models is to identify the extent to which the "total" union effects on compensation and employment, estimated in section 12.3, are attributable to union activity at the higher levels of the municipal budgeting process. Therefore, all equations contain union variables. The specification of exogenous and endogenous variables in the recursive model is represented in figure 12.2. (When "feedback" from lower levels of the process to higher levels are allowed, the arrows between the endogenous variables would no longer be unidirectional.)

Within this specification are a number of different "union effects." First, there are effects of own-unionization on general and function expenditures as well as on compensation and employment. The coefficients of own-union variables in compensation and wage equations are "direct" union effects. Second, the effects of own unionization on

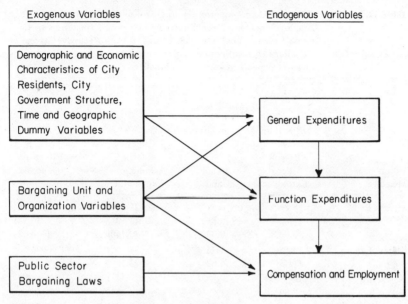

Fig. 12.2   Municipal budgeting model

general and function expenditures will have "indirect" effects on compensation and employment outcomes in the same function. The simple recursive model incorporates two chains that create such "indirect budgetary effects" on the ultimate levels of employment and compensation: the effects of own unionization on function expenditures, coupled with the effects of function expenditures on compensation and employment; and the effects of unions on general expenditures, coupled with the effects of general expenditures on function expenditures and those of function expenditures on compensation and employment. Third, these systems identify "indirect spillover effects"—effects of unionization in one function on outcomes in another—on total function expenditures, compensation, and employment. Specifications of the equation systems are based on much stronger assumptions than are the single-equation models of the previous section. In return, they yield the richer characterization of municipal union effects presented below.

12.4.1   Recursive System

Within the recursive system of figure 12.2, the simplest specification of union effects includes only variables measuring the presence of own-bargaining units or organizations in equations for compensation, employment, function expenditures, and general municipal expenditures. This recursive system is estimated by seemingly unrelated regression analysis. Results of this estimation are presented in table 12.4. Column

Table 12.4   **Effects of Own Unionization on Own Compensation and Employment, Own Expenditures and General Expenditures, No Cross-Unionization Spillovers: Estimates from Recursive System of Equations (*t*-statistics in parentheses; coefficient as percentage of mean of dependent variable, in brackets)**

Union Measure	(1) Effect on Own Payroll Per Employee	(2) Effect on Own Employment Per 10,000 Capita	(3) Effect on Own Function Expenditures	(4) Effect on General Expenditures
Streets B. U.	25.11	0.312	62,327.00***	−97,761.00
	(1.60)	(0.85)	(3.19)	(0.54)
	[0.022]	[0.032]	[0.140]	[−0.024]
Streets Org.	18.56	−1.33***	49,038.00***	−138,990.00
	(1.45)	(4.62)	(3.19)	(0.86)
	[0.016]	[−0.135]	[0.111]	[−0.035]
Police B. U.	59.80***	−1.73***	26,512.00***	55,758.00
	(4.42)	(5.81)	(2.62)	(0.31)
	[0.043]	[−0.071]	[0.051]	[0.014]
Police Org.	42.02***	−0.342	6,050.00	−163,512.00
	(2.27)	(0.84)	(0.46)	(0.80)
	[0.030]	[−0.014]	[0.012]	[−0.041]
Fire B. U.	67.76***	−0.573*	39,157.00***	144,359.00
	(4.27)	(1.84)	(4.95)	(0.85)
	[0.047]	[−0.031]	[0.105]	[0.036]
Fire Org.	83.20***	−0.504	−18,961.00**	367,368.00**
	(4.31)	(1.30)	(2.00)	(2.00)
	[0.057]	[−0.028]	[−0.051]	[0.092]
Sanitation B. U.	29.09*	−0.384	35,319.00***	−335,187.00*
	(1.84)	(1.03)	(3.44)	(1.81)
	[0.027]	[−0.041]	[0.162]	[−0.084]
Sanitation Org.	41.22***	−2.17***	9,432.00	197,761.00
	(3.57)	(8.24)	(1.36)	(1.34)
	[0.038]	[−0.232]	[0.043]	[0.049]

Notes: B. U. = bargaining unit; Org. = organization. Specification of equations and control variables are described by figure 12.2.

***Significant at the 0.01 level, two-tailed test.
**Significant at the 0.05 level, two-tailed test.
*Significant at the 0.10 level, two-tailed test.

1 presents coefficients on own-bargaining unit and own-organization variables in the equations for compensation per employee. Both bargaining units and organizations have significant positive effects on compensation for police, fire, and sanitation workers, when function expenditures are held constant. Effects are positive but insignificant for streets and highways. The percentage estimates given below the t-statistics demonstrate that these direct compensation effects are of similar magnitudes to those of the single-equation models in table 12.2, ranging from 1.6 percent to 5.7 percent of payroll per employee.

In contrast, the employment effects in these models, holding function expenditures constant, are of opposite sign to those of the single-equation models. The coefficients in column (2) demonstrate that either the bargaining unit variable or the organization variable has a significant negative effect on employment in all four functions, holding function expenditures constant.[8] The form of unionization in each of the four functions that has a significant negative effect on employment is the most common form of unionization in that function. For example, organizations have significant negative direct effects on employment in streets and highways and in sanitation. In streets and highways, 17.1 percent of all departments have bargaining units, but 38.5 percent have organizations without bargaining units. In sanitation, the corresponding percentages are 11.5 percent and 42.1 percent. Bargaining units have significant negative direct employment effects for police and fire; 58.4 percent of police and 61.0 percent of fire departments have bargaining units; 8.3 percent of police and 11.4 percent of fire departments have only organizations. These reductions in relative employment in models with total expenditures held constant are particularly large in the functions with fewer employees: organizations cause losses equal to 23.2 percent of mean sanitation employment and 13.5 percent of mean employment in streets and highways.

This budgeting model differs from the single-equation models in that it estimates union effects on higher levels of municipal finance. Their effects on function expenditures are important. The coefficients in column (3) demonstrate that bargaining units have significant positive effects on expenditures in all four functions, holding municipal general expenditures constant. These effects are large; equivalent to at least 5.1 percent of mean expenditures in the case of police, and to as much as 16.2 percent in the case of sanitation.

The equation for general expenditures in this system includes variables for bargaining units and organizations in all four functions. Estimated union effects on general expenditures are inconclusive. The point estimates given in column (4) vary erratically in sign, magnitude, and significance. They sum approximately to zero. However, all eight variables are jointly significant in the equation. These estimates seem to indicate that municipal unions do have significant effects on general expenditures, but that these effects are not well captured by a specification that attributes separate effects to each bargaining unit and organization. These coefficients do suggest, however, that union-induced increases in function expenditures do not cause increases in general expenditures. They may, instead, cause reallocations of general expenditures away from other functions.

If the budgeting process is recursive, as specified in the model from which these estimates are taken, then the estimated union effects in column (2) indicate that the effects of unions on employment, through union activity at the lowest level of the process, are to reduce employment in return for compensation gains. The positive union function expenditure effects of column (3) suggest that the indirect effects of union participation in the budgeting process at the function expenditure level may be responsible for the positive union employment effects observed in the single-equation models. These "indirect budgetary" effects on compensation and employment are the product of union effects on function expenditures, and function expenditure effects on function compensation and employment, as given by:

$$(3) \qquad \frac{\partial(\text{Pay or Emp})}{\partial U} = \frac{\partial(\text{Function Expenditure})}{\partial U}$$
$$\cdot \frac{\partial(\text{Pay or Emp})}{\partial(\text{Function Expenditure})}.$$

Similarly, the consequence of the union effects on general expenditures for employment and compensation outcomes is given by the product of union effects on general expenditures, general expenditure effects on function expenditures, and function expenditure effects on function compensation and employment, as given by:

$$(4) \qquad \frac{\partial(\text{Pay or Emp})}{\partial U} = \frac{\partial(\text{General Expenditure})}{\partial U}$$
$$\cdot \frac{\partial(\text{Function Expenditure})}{\partial(\text{General Expenditure})} \cdot \frac{\partial(\text{Pay or Emp})}{\partial(\text{Function Expenditure})}.$$

According to equations (3) and (4), then, estimates of general expenditure effects on function expenditures, and of function expenditure effects on function compensation and employment, are needed to calculate total union effects. The estimated relationships between general expenditures and expenditures in these four central functions, and between function expenditures and compensation or employment, are significant but not particularly large in absolute terms. Function expenditure effects on compensation and employment, for example, are uniformly positive and significant, with t-statistics exceeding 9.00. Coefficients on the function expenditure variable in compensation equations vary from 0.000307 to 0.000856. With respect to employment, coefficients on function expenditure variables vary from 0.00000373 to 0.0000302. Together, estimated compensation and employment effects imply elasticities of monthly payrolls per capita (compensation per employee per month multiplied by employees per capita) with respect to annual function expenditures that are similar across functions, varying from 0.025 in streets and highways to 0.071 in fire, at mean levels of compensation and employment. Multiplying these elasticities of monthly payrolls by twelve yields elasticities of 0.301 and 0.857 for annual payrolls.[9]

Similarly, general expenditure has uniformly positive and significant effects (all t-statistics exceed 7.00) on expenditures in each of the four functions. These effects indicate that an additional dollar of general expenditure results in additional sanitation expenditures of $0.013, additional fire expenditures of $0.0296, additional police expenditures of $0.0394, and additional streets and highways expenditures of $0.0570. These effects are equivalent to elasticities ranging from 0.24 for sanitation to 0.51 for streets and highways at mean expenditure values.

These relatively low elasticities indicate that union effects on both function and general expenditures will be dampened as they are transmitted through to changes in compensation and employment. Table 12.5 presents the indirect budgetary effects of unions on compensation and employment as calculated from equations (3) and (4). Table 12.5 also lists the "direct effects" of unions on pay and employment in equations that hold general and function expenditures constant (presented previously in table 12.4, columns 1 and 2). The total effect of unions on pay or employment is the sum of the direct effect and the two indirect budgetary effects.

First, the indirect effects on compensation and employment through general expenditures (labeled "Indirect Effect—General Exp.") are uniformly small in comparison to direct effects.[10] Similarly, there is a dampening of the effect of bargaining units on function expenditures before it finally influences compensation outcomes. Nevertheless, these effects (displayed in row 7 of table 12.5, labeled "Indirect Effect—Function Exp.") remain substantial. All indirect effects of bargaining units through function expenditures are positive on compensation, reinforcing the direct effects of unions on compensation. This indirect bargaining unit effect is smallest for police, at 27 percent of the direct union compensation effect. For streets and highways, it attains 76 percent of the direct effect.

Table 12.5 Total Union Effects on Own Payroll Per Employee and Employment Per Capita (total effect as percentage of mean of dependent variable in brackets)

	I. Streets and Highways		II. Police		III. Fire		IV. Sanitation	
	Effect on Payroll Per Employee	Effect on Employment Per 10,000 Capita	Effect on Payroll Per Employee	Effect on Employment Per 10,000 Capita	Effect on Payroll Per Employee	Effect on Employment Per 10,000 Capita	Effect on Payroll Per Employee	Effect on Employment Per 10,000 Capita
Organization:								
1. Indirect Effect—General Exp.	−0.243	−0.00295	−3.88	−0.178	9.1	0.328	0.916	0.0622
2. Indirect Effect—Function Exp.	15.1	0.183	3.64	0.167	−16.2	−0.573	3.39	0.230
3. Direct Effect	18.6	−1.33	42.0	−0.342	83.2	−0.534	41.2	−2.19
4. Total Effect	33.5	−1.15	41.8	−0.353	76.3	−0.779	45.5	−1.90
5. Percent of mean of payroll or employment variable	[0.038]	[−0.117]	[0.030]	[−0.014]	[0.053]	[−0.042]	[0.042]	[−0.203]
Bargaining Units:								
6. Indirect Effect—General Exp.	−1.71	−0.0208	1.31	0.0600	3.66	0.129	−0.644	−0.0437
7. Indirect Effect—Function Exp.	19.1	0.232	16.0	0.732	33.5	1.18	12.7	0.862
8. Direct Effect	25.1	0.312	59.8	−1.73	67.8	−0.573	29.1	−0.384
9. Total Effect	42.5	0.523	77.1	−0.938	105.0	0.736	41.2	0.434
10. Percent of mean of payroll or employment variable	[0.030]	[0.053]	[0.056]	[−0.038]	[0.073]	[0.040]	[0.038]	[0.047]

Equally important, the indirect effects of bargaining units on employment through expenditures are always positive. In the cases of fire and sanitation, positive indirect union employment effects through function expenditures exceed in absolute value the negative direct union employment effects. This produces a net positive effect of bargaining units on employment. In streets and highways, positive indirect effects reinforce positive direct effects. As in the single-equation results of table 12.2, only in police is the net bargaining unit effect on employment negative. For police, the indirect union effect through police expenditures increases employment, but not by enough to nullify the large negative direct union effect.

Indirect effects of organizations through function expenditures are similar to those of bargaining units, but less striking. These indirect effects of organizations on compensation and employment are positive, with the exception of fire fighters. The indirect effects of organizations on compensation are less pronounced than they are for bargaining units. The positive employment effects of organizations through function expenditures are not large enough to reverse negative direct employment effects of organizations for streets and highways, police, and sanitation.

The results obtained from the recursive model of municipal budgeting contain several important insights into the effects of municipal unions. First, unions directly increase compensation and reduce employment when function expenditures are held constant, though union employment effects are positive when function expenditures are not controlled. Second, unions have positive effects on expenditures in their respective functions. Third, for all forms of unionization in all functions (except for the relatively uncommon fire fighter "organization"), there are positive function expenditure effects of unions that increase the demand for labor. The "indirect budgetary" effects of bargaining units are large enough to reverse the negative direct effects of bargaining units on employment in all functions except police.

12.4.2   Cross-Department Union Effects

The recursive thirteen-equation system that generates the results in tables 12.4 and 12.5 is reestimated to allow cross-department spillover effects. Columns (1)–(4) of table 12.6 present the coefficients on all functions' bargaining unit and organization variables in compensation equations for the four functions. The coefficients along the diagonal of columns (1)–(4) correspond to direct "own-department" effects. The coefficients in columns (1)–(4) suggest that police unionization has the strongest effect on compensation in all municipal functions; that is, in all four functions' compensation equations, the coefficient on the police bargaining unit variable is larger than any of the other union variables' coefficients. This suggests that police unionization is

Table 12.6   The Effect of Unions on Payroll Per Employee and Employee Per 10,000 Capita in Own and Other Departments, Estimates from Recursive System of Equations (*t*-statistics in parentheses)

	Payroll Per Employee			
Union Measure	(1) Streets and Highways	(2) Police	(3) Fire	(4) Sanitation
Streets B. U.	72.96** (2.25)	106.32*** (3.40)	93.34** (2.49)	84.49*** (2.76)
Streets Org.	53.09* (1.86)	72.63*** (2.60)	64.70* (1.93)	62.85** (2.29)
Police B. U.	113.42*** (3.78)	110.80*** (3.70)	201.40*** (5.69)	117.46*** (4.04)
Police Org.	121.69*** (3.39)	91.20** (2.54)	130.67*** (3.07)	107.55*** (3.11)
Fire B. U.	56.94** (1.96)	67.39** (2.35)	46.93 (1.35)	80.79*** (2.87)
Fire Org.	9.08 (0.28)	35.55 (1.12)	61.53 (1.59)	− 17.51 (0.56)
Sanitation B. U.	30.00 (0.94)	16.01 (0.50)	5.04 (0.13)	− 2.41 (0.08)
Sanitation Org.	− 15.78 (0.60)	5.04 (0.19)	8.01 (0.26)	2.40 (0.09)

Note: Specification of equations and control variables are described by figure 12.2. B. U. = bargaining unit; Org. = organization.
***Significant at the .01 level, two-tailed test.
**Significant at the .05 level, two-tailed test.
*Significant at the .10 level, two-tailed test.

a critical determinant of compensation of all functions' employees, not just police. Unionization in streets and highways also has important effects on compensation elsewhere. Fire-fighter unionization is less influential, as measured by its effects on own compensation levels and on the compensation levels in other functions. Unions in sanitation have the least pronounced effects on other departments.

The results in table 12.6 demonstrate that, in this specification, unionization in two of the four functions, police and streets and highways, has significant positive effects on compensation levels in their own departments. In both, own compensation effects are larger than those reported in table 12.4, column (1), where no cross-departmental spillover effects were allowed. The positive effects of fire bargaining units and organizations on own compensation are approximately one-quarter less than those of table 12.4 and insignificant. Unionization in sanitation

Table 12.6   (continued)

	Employees Per 10,000 Capita			
	(5) Streets and Highways	(6) Police	(7) Fire	(8) Sanitation
	1.24**	−1.00*	−0.780	−2.73***
	(2.30)	(1.67)	(1.26)	(5.09)
	−0.557	−0.885	−0.490	−2.30***
	(1.15)	(1.64)	(0.88)	(4.80)
	−2.54***	−1.00***	−3.15***	−1.79***
	(4.94)	(5.04)	(5.35)	(3.52)
	−2.10***	−0.774	−0.154	−2.14***
	(3.47)	(1.13)	(0.22)	(3.56)
	−0.815	−0.781	0.362	−2.01***
	(1.64)	(1.41)	(0.63)	(4.09)
	−0.139	−0.564	−0.816	0.0276
	(0.25)	(0.92)	(1.29)	(0.05)
	0.937*	−0.430	−0.902	1.97***
	(1.72)	(0.70)	(1.43)	(3.62)
	0.0336	−0.538	−1.15**	0.00914
	(0.07)	(1.07)	(2.22)	(0.02)

has own compensation effects that are not significantly different from zero.

The off-diagonal elements in columns (1)–(4) of table 12.6 suggest several conclusions about spillover effects on compensation. First, these spillovers are positive. Only 2 out of 24 estimated cross effects are negative. Both are insignificant. The compensation spillover effects attributable to police unionization are most striking. Police bargaining units and organizations significantly increase compensation in all other functions. In addition, the effects of police unionization on compensation in any function are larger than the effects of unionization in any other function, including own-unionization. Similarly, unionization in streets and highways has positive effects on own and other compensation, but the effects of streets and highways unions are smaller and less significant than the effects of police unionization. Fire unionization is less influential; only fire bargaining units have significant spillovers, in all cases smaller than those attributable to bargaining units in streets and highways. Sanitation unionization, which has no effect on sanitation employees' compensation, has no effects on compensation in any other function. Sanitation compensation levels are significantly increased by unionization in all other functions, but not by own unionization. This categorization of spillover strengths suggests that police unionization has the most important implications for the compensation of employees in other functions, followed by unionization in streets and highways, and then by unionization in fire. Sanitation unionization is of little importance in the determination of the compensation levels of municipal employees.

Coefficients for employment spillovers reported in columns (5)–(8) of table 12.6 also reveal a consistent pattern. All but one union variable in equations for other-function employment (i.e., the off-diagonal elements) have negative coefficients. The one positive coefficient is insignificant. Of the 23 negative cross effects, 9 are significant at the 5 percent level, another 2 at the 10 percent level. These negative employment spillovers are the natural counterparts of positive compensation spillovers.

Cross-function union employment effects are analogous to cross-function union compensation effects in another respect; they exhibit the same ordering of functions by union influence. Again, the effects of police unionization on employment in all functions are most striking. Police bargaining units significantly and substantially reduce employment in all functions. Bargaining units in streets and highways increase own employment—though by much less than it is reduced when police have either a bargaining unit or an organization. A streets and highways bargaining unit also reduces police and sanitation employment. In contrast to compensation equations, sanitation unionization has some impacts on employment in own and other functions. However, as with sanitation compensation, spillovers from unionization in other departments are important in the determination of sanitation employment. Sanitation employment is greatly reduced by bargaining units in any other function and by organizations in either streets and highways or police.

The results reported in table 12.6 demonstrate that *union compensation and employment spillovers are important in municipal labor markets.* Compensation spillovers are positive, and employment spillovers are negative, as in the single-equation estimates of table 12.3. Police unions dominate these spillovers, perhaps as a consequence of their public prominence and market power.[11]

12.4.3   Mutually Endogenous Dependent Variables

The model of the budgeting process used to obtain the results in tables 12.4–12.6 is restrictive in that decisions at lower levels of municipal finance are made only after decisions at higher, more aggregate levels. This ordering prohibits budgeting "feedback" which may, in practice, be important. For example, given a predetermined value for general expenditures, a strong department may be able to capture such a large share that it compels the city to increase general expenditures above the limits originally set. Here, general expenditures should be modeled as dependent on function expenditures at the same time that function expenditures are dependent on general expenditures. A strong union might be so successful in obtaining payroll increases that function expenditures have to be increased. In this example, function expenditures, function compensation, and function employment are mutually dependent.

Statistically, the system of exclusions among exogenous variables depicted in figure 12.2 provides sufficient identification to remove these restrictions in the recursive model. The validity of the specified endogeneities can also be tested statistically. Such tests, in themselves, are uninformative with regard to the effects of unions on compensation, employment, and municipal finance. However, it is important to compare the union coefficients in the recursive system above to those obtained from respecifications that permit mutual endogeneity to check whether the union effects in the recursive system are merely artifacts of endogeneities that the recursive model suppresses. If the description of union behavior implied by the recursive model is correct, union coefficients should change predictably as the interactions allowed between dependent variables increase. In particular, compensation equations should show reduced union effects when employment levels are included among the explanatory variables. Union compensation effects should be smaller in this specification because it holds the level of employment constant, when in fact unions achieve their effects at this level by accepting employment reductions. Similarly, the negative union employment effects of the recursive system should be reduced or removed when compensation is held constant. In the absence of compensation increases, unions have no reason to permit employment reductions.

Table 12.7 presents own union coefficients with respect to compensation and employment from a specification including own function employment in compensation equations and own function compensation in employment equations. In addition, general expenditures, as well as own function expenditures, are among the explanatory variables for compensation and employment.[12] The comparisons of these coefficients with those of table 12.4 are entirely consistent with the above predictions. Union effects on compensation are generally smaller and less significant when employment is held constant than when it is not controlled. In all functions, the effects of at least one form of

Table 12.7   **Effects of Own Unionization on Own Payroll Per Employee and Employment Per 10,000 Capita[a] (t-statistics in parentheses)**

Union Measure	Effect on Own Compensation	Effect on Own Employment
Streets B. U.	121.25***	1.90***
	(5.37)	(5.14)
Streets Org.	4.52	−0.0125
	(0.25)	(0.04)
Police B. U.	2.96	0.0494
	(0.21)	(0.17)
Police Org.	45.30**	0.922**
	(2.06)	(2.08)
Fire B. U.	52.63***	0.850***
	(3.00)	(2.87)
Fire Org.	71.22***	1.18***
	(3.18)	(3.11)
Sanitation B. U.	46.56**	0.807**
	(2.07)	(1.96)
Sanitation Org.	−35.42**	−0.694**
	(2.19)	(2.36)

Notes: B. U. = bargaining unit; Org. = organization.

[a]These estimates are taken from a system of equations that permit complete mutual endogeneity among the dependent variables. See text for complete discussion.

***Significant at the 0.01 level, two-tailed test.

**Significant at the 0.05 level, two-tailed test.

*Significant at the 0.10 level, two-tailed test.

unionization on employment are significantly positive when compensation is held constant, while all significant employment effects are negative when it is not.

Statistically, this model severely restricts union activity along all dimensions of the pay determination process. A union in this model affects payroll expenditures only through transfers from other factors used in the function. In one sense, the effects in table 12.7 suggest that, with general expenditures, function expenditures, and employment held constant, municipal unions still have sufficient strength to achieve positive compensation gains. With general expenditures, function expenditures, and compensation held constant, unions are still able to increase employment.[13]

In sum, union direct effects on compensation and employment in models with mutual endogeneity among all dependent variables reinforce the description of direct union effects on compensation and employment obtained from the simpler recursive system of equations. Own union and cross-union effects differ between the recursive and completely endogenous systems, but they differ as predicted under the assumption that, at the level of compensation and employment determination, municipal unions demand higher compensation and accept lower employment levels. In conjunction with single-equation estimates of positive union employment effects, these results provide further support for the conclusion that unions achieve employment gains through increases in demand for services rather than at the bargaining table. This is not to say that a bargaining unit does not obtain some work-force clauses in collective negotiations that serve to increase employment levels. However, such effects must coincide with increases in function expenditures that allow any such work-force clauses to increase the level of employment.

Union effects on function expenditures also depend on the specification of endogeneity. Equation systems including own function payrolls among explanatory variables for function expenditures enrich the description of union activity at this level of the budgeting process beyond that deduced from the recursive model. Own payrolls have significant positive effects (t-statistics all exceed 6.00) when included among explanatory variables for function expenditures. Their inclusion reduces own bargaining unit effects on function expenditures to insignificance. This change confirms that union-induced increases in function expenditures are principally devoted to funding higher payrolls; unions have positive effects when payrolls vary, but no effects when payrolls are held constant.

12.5 Conclusion

The principal theme emerging from the empirical evidence of this study is that municipal unions successfully employ a mix of strategies that rely on collective bargaining and political lobbying activity. Ultimately, this mix of strategies increases relative employment and compensation in the bargaining unit. The results are consistent with a strategy in which unions accept employment reductions in return for compensation increases in collective bargaining negotiations. However, their lobbying activity in the budgetary process has the effect of increasing own function expenditures and thereby increasing derived demand for their own services. This increase in derived demand raises the compensation of municipal employees beyond the increase won at the bargaining table. Furthermore, the increases in function expenditures lead to gains in employment that often exceed the losses in employment attributable to compensation gains won at the bargaining table. On net, then, public sector unions achieve both compensation and employment increases for their own departments. We do not rule out the possibility that these estimated effects are the result of specific contract clauses concerning compensation and employment negotiated at the bargaining table; still our results indicate that even if these contract clauses are sequentially determined first, there must be increases in budget appropriations at some point to accommodate the pay and employment increases.

The second major theme that emerges from this study is that when a municipal union pursues its distinctive strategy of bargaining and lobbying, it can have important implications for municipal employees in other departments. Specifically, bargaining units for police and streets and highways increase pay significantly in other departments as well as their own. For some functions, especially sanitation, these compensation spillover effects are larger than the effect that own unionization has on compensation. These positive pay spillovers coincide with relative reductions in employment levels.

Within this general pattern, we find that bargaining units in some functions achieve most of the increase in compensation through collective bargaining activity; in other functions increases in compensation are more a result of increases in function expenditures; while in still other functions, most of the increase in compensation comes from spillover effects from other functions' bargaining units. For example, while a bargaining unit in any function increases own function expenditures, police bargaining units increase police expenditures by only 5.1 percent of average police expenditures. In the other three functions, bargaining units increase function expenditures by 10.5 percent to 16.2 percent of the mean expenditure level. While police bargaining units have the smallest effect on function expenditures, they have the largest effect on compensation through collective bargaining. They also have the largest effects on other departments' compensation. Increases in the compensation attributable to such spillover effects are larger than those attributable to the direct effects of bargaining units for sanitation workers.

The implications of these effects of municipal unions for public welfare may be positive or negative. Public unions may be effective in pursuing this strategy, in part, because they are abetted by elected and appointed officials whose objectives also include larger government. Governmental unions may achieve these objectives, in part, because citizen-taxpayers on the demand side of markets for municipal services cannot effectively express preferences "at the margin" for smaller governments and fewer taxes. To the extent that municipal union compensation and employment gains rely on these characteristics of the political process, they are exploitative.

These are conventional objections to public sector unionism, but this characterization of the welfare implications of this study's findings may be misleading. Public unions may succeed in their objectives, in part, because organized public sector employees are better prepared than other citizens are to assess service needs and to ensure effective service provision. Citizens support municipal unions with greater expenditures, in appreciation of their contribution to citizen welfare. Expressed somewhat differently, it cannot be determined whether the observed levels of pay and employment in nonunion departments correspond to service levels consonant with taxpayers' desires or to service levels that fall short of desired levels.

This study indicates that the extensive research on the effects of public sector unions should not be interpreted within a "monopoly effects" model of unionism. Rather, in a sector of the economy with distinctive institutional features related to the budget-setting process, unions achieve their objectives by influencing budget expenditures and not just levels of pay.

Statistical Appendix

The *Census of Population and Housing, 1970,* provides all the demographic variables used in this paper: 1970 population; 1960–70 population increase (%); 1960–70 population decrease (%); 1970–80 population increase (%); 1970–80 population decrease (%); 1969 families below poverty level (%); 1969 median family income; 1970 median value, owner-occupied one family homes; 1970 units in one-unit structures (%); 1970 black population (%); 1970 Spanish population (%); 1970 population under 18 years of age (%); 1970 population over 65 years of age (%); 1970 median year of school; 1970 male operative median earnings; 1970 nonworkers/worker ratio; 1970 persons over 23 years of age with more than 3 years high school (%); 1970 white-collar occupations (%); 1970 foreign stock (%).

Annual *Survey of Government* and *Census of Government* published by the U.S. Bureau of the Census report organization and bargaining characteristics of city employees by function, expenditures by function, full-time employment and monthly payroll by function. This information provides the following variables: dummy for streets organization, dummy for police organization, dummy for fire organization, dummy for sanitation organization; dummy for streets bargaining unit, dummy for police bargaining unit, dummy for fire bargaining unit, dummy for sanitation bargaining unit; October payroll/employee, streets; October payroll/employee, police; October payroll/employee, fire; October payroll/employee, sanitation; employment/10,000 capita, streets; employment/10,000 capita, police; employment/10,000 capita, fire; employment/10,000 capita, sanitation; October payroll per 10,000 capita, streets;

October payroll per 10,000 capita, police; October payroll per 10,000 capita, fire; October payroll per 10,000 capita, sanitation; annual expenditures for streets/10,000 capita; annual expenditures for police/ 10,000 capita; annual expenditures for fire/10,000 capita; annual expenditures for sanitation/10,000 capita; and annual general expenditures/10,000 capita.

Two private data sets of the International City Management Association describe local governments. The 1981 "Form of Governments Survey" provides the following variables: years since government form adoption, administration by city manager, nonpartisan city council elections, percent of city council at-large, and direct election of mayor. Its master file of American cities identifies cities in the categories of central city, suburban city, or independent city.

The National Bureau of Economic Research has compiled state laws governing local public sector unionization, as described by Valleta and Freeman (this volume, appendix B). This data set includes descriptions of legal bargaining rights, representation rights, and scope of bargaining for police, fire, and all other employees. This study characterizes the state legal environment with six dummy variables drawn from this compilation: strikes permitted, arbitration available, duty to bargain, bargaining permitted, no legal provisions for bargaining, state has right-to-work law. Variables for police and fire functions describe function-specific laws. Variables for sanitation and other noneducation functions describe the general laws for all other employees.

Notes

1. Local governments are more likely than not to have a civil service procedure. Unions will lobby civil service boards by introducing information during hearings on such matters as what comparison groups will be used in the calculation of "prevailing wages" (Lewin 1983, 133–34).

2. For example, Kochan (1974, 533) found that fire fighters in Madison, Wisconsin, were able to restore parity with police through a civil service board ruling after they had failed to obtain this objective in collective bargaining.

3. Cities that changed their form of government after 1977 are excluded from the sample.

4. Finance variables are drawn from a different data set, the U.S. Census of Governments Annual Survey of Finance. Complete data are not available for all cities included in the analysis of the previous section. The sample size for analyses described in this section is 336 municipalities, each with four functions, in each of five years.

5. Cities must ordinarily run a balanced budget on current account.

6. Municipal output measures are notoriously scarce and imperfect. None are available that cover the range of cities, functions, and years analyzed here.

7. Compensation and employment equations reported here also omit government structure, time, and geographic dummy variables. These exclusions are not necessary for identification of the equation systems.

8. Importantly, these are not arithmetic identities that cause a given variable (e.g., unionization) to have effects with opposite signs on pay and employment once function expenditures are held constant. Specifically, the total functions expenditure variable includes nonpayroll as well as payroll expenditures. In all four functions, there is a significant amount of variation in the payroll's share of total expenditures.

9. The Governments Division of the U.S. Census Bureau warns that the product of twelve and the payrolls in the surveyed month may not be a satisfactory estimate of annual payrolls.

10. In addition, most of the effects labeled "Indirect Effect—General Exp." are based on union coefficients in general expenditure equations that are individually insignificant. See table 12.4, column (4).

11. Union spillovers might also occur in the determination of function expenditures. However, when the recursive model that generates the estimates in table 12.6 is respecified to include measures of unionization in all functions among the exogenous variables in each equation for function expenditures, no particular pattern for the union variables in other departments' total expenditure equations is revealed. Importantly, union coefficients in compensation and employment equations are essentially unaffected by this respecification. The function expenditure equations do show some evidence of spillovers at this level of the budgetary process between police and fire, and between streets and highways and sanitation.

12. The particular specification from which these coefficients are taken permits complete mutual endogeneities: expenditures and payrolls in the four functions are among the explanatory variables for general expenditures; general expenditures and own function payrolls are among the explanatory variables for function expenditures; general expenditures and own function expenditures are among the explanatory variables for compensation and employment; and own compensation and own employment levels appear in each other's equation. This system is estimated using the three-stage least-squares technique. Employment variables in compensation equations and compensation variables in employment equations are all negative, with t-statistics exceeding 40. Estimated elasticities of employment with respect to compensation are -1.13 for police, -1.28 for fire, -1.66 for streets and highways, and -1.92 for sanitation.

13. This pattern of coefficients on the own unionization variables is virtually unaffected when the model is expanded to allow spillovers from other departments' bargaining units in the compensation and employment equations. The magnitudes of the spillover effects, as with the direct effects, are smaller in this model—in which employment is held constant in compensation equations, and compensation is held constant in employment equations—than they were in table 12.6. They are rarely significant. A few of the significant spillovers are of opposite sign of those in table 12.6. With own employment held constant, compensation spillovers can be negative; with own compensation held constant, employment spillovers can be positive. Put differently, the changes observed in the pattern of spillover coefficients (once employment is held constant in compensation equations and compensation is held constant in employment equations) are consistent with the hypotheses that spillovers work by reducing employment in order to match compensation levels in other departments.

References

Courant, Paul N., Edward M. Gramlich, and Daniel L. Rubinfeld. 1979. Public employee market power and the level of government spending. *American Economic Review* 69(5):806–16.

Craft, James A. 1970. Public employee budget negotiations: Budget search and bargaining behavior. *Public Personnel Review* 31(4):244–49.

Derber, Milton, Ken Jennings, Ian McAndrew, and Martin Wagner. 1973. Bargaining and budget making in Illinois public institutions. *Industrial and Labor Relations Review* 27(1):49–62.

Dunlop, John T. 1944. *Wage determination under trade unions*. New York: Macmillan.

Edwards, Linda N., and Franklin R. Edwards. 1982. Public union, local government structure and the compensation of municipal sanitation workers. *Economic Inquiry* 20(3):405–25.

Ehrenberg, Ronald G. 1973. Municipal government structure, unionization, and the wages of fire fighters. *Industrial and Labor Relations Review* 27(1):36–48.

Ehrenberg, Ronald G., and Joshua Schwarz. 1983. Public sector labor markets. NBER Working Paper no. 1179. Cambridge, Mass.: National Bureau of Economic Research.

Fellner, William. 1947. Prices and wages under bilateral monopoly. *Quarterly Journal of Economics* 61:502–32.

Freeman, Richard B. 1986. Unionism comes to the public sector. *Journal of Economic Literature* 24(1):41–86.

Gallagher, Daniel. 1978. Teachers bargaining and school district expenditure. *Industrial Relations* 17(2):231–37.

Hall, Robert E., and David Lilien. 1979. Efficient wage bargains under uncertain supply and demand. *American Economic Review* 69(5):868–79.

Henkel, Jan W., and Normal J. Wood. 1982. Collective bargaining by state workers: Legislators have the final voice in the appropriation of funds. *Journal of Collective Negotiation* 11(3):215–23.

Horton, Raymond D., David Lewin, and James Kuhn. 1976. Some impacts of collective bargaining on local government: A diversity thesis. *Administration and Society* 7(4):497–516.

Kochan, Thomas A. 1974. A theory of multilateral collective bargaining in city governments. *Industrial and Labor Relations Review* 27(4):525–42.

Labor Management Relations Service. 1972. The role of politics in local labor relations: A special report based on a survey of 78 U.S. cities. LMRS Special Report, U.S. Department of Labor. Washington, D.C.: Government Printing Office.

Lewin, David. 1973. Wage parity and the supply of police and firemen. *Industrial Relations* 12(1):77–85.

———. 1974. The prevailing-wage principle and public wage decisions. *Public Personnel Management* 3(6):473–85.

———. 1977. Public sector labor relations. *Labor History* 18(1):133–43.

———. 1983. The effects of civil service systems and unionism on pay outcomes in the public sector. In *Advances in industrial and labor relations,* ed. David P. Lipsky and Joel M. Douglas, vol. 1, 131–61. Greenwich, Conn.: JAI Press Inc.

McDonald, Ian M., and Robert M. Solow. 1981. Wage bargaining and employment. *American Economic Review* 71(5):896–908.

Methe, David T., and James L. Perry. 1980. The impacts of collective bargaining on local government services: A review of the research. *Public Administration Review* 40(4):359–71.

Mitchell, Daniel J. B. 1978. Collective bargaining and wage determination in the public sector: Is Armageddon really at hand? *Public Personnel Management* 7(2):80–95.

Moskow, Michael H., J. Joseph Lowenberg, and Edward Koziara. 1970. *Collective bargaining in public employment*. New York: Random House.

Niskanen, William A. 1975. Bureaucrats and politicians. *Journal of Law and Economics* 18(3):617–43.

Ott, Mach. 1980. Bureaucracy, monopoly, and the demand for municipal services. *Journal of Urban Economics* 18(3):362–82.

Stanley, David T. 1972. *Managing local government under union pressure*. Washington, D.C.: The Brookings Institution.

U.S. Bureau of the Census. 1978, 1979, 1980. *Annual survey of governments*. Washington, D.C.: Government Printing Office (GPO).

———. 1977 and 1982. *Census of governments*. Washington, D.C.: GPO.

———. 1970. *Census of population and housing*. Washington, D.C.: GPO.

Victor, R. B. 1977. The effects of unionism on wage and employment levels of police and firefighters. Santa Monica, Calif.: The Rand Corporation.

Zax, Jeffrey. 1985a. Municipal employment, municipal unions and demand for municipal services. NBER Working Paper no. 1728. Cambridge, Mass.: National Bureau of Economic Research.

———. 1985b. Economic effects of municipal government institutions. NBER Working Paper no. 1657. Cambridge, Mass.: National Bureau of Economic Research.

Comment   Harry J. Holzer

The paper by Jeffrey Zax and Casey Ichniowski is very appealing for a variety of reasons. They present some very straightforward hypotheses on a fundamentally important issue with regards to public sector unionism. These hypotheses are first supported by evidence from the institutional literature on municipal government and union political activities. They are then tested very thoroughly in a variety of statistical formats. It should also be noted that the authors themselves put together the very impressive set of data on municipal unionism which they used in their analysis (see appendix A, this volume).

By and large, I found the results of this work quite convincing. The evidence on own-union and cross-union wage and employment effects in the single-equation (reduced-form) estimates is fairly strong and seems robust.

With regards to the multiple-equations estimates (both recursive and simultaneous), I have a few more reservations. In particular, the use

Harry J. Holzer is assistant professor of economics at Michigan State University and a faculty research fellow of the National Bureau of Economic Research.

of own-service expenditures as a control variable in wage and employment equations may be problematic. The authors interpret this measure as a proxy for total value of output in that service, which in turn should reflect the shifts in demand that municipal unions are hypothetically causing through their political efforts. Indeed, the inclusion of this variable in the employment equations turns the original positive estimate of own-union effects into a negative one in most cases. However, it is at least possible that most of the variance in expenditures represents variance in employment for that service. If this is the case, the strong positive correlation between expenditures and both unions and employment may be causing the negative estimate of the union employment effect in these equations. It also may be causing the large demand elasticities (see Zax and Ichniowski, note 12) observed in the simultaneous equations. (On the other hand, the negative cross-union effects on employment observed even in the reduced-form estimates suggest that demand effects are not all spurious.)

The doubts I have about the existence of these negative employment effects in the own-union context raise another question in my mind: Is the labor demand framework the correct one for analyzing these issues? While the authors briefly mention the "efficient contracts" notion, it may deserve more consideration. This framework provides an alternative explanation for the absence of observed negative employment effects of unions—namely, that outcomes lie on a "contract curve" for bargaining which is not negatively sloped. If the latter is true, it would suggest that union work rules and other contract clauses are responsible for the observed union-employment relationship rather than their political activities. Sorting out these interpretations would require data on such activities as well as on nonwage components of union contracts. While obviously beyond the scope of this paper, it seems a worthwhile topic for further research.

Given the data that the authors have collected, a few other recommendations can be made. While the authors occasionally mention the correlations in unionization across services of the same city, a full listing of these (or of conditional probabilities of unionism in each function given that it is present in others) would have been quite useful. For it is possible that the absence of significant union effects on general expenditures might reflect multicollinearity between the union variables. An aggregate measure of municipal unionism (e.g., a weighted average across the four functions) might have been more appropriate in this case. Estimation of employment effects, with and without the legal measures included, would also have provided a direct test of whether or not the unions' political activities are the source of their ability to maintain employment despite rising wages. Finally, the authors might have made better use of the panel nature of their data by estimating some fixed-effect equations for wages and employment. These equations would have eliminated at least some of the unobserved characteristics of cities (e.g., tastes for municipal services) which might be correlated with both unionism and those outcomes.

Having said this, I emphasize once again that the analysis presented presents several important and relatively convincing findings. I commend the authors for their efforts.

Appendix A
Collective Organization of Labor in the Public Sector

Richard B. Freeman, Casey Ichniowski,
and Jeffrey Zax

Between 1960 and 1980 the public sector in the United States experienced a dramatic spurt in unionism, which changed it from one of the least organized to one of the most heavily organized parts of the economy. What is the current extent of public sector organization in this country? Has the dramatic spurt leveled off or been reversed? How do organized public sector workers and jurisdictions differ from unorganized workers and jurisdictions?

These basic questions are not easy to answer. Unlike the private sector where the National Labor Relations Act (NLRA) and Railway Labor Act (RLA) provide standardized federal-level criteria for defining the existence and activities of unions, there are vast differences in public sector labor laws across states, occupations, and time which lead to considerable differences in the meaning of public employee "unionism" or "bargaining." For example, some state laws prohibit employees from striking and provide no alternative mechanism for resolving bargaining impasses. Other laws permit the right to strike or provide dispute resolution mechanisms, such as mediation, fact-finding, or arbitration. Still others outlaw public employee bargaining altogether. Federal policy permits federal employee bargaining, but in most cases not over wages. While collective bargaining resulting in written

Richard B. Freeman is professor of economics at Harvard University and a research associate of the National Bureau of Economic Research. Casey Ichniowski is associate professor of the Graduate School of Administration of Columbia University and faculty research fellow of the National Bureau of Economic Research. Jeffrey Zax is assistant professor of economics at Queens College, City University of New York, and research economist of the National Bureau of Economic Research.

The authors would like to thank Roo Canfield, Leslie Kimerling, Seung Lim, John Smith, and Robert Valletta for valuable research assistance on this paper.

contracts exists in all such environments—even where the state law outlaws bargaining—these differences in labor laws radically alter the meaning of public sector "unionism." Moreover, in contrast to private sector unions, many public sector labor organizations have dues-paying members who are not covered by bargaining agreements.

To deal with these problems and to develop a better picture of union organization in the public sector, this appendix presents a comprehensive analysis of the basic quantitative data on collective organization in the public sector. Section I describes the major institutions involved in public sector labor relations. Section II assesses the sources of data on public sector unionism and contrasts the levels and trends in the public sector unionization from these sources. Section III summarizes information on organization by level of government, occupation, and type of labor law. Finally, section IV considers differences in the characteristics of organized and unorganized workers and jurisdictions and explores the relationship between unionism and selected economic outcomes.

I. Organizations and Institutions Involved in Public Sector Labor Relations

As in the private sector, three types of institutions are involved in labor relations in the public sector: labor organizations, management organizations, and governmental agencies that oversee the unionization and collective bargaining process.

Labor Organizations

Table 1 records the membership in labor organizations with a large representation in the public sector in 1982–85, using data from the Bureau of National Affairs (BNA), the *Union Sourcebook,* and information obtained directly from largely private sector unions on their public sector membership. The majority of public sector workers who are members of labor organizations are in organizations serving well-defined groups of public employees. In jurisdictional terms, many are more like craft than industrial labor organizations, being organized along occupational lines (i.e., separate unions for postal workers, teachers, police, fire fighters, and nurses). Membership includes an exceptionally large number of white-collar workers, even if one excludes teachers. Some public sector labor organizations, such as unions of federal employees outside the postal service or federal authorities, cannot legally sign agreements covering wages and fringe benefits; while some state and local government employees cannot legally enter into a collective bargaining agreement of any kind.[1]

Table 1   **The Public Sector Unions, 1982–85**

	BNA Reported Membership	Sourcebook Reported Membership
Teachers		
American Federation of Teachers	573,644	458,630
National Education Association	1,641,168	1,443,970
American Association of University Professors	62,850	60,590
Public Safety		
International Association of Fire Fighters	162,792	155,930
Fraternal Order of Police	160,000	150,000
State and Local Government		
American Nurses Association	160,357	170,000
American Federation of State, County, and Municipal Employees	950,000	934,370
Assembly of Government Employees	250,000[a]	341,000
Primarily Private Sector		
Service Employees International Union (1986) including National Association of	450,000[a]	—
Government Employees which joined Service Employees in 1982	200,000	—
Teamsters (1985)	150,000[a]	—
Laborers (1985)	85,000[a]	—
Federal Non Postal		
American Federation of Government Employees	210,000	212,850
National Federation of Federal Employees	52,000	33,420
National Treasury Employee's Union	55,000	46,040
Postal and Federal	20,000	18,420
Postal Unions		
American Postal Workers Union	248,000	244,560
National Association of Letter Carriers	175,000	214,460

Sources: Bureau of National Affairs (1984, 13–43) and Troy and Sheflin (1985), unless otherwise noted.

Note: Numbers are rounded to nearest thousand.

[a]Estimates on the public sector membership in Service Employees International, Teamsters, Laborers, and Assembly of Government Employees are from union officials.

Finally, some public sector labor organizations only serve as a kind of intermediate affiliation. For example, the International Brotherhood of Police Officers (IBPO) members actually paid dues to the National Association of Government Employees (NAGE) with whom IBPO was affiliated until 1982. After 1982, IBPO members were affiliated with Service Employees International Union (SEIU) since NAGE was absorbed by SEIU. There are also umbrella organizations at the national level. For example, many municipal police who are already members of local- and state-level labor organizations may also belong to the International Union of Police Associations (IUPA)—an AFL-CIO affiliate that was chartered after the International Conference of Police Associations had dissolved over the issue of AFL-CIO affiliation (U.S. Bureau of Labor Statistics 1980, 51). Clearly, there may not be a straightforward answer to the question: "To what labor organization do you belong?" for the organized public employee.

Management Organizations

In government jurisdictions below the state level, managers also belong to state-level organizations. Municipal leagues, in particular, will often be involved in labor relations activities by collecting and disseminating data on pay and employment practices across local jurisdictions, sponsoring conference activity, and lobbying on behalf of management in state legislatures. According to information supplied by the International City Managers' Associations, all states except Hawaii have a Municipal League, such as the Alabama League of Municipalities or the Vermont League of Cities and Towns, and a City Managers Association, such as the Colorado Sector of the International City Management Association or the Tennessee City Management Association. In addition, separate organizations exist for specific classes of management officials. In Massachusetts, for example, there are separate state associations for city mayors, chief financial officers of municipalities, and towns' selectmen. Furthermore, there are regional associations for managers that span several states.

Government Agencies

States that regulate public sector collective bargaining have set up state public employment relations boards (PERBs) or similar organizations. These agencies are generally patterned closely after the National Labor Relations Board (NLRB), but in addition they often devote considerable time and effort to mediation, fact-finding, and arbitration of collective bargaining impasses. At the federal level, the key institutions in regulating labor relations are the Federal Labor Relations Authority (FLRA) and the Federal Services Impasses Panel. The FLRA determines units for purposes of representation, supervises elections, and judges charges of unfair labor practices, much as the NLRB does in the private sector. In addition, the FLRA also rules on disputes over which issues are subject to bargaining. The Federal Services Impasses Panel has the role of resolving disputes when negotiations break down. It can impose settlements when the federal union and governmental agency are unable to reach agreement, thereby providing the equivalent of compulsory arbitration in the federal sector (Levitan and Noden 1983).

II. Economy-Wide Estimates of Public Sector Unionism

There are four basic sources of data on organization in the public sector.

1. *Directory of National Unions and Employee Associations* (Bureau of Labor Statistics). Until 1981 the U.S. Bureau of Labor Statistics (BLS) gathered data on union membership from a questionnaire to national unions, employee associations, and AFL-CIO state organizations. The questionnaire asked for the "annual average dues-paying members" of the relevant organization as well as other data, including estimated membership by state and industry, and, in some years, numbers covered by collective bargaining agreements. From 1958 to 1968, the BLS data covered national and international "unions" only; in 1968, associations of professionals and of state public employees "believed to be engaged in collective bargaining or representational activities" were included in the BLS survey.

The Bureau of National Affairs (BNA) published the results of the 1981 BLS survey and conducted its own independent survey of labor organizations in 1983. These two BNA publications do not report separate statistics for the public sector. (They do, however, publish data for individual labor organizations, as presented in table 1, and evaluate the membership in those organizations with a large number of public employees.)

The BLS data have several drawbacks for gauging the extent of public sector organization. First, the survey excludes independent municipal and local government unions. If local government employees are not members of any of the national or international unions surveyed, they are not counted. The BLS estimated that in 1978 there were 235,000 local government employees who were members of such independent unions or associations (BLS 1980, 57)—or 3.9 percent of the total number of organized government employees estimated for the organizations that were surveyed by the BLS. This, however, is probably a considerable underestimate of the total number of members in unaffiliated labor organizations in 1978 given the crudeness of BLS's procedure to derive this figure.[2] As the BLS's reported public sector figures never include the estimates of such members in its totals of organized public employees, these figures underreport the level of membership.

A second major drawback with the BLS estimates is that the figures on public sector organization are derived from a question asking union officials for the "approximate percentage of all union members" in various industries. Officials' approximations of the percentage of their members in the government sector is a potentially sizeable source of error whose direction is unclear.

Third, errors could occur because the figures are reported by unions who may exaggerate their own strength; indeed, Thieblot's comparison of the numbers reported by unions to the BLS and to the AFL-CIO convention (on which they pay per capita dues) between 1965 and 1975 showed differences of 20 percent (Thieblot 1978). Such exaggeration may be particularly common in situations involving jurisdictional disputes between unions. For example, Thieblot reports that both the American Federation of Teachers and the National Education Association claimed New York's 200,000 teachers as members from 1972 to 1976.

Fourth, the BLS's distinction between "union" and "association" does not reflect a difference between bargaining and nonbargaining labor organizations. Specifically, membership of every labor organization is counted exclusively as either association or union membership. For example, the Fraternal Order of Police (FOP) is an "association," while the International Association of Fire Fighters (IAFF) is a "union." However, largely attributable to the differences in state collective bargaining laws, both the FOP and the IAFF have members who are and are not covered by collective bargaining agreements.

Finally, the BLS reports increased public sector membership over time as new labor organizations are added to the universe surveyed, not just because more employees joined a fixed number of organizations. (See for example note 3 of table 4 in BLS 1979, 57). The year that BLS adds an organization to the survey does not necessarily correspond to the initial charter of the organization, nor to the onset of bargaining within that organization.

Despite these drawbacks, the BLS surveys cover a large number of labor organizations and a lengthy time period. For many years they are the only basis for national estimates of unionization in the United States.

2. *Union Sourcebook* (Troy and Sheflin 1985). While the *Union Sourcebook* parallels the BLS survey in some respects and therefore suffers from some of the same limitations, it differs in other ways. The principal difference is that, in an attempt to provide "a consistent, objective basis for membership determination," Troy and Sheflin derive their figures largely from standardized, annual financial reports as required under the Labor Management Reporting and Disclosure Act of 1959 (LMRDA). The *Sourcebook* uses the ratio of total dues reported

by a union to a full-time member's dues rate to measure "the average annual, dues-paying, full-time equivalent membership."

There are two problems with this methodology. First, since unions do not report the proportion of dues paid by public as opposed to private sector workers, it is necessary to estimate the number of organized government workers who are members of predominantly private sector unions. Troy and Sheflin appear to use the unpublished "approximate percentage" estimates given in the 1979 BLS *Directory of National Unions* (1980) and apply those same percentages to the entire 1962–83 period. As described below, this fails to capture the growth in the share of certain unions' ranks coming from the public sector. Notable among these, the Service Employees International Union (SEIU) over the 1978 to 1983 period changes from a predominantly private sector union to a predominantly public sector union.[3]

The second problem is that labor organizations that are interstate in scope do not file financial records under LMRDA. In the *Sourcebook* an estimate of organized municipal employees who are not counted in the ranks of reporting unions is "derived by extending the percentage that such organizations represented of total union membership for a single year (obtained from a BLS survey of such organizations) to the years 1962–82" (Troy and Sheflin 1985, 3-3). From a review of the separate membership series reported in the *Sourcebook* for municipal and local organizations between 1962 and 1984 (Troy and Sheflin 1985, B-11), it appears that this means that the *Sourcebook* uses the same underestimate of unaffiliated local government membership from BLS Bulletin no. 1702 (1971), described above. In each year from 1962 to 1980, the total number of unaffiliated municipal and local members is approximately 5.6 percent of the total number of public sector members (Troy and Sheflin 1985, 3-20 and B-11). Again, this probably causes an underreporting of overall membership in state and local government. A conservative estimate of the magnitude of the underreporting of state and local government membership is 263,000 in 1982.[4] Moreover, if state and local government membership outside the surveyed unions was growing at a different rate from that in the surveyed unions, the growth rate in public sector membership is also biased.

In comparing the BLS and *Sourcebook* methods, there are reasons to expect that *Sourcebook* estimates of total membership in labor organizations in the government might be above or below BLS membership estimates. On the one hand, the *Sourcebook* estimates should be below BLS estimates since the *Sourcebook* reports "full-time equivalent" members and the BLS simply reports members. However, the *Sourcebook* identifies a significantly larger number of labor organizations than does the BLS—presumably through the LMRDA files—

which would cause *Sourcebook* figures to exceed those of the BLS. Finally, as with the BLS data, the *Sourcebook*'s distinction between "association" and "union" membership does not reflect a difference in bargaining and nonbargaining organizations.

3. *The Current Population Survey* (CPS). The CPS asks household respondents about the union status and collective bargaining coverage of persons in the household. Until 1976 the question was limited to unionization per se: "on this job, is . . . a member of a labor union?" In 1977, the phrase ". . . or employee association" was added to the question. Beginning in 1978, an additional question asked whether household members who did not belong to a union or association were covered by a collective bargaining agreement: "On this job, is . . . covered by a union or employee association contract?" From 1978 to 1981, "don't know" was considered a valid response; after 1981, respondents could not answer "don't know."

The major disadvantages of these data are: (1) the household respondent may not be fully aware of the union, association, or coverage status of other household members; (2) precise definitions of "union" and "association" are not given to respondents; (3) in no year can the extent of "union" membership be compared to the extent of "union or association" membership; (4) until 1983 it was not possible to determine the breakdown of public sector workers between state, local, and federal public employees outside of public administration; and (5) the coverage question is asked only of workers who are not members of unions or employee associations, which fails to account for the fact that in the public sector dues-paying members of labor organizations may not be covered by a collective bargaining agreement.

The CPS data have two advantages. They are obtained from a rigorous survey design—a particularly desirable feature when estimating the proportion of public employees who are members; and they contain diverse measures on individuals' demographic characteristics and economic status, so that personal correlates of unionism can be measured.

4. *Survey of Governments* (SOG), conducted by the U.S. Bureau of the Census. The Census Bureau has collected labor relations data by function of employee from: "a canvass of all State governments . . . all local governments which reported 50 or more full-time employees in the 1977 Census of Governments"; a subsample of the small governmental units that reported less than fifty employees; and data from the 1977 Census of Governments for unsurveyed small governments (U.S. Bureau of the Census 1980, 5).

The SOG is the only source that recognizes some of the features that distinguish public sector labor relations from private sector labor relations. It distinguishes coverage by contracts from membership in other types of "organizations"[5] that do not necessarily bargain. It does not erroneously assume that membership implies bargaining as the CPS does; nor does it assume that a given labor organization must be exclusively a "union" or exclusively an "association" as the BLS and *Sourcebook* do. In addition, it asks about "bargaining units" in the city,[6] numbers of contractual agreements, and "memoranda of understanding."

There are three basic problems with the SOG. First, the distinctions among different kinds of public sector labor organizations are not as detailed as would be desired. "Membership" in organizations that bargain for formal contracts is not assessed—only coverage; furthermore, it is not possible to obtain separate contract coverage estimates for specific functions or occupations within municipalities—only for the municipality.[7] Second, the SOG contains no information on the federal government. Third, employers' estimates of the degree to which their employees are members of labor organizations may be inaccurate. As reported with the analysis of SOG data tapes in section III, this appears to be an important source of error that tends to understate the level of organization in the public sector.

Economy-Wide Estimates

Table 2 records measures of public sector unionism from the aforementioned sources. Different measures can be contrasted at a point in time and over time. Taking differences at a point in time within any survey source, union and association membership invariably exceeds union membership. In the BLS and *Union Sourcebook,* this simply reflects the fact that a larger number of labor organizations are included once "associations" are considered. For the CPS, individuals reported significantly more membership in "unions or associations" in 1977 (33.4 percent) than in "unions" in the previous year (25.8 percent).

Comparing coverage and membership, the CPS figures show that many nonmembers are covered by collective bargaining agreements: coverage is always about ten percentage points above membership figures. Since the CPS asks the coverage question only of nonmembers, however, this does not imply that coverage exceeds membership. Many union members could be *not* covered. By examining the SOG data on state and local governments, it is clear that, in fact, this is the case. Specifically, in 1982, when the SOG collected membership and contract coverage data for the same "all worker" population, membership (37.5 percent) exceeded contract coverage (34.8 percent) at the state and local levels. If, two plus percentage points of the 39.5 percent of all workers "represented" by bargaining units in 1982 are actually nonmembers, then total membership would exceed "bargaining unit coverage." Unfortunately, as the SOG does not calculate membership in organizations that bargain contracts, it is not possible to give a precise estimate of the extent of "membership without contracts."

Table 2   Alternative Estimates of the Percent of "Organized" Public Sector Employees, Economy-Wide Estimates[a]

	Survey of Governments			Current Population Survey		
	(1)	(2)	(3)	(4)	(5)	(6)
			Full-time Workers-			
		Covered	Unions		Union	
	Bargaining	by	and	Union	and	C-B
Year	Units	Contracts	Assoc.	Member	Assoc.	Coverage
1950						
1956						
1957						
1958						
1959						
1960						
1961						
1962						
1963						
1964						
1965						
1966						
1967						
1968						
1969						
1970						
1971						
1972			50.4			
1973			—	22.7		
1974	31.4		51.5	24.8		
1975	34.9	26.0	49.9	25.1		
1976	35.8	27.7	49.8	25.8		
1977	37.0	29.4	47.8		33.4	
1978	37.9	31.1	48.1		34.1	44.1
1979	38.0	31.5	47.9		36.6	46.6
1980	38.4	32.1	48.8		35.8	46.0
1981	—	—	—		34.5	46.4
1982	39.5	34.8	45.7(37.5)[b]	—	—	
1983				37.5	45.6	
1984				35.4	44.2	
1985				35.8	43.1	
1986				36.0		

Sources: Columns (1)–(3), U.S. Bureau of the Census, *Survey of Governments, Labor-Management Relations in State and Local Government* (various years, table 1). Columns (4)–(6), U.S. Bureau of Labor Statistics, *Current Population Survey* (various years, computer tapes). Columns (7)–(8), U.S. Bureau of Labor Statistics (1979). Columns (9)–(10), Troy and Sheflin (1985, appendix table A and table 3.91).

[a]*Survey of Governments'* figures do not cover employees of the federal government.

[b]All workers.

Table 2   (continued)

| Year | Bureau of Labor Statistics | | Union Sourcebook | |
	Union Member (7)	Union and Assoc. (8)	Union Member (9)	Union and Assoc. (10)
1950		12.3		
1956	12.6		11.1	
1957			10.7	
1958	13.2		10.6	
1959			10.5	
1960	12.8		10.8	
1961			10.6	
1962	13.8			24.3
1963				25.1
1964	15.1			26.0
1965				26.1
1966	15.9			26.1
1967				27.0
1968	18.2	32.6		27.3
1969				26.9
1970	18.5	32.5		32.0
1971				33.0
1972	18.4	33.9		35.4
1973				37.0
1974	20.6	37.7		38.0
1975				39.6
1976	20.3	39.4		40.2
1977				38.1
1978	23.4	39.4		36.7
1979				36.4
1980				35.1
1981				35.4
1982				35.1
1983				34.1
1984				33.1
1985				
1986				

Turning to the federal government, it appears that the extent of coverage by bargaining agreements (agreements severely limited in scope by Executive Order no. 10988) exceeds membership. Burton (1979) estimates that total membership was 1,332,000 in 1976 —or 48.7 percent of federal government employment, while the number of employees of the executive branch and the postal service who were covered by agreements was 1,639,000.[8] "Coverage" in the federal sector, however, has not always exceeded membership. For example, in 1968, there were 1,391,000 members, but only 1,176,000 covered employees in the executive branch and postal services (Burton 1979). The dramatic increase in coverage by agreements from 1968 to 1976 is attributable to the growth in the percentage of employees in exclusive representation units that became covered by labor agreements.

Finally, for the current level of the membership "density or penetration rate" in the public sector, the SOG reports that 37.5 percent of all state and local government workers were members in 1982. The CPS estimates that the same percentage of all government workers (including those in the federal government) were members in 1983. Since the *Union Sourcebook* reports that among federal workers (included in the SOG data), 38.0 percent and 37.1 percent were members in 1982 and 1983, respectively,[9] we judge that *37.5 percent is a good estimate for the level of membership in the entire government sector in 1982–83*. In 1982, the level of the "membership density rate" (37.5 percent) exceeded "contract coverage" (34.8 percent) but was below the level of "bargaining unit representation" (39.5 percent) at the state and local level, while at the federal level, "agreement coverage" rates surpass membership rates. Examination of trends over time also suggests that membership rates for the state and local sector may also soon be surpassed by all "coverage rate" figures.

Trends

While there is reasonable consistency in estimated membership and coverage in the 1980s among sources, figures in earlier years differ among surveys, producing some disagreements over trends. As can be seen in table 2, during the 1960s and through the early 1970s, the various measures show steady increases in union or union and association density in the public sector.[10] Thereafter, disagreements emerge. The BLS union and association membership series shows a leveling off between 1976 and 1978. The CPS membership series shows continued growth through 1979 and irregular declines and advances thereafter. In 1986, 36.0 percent of all public employees were members according to the CPS—approximately the same penetration rate for 1979. By contrast, SOG data show that state and local level membership of full-time workers declined from a high-water mark of 51.5 percent in 1974, to

48.8 percent in 1980 to 45.7 percent by 1982. The *Sourcebook* also records a drop in public sector membership from a peak of 40.2 percent in 1976 to 33.1 percent in 1984.

Which of these trends is more likely to be correct—the individual-based CPS and union-based BLS figures, or the dues-based *Sourcebook* or employer-based SOG figures? Our analysis suggests that, at the minimum, the drop in the *Sourcebook* figures overstate any possible drop in membership. First, the *Sourcebook* assumption that predominantly private sector unions have had a fixed share of their members coming from the government sector appears incorrect, as unions such as the Laborers, Teamsters, and especially the SEIU have had increases in the share of their membership from government ranks. Adjusting for the increase in public sector membership of these three unions would increase overall public sector density by about two percentage points at the end of the series—or about 30 percent of the decline reported in the *Sourcebook* between 1975 and 1984.[11]

Whether the remainder of the decline represented in the *Sourcebook* is correct or due to the growth in labor organization members in local government not represented in LMRDA financial statistics is difficult to tell. As for the decline in the SOG data, our analysis in section III indicates that some of the decline is due to reporting errors by employers. Still, we suspect that the decline in membership density is real for specific occupations and levels of government. For example, the *Sourcebook* reports a decline in teacher union membership, which seems reasonable in light of our analysis of state and local government figures.

While we are unable to satisfactorily resolve the inconsistency between the CPS and *Sourcebook* series, we stress that even if membership density is declining, *collective bargaining continues to increase in the government sector.* For example, the SOG series on state and local bargaining unit representation and contract coverage grows steadily through 1982. On net, there seems to be a decline in "nonbargaining members" and an increase in "covered nonmembers."

III.   New Estimates of Public Sector Unionization

As noted, the most extensive estimates on public sector organization by level of government (other than the federal level) are collected in the SOG. Data for all labor organizations including "associations" cover the period from 1972 to 1982; there are data specifically on bargaining units and on contractual agreements from 1977 to 1982. (Again, in the SOG, bargaining units include units that "meet and confer" with their government employers.) It is not possible to identify which functions of employees in different government jurisdictions are covered by contractual agreements from the SOG data files, but only the total number of employees covered by contracts across all functions. However, the SOG does identify which functions have employees in associations or in bargaining units. For municipalities and townships for a given function of employees, the presence of an association or bargaining unit probably means that most employees in that function are "covered" by the activities of that local public employee organization. However, at higher levels of government, it is less likely that all employees in a given function are covered by the activities of an existing organization or bargaining unit. Therefore, we will estimate "function-specific" figures only for municipalities and townships.

SOG-based estimates of public employee density for "organizations," "bargaining units," and "contractual agreements" by level of government are given in panels A, B, and C of table 3, respectively. The figures in panel A give the percentage of full-time employees who are members of any employee organization or association. Across the various levels of government, municipalities and townships are more organized than the column (1) average for all levels of government, while counties, special districts, and states are consistently below the column (1) average. The decline in school district membership from 1980 to 1982 underlies much of the decline in the overall public sector "membership density" reported in table 2.

The bargaining unit figures in panel B give the percentage of full-time and part-time employees in the bargaining units. Unlike membership, bargaining unit coverage increases for nonfederal public employees between 1977 and 1982. The biggest increase in bargaining unit coverage occurs for state employees, while the highest coverage level is found among municipalities and school districts. Because the bargaining unit statistics include part-time employment while association statistics do not, it would be incorrect to attribute differences between the figures in panel A and panel B across the various levels of government strictly to changes over time in the percentage of all associations that engage in bargaining unit activities. Importantly, for all levels of government, bargaining unit representation was either increasing or, at a minimum, stable between 1977 and 1982.

Finally, panel C of table 3 reports the percentage of full-time and part-time employees covered by contractual agreements for the different levels of government. Since those "bargaining unit" employees that engage only in "meet and confer" discussions with their employers without negotiating a contractual agreement are excluded from the numerator of these percentages, these figures are consistently below those in panel B. For all state and local government employees, there has been an even greater increase in the percentage of employees covered by contractual agreements than in the percentage covered by bargaining units. Between 1977 and 1982, the percentage covered by contractual agreements increased by 5.4 percentage points from 29.4

Table 3   **Estimates of Membership in Associations or Unions by Level of Government,** *Survey of Governments* **Data**

Year	(1) Economy-Wide	(2) State	(3) County	(4) Municipal	(5) Township	(6) Special District	(7) School District
Panel A: Percent of Full-Time Public Employees Who Are Members of Associations or Unions, 1972–1982							
1972	50.4	40.8	39.0	54.4	51.6	33.2	62.1
1975	49.9	39.6	38.1	52.9	56.4	28.9	63.4
1976	49.6	38.2	36.6	53.5	57.1	37.3	64.2
1977	47.8	37.7	34.6	53.1	58.9	34.9	59.9
1978	48.1	38.1	34.5	53.8	58.5	36.5	60.3
1979	47.9	38.7	34.1	53.5	56.1	35.9	59.9
1980	48.8	40.5	34.9	53.9	58.6	37.8	60.2
1982	45.7	37.4	35.1	52.7	62.4	36.4	53.8
Panel B: Percent of All Public Employees Who Are Represented by Bargaining Units, 1977–1982							
1977	37.0	24.8	30.1	44.1	39.0	29.2	46.4
1978	37.9	24.8	30.3	46.7	34.0	30.1	48.2
1979	38.0	25.8	30.9	45.6	35.6	28.9	48.5
1980	38.4	26.7	31.4	46.1	36.8	30.6	48.2
1982	39.5	31.0	31.9	48.9	38.9	31.5	46.1
Panel C: Percent of All Public Employees Covered by Contractual Agreements, 1977–1982							
1977	29.4	21.3	18.4	34.3	37.0	25.1	37.7
1978	31.1	21.5	19.1	36.9	32.5	25.1	41.6
1979	31.5	21.8	20.3	37.7	33.8	24.4	42.5
1980	32.1	22.1	19.6	38.7	35.4	24.0	42.7
1982	34.8	28.1	26.4	41.8	37.7	25.1	41.2

Source: U.S. Bureau of the Census, *Survey of Governments, Labor-Management Relations in State and Local Governments* (various years, table 1).

percent to 34.8 percent—an 18.4 percent increase, with especially dramatic gains for state, county, and municipal employees. Only for special district employees, where the percentage covered by contractual agreements is 25.1 percent in both 1977 and 1982, is there no increase over this period.

Overall, table 3 shows that *the more one focuses on the process of collective bargaining leading to actual contracts and the less one includes other sorts of employee organizations that do not bargain, the more it becomes evident that public employee "unionism" continued to grow even through the early 1980s.*

New Estimates

For the six functions for which data are collected (police, fire, sanitation, streets and highways, public welfare, and hospitals), we estimated separate figures for organization membership, bargaining unit coverage, and the percentage of *departments* (rather than employees) that have an organization or a bargaining unit present. In these calculations, we assumed that if more than 10 percent of the employees in the function are members of an association or covered by a bargaining unit, then the municipal department for that function has an association or bargaining unit. While this may be a misleading assumption in some situations (e.g., for hospital workers who cover a wide range of occupations), it should provide reasonable estimates of the extent to which departments are "organized." By comparing survey responses for the same municipal function over several years, we are able to examine the consistency of responses for a given municipal function at one point in time across the range of unionization questions and for a given municipal function over time for the same unionization question.

Our analysis turned up two kinds of questionable patterns that we investigated through telephone interviews: (1) municipal functions report a bargaining unit but no employee organization in a given year; and (2) municipal functions report losing and often regaining an "organization" or "bargaining unit" over time. Of the 9,984 municipal functions that report employment in each of the eight surveys between 1972 to 1982, 334 indicated that a bargaining unit was present, but that they had *no* labor organization! We interviewed representatives for approximately 20 percent of these municipal functions and found that in each case "organizations" were indeed present. The error generally stemmed from respondents interpreting the bargaining unit and organization questions as mutually exclusive.

Tables 4 and 5 report estimates of unionization with and without various adjustments for the survey error. Panel A of table 4 records the percentages of all municipal *functions* that have some kind of labor organization. The only adjustment for the survey response error that we make in the data for 1972–82 is to reclassify the organization data for the 334 municipal functions in those years when they report a bargaining unit but no organization. Panel B of table 4 shows the percentage of full-time employees—rather than the percent of departments—who are members of an organization. The data reported on the lines for 1972–82 are completely unadjusted; that is, for the 334 municipal functions that report a bargaining unit but no organization in some years, we did not adjust the reported number of full-time employees who are members.

In terms of trends, the unadjusted percentage of full-time employees in municipalities and townships who are members declines from 65.0 percent in 1972 to 62.1 percent (table 4, panel B), but this does not reflect a decline in the percentage of municipal (or township) functions in which an organization is present. As shown in table 4, panel A, all functions except hospitals (which is based on only 104 observations) experience an increase in the percentage of "organized departments" from 1972 to 1982.[12] The decline in unadjusted organization membership also does not reflect any decline in bargaining unit activity in municipal and township functions. As shown in table 5, there has been an *increase* in the percent of functions with bargaining units present and in the percent of full-time employees represented by bargaining units between 1977 and 1982, the years for which SOG bargaining unit data are available. Only the employee-based figure for sanitation workers shows a decline in bargaining unit representation between 1977 and 1982. As for the difference between association membership (table 4, panel B) and bargaining unit representation (table 5, panel B), the smallest differences are for the highly organized protective service employees. For the four nonprotective service functions, a considerable number of dues-paying members are not represented by a bargaining unit.

Survey Error in the Decline in Membership Density

The only unionization series in these SOG local government data that declines is the percent of full-time employees who are members of any kind of association or organization. We investigated the possibility that the decline in the percentage of employees in organized departments that are dues-paying members was due to organized departments becoming unorganized and found a surprising number of city functions that report losing (and regaining) an organization or bargaining unit. The small percentage changes between any two years for any function in the table 4 organization figures or the table 5 bargaining unit figures mask a much greater degree of loss of union status reported by individual functions over time. Specifically, 20.8 percent of the 9,984 municipal function observations report some pattern of losing (and regaining) an association over the 1972–82 period. For the bargaining unit responses for the 1977–82 period, 10.6 percent of the 9,984 municipal functions reported losing a bargaining unit in one or more years.

To investigate these patterns of switching, we conducted telephone interviews that provided information on 258 cases which reported losing an organization or bargaining unit among its employees.[13] With 2,073 instances of organization loss and 1,057 instances of bargaining unit loss reported in the 9,984 SOG observations, the 258 telephone interviews account for 8.2 percent of all cases that report loss of some form of unionism. Importantly, out of the 258 governments telephoned, *in no case was the loss of an organization or a bargaining unit an accurate reflection of the labor relations history in the municipal function.*[14] Those interviewed were confident about one of two points: either they had never had an organization or bargaining unit present, or they had never lost such unionization.

Table 4   **Estimates of Employee Organization in Municipalities and Townships, by Function, *Survey of Governments*, 1972–82**

Year	(1) All Municipal and Township (Six Function Total) (N = 9,984)	(2) Police (N = 3,208)	(3) Fire (N = 1,936)	(4) Sanitation (N = 1,615)	(5) Streets and Highways (N = 3,007)	(6) Welfare (N = 114)	(7) Hospitals (N = 104)
	*Panel A: Percent of Municipal Functions with Organizations—Adjustment A**						
1972	40.5	41.2	53.9	36.0	34.7	23.7	28.8
1975	45.3	46.9	56.5	40.1	40.6	28.9	27.9
1976	47.8	49.8	57.7	43.2	43.0	33.3	34.6
1977	48.9	51.5	59.0	42.3	44.3	32.5	34.6
1978	49.1	51.7	58.7	42.5	45.4	22.8	29.8
1979	49.9	52.7	59.4	43.2	46.0	23.7	29.8
1980	51.0	54.4	60.2	43.3	47.3	28.9	29.8
1982	52.3	56.3	61.1	44.3	48.2	35.1	27.9
1982 ADJ B*	63.7	67.3	73.9	57.5	57.7	49.1	44.2
1982 ADJ C*	59.4	63.1	73.5	52.2	53.8	44.0	27.9

			Panel B: Percent of Full-Time Municipal Employees Who Are Members of Organizations —Unadjusted				
1972	65.0	64.4	78.0	54.5	49.9	76.0	65.6
1975	65.5	65.9	78.6	57.8	47.5	76.6	63.8
1976	66.1	65.9	78.8	59.6	51.5	76.4	61.5
1977	65.1	65.1	79.3	53.9	52.2	71.4	62.7
1978	61.3	60.6	74.1	49.4	51.2	71.3	58.5
1979	59.6	59.4	72.4	48.2	47.4	70.0	56.7
1980	60.3	59.8	73.0	50.5	49.0	71.8	54.9
1982	62.1	62.5	73.2	52.5	52.1	71.9	54.8
1982 ADJ B*	74.8	74.2	91.8	62.5	62.4	80.6	65.6
1982 ADJ C*	70.0	69.7	91.2	58.5	58.2	77.4	54.8

*Notes on adjustments used in table 4:

ADJ A: The presence of a bargaining unit implies the existence of an employee organization within any municipal or township function.

ADJ B: The given unionization measure is assumed to continue to exist in subsequent years after it is first reported by a municipal or township function. This leads to an overestimate of the extent of unionization.

ADJ C: A certain percentage of municipal or township functions that are assumed to be unionized according to ADJ B are treated as nonunion to correct for the overestimate caused by the ADJ B procedure. See text for a discussion of how data from telephone interviews were used to construct ADJ C.

Table 5   **Estimates of Bargaining Unit Representation in Municipalities and Townships, by Function, *Survey of Governments*, 1977–82**

Year	(1) All Municipal (N = 9,984)	(2) Police (N = 3,208)	(3) Fire (N = 1,936)	(4) Sanitation (N = 1,615)	(5) Streets and Highways (N = 3,007)	(6) Welfare (N = 114)	(7) Hospitals (N = 104)
Panel A: Percent of Municipal Functions with Bargaining Units—Unadjusted							
1977	28.0	40.4	43.6	7.1	16.9	7.0	24.0
1978	32.5	46.1	49.4	9.1	20.9	6.1	25.0
1979	33.8	47.7	51.1	9.3	22.2	6.1	24.0
1980	36.2	49.1	52.5	12.4	26.1	7.0	24.0
1982	35.0	49.3	51.4	10.8	23.7	7.0	23.1
1982 ADJ B*	43.1	54.6	57.9	20.6	34.8	14.9	29.8
1982 ADJ C*	41.4	53.6	56.3	18.4	32.6	14.6	28.2
Panel B: Percent of Full-Time Municipal Employees Who Are Represented by Bargaining Units—Unadjusted							
1977	44.1	52.5	60.9	22.0	31.7	38.8	23.9
1978	49.6	58.5	66.2	31.0	53.5	1.1[a]	22.6
1979	49.8	59.2	67.1	29.4	47.7	4.6[a]	25.4
1980	51.3	58.8	69.3	28.6	58.8	1.1[a]	25.1
1982	51.5	64.0	69.7	20.8	44.9	4.5[a]	28.6
1982 ADJ B*	62.0	67.9	74.5	44.1	60.1	75.5	30.8
1982 ADJ C*	59.4	67.2	73.3	38.9	57.6	72.8	30.3

*See notes for table 4 for explanation of ADJ B and ADJ C.

[a] The sharp decline in public welfare bargaining unit membership figures after 1977 is strictly a result of New York City reporting virtually no bargaining unit representation from 1978 to 1982.

These responses led us to consider two rules for recoding the data: (1) turn union-losing cases into strictly nonunion observations; or (2) turn union-losing cases to unionized observations following the year in which unionization is first reported. Adopting the first rule would underreport unionization, while the second would overreport unionization. To minimize these biases, we identified six different patterns of union losing in the longitudinal organization and bargaining unit data.[15] For the 258 interviews, we calculated the percentage of cases in each of the six switching categories that would be miscoded if the first and second recoding rules were adopted. In all six switching categories for organization and bargaining unit data, the 1982 unionization status of the 258 municipal functions is more accurately captured by changing nonunion observations to union observations after the initial report of unionization. Only for one switching pattern (0's → 1's → 0's in the organization data) was the percentage of municipal functions miscoded equal under the two recoding rules.[16] The percentages of all departments with an organization or bargaining unit present in 1982 after making this recoding adjustment are given in each panel of tables 4 and 5 in the row headed "1982, ADJ B."

Given the nature of this adjustment, the percentages in the row "1982, ADJ B" will overestimate the degree of unionization at the end of the period, while the figures in the "1982" row line underestimate unionization according to our telephone interviews. We make one final adjustment to the "1982, ADJ B" figures to account for the overreporting of unionization caused by the recoding rule. Specifically, for the cases contacted by telephone, we calculate the percentage of times that we incorrectly changed an observation to unionized when the telephone interviews actually reported no unionization. These percentages are calculated within each of the six switching categories for each of the six functions—a total of thirty-six "function-switching category" cells. Finally, these percentages are applied to the total number of observations in the thirty-six cells in the data set.

This final adjustment is listed in the row "1982, ADJ C" in each panel of tables 4 and 5. Overall the adjustments that we make based on our telephone interviews indicate that municipal and township functions are *more highly unionized* than the SOG data indicate because of reporting errors by local government officials. Specifically, we calculate that another 7.1 percent of all municipal functions have an organization of some kind present in 1982 beyond the percentage reported in the 1982 SOG data tapes. For bargaining units, our calculations cause an adjustment of 6.4 percentage points. After these adjustments are made, the percentage of full-time employees who are members of an organization in municipalities and townships (table 4, panel B) *no longer declines* between 1972 and 1982.[17] Still, this series does not show the kinds of increases between 1977 and 1982 that the bargaining unit representation figures indicate.

Can survey response error account for all the decline shown in the SOG data on organization membership density? As we have not analyzed the school district responses to the SOG, which showed the greatest fall, we can make no definitive statement. However, if the pattern we uncovered in which employers erroneously report no organization present, apparently because they interpreted contract coverage as precluding organization, it may very well be that response error underlies not only the drop in membership density for municipalities but also for school districts and, thus, overall organization membership density.

CPS Data

Estimates of the percentage of workers who are members or who are covered by collective bargaining agreements in the CPS data are given in table 6 for various occupations and for workers in public administration. We use the May CPS surveys to tabulate these figures, using the sample weights indicated in CPS surveys; for 1984 we also report figures from the 12-month CPS file in table notes. The CPS membership figures in panel A provide additional support for the adjustments made to the SOG data. Specifically, between 1978 and 1984, all categories report increases in organization membership. Taking the CPS and SOG data together, it appears that in the late 1970s and early 1980s membership density for public sector labor organizations has been fairly stable.[18]

As with the SOG bargaining-unit representation figures and contract coverage figures, the CPS coverage statistics reveal a generally increasing pattern for specific occupations. Changes in employment in different occupations produce a rough stability in total coverage among all CPS government workers. Again, for estimates of the level of coverage, we place greater weight on the SOG estimates in various tables, since the CPS does not allow for noncoverage of dues-paying members.[19]

Coverage and the Law

Clear patterns link our estimates of public sector organization to the legal environment governing public sector labor relations. Table 7 presents SOG data for the four functions with a large number of departments at the municipal level—police, fire, sanitation, and streets and highways—and shows higher levels of organization and bargaining in states with more favorable bargaining laws.[20] The law categories are based on laws that apply to the given employee group, as described in the NBER Public Sector Labor Law Data Set (Valletta and Freeman, Appendix B, this volume). Consider first police and fire, the two func-

Table 6   **CPS Estimates of Union Membership and Collective Bargaining Coverage of State and Local Government Employees, 1978–84, by Function**

	1978	1979	1980	1981	1983[a]	1984[b]
	Panel A: Union Membership					
Total	0.33	0.37	0.36	0.34	0.39	0.37
Local Police	0.50	0.57	0.55	0.49	0.53	0.69
Local Fire Fighters	0.74	0.74	0.76	0.76	0.69	0.85
Teachers	0.55	0.61	0.59	0.60	0.67	0.65
Total Public Administration	0.32	0.37	0.33	0.31	0.39	0.36
State Public Administration	0.31	0.33	0.26	0.24	0.37	0.38
Local Public Administration	0.33	0.39	0.37	0.34	0.41	0.36
	Panel B: Collective Bargaining Coverage					
Total	0.43	0.47	0.47	0.46	0.46	0.45[c]
Local Police	0.63	0.64	0.64	0.56	0.56	0.77
Local Fire Fighters	0.82	0.78	0.82	0.87	0:76	0.92
Teachers	0.71	0.75	0.74	0.74	0.75	0.75
Total Public Administration	0.41	0.46	0.42	0.42	0.44	0.44
State Public Administration	0.40	0.43	0.35	0.38	0.42	0.47
Local Public Administration	0.41	0.47	0.45	0.44	0.45	0.42

Source: Tabulated from the U.S. Bureau of Labor Statistics, Current Population Survey, May 1978–84. All estimates are calculated using sampling weights indicated in the CPS surveys.
[a]Union and coverage questions were not asked in 1982.
[b]Comparable figures from the 12-month CPS file are, in order: 0.37, 0.62, 0.81, 0.63, 0.36, 0.33, 0.38.
[c]Comparable figures for 1984 collective bargaining coverage from the 12-month CPS file are, in order: 0.45, 0.70, 0.86, 0.75, 0.43, 0.41, 0.45.

tions with the highest organization density. Twenty-nine state laws for fire fighters have some kind of duty-to-bargain provision; twenty-seven states have this type of bargaining right for their local police, generally with compulsory interest arbitration rather than the right to strike, or some impasse resolution mechanism other than interest arbitration. Among these protective service workers, those in states with arbitration mechanisms are the most likely to be in associations or covered by a bargaining unit. Interestingly, even where bargaining is legally prohibited, some police and fire fighters (as well as employees in other functions) have bargaining units.

Table 7   Estimates of Public Sector Organization and Coverage in
Associations and Unions, by Function and Nature of Bargaining
Law, *Survey of Governments*, 1982

	(1)	(2)	(3)
Bargaining Law	Number of States	Number of Municipal Departments	Number of Full-Time Employees
Panel A: Police			
1. Strikes Permitted	1	18	623
2. Arbitration	14	1,122	108,847
3. Duty-to-Bargain	12	813	89,729
4. Bargaining Permitted	11	530	49,275
5. No Provisions	8	485	37,896
6. Bargaining Prohibited	4	239	19,852
Panel B: Fire Fighters			
1. Strikes Permitted	1	14	484
2. Arbitration	17	560	57,446
3. Duty-to-Bargain	11	577	56,107
4. Bargaining Permitted	13	484	36,076
5. No Provisions	5	184	14,747
6. Bargaining Prohibited	3	116	11,055
Panel C: Sanitation Workers			
1. Strikes Permitted	8	150	6,152
2. Arbitration	5	112	1,759
3. Duty-to-Bargain	11	500	29,367
4. Bargaining Permitted	12	308	11,986
5. No Provisions	9	295	11,150
6. Bargaining Prohibited	5	249	15,590
Panel D: Streets and Highways			
1. Strikes Permitted	8	453	12,056
2. Arbitration	5	284	6,712
3. Duty-to-Bargain	11	1,046	37,902
4. Bargaining Permitted	12	509	15,326
5. No Provisions	9	430	12,425
6. Bargaining Prohibited	5	284	13,900

For sanitation workers and streets and highways employees, the
ranking of bargaining unit coverage across the law categories is similar
to the ranking observed for police and fire fighters. Various kinds of
duty-to-bargain states tend to have higher levels of bargaining unit
coverage than do states without such provisions. Among states with
duty-to-bargain provisions, states with arbitration provisions have the
highest or second highest percentage of sanitation workers and streets
and highways workers covered by a bargaining unit.

Table 7   (continued)

(4) Percentage of Depts. with Assoc.	(5) Percentage of Employees Who Are Members in Associations	(6) Percentage of Depts. with Barg. Units	(7) Percentage of Employees Represented by Barg. Units
0.500	0.547	0.500	0.546
0.850	0.856	0.817	0.943
0.621	0.616	0.538	0.579
0.281	0.504	0.202	0.454
0.293	0.425	0.213	0.292
0.096	0.211	0.029	0.156
0.429	0.700	0.429	0.694
0.820	0.924	0.770	0.947
0.704	0.708	0.610	0.616
0.370	0.582	0.258	0.537
0.554	0.315	0.429	0.296
0.155	0.302	0.017	0.184
0.713	0.868	0.227	0.299
0.598	0.733	0.143	0.694
0.676	0.797	0.154	0.135
0.260	0.259	0.075	0.229
0.271	0.428	0.064	0.269
0.116	0.172	0.020	0.078
0.603	0.665	0.391	0.382
0.592	0.574	0.412	0.690
0.671	0.720	0.313	0.705
0.244	0.364	0.112	0.194
0.267	0.466	0.074	0.444
0.099	0.086	0.004	0.007

Similar figures on public employee organization by collective bargaining law were also tabulated using the CPS data files. These figures, presented in table 8, are consistent with the SOG data: coverage is higher, group by group, under more favorable legal environments. The CPS data show that a large number of teachers and other local employees, who are covered by contract, work in states where bargaining is prohibited. As the CPS implicitly assumes that all members are covered, we suspect that a relatively large proportion of the members in bargaining-prohibited environments are in fact not covered by collective bargaining contracts. While the SOG and CPS data indicate that public sector unionism is more common where laws are more favorable, they also reveal that organization and collective bargaining exist in all legal environments. As a result of these legal differences, the nature

Table 8   State and Local Public Sector Collective Bargaining Coverage, by Function and Nature of Bargaining Environment, 1984

Bargaining Law	Number of States	Number of Workers	Percentage Covered
State Employees			
Strikes Permitted[1]	6	226,890	0.58
Arbitration[2]	5	61,789	0.71
Duty to Bargain	13	861,575	0.52
Bargaining Permitted[3]	10	604,459	0.31
No Provision	8	400,959	0.23
Bargaining Prohibited	8	730,528	0.13
Local Police			
Strikes Permitted[1]	1	620	1.0
Arbitration[2]	14	112,773	0.89
Duty to Bargain	12	119,705	0.72
Bargaining Permitted[3]	11	28,075	0.29
No Provision	8	42,836	0.58
Bargaining Prohibited	4	24,117	0.18
Local Fire Fighters			
Strikes Permitted[1]	1	373	0.93
Arbitration[2]	17	38,262	0.93
Duty to Bargain	11	49,470	0.87
Bargaining Permitted[3]	13	24,027	0.74
No Provision	5	18,966	0.88
Bargaining Prohibited	3	5,067	0.48
Teachers			
Strikes Permitted[1]	8	215,749	0.88
Arbitration[2]	5	32,396	0.90
Duty to Bargain	18	897,742	0.85
Bargaining Permitted[3]	12	556,951	0.58
No Provision	3	43,862	0.47
Bargaining Prohibited	4	253,456	0.48
Other Local			
Strikes Permitted[1]	8	457,848	0.49
Arbitration[2]	5	39,494	0.44
Duty to Bargain	11	2,118,444	0.54
Bargaining Permitted[3]	12	441,967	0.15
No Provision	9	814,481	0.27
Bargaining Prohibited	5	859,274	0.13

Table 8   (continued)

Bargaining Law	Number of States	Number of Workers	Percentage Covered
Total			
Strikes Permitted[1]	—	901,563	0.79
Arbitration[2]	—	284,172	0.61
Duty to Bargain	—	4,046,936	0.62
Bargaining Permitted[3]	—	1,655,479	0.36
No Provision	—	1,321,104	0.28
Bargaining Prohibited	—	1,872,442	0.18

Sources: BLS Current Population Survey, 1984 (weighted); Valletta and Freeman (appendix B, this volume).

[1]This category includes states that have a duty-to-bargain provision and allow strikes, typically under very limited circumstances.

[2]This category includes states that have both a duty-to-bargain provision and a final and binding arbitration mechanism which is mandatory at a certain point in the impasse, either automatically or at the request of one of the parties.

[3]This category includes states which have "meet and confer," "right to present proposals," or "bargaining permitted" provisions.

of unionism and labor-management relations that does exist in the different legal environments will be extremely different.

IV.   Comparison of Organized and Unorganized Workers and City Functions

Are the characteristics of unionized workers or city functions markedly different from nonunion workers or functions? How do public sector union workers differ from private sector union workers? Are union/nonunion differences in characteristics of workers greater in the public than in the private sector? In this section we present some simple comparisons of workers and cities to answer these questions.

Table 9 compares the characteristics of union and nonunion workers in the CPS in 1984 and, for purposes of contrast, the characteristics of union and nonunion private sector workers as well. The data show:

(1) that public sector unionists have higher wages than their nonunion peers, though with a smaller percentage advantage than unionists have in the private sector;

(2) that in the government as well as in the private sector, unionists have markedly lower wage dispersion than do nonunion workers;

(3) that in the public sector union members are modestly older than nonunion members, whereas in the private sector they are 4.5 years older on average, indicating in part the greater inability of

Table 9   **Comparison of Characteristics and Economic Position of State and Local Public Sector Workers, by Unionization, vs. Private Sector Workers (1984, employed workers only)**

	State and Local Public Sector		Private Sector	
	Union	Nonunion	Union	Nonunion
Sample Size	9,159	15,608	21,238	120,446
Economic				
Part-Time	0.041	0.194	0.053	0.177
Hourly	0.315	0.429	0.848	0.587
Hourly Wage[1]	8.63	6.18	9.93	5.87
Usual Weekly	406.34	303.29	404.33	298.42
Earnings	40.37	36.14	39.93	37.42
Usual Weekly Hours	9.76	7.83	9.74	7.38
Usual Hourly Earnings[2]	41.3	59.1	41.4	65.0
Dispersion[3]				
Demographic Characteristics				
Age	40.91	39.22	39.52	35.07
% < 34	0.289	0.387	0.363	0.536
% > 55	0.125	0.145	0.129	0.101
Experience	20.26	19.42	21.69	16.40
% < 15	0.379	0.436	0.348	0.544
% > 36	0.111	0.143	0.165	0.111
% College Grads	0.541	0.413	0.086	0.223
% HS Grads	0.947	0.909	0.813	0.865
% Female	0.525	0.569	0.271	0.486
% White	0.845	0.854	0.847	0.896
% Black	0.120	0.110	0.119	0.074
% South	0.152	0.365	0.183	0.309
% West	0.273	0.243	0.231	0.230
% Married	0.732	0.671	0.730	0.596
% Veteran	0.419	0.365	0.406	0.287
Occupation				
% White Collar	0.689	0.692	0.227	0.556
Professional	0.526	0.424	0.063	0.202
Clerical	0.139	0.223	0.093	0.176
Sales	0.005	0.010	0.049	0.142
Technical	0.020	0.035	0.022	0.035
% Blue Collar	0.311	0.308	0.773	0.444
Craft	0.046	0.044	0.262	0.113
Machine	0.006	0.007	0.223	0.075
Handlers	0.047	0.055	0.202	0.082

Source: Tabulated from BLS Current Population Survey, 1984 (unweighted).
[1]For hourly workers only.
[2]Calculated as usual weekly earnings divided by usual weekly hours for all workers.
[3]Dispersion is measured by the coefficient of variation of usual hourly earnings.
[4]Calculated as (age − education − 5).

private sector unions to organize new plants and younger employees;

(4) that in the public sector over half of union members are college graduates (reflecting in large part organization of teachers) with union employees better educated than nonunion employees, while union members are markedly less educated than nonunion members in the private sector;

(5) with respect to women, in the public sector but not in the private sector, unions have organized roughly a proportionate share of female and male workers.

In sum, very few of the union/nonunion differentials in table 9 are similar in the private and public sectors. In fact, the only characteristics that show similar union/nonunion differentials between the sectors are region, where the proportion of all union workers in the South is markedly below the proportion of all nonunion workers in the South in both sectors, and characteristics associated with a more stable and permanent group of employees. For example, the proportion of union workers who are married or who are veterans is higher than the comparable proportions of nonunion workers, while the fraction who are part-time workers is markedly lower among unionized employees in both the private and public sector.

Turning to differences between organized and unorganized cities and functions, table 10 compares salary levels and department sizes for departments without organized units, departments with an association but no bargaining unit, and departments with bargaining units. With

Table 10   Comparison of Pay and Employment in Municipal Functions, by Unionization Status, Survey of Governments Data, 1982

		Unorganized	Association Only	Bargaining Unit
1.	Police—Monthly Pay	1352.23	1579.93	1802.84
2.	Police—Department Size	43.32	98.40	143.76
3.	Fire—Monthly Pay	1432.50	1611.16	1892.44
4.	Fire—Department Size	41.65	80.58	131.51
5.	Sanitation—Monthly Pay	1114.57	1388.29	*1361.38
6.	Sanitation—Department Size	28.16	71.89	75.29
7.	Streets and Highways—Monthly Pay	1223.89	1490.93	1429.53
8.	Streets and Highways—Department Size	20.11	46.48	47.29
9.	Public Welfare—Monthly Pay	1170.35	1215.28	1257.28
10.	Public Welfare—Department Size	92.28	866.47	469.63
11.	Hospitals—Monthly Pay	1164.96	1255.75	1379.49
12.	Hospitals—Department Size	410.47	507.40	2702.33

Table 11   Comparison of Demographic Characteristics of Municipalities, by Unionization Status, Survey of Governments Data

	Unorganized	Association	Bargaining Unit
1. 1970 population	44,517	82,240	138,041
2. Median family income, 1970	$8,887	$9,527	$10,142
3. Median values of owner-occupied single-family housing, 1970	$15,268	$16,017	$18,693
4. Male operatives' median earnings, 1970	$7,039	$7,414	$8,294
5. Persons with more than three years of high-school, 1970 (%)	53.0	57.5	58.5
6. Central cities (%)	26.0	35.8	44.6

few exceptions, the stronger the unionization, the larger and better paid are the municipal departments.

Finally, table 11 presents several demographic characteristics of organized and unorganized municipalities and their citizens. A municipality is classified as unorganized if there are no associations or bargaining units in any function. The association column consists of municipalities that have no bargaining units in any of their functions, but at least one function has an association present. The bargaining unit column consists of municipalities that have a bargaining unit present in one or more of their functions.

The most important fact shown in the table is that larger municipalities have stronger unionization. Municipalities with at least one bargaining unit are over three times larger than municipalities with no organization. Moreover, strong unionization is also associated with wealthier or higher cost cities, as judged by median family income, median housing value, and median earnings of male operatives. Unorganized municipalities have the lowest high-school education rates, and bargaining unit municipalities, the highest. Bargaining unit municipalities are also most likely to be central cities.

Conclusion

There are significant problems in defining and measuring unionization in the public sector, resulting in occasional contradictory pictures of developments in the area. This appendix has compared the major sources of public sector organization data and explained, where possible, the differences in estimated collective organization across the data sets. It finds that:

1. After nearly two decades of rapid growth, membership density has leveled off and possibly declined. Collective bargaining coverage, however, continues to increase. By the early 1980s, the membership density was approximately 38 percent among all government workers.
2. Organizational density differs significantly by level of government and the function or occupation of employees.
3. Organization is much stronger in areas with more favorable laws than in areas with less favorable laws.
4. Public sector unionists differ significantly in education and occupation from private sector unionists. However, along many dimensions, the differences between union and nonunion employees in the public sector are less pronounced than the differences between union and nonunion workers in the private sector. Organized public sector workers are higher paid and tend to work for larger and wealthier jurisdictions.

Notes

1. There are other labor organizations below the level of national and international unions to which public employees "belong"—particularly for municipal and other local government employees. For example, local police may bargain with their municipal employers as members of the Fraternal Order of Police (FOP), International Brotherhood of Police Officers (IBPO), Teamsters, AFSCME, or other organizations. Local police may also belong to state-level umbrella organizations that span the membership of individual labor organizations of cities and towns. These organizations, such as the New Jersey Police Benevolent Association (NJPBA) or the Massachusetts Police Association (MPA), are involved in lobbying activities in state legislatures. They may also include independent municipal locals unaffiliated with national labor organizations.

2. First, the figure is derived from BLS Bulletin no. 1702 (BLS 1971) concerning public employee membership in associations during 1968–69—not 1978. Therefore, any growth in such membership between 1969 and 1978 is completely missed. More importantly, the sample from which this figure is derived is far from a universe of all local government employee associations, and no attempt to adjust for the incompleteness of the subsample is made in the BLS estimate. Specifically, this association survey was mailed only to associations in municipalities that reported having an association in a separate International City Managers Association (ICMA) survey, which itself was an incomplete survey of municipalities. Moreover, any organization of local employees that referred to themselves as a "union" were intentionally deleted from the sample. It certainly cannot be assumed that these union members were all included in some national or international union surveyed by the BLS. Ultimately this survey of local government "associations" covered only 662 local associations in only 438 cities—and it intentionally excludes members of "unions"; 235,000 of the 264,366 members in these 662 associations are the basis of the BLS

estimate. Apparently, the BLS excluded the membership of the Fraternal Order of Police and two nurses unions to arrive at their estimate of 235,000 "unaffiliated" members. The magnitude of the underestimate can be illustrated by considering the fact that the U.S. Bureau of the Census (1974) reports that even just among full-time state and local government employees, 4,319,941 were organized in 1972, only three years after the date of BLS Bulletin no. 1702. While it is unknown how many of the over four million organized public employees in 1972 were captured in the BLS survey of national and international unions, the crudeness of the BLS estimate and the potential for extreme undercounting of these workers are clear.

3. The actual percentage breakdown of SEIU members in the government is not reported for the 1979 BLS *Directory,* so the estimate used by Troy and Sheflin to calculate the number of SEIU members who are government employees is not known precisely. However, the 1979 BLS *Directory* does report that 65 percent of SEIU's members were in private sector service industries (BLS 1980, 106) so that the percentage that Troy and Sheflin apply to SEIU membership figures is at most 35 percent. For this particular union, and presumably others as well, applying a fixed 1979 percentage to calculate the number of government employees in certain unions will underestimate the number of organized government employees after 1979 and overestimate the number of organized government employees before 1979. For example, the percentage of SEIU members coming from the government was 30 percent in 1977 (BLS 1979, 117–18)—not the fixed (approximately) 35 percent figure used by Troy and Sheflin. According to the Research Department of SEIU, its total membership in 1986 was 850,000 with 450,000 members from the public sector—or 52.9 percent of its total membership. Their 450,000 public sector members, however, include members gained through mergers and absorption with such unions as the National Association of Government Employees (NAGE).

4. The Survey of Governments (SOG) reports that in 1982 there were 4,645,000 organized full-time employees and 4,868,000 organized employees on full-time or part-time schedules in 1982 (see U.S. Bureau of the Census 1982). In contrast, Troy and Sheflin estimate 4,382,000 organized full-time equivalents in 1982 at the state and local levels. Furthermore, based on our telephone interviews with municipalities that reported switching back and forth between union and nonunion status in the SOG, we believe that the membership figures reported in SOG publications for local governments are underestimates of the actual levels of membership (see discussion in section III accompanying tables 4 and 5).

5. It defines an "employee organization" as: "Any organization . . . which exists for the purpose in whole or in part of dealing with the employer concerning grievances, personnel policies and practices, labor disputes, wages, rates of pay, hours of employment, or work."

6. A bargaining unit is defined as: a "group of employees recognized as appropriate for representation by an employee organization for the purpose of collective bargaining or other discussions."

7. The question on "bargaining units" (which refers to units that have contracts or that engage in "meet and confer" discussions) also seems to be a "coverage-type" question, since it specifically asks for the number of employees "represented" by the organizations. Still, it is possible that this language could be interpreted as a membership question. The employee organization question clearly asks for the number of employees who are "members" of an organization, but through 1980, this question—unlike the contract and bargaining unit questions—referred only to full-time employees.

8. These two groups accounted for 99.3 percent of all federal employment in 1976. The 1,639,000 membership figure is the sum of 1,060,000 employees in the executive branch "under agreement" and 579,000 postal employees in "exclusive units" (Burton 1979, 18).

9. Troy and Sheflin's (1985) estimates for the federal sector appear to be somewhat below those assembled earlier by Burton (1979). For 1976, Burton estimates 1,332,000 out of 2,733,000 federal employees (or 48.7 percent) were members, while Troy and Sheflin estimate 1,133,000 of 2,682,000 federal employees (or 41.5 percent) were members in the same year. Since 1976, the membership penetration rate in the federal government seems to have declined.

10. For these early years, the individual BLS series covers fewer organizations than does the *Sourcebook*, but the trends in the BLS series are likely to be more accurate as they are not affected by the imprecise extrapolations used in the *Sourcebook* to gauge membership in independent municipal organizations and membership of government employees in predominantly private sector labor organizations.

11. This is obtained by comparing 1985 figures on public sector membership of these three unions in table 1 with 1975 figures reported by Stern (1979). Between 1975 and 1985, SEIU representation in the public sector rose by 270,000; Teamsters representation grew by 50,000, and Laborers by 5,000, giving a total growth of 325,000 for those unions. This is 2.03 percent of 16 million public sector employees used as the base for the public sector density for 1984 in the *Sourcebook* (table 3.91).

12. The percentages in table 4, panel A are very similar whether or not the 334 municipality functions that report a bargaining unit but no organization are classified as having an organization.

13. Only when telephone respondents indicated that they were familiar with the labor relations history of the municipal function in question was information collected from a municipal representative. Usually, such an employee in the municipality could be identified after several telephone calls.

14. Occasionally, we interviewed a representative of municipal management who indicated that he or she completed the SOG survey in some but not all survey years, so that changes in the respondent to the SOG survey is at least one of the reasons for the measurement error on the SOG unionization data.

15. Letting zero reflect nonunion status, and one reflect union status, these six patterns are: (1) 1's → 0's; (2) 1's → 0's → 1's; (3)1's → 0's → 1's → 0's; (4) 0's → 1's → 0's; (5) 0's → 1's → 0's → 1's; (6)0's → 1's → 0's → 1's → 0's. As one might expect, there are fewer instances in those categories characterized by more frequent switching.

16. There were 498 municipality-function observations that reported this pattern of switching in their organization data over time; 78 of these cases were contacted; 39 reported that employees belonged to an organization in 1982, and the other 39 reported that no type of organization had ever existed among employees in the given function.

17. When we extend adjustment B to the employee-based figures in panel B of tables 4 and 5, we assume that for those municipality-function-years, when we reclassify nonunion status as unionized, the percentage of full-time employees who are members of an organization or who are represented by a bargaining unit equals the average of the year before and the year after the reclassified municipality-function-year observation. If these adjoining years are also being reclassified, we go to the nearest adjoining year that is not being reclassified. When we reclassify these percentages for observations in 1982, we use the percentage from the most recent year that is not being reclassified.

18. The CPS figures call into question the decline in membership among teachers reported in the unadjusted SOG data in table 3, panel A, between 1980 and 1982. Since we conducted no interviews with school districts, we do not know how much of the decline in membership in table 3, panel A, column (7), is a result of reporting errors by school district managers.

19. CPS figures, therefore, would tend to overestimate coverage. For example, for police and fire fighters in 1978, 1979, and 1980 (the only direct points of comparison between function-specific SOG and CPS estimates), the CPS collective bargaining contract coverage figures in table 6, panel B, exceed the SOG bargaining unit representation figures in table 5, panel B. This is true even though the SOG figures specifically include meet and confer arrangements as bargaining units in the numerator of their percentages. Furthermore, part-time workers who are less likely to be unionized are excluded from the SOG calculations.

20. The only adjustments applied to the original data on the 1982 SOG data tapes are to assume that an "association" exists in all cases where a "bargaining unit" is reported.

References

Bureau of National Affairs. 1982. *Directory of U.S. labor organization, 1982–83 edition*, Washington, D.C.: BNA, Inc.

———. 1984. *Directory of U.S. labor organization, 1984–85 edition*, Washington, D.C.: BNA, Inc.

Burton, John F. 1979. The extent of collective bargaining in the public sector. In *Public sector bargaining,* eds. Benjamin Aaron, Joseph R. Grodin, and James L. Stern. Washington, D.C.: BNA, Inc.

Levitan, Sar, and Alexandra Noden. 1983. *Working for the sovereign.* Baltimore, Md.: John Hopkins University Press.

Stern, James L. 1979. Unionism in the public sector. In *Public sector bargaining,* eds., Benjamin Aaron, Joseph R. Grodin, and James L. Stern. Washington, D.C.: BNA, Inc.

Thieblot, Armand J. 1978. An analysis of data on union membership. Working Paper no. 38. St. Louis: Washington University Center of American Business.

Troy, Leo, and Niel Sheflin. 1985. *Union sourcebook.* West Orange, N.J.: Industrial Relations Data and Information Services.

U.S. Bureau of the Census. 1974. *1972 Survey of governments: Public employment, management-labor relations in state and local governments.* Washington, D.C.: Government Printing Office (GPO).

———. 1980. *Survey of governments: Labor-management relations in state and local governments: 1980.* Washington, D.C.: GPO.

———. 1982. *Survey of governments: Labor-management relations in state and local governments: 1982.* Washington, D.C.: GPO.

U.S. Bureau of Labor Statistics (BLS). 1971. *Municipal public employee association.* Bulletin no. 1702. Washington, D.C.: GPO.

———. 1979. *Directory of national unions and employee associations 1977.* Bulletin no. 2044. Washington, D.C.: GPO.

———. 1980. *Directory of national unions and employee associations 1979,* Bulletin no. 2079. Washington, D.C.: GPO.

Appendix B
The NBER Public Sector Collective Bargaining Law Data Set

Robert G. Valletta and Richard B. Freeman

The NBER Public Sector Collective Bargaining Law Data Set provides a comprehensive source that describes the status of state public sector collective bargaining policies for five main functional groups in all fifty states from 1955 to 1985.[1] Building on previous works by the Department of Labor, the American Federation of State, County, and Municipal Employees, Berkeley Miller of the University of South Florida, and John Burton of Cornell University, we have constructed this data set to provide longitudinal as well as cross-sectional information about state labor laws.[2] In its completed form, the data set embodies legal provisions for the five main public employee functions in all fifty states since 1955. The five groups covered are: state employees, municipal police, municipal fire fighters, noncollege teachers, and other local employees. Some laws may cover other groups (such as prison guards, hospital employees, state police, etc.), but these five groups were the primary ones mentioned. Many states have comprehensive laws which cover all five groups; however, some make distinctions between these groups, as we shall discuss below.

We chose fourteen variables to represent relevant dimensions of the laws; a numerical coding scheme was devised for each in order to allow the proper distinctions to be made in the data set. These variables are divided into five main categories: contract negotiation (bargaining rights), union recognition, union security, impasse procedures, and strike policy.

Richard B. Freeman is professor of economics at Harvard University and the director of labor studies at the National Bureau of Economic Research. Robert G. Valletta is a visiting assistant professor of economics at the University of California, Irvine.

The authors wish to thank Eric Larson for aiding in the construction of the data set, and particularly Lee Simmons for designing the data set and performing much of the research.

Coding sheets for these five categories, along with explanatory notes, are provided in tables 1A–1E.[3]
To illustrate the nature of the data set and its contents, we have compiled a number of descriptive tables. Tables 2A and 2B indicate contract negotiation provisions (bargaining rights and scope) in the fifty states as of January 1984 and January 1969, respectively.[4] The states are arranged from those with the strongest bargaining provisions to those that prohibit collective bargaining. In table 2A, the first feature to stand out is the high degree of consistency for bargaining provisions across different functional groups within a state; this is particularly true for states that provide strong bargaining rights. Of the thirty-five states that provide strong bargaining rights and include wages as a subject of bargaining (values 5 and 6) for at least one functional group, twenty-four do so for at least four functional groups; of those twenty-four, twenty-one provide strong bargaining rights for all five groups.

Despite this consistency across functional groups within many states, there is variation between bargaining provisions within states. For example, in table 2A, Texas and Kentucky provide strong bargaining rights only for police and fire and prohibit collective bargaining for at

Table 1A   Coding Sheet for Contract Negotiation Provisions

Variable	Value
(1) Collective Bargaining Rights	0 = No provision
	1 = Collective bargaining prohibited
	2 = Employer authorized but not required to bargain with union
	3 = Right to present proposals
	4 = Right to meet and confer
	5 = Duty to bargain I (implied)
	6 = Duty to bargain II (explicit)
(2) Scope of Bargaining	0 = No provision
	1 = Excludes compensation
	2 = Includes compensation

Notes: This section originally contained an additional variable, intended to represent the extent to which collective bargaining agreements were subject to legislative recall. After some preliminary coding, this variable was abandoned; consistent distinctions could not be made across different state laws.

Values 3, 4, 5, and 6 under variable (1) can sometimes be difficult to distinguish between. For 3 and 4, one needs to look for the key phrases; however, in both these cases the public employer is still free to unilaterally set the terms and conditions of employment (i.e., there is no obligation for the employer to actually bargain). Value 5 means that although there is no explicit statutory provision stating that the parties must come to an agreement, it is implied (frequently through specifying a ratification procedure or through listing failure to bargain in good faith under "Unfair Practices") that they must attempt to do so. Value 6 means that there is explicitly stated (frequently in the definition of "collective bargaining") an obligation for the parties to come to a written agreement.

Table 1B   **Coding Sheet for Union Recognition Provisions**

Variable	Value
(1) Representation and Election	0 = No provision 1 = Nonexclusive allowed or required 2 = Exclusive; petition and election procedure not specified 3 = Exclusive; petition and election procedure specified
(2) Term of Recognition (minimum period guaranteed until another election can be called)	0 = No provision 1 = Any time after certification 2 = At least 12 months since last election 3 = At least 12 months since last election and previous collective bargaining agreement has expired 4 = At least 24 months since last election (may or may not include contract expiration clause)

Notes: The election procedure specified typically includes provisions for the following: initial petition for certification (percentage necessary for acceptance, usually 30 percent), additional petitions to appear on ballot (usually 10 percent of members of bargaining unit must sign for organization to appear), posted notices, timing of election and other procedures, place of election, restrictions on who can vote, employer or employee organization noninterference, and runoff elections.

"Nonrepresentation" is invariably a voting choice, and certification can be legally revoked during the term of recognition.

Petition and election procedures can generally be avoided if the public employer voluntarily recognizes an employee organization and there is no challenge.

Despite exclusive representation, most laws contain a clause stating that employees can individually present grievances (although a union representative frequently must be present).

least one other group, while Maryland and North Dakota provide bargaining rights only for teachers. Other states may provide weaker "meet and confer" or other provisions for some groups but not for others. Thus, the variation in bargaining rights allows for cross-sectional investigations to be performed both across and within states.

The longitudinal nature of the data set is illustrated by a comparison of tables 2A and 2B. Of the twenty-one states which had comprehensive strong bargaining laws in 1984, only twelve had strong bargaining laws for at least one group in 1969; of those twelve, only five had strong bargaining provisions for all five functional groups. Similar variation exists for states with other types of provisions. For example, Minnesota switched from "meet and confer" in 1969 for all five functional groups to strong bargaining rights by 1984, while Virginia changed from a "permissive" (value 2) status for four groups in 1969 to *prohibiting* collective bargaining for all five groups by 1984. In general, the trend is toward more probargaining laws (see table 3), although antibargaining

Table 1C   Coding Sheet for Union Security Provisions

Variable	Value
(1) Agency Shop	0 = No provision
	1 = Agency shop prohibited
	2 = Agency shop negotiable
	3 = Agency shop compulsory
(2) Union Members' Dues Checkoff	0 = No provision
	1 = Dues checkoff prohibited
	2 = Dues checkoff negotiable
	3 = Dues checkoff compulsory
(3) Union Shop	0 = No provision
	1 = Union shop prohibited
	2 = Union shop negotiable
	3 = Union shop compulsory
(4) "Right-to-Work" Law	0 = has no "right-to-work" law applying to public employees
	1 = has a "right-to-work" law applying to public employees

Notes: The term "fair-share agreement" is synonymous with "agency shop."
  Agency shop provisions typically stipulate that the service fee shall be deducted from nonmembers salaries. Such provisions are distinct from dues checkoff, which stipulates that union members' dues shall be deducted from their salaries; the two types of provisions often exist separately.
  "Maintenance of membership" is another type of provision relating to union membership; it stipulates that employees who join the union must maintain their membership for the duration of the collective bargaining agreement. We decided this was not important enough to code, although several states do have such provisions.
  Agency shops, dues checkoff, and union shops are "negotiable" when the law stipulates that public employers and public employee unions may settle contracts that include such provisions. "Prohibited" and "compulsory" are self-explanatory, except that dues checkoff is also coded as "compulsory" when the public employer must deduct union dues at the request of either the union or individual employees. Also, individual employee consent is generally required by the law.

Table 1D   **Coding Sheet for Impasse Procedures**

Variable	Value
(1) Mediation: Availability	0 = No provision
	1 = Specifically prohibited
	2 = Voluntary (both parties must consent)
	3 = Discretionary: Administrative agency may initiate, either unilaterally or upon request of a party to impasse.
	4 = Mandatory: Required by statute
(2) Fact-finding: Availability	(same as mediation)
(3) Arbitration: Availability	(same as mediation)
(4) Arbitration: Scope	0 = No provision
	1 = Issues other than compensation
	2 = All negotiable issues
(5) Arbitration: Type	0 = No provision
	1 = Conventional
	2 = Final offer—Issue basis
	3 = Final offer—Package basis
	4 = Any one of these types may be used

Notes: The coding is intended to reflect the actual nature of the process provided for in law and may in some cases differ from the *wording* used in the law where that deviates from common usage. For example, Alaska's teachers' law does not explicitly provide for fact-finding, but their so-called mediation process clearly includes fact-finding. The most important example of this is arbitration. We *define* arbitration as being final and binding. Some states have so-called arbitration procedures that are merely advisory, hence no different from fact-finding; we have coded such procedures as "fact-finding."

Table 1E   **Coding Sheet for Strike Policy Provisions**

Variable	Value
(1) Strike Policy	0 = No provision
	1 = Prohibited with penalties specified
	2 = Prohibited with no penalties specified (discretion of court)
	3 = Permitted (with qualifications)

Notes: The values for this variable represent broad categories. However, the types of penalties and qualifications used are very consistent across states, and the values represent as fine a distinction between state policies as we are accurately able to construct from the laws. Researchers should note that depending on the state, court-imposed penalties may be more severe than those provided for by law.

In general, the penalties specified include one or more of the following: loss of union certification, loss of dues deduction, loss of wages during strike (or twice wages), termination of employment, fines for union and/or individual employees, and rehire on probation.

No state permits its public employees to strike without qualifications. Typical qualifications include: the previous collective bargaining agreement has expired and no new one has been reached; impasse procedures have been fully complied with; and at least XX days have elapsed since issuance of the fact-finders' report. Such strikes can usually be enjoined if the courts decide that they have caused a threat to public safety or health.

Table 2A   Bargaining Rights and Scope (as of January 1984)

State	State Employees	Police	Fire	Teachers	Other Local
Alaska	6	6	6	6	6
Delaware	6	6	6	6	6
Florida	6	6	6	6	6
Montana	6	6	6	6	6
Pennsylvania	6	6	6	6	6
Washington	5	6	6	5	6
Connecticut	5	5	5	5	5
Hawaii	5	5	5	5	5
Iowa	5	5	5	5	5
Maine	5	5	5	5	5
Massachusetts	5	5	5	5	5
Michigan	5	5	5	5	5
Minnesota	5	5	5	5	5
New Hampshire	5	5	5	5	5
New Jersey	5	5	5	5	5
New York	5	5	5	5	5
Oregon	5	5	5	5	5
Rhode Island	5	5	5	5	5
South Dakota	5	5	5	5	5
Vermont	5	5	5	5	5
Wisconsin	5	5	5	5	5
California	4	5	5	5	5
Nebraska	5	5	5	2*	5
Oklahoma	0	5	5	5*	0
Idaho	0	2*	5	6*	2*
Nevada	1	5	5	5	5
Kansas	4	4	4	5	4
Kentucky	1	5	5	2*	0
Texas	1	5	5	2*	1
Maryland	0	0	0	5	0
North Dakota	0	0	0	5	0
Wyoming	0	0	5	0	0
Missouri	4	0	4	0	4
Utah	3*	3*	3*	3*	3*
New Mexico	5**	2*	2*	2*	2*
Arizona	2	2	2	2	2
West Virginia	2	2	2	2	2
South Carolina	2*	2*	2*	2*	2*
Arkansas	2*	2*	2*	2*	2*
Illinois	5	2*	2*	2*	2*
Indiana	2*	2*	2*	5	2*
Louisiana	2*	2*	2*	2*	2*
Colorado	0	0	0	2*	0
Ohio	0	0	0	2*	0
Mississippi	0	0	0	0	0
Tennessee	1	1	1	5	1
Georgia	1	0	4	1	0
Alabama	1	1	3	1	1

Table 2A   (continued)

State	State Employees	Police	Fire	Teachers	Other Local
Virginia	1	1	1	1	1
North Carolina	1	1	1	1	1

Key:
    6 = Duty to bargain II (explicit)
    5 = Duty to bargain I (implied)
    4 = Right to meet and confer
    3 = Right to present proposals
    2 = Employer authorized but not required to bargain with union
    1 = Collective bargaining prohibited
    0 = No bargaining provision
    * = No provision as to the scope of bargaining
    ** = Wages are a prohibited subject of bargaining

Table 2B   **Bargaining Rights and Scope (as of January 1969)**

State	State Employees	Police	Fire	Teachers	Other Local
Alaska	2	2	2	2	2
Delaware	6	6	6	0	6
Florida	0	0	0	0	0
Montana	0	0	0	0	0
Pennsylvania	0	6	6	0	0
Washington	5	6	6	6	6
Connecticut	0	5	5	5	5
Hawaii	0	0	0	0	0
Iowa	0	0	0	0	0
Maine	0	0	5	0	0
Massachusetts	5*	5	5	5	5
Michigan	0	5	5	5	5
Minnesota	4*	4*	4*	4	4*
New Hampshire	2*	2*	2*	2*	2*
New Jersey	5	5	5	5	5
New York	5	5	5	5	5
Oregon	2	2	2	4	2
Rhode Island	5	5	5	5	5
South Dakota	0	0	0	0	0
Vermont	0	5	5	5	5
Wisconsin	5**	0	5	5	5
California	4	2	4	4	4
Nebraska	0	0	0	2*	0
Oklahoma	0	0	0	0	0
Idaho	0	2*	2*	2*	2*
Nevada	1	1	1	1	1
Kansas	0	0	0	0	0
Kentucky	1	0	0	2*	0
Texas	1	1	1	2*	1

Table 2B   (continued)

State	State Employees	Police	Fire	Teachers	Other Local
Maryland	0	0	0	0	0
North Dakota	0	0	0	0	0
Wyoming	0	0	5	0	0
Missouri	4	0	4	0	4
Utah	3*	3*	3*	3*	3*
New Mexico	0	2*	2*	2*	2*
Arizona	0	0	0	0	0
West Virginia	2	2	2	2	2
South Carolina	0	0	0	0	0
Arkansas	2*	2*	2*	2*	2*
Illinois	2	2*	2*	2*	2*
Indiana	0	0	0	0	0
Louisiana	0	0	0	0	0
Colorado	0	0	0	0	0
Ohio	0	0	0	0	0
Mississippi	0	0	0	0	0
Tennessee	0	0	0	0	0
Georgia	0	0	0	2*	0
Alabama	1	1	3	1	1
Virginia	1	2*	2*	2*	2*
North Carolina	1	1	1	1	1

Key:
  6 = Duty to bargain II (explicit)
  5 = Duty to bargain I (implied)
  4 = Right to meet and confer
  3 = Right to present proposals
  2 = Employer authorized but not required to bargain with union
  1 = Collective bargaining prohibited
  0 = No bargaining provision
  * = No provision as to the scope of bargaining
 ** = Wages are a prohibited subject of bargaining

Table 3   **State Counts by Pro- or Antibargaining, 1969 and 1984**

	1969	1984
States all probargaining	5	21
States mostly probargaining	5	4
States mostly prohibiting bargaining	4	4
States all prohibiting bargaining	1	2

Note: To be counted as all probargaining, states must have strong bargaining rights (values 5 or 6) for all five functional groups. To be counted as mostly probargaining, states must have 3 or 4 strong bargaining groups. The same scheme was used for the "prohibiting" categories, using the value 1.

states in some cases adopted more explicit or stringent antibargaining provisions. Overall, there is enough longitudinal variation to perform both within-state longitudinal and panel investigations.

Several states stand out as early probargaining states: Washington, Massachusetts, New Jersey, New York, and Rhode Island. These states currently have broad probargaining laws that also extend to our other dimensions, such as impasse procedures. Not surprisingly, police and fire fighters were typically among the earliest groups to be covered by strong bargaining laws, in addition to sometimes being the only groups covered in a state (see table 2A). Several states have recognized explicitly in their laws the importance of assuring uninterrupted police and fire-fighting services and have instituted strong bargaining rights for these groups in the belief that such provisions, along with extensive impasse procedures and antistrike laws (see below, tables 6A and 6B), would assure smoother labor relations. Whether they have succeeded is the type of testable hypothesis that the data set will enable researchers to investigate.

Tables 4A and 4B list union security provisions as of January 1984 and January 1969, respectively; the states are listed in the same order as in tables 2A and 2B. The incidence of these provisions within and across states follows patterns similar to those of the bargaining rights provisions in tables 2A and 2B. It should be noted that tables 4A and 4B list only the strongest union security provision in effect for each functional group. However, as states with strong union security provisions, such as required agency shops, also tend to have provisions for weaker union security arrangements, such as dues checkoff, the data set itself includes values for all union security mechanisms. Also, some states with right-to-work laws, which typically prohibit union and agency shops, have other security provisions, such as allowing or requiring dues checkoff; these states have two numbers listed in tables 4A and 4B.

Comparing tables 2 and 4, we see that the states with stronger bargaining laws also tend to have stronger union security provisions. States with right-to-work laws are more likely to have weak bargaining provisions or to prohibit bargaining, supporting the use of right-to-work laws as an indicator of antibargaining attitudes. The obvious exceptions to this are Florida, South Dakota, and Nebraska, each of which is a strong bargaining state but has a right-to-work law still on the books. Florida's comprehensive 1975 law (preceded briefly by a 1973 law for fire fighters) enacted very strong bargaining rights in a state that previously had only a right-to-work law on the books.

In contrast, a comparison of tables 4A and 4B indicates that many states enacted stronger union security provisions during the years between 1969 and 1984. In 1969, only two states (Massachusetts and

Table 4A   Union Security Provisions (as of January 1984)

State	State Employees	Police	Fire	Teachers	Other Local
Alaska	5	5	5	0	5
Delaware	3	3	3	3	3
Florida	1,3	1,3	1,3	1,3	1,3
Montana	4	4	4	4	4
Pennsylvania	2	2	2	2	2
Washington	5	5	5	5	5
Connecticut	6	2	2	4	2
Hawaii	6	6	6	6	6
Iowa	1,2	1,2	1,2	1,2	1,2
Maine	4	0	0	0	0
Massachusetts	4	4	4	4	4
Michigan	4	4	4	4	4
Minnesota	4	4	4	4	4
New Hampshire	0	0	0	0	0
New Jersey	4	4	4	4	4
New York	6	4	4	4	4
Oregon	4	4	4	4	4
Rhode Island	6	0	0	6	0
South Dakota	1	1	1	1	1
Vermont	0	4	4	0	4
Wisconsin	4	4	4	4	4
California	4	4	4	4	4
Nebraska	1	1	1	1,3	1
Oklahoma	0	0	0	0	0
Idaho	0	0	0	0	0
Nevada	0	2	2	2	2
Kansas	1	1	1	1	1
Kentucky	0	0	4	0	0
Texas	1	1,2	1,2	1,2	1,2
Maryland	0	0	0	0	0
North Dakota	1	1	1	1,3	1
Wyoming	1	1	1	1	1
Missouri	0	0	0	0	0
Utah	1,3	1,3	1,3	1,3	1,3
New Mexico	2	0	0	0	0
Arizona	1,3	1	1	1,2	1
West Virgina	3	0	0	0	0
South Carolina	1,2	1,2	1,2	1,2	1,2
Arkansas	1,2	1	1	1	1
Illinois	2	2	2	2	2
Indiana	0	0	0	4	0
Louisiana	2	2	2	2	2
Colorado	0	0	0	0	0
Ohio	2	2	2	4	2
Mississippi	1	1	1	1	1
Tennessee	2	0	0	2	0
Georgia	0	0	0	0	0
Alabama	1	1	1	1,3	1

Table 4A   (continued)

State	State Employees	Police	Fire	Teachers	Other Local
Virginia	1	1	1	1	1
North Carolina	0	0	0	0	0

Key:
  6 = Agency shop compulsory
  5 = Union shop negotiable
  4 = Agency shop negotiable
  3 = Dues checkoff compulsory
  2 = Dues checkoff negotiable
  1 = Right-to-work law (prohibits union shop and typically agency shop)
  0 = No union security provisions (union and agency shops may be prohibited)

Table 4B   **Union Security Provisions (as of January 1969)**

State	State Employees	Police	Fire	Teachers	Other Local
Alaska	0	0	0	0	0
Delaware	3	3	3	0	3
Florida	1	1	1	1	1
Montana	0	0	0	0	0
Pennsylvania	0	2	2	0	0
Washington	3	3	3	3	3
Connecticut	0	2	2	0	2
Hawaii	0	0	0	0	0
Iowa	1,2	1,2	1,2	1,2	1,2
Maine	0	0	0	0	0
Massachusetts	3	4	4	4	4
Michigan	0	0	0	0	0
Minnesota	0	0	0	0	0
New Hampshire	0	0	0	0	0
New Jersey	0	0	0	0	0
New York	3	3	3	3	3
Oregon	0	0	0	0	0
Rhode Island	3	0	0	0	0
South Dakota	1	1	1	1	1
Vermont	0	4	4	4	4
Wisconsin	2	0	0	0	0
California	0	0	0	0	0
Nebraska	1	1	1	1	1
Oklahoma	0	0	0	0	0
Idaho	0	0	0	0	0
Nevada	0	0	0	0	0
Kansas	1	1	1	1	1
Kentucky	0	0	0	0	0
Texas	1	1,2	1,2	1,2	1,2
Maryland	0	0	0	0	0
North Dakota	1	1	1	1	1

Table 4B   (continued)

State	State Employees	Police	Fire	Teachers	Other Local
Wyoming	1	1	1	1	1
Missouri	0	0	0	0	0
Utah	1	1	1	1	1
New Mexico	0	0	0	0	0
Arizona	1	1	1	1	1
West Virginia	3	0	0	0	0
South Carolina	1,2	1,2	1,2	1,2	1,2
Arkansas	1	1	1	1	1
Illinois	2	2	2	2	2
Indiana	0	0	0	0	0
Louisiana	2	2	2	2	2
Colorado	0	0	0	0	0
Ohio	2	2	2	2	2
Mississippi	1	1	1	1	1
Tennessee	0	0	0	0	0
Georgia	0	0	0	0	0
Alabama	1	1	1	1	1
Virginia	0	0	0	0	0
North Carolina	0	0	0	0	0

Key:
6 = Agency shop compulsory
5 = Union shop negotiable
4 = Agency shop negotiable
3 = Dues checkoff compulsory
2 = Dues checkoff negotiable
1 = Right-to-work law (prohibits union shop and typically agency shop)
0 = No union security provisions (union and agency shops may be prohibited)

Vermont) had union security mechanisms permitting agency shops. By 1984, nineteen states had union security provisions that were at least as strong as permitting agency shops (see table 5). Again, the general trend during these years was toward stronger probargaining provisions.

Tables 6A and 6B list final impasse resolution and strike policy provisions as of the years 1984 and 1969, respectively; once again, the states are listed in the same order as in tables 2A and 2B. Only the *final* impasse procedure is listed. However, states with arbitration provisions often have mediation and fact-finding provisions, and states with fact-finding often have mediation provisions; the data set itself includes values for all these mechanisms for each state-function. For mediation and fact-finding, only their availability (i.e., whether the mechanism is mandatory, discretionary—requiring the request of one of the parties, or voluntary—requiring the consent of both parties) is shown. For arbitration, the scope and type of arbitration is also shown.

Table 5   **State Counts for Union Security Provisions**

	1969	1984
Agency shop negotiable or compulsory	2	19
Dues checkoff negotiable or compulsory	14	18
Right-to-work law	14	15
No provision	24	9

Note: Columns do not sum to fifty since some states have both a right-to-work law and dues checkoff provisions.

Once again, states with stronger bargaining rights are more likely to have strong third-party impasse resolution procedures (where "strong" is defined by both the mechanism used and its availability). There are many more blanks as we move down tables 6A and 6B and fewer functions with arbitration provisions.

The patterns in impasse and strike provisions within and across states are similar to those in bargaining and union security provisions. However, there is less consistency across functional groups for impasse procedures than there is for the other two dimensions. In particular, police and fire fighters are more likely to be provided with mandatory or discretionary arbitration than are the other functional groups (see table 7).

Police and fire fighters are also much less likely to be granted a limited right to strike than are the other groups. As of 1984, only two states (Montana and Idaho) grant such a right to police or fire fighters, while nine states grant a limited right to strike to at least one of the other groups. However, most states prohibit strikes by public employees; of the forty-one remaining states, only three have no explicit strike provisions, leaving thirty-eight states as of 1984 that specifically prohibit strikes by at least one functional group and do not explicitly permit strikes by any (see table 8).

Finally, table 7 reveals once again the longitudinal change since 1969 toward broader provisions; the general movement is away from no provision and toward some combination of mediation, fact-finding, and arbitration in most states. Mandatory and discretionary arbitration provisions were virtually nonexistent in 1969, and only conventional arbitration was mentioned. Table 8 indicates a similar phenomenon for strike policy provisions; the general movement is toward more explicit provisions, with many more states specifically prohibiting or allowing strikes in 1984 than in 1969.

Our final descriptive table is table 9; it provides a rough summary statistic indicating the public sector bargaining environment, as measured by our variables, in all fifty states. In general, a higher variable value in our data set indicates a stronger probargaining provision. The

Table 6A   **Final Impasse Resolution and Strike Policy (as of January 1984)**

State	State Employees	Police	Fire	Teachers	Other Local
Alaska	M:D,Pm	A:M,C,P	A:M,C,P	F:D,Pm	M:D,Pm
Delaware	A:V,C*,P	A:V,C*,P	A:V,C*,P	F:D,PP	A:V,C*,P
Florida	F:M,PP	F:M,PP	F:M,PP	F:M,PP	F:M,PP
Montana	A:V,NP,Pm	A:V,NP,Pm	A:V,NP,P	A:V,NP,Pm	A:V,NP,Pm
Pennsylvania	A:V,NP,Pm	A:D,C,PP	A:D,C,PP	A:V,NP,Pm	A:V,NP,Pm
Washington	P	A:M,C,P	A:M,C,P	A:V,C,P	P
Connecticut	F:D,P	A:M,FOI,P	A:M,FOI,P	A:M,FOI,P	A:M,FOI,P
Hawaii	A:V,C,Pm	A:V,C,P	A:M,FO,P	A:V,C,Pm	A:V,C,Pm
Iowa	A:D,FOI,PP	A:D,FOI,PP	A:D,FOI,PP	A:D,FOI,PP	A:D,FOI,PP
Maine	A:D,C*,P	A:D,C*,P	A:D,C*,P	A:D,C*,P	A:D,C*,P
Massachusetts	A:V,NP,P	A:V,NP,PP	A:V,NP,PP	A:V,NP,PP	A:V,NP,PP
Michigan	M:M,PP	M:M,PP	M:M,P	M:M,P	M:M,P
Minnesota	A:V,C&F,Pm	A:D,C&F,PP	A:D,C&F,PP	A:V,C&F,Pm	A:V,C&F,Pm
New Hampshire	F:M,P	F:M,P	F:M,P	F:M,P	F:M,P
New Jersey	F:M,P	A:M,C&F,P	A:M,C&F,P	F:M,P	F:M,P
New York	A:V,NP,PP	A:D,C,PP	A:D,C,PP	A:V,NP,PP	A:V,NP,PP
Oregon	A:V,C,Pm	A:M,C,P	A:M,C,P	A:V,C,Pm	A:V,C,Pm
Rhode Island	A:M,C*,P	A:M,C,P	A:M,C,P	A:D,C*,P	A:D,C*,P
South Dakota	F:D,PP	F:D,PP	F:D,PP	F:D,PP	F:D,PP
Vermont	A:M,FO,P	A:V,C,P	A:V,C,P	F:D,Pm	A:V,C,Pm
Wisconsin	F:V,PP	A:D,FO,PP	A:D,FO,PP	A:D,FO,Pm	A:D,FO,Pm
California	M:D,P	M:D,P	M:D,P	A:V,NP,P	M:V,P
Nebraska	A:D,C,PP	A:D,C,PP	A:D,C,PP	A:D,C,PP	A:D,C,PP
Oklahoma	—	—	F:D,PP	F:M,PP	—
Idaho	—	—	F:M,Pm	F:D	—
Nevada	—	A:V,NP,PP	A:M,FO,PP	A:V,NP,PP	A:V,NP,PP

State					
Kansas	P	F :M,P	F :M,P	F :D,P	F :M,P
Kentucky	P	P	F :D,P	P	P
Texas	PP	A:V,C,PP	A:V,C,PP	PP	PP
Maryland	M:D,P	—	—	M:D,PP	—
North Dakota	M:D,P	M:D,P	M:D,P	F:D,PP	M:D,P
Wyoming	—	—	A:M,C	—	—
Missouri	P	P	P	—	P
Utah	PP	PP	PP	PP	PP
New Mexico	F:D,PP	—	—	—	—
Arizona	—	—	—	P	—
West Virginia	—	P	—	—	—
South Carolina	P	P	P	P	P
Arkansas	P	P	P	P	P
Illinois	PP	PP	F:M,PP	PP	PP
Indiana	—	—	—	A:V,NP,PP	—
Louisiana	P	P	P	—	P
Colorado	P	P	P	P	P
Ohio	PP	PP	PP	PP	PP
Mississippi	—	—	—	—	—
Tennessee	PP	—	—	F:D,PP	—
Georgia	PP	F:M,P	F:M,P	—	—
Alabama	P	P	P	P	P
Virginia	PP	PP	PP	PP	PP
North Carolina	—	—	—	—	—

Key: The first letter indicates whether there is mediation (M), fact-finding (F), or arbitration (A). The first letter after the colon indicates whether the procedure is mandatory (M), discretionary (D), or voluntary (V). For arbitration, the next symbol indicates the type of arbitration: conventional (C), final offer by package (FO), final offer by issue (FOI), conventional or final offer (C&F), no provision on the type (NP). An asterisk indicates that wages are an excluded issue for arbitration. Finally, the last letter indicates strike policy: prohibited with penalties (PP), prohibited (P), permitted with qualifications (Pm).

Table 6B   **Final Impasse Resolution and Strike Policy (as of January 1969)**

State	State Employees	Police	Fire	Teachers	Other Local
Alaska	—	—	—	—	—
Delaware	A:V,C*,P	A:V,C*,P	A:V,C*,P	—	A:V,C*,P
Florida	P	P	P	P	P
Montana	—	—	—	—	—
Pennsylvania	PP	A:D,C,PP	A:D,C,PP	PP	PP
Washington	P	P	P	P	P
Connecticut	—	F:D,P	F:D,P	F:M,P	F:D,P
Hawaii	—	—	—	—	—
Iowa	—	—	—	—	—
Maine	—	—	F:M,P	—	—
Massachusetts	F:D,P	F:D,P	F:D,P	F:D,P	F:D,P
Michigan	M:D	M:D,P	M:D,P	M:D,P	M:D,P
Minnesota	M:D,PP	M:D,PP	M:D,PP	M:D,PP	M:D,PP
New Hampshire	P	P	P	P	P
New Jersey	A:V,NP,P	A:V,NP,P	A:V,NP,P	A:V,NP,P	A:V,NP,P
New York	F:D,PP	F:D,PP	F:D,PP	F:D,PP	F:D,PP
Oregon	M:D,P	M:D,P	M:D,P	M:D,P	M:D,P
Rhode Island	A:M,C*,P	A:M,C,P	A:M,C,P	A:D,C*,P	A:D,C*,P
South Dakota	—	—	—	—	—
Vermont	—	A:V,NP,P	A:V,NP,P	A:V,NP,Pm	A:V,NP,Pm
Wisconsin	F:D,P	F:D	F:D,P	F:D,P	F:D,P
California	—	—	P	—	—
Nebraska	P	P		P	P
Oklahoma	—	—	—	—	—
Idaho	—	—	—	—	—
Nevada	—	—	—	—	—
Kansas	—	—	—	—	—
Kentucky	—	—	—	—	—
Texas	PP	PP	PP	PP	PP
Maryland	—	—	—	—	—
North Dakota	M:D,P	M:D,P	M:D,P	M:D,P	M:D,P
Wyoming	—	—	A:M,C	—	—
Missouri	P	—	P	—	P
Utah	PP	PP	PP	PP	PP
New Mexico	—	—	—	—	—
Arizona	—	—	—	—	—
West Virginia	—	—	—	—	—
South Carolina	—	—	—	—	—
Arkansas	P	P	P	P	P
Illinois	P	P	F:M,P	P	P
Indiana	—	—	—	—	—
Louisiana	—	—	—	—	—
Colorado	—	—	—	—	—
Ohio	PP	PP	PP	PP	PP
Mississippi	—	—	—	—	—
Tennessee	—	—	—	—	—
Georgia	PP	—	—	—	—
Alabama	P	P	P	P	P

Table 6B   (continued)

State	State Employees	Police	Fire	Teachers	Other Local
Virginia	—	—	—	—	—
North Carolina	—	—	—	—	—

Key: The first letter indicates whether there is mediation (M), fact-finding (F), or arbitration (A). The first letter after the colon indicates whether the procedure is mandatory (M), discretionary (D), or voluntary (V). For arbitration, the next symbol indicates the type of arbitration: conventional (C), final offer by package (FO), final offer by issue (FOI), conventional or final offer (C&F), no provision on the type (NP). An asterisk indicates that wages are an excluded issue for arbitration. Finally, the last letter indicates strike policy: prohibited with penalties specified (PP), prohibited (P), permitted with qualifications (Pm).

Table 7   **State Counts for Final Impasse Resolution Procedures, 1984 and 1969**

	Mandatory or Discretionary Arbitration	Voluntary Arbitration	Mediation or Fact-finding	None
1984				
Police	14	7	7	22
Fire	17	5	11	17
State employees	5	8	11	26
Teachers	6	11	14	19
Other local	6	10	9	25
1969				
Police	2	3	8	37
Fire	3	3	10	34
State employees	1	2	7	40
Teachers	1	2	8	39
Other local	1	3	8	38

Table 8   **State Counts for Strike Policy**

	1969	1984
Permitted with qualifications	1	9
Prohibited	18	15
Prohibited with penalties	7	23
No provision	24	3

Table 9   Summary Bargaining Environment Statistic (sum of all variables)

State	1984	1969
Alaska	156	80
Delaware	129	118
Florida	135	55
Montana	158	70
Pennsylvania	132	80
Washington	146	121
Connecticut	160	118
Hawaii	162	70
Iowa	135	60
Maine	123	77
Massachusetts	137	127
Michigan	131	108
Minnesota	142	84
New Hampshire	125	70
New Jersey	132	115
New York	130	115
Oregon	160	92
Rhode Island	126	114
South Dakota	105	60
Vermont	143	130
Wisconsin	129	96
California	119	81
Nebraska	113	54
Oklahoma	91	70
Idaho	92	74
Nevada	104	65
Kansas	115	60
Kentucky	87	70
Texas	69	51
Maryland	79	70
North Dakota	70	60
Wyoming	63	63
Missouri	82	82
Utah	65	55
New Mexico	82	74
Arizona	62	55
West Virginia	82	82
South Carolina	60	60
Arkansas	56	55
Illinois	77	79
Indiana	88	70
Louisiana	79	75
Colorado	66	70
Ohio	58	65
Mississippi	55	55
Tennessee	72	70
Georgia	73	69
Alabama	51	49
Virginia	40	73
North Carolina	65	65

exceptions are the "0" and "1" values of the variables; the value "1" generally represents a restriction on the relevant activity, while "0" typically represents "no provision." Thus, with a recoding so that the 0's and 1's in the variables are interchanged, a simple sum of all the variable values across all five functions in a state is a good overall indicator of how amenable the state is to public sector unions and collective bargaining.[5] The value of this statistic is shown for both the years 1984 and 1969.

The states listed first tend to have higher values in this table, although not in exact order. Again, this indicates that states with strong provisions in one area also tend to have them in others; the same holds true for states with weak, antibargaining, or no provisions. The general trend toward stronger and more provisions is illustrated by a comparison of the two columns in table 9. Most states' summary statistics increased significantly between 1969 and 1984, while a few remained the same or decreased over the period. The states with the most pro-bargaining environments as of 1984 are Hawaii, Connecticut, and Oregon. The early leaders in this area are Vermont, Massachusetts, and Washington. Of the remaining states, almost all experienced a significant change in their public sector bargaining environments.

In sum, the 1970s were a period of tremendous growth in laws protecting the existence and activities of public sector unions. Although the laws written during this period demonstrate marked consistency in the language used and issues addressed, the range of different bargaining environments is quite broad, whether we compare across functions, across states, or over time. This evolving legal framework is a rich source for investigations, whether they concern wages, strikes, or any other outcome associated with public sector collective bargaining. Our data set is intended to make such investigations easier to design and implement and also to allow further research into the evolution of the laws themselves.

Notes

1. Previous attempts to provide similar information in compact form exist. The U.S. Department of Labor's *Summary of Public Sector Labor Relations,* published approximately every second year since 1971, contains descriptions of public sector collective bargaining policies in the fifty states plus the District of Columbia and several territories. It is a particularly useful reference since it includes descriptions not only of codified laws, but also of important case decisions and Opinions of State Attorneys General, each of which is often used to define state policy.

The AFSCME Research Division provided us with a computer printout of the fifty states' legal provisions as of March 1985. Their information covers most of the relevant dimensions of the laws but does not indicate when changes occurred nor list provisions specifically prohibiting bargaining or union security arrangements.

A broader attempt, which includes the coding of provisions into numerical form and covers the fifty states in the years 1966 and 1979, was made in December 1984 by Berkeley Miller of the University of South Florida. This data set aids longitudinal investigation but omits important dimensions of the laws, particularly in the areas of union security and impasse procedures.

Finally, John Burton of Cornell University has recorded the status of most of the relevant dimensions of the laws since about 1950 and has provided us with tables summarizing the laws and when changes occurred. Our data set is closest in form and content to his information, although ours has been coded into numerical form and stored on computer disk.

2. Our procedure was to use the U.S. Department of Labor's (DOL) *Summary of Public Sector Labor Relations* to discern which states had codified laws and where these laws could be found in the statutes, then to review the statutes. Since some laws had been repealed and hence were not listed in the DOL *Summary*, we were careful to use all available sources to locate and copy any previous laws not currently on the statutes.

Constructing complete legislative histories entailed difficulties. Many of the laws had significant amendments. Since the state statutes contained only current versions of the laws and typically did not explain any amendments made, we had to look up most amendments in the session law files to see when and if significant revisions were made. Frequently, we would read an amendment only to discover that it simply changed a wording.

The laws were then carefully read and the dimensions that we deemed relevant (see tables 1A–1E) were noted. Using fourteen variables and a numerical coding scheme of our own design, the laws were translated onto code sheets. For those states which did not have laws on the books, we used the DOL *Summary* and other sources to find relevant cases and Office of Attorney General (OAG) rulings. Where the laws and cases were ambiguous, we telephoned a source in the state (usually the state Public Employment Relations Board or the Office of the Attorney General) to obtain an accurate interpretation.

3. The data set is arranged as follows. Each observation contains the status of all fourteen variables for a particular functional group in a particular state for one year. The states are ordered alphabetically, and within each state the functional groups are ordered as follows: state employees, police, fire fighters, teachers, other local employees. For example, the first observation is for state employees in Alabama during the year 1955; the 30th observation is for Alabama state employees in the year 1984; the 151st observation is for Alaska state employees in the year 1955, etc. To avoid confusion, each observation includes eighteen variables; the fourteen legal variables, plus variables indicating the state, functional group, month, and year. For years in which no change in the law occurs, the month variable is coded as "00"; for years in which the law changes, the month variable is coded as the month that the change became effective. For some cases and OAG decisions, the exact effective date is unknown; the month is coded as "13" in these instances, making it clear that a change has occurred. Finally, since states varied in the up-to-dateness of their available statutes, the final observation for different state-functional groups typically corresponds to different dates. The earliest date is January 1984, the latest is April 1985, hence some state-functional groups contain thirty-one rather than thirty observations.

4. January 1984 is the most recent date we could use and still insure complete accuracy for all fifty states. Researchers should note that Ohio passed a comprehensive law effective April 1984, and Illinois passed a law effective January 1984 for teachers and July 1984 for all other groups. These laws are included in the data set, but they are not included in the tables presented here.

5. For example, the collective bargaining rights variable was recoded so that the value 0 represents "collective bargaining prohibited" and the value 1 represents "no provision on collective bargaining." This recoding was done for all variables except for "type of arbitration" and "strike policy." The "type of arbitration" variable was excluded from calculation of the summary statistic presented in table 9, as no natural ordering exists for this variable. The strike variable was recoded so that the value 2 represents "no provision," the value 0 "prohibited with penalties specified," and the value 1 "prohibited with no penalties specified." Data set users may want to devise similar recoding schemes.

References

Miller, Berkeley. 1984. Economics vs. Politics: The growth of public sector collective bargaining laws in the American states, 1966–1979. University of South Florida. Mimeo.

U.S. Department of Labor (Labor Management Services Administration). 1971, 1973, 1977, 1979, 1981. *Summary of public sector labor relations*. Washington: Government Printing Office.

Contributors

John M. Abowd
New York State School of Industrial
and Labor Relations
Cornell University
Ives Hall
Ithaca, NY 14851-0952

Steven G. Allen
Department of Economics and
Business
North Carolina State University
Box 8110
Raleigh, NC 27695-8110

Joseph G. Altonji
Department of Economics
Northwestern University
2003 Sheridan Road
Evanston, IL 60208

David E. Bloom
Department of Economics
Columbia University
420 W. 118 Street, 10th floor
New York, NY 10027

Charles C. Brown
Institute for Social Research
Department of Economics
University of Michigan
P.O. Box 1248
Ann Arbor, MI 48109

Richard P. Chaykowski
School of Industrial Relations
Queen's University
Kingston, Ontario, K7L 3N6
Canada

William T. Dickens
Department of Economics
University of California
Berkeley, CA 94720

Randall W. Eberts
Federal Reserve Bank of Cleveland
P.O. Box 6387
Cleveland, OH 44101

Ronald G. Ehrenberg
New York State School of Industrial
and Labor Relations
Cornell University
Ithaca, NY 14851-0952

Henry S. Farber
Department of Economics
Massachusetts Institute of
Technology
E52-252F
Cambridge, MA 02139

Richard B. Freeman
National Bureau of Economic
Research
1050 Massachusetts Avenue
Cambridge, MA 02138

Zvi Griliches
Department of Economics
125 Littauer Center
Harvard University
Cambridge, MA 02138

Daniel S. Hamermesh
Department of Economics
Marshall Hall
Michigan State University
East Lansing, MI 48824

Harry J. Holzer
Department of Economics
Michigan State University
East Lansing, MI 48824

Morris A. Horowitz
Department of Economics
301 Lake Hall
Northeastern University
Boston, MA 02115

Casey Ichniowski
Graduate School of Business
Columbia University
713 Uris Hall
New York, NY 10027

Morris M. Kleiner
Hubert H. Humphrey Institute of
    Public Affairs
Humphrey Center
University of Minnesota
301 19th Avenue South
Minneapolis, MN 55455

Alan B. Krueger
Department of Economics
Princeton University
Princeton, NJ 08544

H. Gregg Lewis
Department of Economics
Duke University
Durham, NC 27706

Lisa M. Lynch
Sloan School of Management
Massachusetts Institute of
    Technology
E52-563, 50 Memorial Drive
Cambridge, MA 02139

James L. Medoff
Department of Economics
Littauer Center 115
Harvard University
Cambridge, MA 02138

Richard J. Murnane
Gutman Library 461
Graduate School of Education
Harvard University
Cambridge, MA 02138

Daniel L. Petree
School of Business
Rockhurst College
5225 Troost Avenue
Kansas City, MO 64110

Harvey S. Rosen
Department of Economics
Princeton University
Princeton, NJ 08544

Gregory M. Saltzman
Institute of Labor and Industrial
    Relations
Victor Vaughan Building
University of Michigan
Ann Arbor, MI 48109

Joe A. Stone
420 PLC, Department of Economics
University of Oregon
Eugene, OR 97403

Robert G. Valletta
Department of Economics
School of Social Sciences
University of California
Irvine, CA 92717

Jeffrey Zax
National Bureau of Economic
    Research
269 Mercer Street, 8th Floor
New York, NY 10003

Author Index

Subject Index